THE SOUL OF THE ENTERPRISE

THE SOUL OF THE ENTERPRISE

CREATING A DYNAMIC VISION FOR AMERICAN MANUFACTURING

ROBERT HALL

HarperBusiness
A Division of HarperCollinsPublishers

HarperCollins books may be purchased for educational, business, or sales promotional use. For information please write: Special Markets Department, HarperCollins Publishers, Inc., 10 East 53rd Street, New York, NY 10022.

FIRST EDITION

Library of Congress Cataloging-in-Publication Data

Hall, Robert W.
    The soul of the enterprise : creating a dynamic vision for
American manufacturing / Robert Hall. — 1st ed.
      p. cm.
    Includes bibliographical references and index.
    ISBN 0-88730-563-6
    1. United States—Manufactures—Management. 2. United States—
Manufactures—Quality control. I. Title.
HD9725.H283   1993
670′.068—dc20   91-58505

93 94 95 96 97 AC/HC 10 9 8 7 6 5 4 3 2 1

Contents

LIST OF ILLUSTRATIONS   *xi*

PREFACE   *xiii*

1   CATCHING A NEW WAVE   *1*
    □   Is the United States Losing Economic Strength?   2
      Slow Growth   4
      The End of Growth as a Driver   6
    □   Evolution Toward a System of Remanufacturing   7
      The Soul of the Enterprise   8
      The American System   9
      Increasing Economy of Scale   12
      Mass Production   15
      The Legacy of Mass Production   16
      The Rise of Lean Manufacturing   20
      The New Challenge: Holistic Remanufacturing   22
      Signs of the Times   24
      A New Form of Enterprise   24
      In Search of a New Soul   26

2 BEYOND THE ACRONYMS—THE THREE-DAY CAR 30
   ☐ New Enterprise, New Soul 32
      The Soul of the Enterprise 35
      Open-System Enterprise 37
      Why Open-System Enterprise Must Be Different 38
   ☐ Where Are We Going? 39
      Escaping the Imperial Court 41
   ☐ The Challenges of Twenty-first–Century Visions 43
      General Projections 44
      UltraComm 47
      Application-Specific Integrated Circuits (ASICs) 48
      Chemicals Without Muss or Fuss 50
      The Three-Day Car 52
      Flexibility: A First Step for the 1990s 54
      Intelligent Body Systems 55
      The Manufacturing 21 "Three-Day Car" 56
      Ordering a Three-Day Car 57
      Engineering, Production, and Delivery 59
      The Agile Manufacturing Version 61
      The Plot Thickens 62
      So What? 64

3 QUALITY GROWTH 67
   ☐ Expanding Toward a Global Vision of Quality 69
      Information-Wave Improvement Processes 74
   ☐ Growth in Practicing Quality Processes 75
      The Search for the Japanese Mystique 77
      Redefining Quality 78
      Different Kinds of Customers and Suppliers 81
      The Evolution of Quality Performance
        Measurement 84
      Ultimate Manufacturing Quality 86
      No Shirt, No Shoes, No Service 87

☐ Growth in the Quality of Life 89
    Quality Growth in Governments and Services 92
    Quality of Life as an Economic Challenge 95

4 CATCHING UP WITH THE TIMES 101
☐ The Mysteries of JIT 103
☐ The Time-Based Organization 104
    Why We Need Open-System Enterprise 108
    Different Senses of Time 110
    The Floating Crap Game 111
☐ Learning Is a Time-Based Concept 113
    Improvement Cycles 114
    Cumulative Learning 115
☐ Information Is the Ultimate Waste 116
☐ Reducing Times-to-Change 119
    Lead Times and Cycle Times 121
☐ Firing Up the Afterburner on Fundamental JIT 127
    Visibility Systems 128
    Scheduling Improvement Cycles 130

5 REVERSE UTOPIA: ENVIRONMENTALISM 136
☐ Growth-Versus-Green Debates 138
☐ Growth: The Industrial-Wave Utopia 139
    Reverse Utopia: Environmentalism 143
☐ Ecological Roulette: Risks and Unknowns 147
☐ Closed-Loop, Zero-Discharge Materials-Use
Cycles 151
☐ The Case for Remanufacturing and Recycling 154
☐ Organizations Spanning the Material-Use Cycle 156
    Design for Material Reuse Cycles 157
    Open-System Information 159
    The Limits of Regulations 161
    Discovering the Unknowns in a Process 163

☐ Manufacturing Excellence Leads to Environmental
   Excellence   165

6 THE HIGH-TECH RAT RACE   170
☐ Incentives to Innovate   171
   Intellectual Capital   173
   High-Tech Rat Races   177
   Our Limits Are Ourselves   179
☐ Paying for the Innovation Process   182
   Sharing the R&D Risk and Expense   183
   Consortia   184
   High-Pressure Research   186
☐ Cutting the Time to Innovate   189

7 THE OPEN SYSTEM—LEARNING TO BE A NONSELLER   200
   The Quest for the Open System   201
☐ The Consequences of Closed Systems   202
   The High Cost of Distrust   204
   Why Cooperate in an Open System   206
   Limits to an Open System   207
☐ Learning Organizations and Learning Competition   208
   Benchmarking   212
☐ Characteristics of an Open System   214
   Open Computing Systems   214
   Automating the Past   216
☐ Open-System Enterprise and the Nature of
   Competition   221
   Why Have Open-System Enterprise?   222

8 ASSOCIATES OF THE WORLD, ARISE!   227
   *The Trouble with Silos, Chimneys, and Pigeon
   Roosts*   229
   Letting Go   231

Recognition 235
Picking Up 238
Pay and Reward Systems 239
Open-System Organizations 243
Migration to the Open System 245
Order-of-Magnitude Reorganization 247
Enterprise Organization 248
Migrating Toward a New Enterprise 250

9 CUSTOMERS, SUPPLIERS, AND OPEN-SYSTEM
ENTERPRISE 254
Internal Customers 256
First Step: Becoming a World-Class Customer 260
Types of Partners 265
Open Systems and Trust 267
Lessons from Japanese Supplier Relations 269
Selecting the Japanese Supplier 271
Japanese Supplier Associations 272
Weaknesses of the Japanese Supplier System 273
The Beginnings of Open-System Operations 274
Open-System Enterprise 276
Structure of Open-System Enterprise 278
Example of a Long-Term Open-System Enterprise 279
More than Restructuring 284

10 SUBSTANCE OVER STYLE 287
Directionless Financial Management 289
Control by Misbegotten Measurements 291
Types of Performance Comparisons 293
Measurement for Improvement 297
Balanced Performance Measures 298
From Vision to Reality 303
Vision Deployment and Performance Drivers 309

*Toward a Universal Operating-Performance
    Assessment*   310

11 TRUST BETWEEN THE STAKEHOLDERS   317
    A Small Manufacturer's Plight   319
    The Big-Company Example: General Motors   321
    The Investment Mind-Set   325
    Profits and Interest Used as a Tax System   330
    Lessons from Japan on Governance   334
    The New Financial Order   336
    *Entrepreneurship and the Open-System
        Enterprise*   337
    Buy-In   341

12 ESCAPING THE BLACK HOLE   344
    Black Hole Economics   348
    Inflation and the Value-City Economy   350
    What Has Changed?   352
    Reinflation with High-Margin Business   355
    Investing in Human Capital   358
    The High-Margin Enterprise   359
    Private Taxation   362
    Migrating to Open Systems   363
    Forging Ahead   367

INDEX   369

ILLUSTRATIONS

FIGURE 1-1. Erosion of the U.S. Share of Technology Markets   3

FIGURE 1-2. Estimates of Production and Licensed Stock of Motor Vehicles   5

FIGURE 1-3. Development from American System to Holistic Remanufacturing   10

FIGURE 2-1. Everything Isn't the Way It Used to Be   33

FIGURE 2-2. Themes of the New Soul of the Enterprise   40

FIGURE 2-3. World View of the Chinese Circa 500 B.C.   42

FIGURE 3-1. Expanding toward a Global Understanding of Quality   70

FIGURE 3-2. Example of a Stepwise Improvement Process   71

FIGURE 3-3. Four Classifications of Quality from Kano   80

FIGURE 3-4. Different Types of Customers and Suppliers   82

FIGURE 3-5. Quality of Life Defined as Fundamental Social Concerns   91

FIGURE 4-1. Cost-Time Profiles at Westinghouse   105

FIGURE 4-2. Hypothetical Financial Statements Showing Effects of Time Compression   109

FIGURE 4-3. Product-Development Lead Times and Cycle Times   122

FIGURE 4-4. Relationship Diagrams   124
FIGURE 4-5. Time-Flow Diagrams   126
FIGURE 5-1. Life Expectancy at Birth (1980–1985) by Gross
             National Product per Capita, 1983   140
FIGURE 5-2. Life Span in Industrial Regions throughout
             History   142
FIGURE 5-3. Emissions of Selected Pollutants in the United
             States, 1950–1987; Carbon Emissions from Fossil
             Fuels, 1950–1989   144
FIGURE 5-4. Classification of Selected Environmental Risks   146
FIGURE 5-5. Definitions of Material-Use Cycles   153
FIGURE 5-6. Environmental Benefits of "Manufacturing
             Excellence" Practices   167
FIGURE 6-1. Summary: Ideals of Combining Product and
             Process Design   190
FIGURE 6-2. The Ideal Product/Process Design Service System   191
FIGURE 8-1. Myers's Three-Dimensional Reward Structure   241
FIGURE 9-1. Stages of Customer–Supplier Development   257
FIGURE 9-2. Characteristics of a Good Customer Company
             (Circa 1992)   262
FIGURE 9-3. Critical and Less Critical Suppliers   266
FIGURE 9-4. Open-Systems Comparisons   280
FIGURE 9-5. Comparison of Information Normally Kept Secret   282
FIGURE 10-1. Examples of a Balanced Array of Performance
             Measures   300
FIGURE 10-2. Maturity Matrices for Quality Assessments   305
FIGURE 10-3. An Example Performance Rating Using a
             Maturity Index   306
FIGURE 10-4. Achieving Quality of Life and Enterprise Visions
             Is a Cumulative Development of Ourselves   308
FIGURE 10-5. Vision Deployment and Performance Drivers   311
FIGURE 10-6. Framework of a Universal Performance-
             Measurement System   313
FIGURE 12-1. Elements of the Open-System Enterprise   346

PREFACE

THIS BOOK IS NOT FINISHED. IT IS INTENDED TO FURTHER A PROCESS THAT WE must pursue more vigorously and with much more participation from diverse people. Despite its futurist nature, this book is intended not for idle dreamers but for those who are going to make a future rather than merely waiting for it to happen.

The visions are derived more from business operational considerations than economic theory or scientific possibility. The demands of operating excellence are becoming so stringent that we are approaching a condition where we need a common operating system, not just the common marketing and financial systems on which business is based today.

The book is incomplete for many reasons. One is that all kinds of industry and all vital considerations cannot possibly be addressed by one person alone, nor can they be adequately considered in one book. For example, a strong case for preserving biological diversity was hardly touched.

Furthermore, all the system changes needed in industry itself could not be covered in detail. For example, the book barely mentions the kind of distributed planning and control necessary in the new manufacturing. What's needed is neither "pull" or "push," as those systems are now regarded by manufacturing folk, but an orchestration of all functions—marketing, engineering, and production, across multiple boundaries—in lot sizes of one. That is a book in itself.

The projections of future technology or future systems in this book are rather conservative. The reason for the title, *The Soul of the Enterprise*, is that considering such issues rapidly leads to the conclusion that our problems as we enter the twenty-first century are not so much technology as us. Solving them will not be mere economic tinkering, behavioral tweaking, or morale uplifting.

The author and many other technically oriented people wish it were not so. Innovations confined to rational inanimate materials are easier than revising how *we* make things work differently. Changing the way we work is painful because most of us prefer to continue doing whatever brought us success in the past—only better. Venturing into something we have never done before takes clear vision and strong motivation. Would that the conclusion were otherwise, for this author is not by nature a revolutionary.

Whether change is more tumultuous now than at any other time in the last three hundred years is doubtful. However, the business world cannot continue to work the same way, and the nature of this change must be shaped by a new kind of entrepreneurship. Whatever this new system may become, it must evolve from the trials and triumphs of people who make things work. A "new world order" devised and imposed by the uninvolved is a disaster. The Soviets began such an adventure in 1917.

Ideas are rarely original. Those in this book are no exception. Some surely came from references read in the past and the source is forgotten. The credit list or colleagues who have contributed ideas and inspiration could be longer than the book. Regrettably, the exact source of some ideas is now vague because the book was in gestation a long time, and some conversations occurred when the author was not consciously "doing research."

The original idea for writing this book came from the efforts of the Manufacturing 21 working group at Waseda University, Tokyo, and particularly Professor Jinichiro Nakane, who took much of his time to share with me their inspiration and frustration as they sought a new direction for Japanese manufacturing. A second source of ideas has been the Agile Manufacturing Enterprise Forum at Lehigh University. The forum is exerting considerable energy and creativity to find a new direction for American manufacturing.

The "godfather" of the book is Ken Stork of Kenneth J. Stork and Associates (formerly of Motorola). For two years, Ken read drafts, discussed ideas, suggested organization, and generally prodded the effort whenever it stalled.

Ideas came from many people. A few were interviewed. Others simply contributed through conversation for other reasons. A short list would include Leonard Allgaier (General Motors and the Agile Manufacturing Enterprise Forum), Vaughn Beales (retired CEO of Harley-Davidson Motor Co.), James Childs (the original editor who smiled on the idea of the book), Robert Costello (former undersecretary of defense for procurement), Jack Sweeney (president, Labeco), William J. Kennedy (chairman and CEO of Analytical Technologies), Jack Warne (retired CEO of Omark Industries), and Bill Wheeler (Coopers & Lybrand).

Finally, I thank my wife, Kay, and my secretary, Jan Cashion, both of whom endured considerable frustration during the writing process. They may endure a great deal more if the book stirs up controversy.

ROBERT W. HALL
Plainfield, Indiana

1

CATCHING A NEW WAVE

IT'S TIME TO CHANGE THE BASIC PRECEPTS UNDERLYING BUSINESS INSTITUTIONS. Our current ones are not up to twenty-first century challenges. "Catching a new wave" sometimes means chasing a fad, but in this case the wave seems to be a fundamental change in how the world's work is done. This new wave won't wash over us by itself. Human energy must make it rise.

Signs of a different wave are all around. The American economic malaise of the early 1990s has a different feel from that of earlier recessions. Even the great world recession of the 1930s was considered a lull in an inexorable long-term growth trend. This time people are not so sure. Companies discover that they have to improve customer satisfaction while running leaner. They downsize, delayer, and outsource. General Motors, IBM, Xerox, American Express, and many other famous names—once solid growth performers—all announce reductions in force.[1] Even healthy, growing companies openly state goals such as doubling sales without adding employees.

One reaction is the desire to create a future that resembles the past—of about 1960. Some find it easy to blame the Japanese—or any foreign company—and wrap their sales pitches in the flag. However, try as they might, major companies can rarely repeat their founders' rushes of heady growth; 1900, or 1920—or 1960—won't come around again. Instead, we need to follow one of the best approaches to creative problem solving: think about the situation differently.

IS THE UNITED STATES
LOSING ECONOMIC STRENGTH?

Among the economic arguments of recent years is whether the United States is slipping in manufacturing, and if so, whether the eclipse of manufacturing by a service company is a good thing. "Losing manufacturing" is a state of mind. Optimists point to improved productivity growth. (Average productivity automatically improves if one simply sends the low-productivity jobs elsewhere.) Pessimists see it as merely the natural result of outsourcing. Optimists see GNP increasing. Pessimists note the relative decline of key industries: computers, machine tools, semiconductors, autos, steel, and so forth, as shown in Figure 1-1. When the market share of American-produced items such as tape recorders and VCRs hit zero, the Department of Commerce simply stopped tracking them.

Manufacturing insiders are more interested in the health of manufacturing know-how than in current output. Know-how grows from actual practice, not abstract study. For instance, at the turn of the century, one could buy an American-built machine tool almost anywhere—almost like ordering seeds from a catalogue. Today, the total capitalization of all American machine tool companies is less than $1 billion, and probably closer to half that, an insignificant tick in the national income accounts.[2]

More disturbing is the loss of competitive know-how. Production equipment has rapidly become computerized. Stodgy competitors have dropped out, but few thriving entrepreneurs seem ready to take their places. This kind of enterprise is now less easily built on solitary genius than it once was, nor can expertise as easily be confined to a single company. But too few manufacturers and their equipment suppliers form partnerships to probe leading-edge practice. (Buying key equipment from competitors is almost always buying hand-me-down know-how.)

FIGURE 1-1
EROSION OF THE U.S.
SHARE OF TECHNOLOGY MARKETS

(Percent U.S. share of domestic American
market in products pioneered by U.S. firms.)

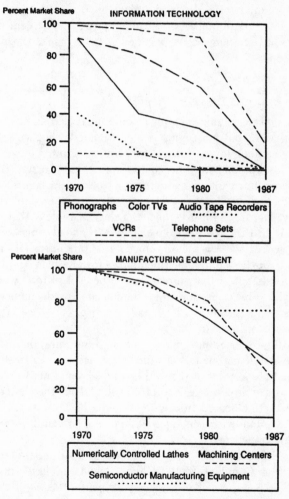

SOURCE: *United States Department of Commerce International Trade Administration.*

On the bright side, educational institutions are seeing a resurgence of interest in manufacturing. "Centers of excellence" and numerous training programs are growing. Almost everyone realizes that wherever manufacturing is headed skilled, educated work teams are its capital of tomorrow. As Americans adjust to increasingly intense competition, they must consistently achieve levels of operating performance that tax the full nature of man and that were rarely if ever attained in the past. We are ill-prepared to enter the twenty-first century. The first step in becoming better prepared is to recognize the need for preparation.

Slow Growth

In real dollars, American family incomes increased slightly between 1973 and 1989, but per capita income declined. Slippage was most noticeable among under thirties and minorities, but yuppies exiting once rock-solid companies began to interpret growth statistics with the same confidence they had in penny stock prospectuses.[3]

Perhaps the slowdown is part of a natural evolution in the U.S. economy. The auto industry provides a clear example of that process. From 1919 to 1929, the stock of vehicles on the road tripled to almost 27 million. In 1925, 4.4 million vehicles were produced. This number was less than the 9.8 million (including Japanese plant production) built in 1990, but at that time it was 87 percent of total world production. As vehicles accumulated, they needed roads, refineries, gas stations, repair garages, parking spots—and places to go. Wind-in-your-face, joyous growth![4]

Gradually the U.S. auto market matured, meaning that it leveled out, thus stabilizing the rate at which we added vehicles to stocks. At the same time the rest of the world had discovered mass production and the joys of driving after World War II. Outside the United States auto production soared from ground zero. The result was that by 1990, U.S. production was only 20.7 percent of world output. The wind blew elsewhere.

From 1925 to 1990 the overall stock of vehicles in the United States swelled from 20 million to 190 million (while population doubled), but the U.S. vehicle market grew very little after the 1960s. Allowing for scrap, 3 to 5 million vehicles per year are still being added to

FIGURE 1-2

ESTIMATES OF PRODUCTION
AND LICENSED STOCK OF MOTOR VEHICLES

(All figures are millions of units)

Year	UNITED STATES			REST OF WORLD		WORLD TOTALS	
	Prod.	Market	Stock	Prod.	Stock	Prod.	Stock
1925	4.4	—	20	0.5	—	4.9	—
1930	3.6	—	27	0.5	6	4.1	33
*	—	—	—	—	—	—	—
1950	8.0	—	49	2.6	—	10.6	—
1960	7.9	7.6	74	8.6	32	16.5	106
1970	8.3	10.2	108	21.2	86	29.4	194
1980	8.8	11.5	156	30.0	165	38.5	321
1980	9.8	14.1	190	37.5	240	47.3	430

The years 1970, 1980 and 1990 were all down years for Detroit. During the two decades, the American auto industry became accustomed to sales in the range of thirteen to fifteen million units per year, but when Detroit production slackened, imports took more market share. In 1925, Detroit production was 87 percent of a very small world. In 1990, it was 20.7 percent of a vastly bigger and fast-growing world. The market versus registration figures also hint that from 1960 to 1990, the purchase-to-scrap lifetime of the average car increased from a little under ten years to over thirteen years.

* Numbers not available for 1940.
SOURCE: *Prepared with data from Paul Zajac, Motor Vehicle Manufacturers Association, Detroit, MI.*

rolling stock, about twice as many per year as in the roaring Twenties.[5]

In 1970, 56 percent of the cars in the world were still in the United States. By 1990, that had dropped to about 44 percent, while world car population more than doubled. Much of the rest of the world is still selling to first-time buyers, while the United States has become largely a replacement market.

Not long ago America's economy dwarfed the world's. In 1930, 6 percent of the world's population produced (and mostly consumed)

70 percent of the oil, 80 percent of the cars, and so on.[6] Economically, the United States was half the world. During World War II, it was only a matter of time before the Axis powers were swarmed under by American equipment. America's preeminent status could not last forever, but somehow Americans seemed to feel that even though other nations grew, the United States would always run half the world's economy.

During the Great Depression Americans learned that they had to become prodigious consumers if they were to keep mass production going. They were successful at it. As late as 1988, for example, Americans still consumed 40 percent of all the motor fuel used in the world.

Environmental considerations are also starting to have a serious effect on growth. The auto industry is facing a major technological shift to accommodate a replacement market. In California, the South Coast Air Quality Management District's stringent air pollution control plan announced in 1989 is prodding the development of battery-powered cars. To support the plan, the Southern California Association of Governments in 1990 initiated zoning to decrease average commuting distance and traffic density. The love affair with the automobile has not ended, but a houseful of whiny children is spoiling the romantic mood.

The story of many mass-produced items roughly parallels that of automobiles. Television grew to maturity in the 1960s, then dwindled to a replacement and second-set market. Refrigerators are mature, but the industry has a huge challenge replacing ozone-depleting CFC refrigerants. Personal computers are somewhere in the same cycle. Americans became accustomed to product-centered growth sprees with few aftereffects. Another new technology, another whoopee on the roller coaster. We can no longer bury problems under fresh economic growth, leaving our mess behind.

The End of Growth as a Driver

For U.S. manufacturing *output* to return to its dominant position of 1920–1970, the United States would either have to produce for the rest of the world (which has no money to buy), or the rest of the world would have to reverse its manufacturing growth. Neither expectation is reasonable—not without wishing for a world disaster everywhere but in the United States, like a rerun of World War II or the Gulf War multiplied many times over. We are in danger of trying to refight yesterday's wars. It is time to do something different.

The situation is analogous to Olympic basketball. Invented in the United States, basketball caught on around the world. No longer do foreigners need to come here to learn the game, nor can we expect to beat the world's best with a squad of college all-stars.

Politically, many Americans have yet to catch up to this new reality. They would prefer to go "back to the future" of about 1960, when everyone else in the world feared that Americans would overrun them economically, a condition similar to the current "Japan panic." Both America's quest for a dominant world position and other nations' fear of being subjected to it lead to maximum conflict and minimum progress. Furthermore, many of the problems can no longer be smothered with overall economic growth. We must create a different set of aspirations.

It's time to ask tough questions. What does more production mean, and to whom? What are we trying to accomplish? It's time to grope our way to a different system for the world's work.

EVOLUTION TOWARD A SYSTEM OF REMANUFACTURING

A new movement, or perhaps a set of movements, is struggling to cope with the "information wave." The wave analogy signifies that it is difficult to determine exactly when and how a broad sweeping movement begins or ends. The analogy is taken from Alvin Toffler, the well-known futurist, in *The Third Wave.* He classified recorded, European-centered history into three ages, or waves: (1) agricultural, a long wave from the dawn of history until around 1800; (2) industrial, a wave beginning in the 1700s and now believed to be past maturity; and (3) informational, which is just beginning.[7]

Daniel Bell described this third wave as "postindustrial," but he takes pains to point out that he does not mean that industry has become unimportant.[8] Likewise, Toffler does not believe that agriculture has stopped being important. Rather, in the information wave computer technology is profoundly transforming agriculture, industry, and everyday life, just as industry radically transformed agricultural societies two centuries ago.

Theories about how an economy should work emerged early in the industrial wave, when computers, Total Quality Management, and other new managerial ideas were too far out to imagine. For instance, Adam Smith's thinking was shaped by his observations of entrepreneurial manufacturers very early in the Industrial Revolution. Karl Marx was certainly influenced by industrial sweatshops later in that age. Western economic theory and practice developed during the industrial wave assumed that independent companies, each independently working at arm's length to maximize its own profit, produce an optimum social benefit. In general, that benefit was maximum growth with minimum effort and communication. That system has been particularly effective in stimulating entrepreneurial companies to convert material to human use with the least effort possible. Provided the entrepreneurs have foresight, these goals can even be accomplished while pleasing customers and tending to the environment.

However, a number of the assumptions underlying the system are changing. People in different companies may communicate with each other more effectively than they do within their own companies. Efficiency of distribution is enhanced by sharing data across company boundaries. If everyone has access to data about a company and its products, the emphasis begins to change from making money (still important) to pleasing customers. The same is true of environmental protection. Nothing forces management to wake up to environmental issues faster than public scrutiny—whether factually based or not.

The Soul of the Enterprise

The changes of the late twentieth century are forcing us to contemplate the capabilities and limits of humanity in new ways. The future is always derived from the past, for people do not change quickly. But the future is not a replica of the past using faster technology.

A bare-bones vision of the future without a precise timetable will do. No one can forecast in detail. A vision need only provide a sense of direction. Technology has an enormous impact on the future, but the major challenge of that future is to human motivations and human institutions. To see where we are going, a brief historical review is useful. Figure 1-3 is a quick recap of various stages of the industrial wave leading to the new era of "holistic remanufacturing." The actual process of working into holistic remanufacturing will be pragmatic work by multitudes of people. We need a rapid process to find out what really works and spread it quickly.

Each of these stages of development is marked by very powerful social motivations that are virtually unchallenged at the time, at least by the people doing most of the economic building. These strong motivations are the "soul of the enterprise"—the universal drivers—of that stage. Vague as it may be, the soul of enterprise encapsulates a spirit that guides social change and the development of economic institutions.

A practical trial and error approach to development will work if the enterprise's constituents have somewhat common visions and overall goals. One of the major reasons for the failure of the Communist system was that while it extolled the workers, it maintained a belief in the omnipotence of central control, while many capitalist companies have failed because individuals "ran companies" until they overran their own capabilities.

Many fact-seeking, data-driven managers don't like to consciously think about a "soul of the enterprise." They do it indirectly. The soul of the enterprise is the basis of almost any assumption made in a business venture.

The American System

The United States virtually began as a corporation. The British chartered companies that allowed people with money to fund a venture into uncharted lands and financially share in its risks and rewards. That set the theme of expansion and growth from the beginning. However, the earliest factories were too small in scale to require organizations beyond the family farm model often used by owner-operators. At its best, the American system was cowboy capitalism run by handshake transactions.

As the ability to capture fuel energy improved, products became

FIGURE 1-3

DEVELOPMENT
FROM AMERICAN SYSTEM
TO HOLISTIC REMANUFACTURING

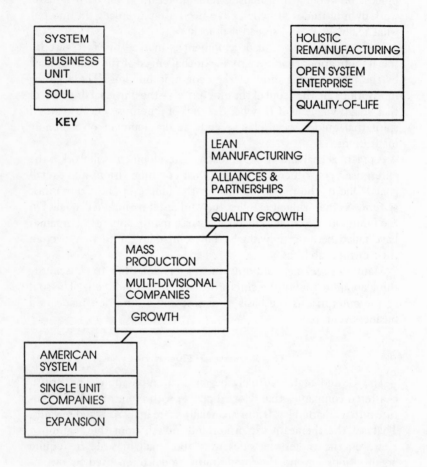

SYSTEM

BUSINESS UNIT

SOUL

KEY

HOLISTIC REMANUFACTURING

OPEN SYSTEM ENTERPRISE

QUALITY-OF-LIFE

LEAN MANUFACTURING

ALLIANCES & PARTNERSHIPS

QUALITY GROWTH

MASS PRODUCTION

MULTI-DIVISIONAL COMPANIES

GROWTH

AMERICAN SYSTEM

SINGLE UNIT COMPANIES

EXPANSION

too complex for craft shop systems. By the middle 1800s the growing factories turned to familiar models to learn how to organize. They generally began by unifying large factories in one location. Most of the models came from railroads, textile mills, and armories.

Financiers were seldom cut out to run operations, so as manufacturing became larger in scale, professional managers soon became necessary. Samuel Slater, who copied Richard Arkwright's spinning mills (copying has always been the best way to start), was financed by Moses Brown to construct and operate the first spinning mill in the United States. Slater's mill typified many early start-ups. He soon became wealthy himself, but as long as the scale of operations was small, he was an integral part of mill-town society. Early mills were an extension of the surrounding agricultural countryside, so someone leaving a job could easily go back to the land—an attitude that still persists.

The soul of that age was expansion. People moved west, cleared farms, and started small manufacturing ventures. Most managed as it came naturally.

The soul of that early system was typified by the Boott Mill, opened in 1836 in Lowell, Massachusetts. It began as a planned industrial community, serving as an example to similar English communities. Drinking and other vices were prohibited in company boarding houses.

Contrary to the plan, however, a latter-day version of feudalism emerged. Absentee owners hired a manager to run the business based on returns to ownership, just as was done in Europe. It was a time when today's "old money" was made. The soul that existed at Boott depended on the manager of the time, a condition that corporate denizens still recognize today.

Because Boott Mill was run as a cash cow for the investors, no one could ever justify putting more money into it than was necessary. Layout, materials handling, and the vibration of the structure itself were exceedingly wasteful, but no ROI calculus ever recommended renovation. During the long history of Boott, owner imagination was always constricted by rate-of-return thinking. "Short-termism" is an old phenomenon.

The American system was designed to exploit any new opportunity, as in oil exploration, real estate speculation, and genetic engineering ventures. It was not designed for long-term preservation or for continuous improvement, though farsighted individuals can correct for system bias. Renewal comes when an entrepreneur fires up a new venture to compete against the old.

For example, the Boott operated for many dismal but generally profitable years, always competing with mills in the South after 1900. The most profitable action was to ride it down. Positive cash flow dragged on until 1950, when the mill "went south," the easiest course of action for the owners.[9]

Fortunately, the country had many, many inventors and entrepreneurs. The stagnation of the Boott was more than offset by the start-up of all kinds of ventures, a few doubtless financed by cash thrown off by the Boott. The soul of the time was growth, expansion, and adventure. If stifled in one endeavor, the ambitious could leave it all behind and find another area of virgin growth. No one needed to worry about perfect quality, worker displacement, ecology, coordination with other enterprises, and so on, so the system worked.

Increasing Economy of Scale

The beginning of mass production dates to about the 1880s, when numerous manufacturing operations began growing beyond the ability of unassisted natural leadership to manage them. At the time, the railroads were also consolidating and cooperating on standard systems (standard track gauges, exchanges of cars, and so on) to quickly move freight nationwide, thus creating the means for mass distribution of manufactured goods.

Thus began a period of industrial growth still comparatively unsurpassed. However, aggregate numbers that would summarize that growth are less meaningful than the story of Carnegie Steel.

Andrew Carnegie is remembered today principally as a rich old philanthropist. However, his leadership typified the soul of the maturing industrial wave. Carnegie was a numbers-watcher whose accounting systems were widely copied. After early experience on the Pennsylvania Railroad, widely touted as the best-organized company of its time, Carnegie began to buy established iron foundries and mills just to make money.

However, after seeing an open-hearth furnace in Scotland, he instantly "got the vision" to advance steelmaking in the United States—and on a scale befitting a big country. Carnegie was a leader who inspired both financiers and working men. He assembled a talented core of managers to oversee one of the fastest industrial run-ups in history. Virtually all their improvements were in temperatures achieved, management controls, layouts, handling, and material flow. Results were astounding. Output from the same furnace increased as much as eight times in twenty years.[10] In 1885 Great Britain led the world in steel production. By 1900, only fifteen years later, the steel output from Carnegie's companies *alone* far surpassed the total British output. (Americans astonished by the Japanese rise of the 1980s are usually unaware that they subjected the British to an even more dramatic blowout a century earlier.)

So great was the advantage of steel over iron, and so great the market for steel in a rapidly growing country, that strikes and conflicts were mere blips in Carnegie's growth curve. In 1900 Carnegie cashed in, selling his company to J. P. Morgan, who in turn rapidly tripled its value in the stream of transactions that created U.S. Steel.[11]

Andrew Carnegie's accomplishment was the prototype for the kind of career that MBAs have coveted ever since. Turn-of-the-century factories followed Carnegie's lead, spewing out construction material, railcars, bicycles, wagons, and farm machinery. Many entrepreneurs created booms and minibooms in a fashion similar to Carnegie, leaving now-old libraries, museums, universities, and other objects of their philanthropy in their wake. The factory system of the day was hard work, but it beat plowing with a mule. People were caught up in the enthusiasm of creating a vibrant, pulsating new country. The soul of America and its industry was growth—untrammeled, pell-mell, set-a-record-or-bust growth.

However, without new management systems, the monstrous new factories were chaotic until the rise of "Taylorism," which refers to the method of running shops and large industrial organizations that today is considered business-as-usual. Taylorism crawled out of a quagmire of conflicting practices and free market flimflam from roughly 1880–1920. Fredrick Winslow Taylor's name defines the movement, though many other persons participated.

Taylorism developed in response to the chaos of earlier management practice. In 1880, many industrialists contracted work to multiple inside foremen, who in turn hired and paid workers. Mid-nineteenth-century contractor-foremen were prosperous entrepreneurs who wore suits to work. Letting out work to an "internal market" attracted capable people to perform critical work, but it also invited scams. The ambitious bid low for work, then figured out how to do it later. Experienced contractors bid high for work that only they understood well, then gained a fat margin while working well below their capability. "Soldiering," the Taylorists called it.[12]

Machinists learned their trade by guess and by golly. For every skilled one, an inept one heaped scrap. Only a few factories, except watchmakers and armories, actually made interchangeable parts. Singer sewing machines, for instance, were assembled by a roomful of people filing parts to fit.[13]

As factories became large and products complex, expediting work through a labyrinth of inside contractors became intolerable. To gain control of the chaos, engineer-managers experimented with shop accounting systems, worker payment systems, and production planning and control. The American Society of Mechanical Engineers (ASME) became the seedbed of Taylorism. These issues were openly discussed at meetings by those experimenting with new insights.

The contractor system was broken by incentive plans. In 1889 Henry Towne reported to ASME a gainsharing plan that had been introduced earlier at Yale and Towne Lock Company. Rather than contracting a piece rate with foremen, reductions in overall unit costs were shared with the workers and foremen. Various companies experimented with different plans, and gainsharing was soon abandoned because many workers could see little relationship between *individual* effort and pay—a hundred years before teamwork became a buzz-word. Only a few owners adopted profit sharing. Most would not disclose profits, much less share them. The most common choice: individual output incentives.

The incentive systems rapidly destroyed internal contracting, though a few machine shops contracted highly skilled work well into the twentieth century. To administer incentive systems, plants established detailed cost systems and job-shop production-planning control systems. Soon both the foremen and the workers were controlled by these systems, and the bureaucracy needed to administer them began to grow.

These basic factory-control systems have been used through most of the twentieth century, and descendants of them are still in use. They are representative of the mind-set we are now trying to break.[14]

Taylor himself became famous for setting the standards on which pay systems (and budgets) were based. Initially, he experimented with machine tooling, feeds, and speeds to create universal standards that would displace "black art," the unsubstantiated personal know-how varying greatly by individual and often kept secret for bargaining. Shops adopting his scientifically determined machining standards usually inherited better machining methods.

Taylor went on to study many kinds of work, from shoveling to parts inspection. He held that by study and experiment, engineers could find a "best way" to perform any job, just as he had done in machining. Rather than bonuses for beating their own prior performance, workers received incentives to conform to these "scientific" methods and a bonus if they were able to beat them. The use of standards further shrank the powers of foremen. Over time the standards often degenerated to poorly established budgetary standards by which staff numerically controlled companies by remote control.[15]

In practice, factories extended and modified Taylor's concepts, and managers adapted Taylorism to run entire companies of all kinds, installing the isolated line-and-staff hierarchies that endure today. Despite its faults, at the turn of the century Taylorism enabled managers to plan and control an enormous chunk of the world economy at the time. It was a vast improvement over the chaos of internally contracting everything.

Mass Production

Though continuous-process machines of many kinds were introduced from the 1870s onward, Ford's assembly line has symbolized mass production. The genius of Henry Ford was simplicity. He envisioned the Model T as a simple car affordable by the common man, and he designed it with a minimum number of parts, precisely engineered so that they would be absolutely interchangeable. (Almost as important, the Master Mechanic fought and won a series of legal battles to avoid paying hefty royalties on each car produced. Losing might have kept the auto a small-volume toy for the rich.)

Once the basic design was in production, Ford supervisors kept changing layouts and equipment until they struck on the basic idea of line production. The first line was for producing a magneto. The continuous final-assembly line followed soon after. Assembly lines draw a big yawn today, but in 1913 they were the realization of a dream. Many other industries experimented with mass-production concepts, some much earlier than Ford, and set the United States off on an industrial growth binge that dominated the world through subsequent decades until Americans considered it a normal way of life.

No grand plan existed for the development of mass production and economy of scale. Rather, a number of leaders worked toward a vision themselves and inspired others to do the same. Their actual accomplishments came about through a series of experiments with reality— some semiscientific, like Frederick Taylor's, some systematic like Andrew Carnegie's, and others a mechanic's trial and error like Henry Ford's.

With mass production, mass distribution, and mass media came massive, multidivisional business organizations. The Pennsylvania Railroad was recognized as an excellent multidimensional operation as early as 1873. Pierre Du Pont and Alfred Sloan crafted the classic multidivisional organization at General Motors in the 1920s. The big organizations intensified both the seemingly eternal conflict between functions and arguments over control systems that still plague big organizations today. Furthermore, the baggage of Taylorism tended to bloat the staff bureaucracies.

The soul of mass production has been growth—growth and size. Stock prices are supposed to appreciate—quickly rather than slowly. Investment analysts normally expect a company to grow, and the faster the better. If not, the analyst picks on the perceived faults of management. Prestige attaches to being a Fortune 500 company. An executive of a company with over 100,000 employees is more highly regarded than one with only 100 employees.

The Legacy of Mass Production

The spirit of American mass production was never more glorious than during World War II. When the war broke out, experienced production people took over military procurement. Many of the most stupendous feats resulted from unprecedented cooperation between companies. Engineers and others with know-how disregarded control systems when it was time to get something done. Plans, tooling, techniques, equipment, and expertise were exchanged whenever needed. Younger Americans briefly saw a miniversion of that same spirit during the 1991 Gulf War.

Some of those involved in war production later wondered how they had done it. (Some of the obvious factors were minimal goldbricking, multiple shifts, expediting, or bypassing the usual decision processes, extensive training, and pressure to innovate.) In thirty-five years before the war the United States had produced only 30,000 aircraft. During the war, it produced 300,000.[16]

The most famous defense plant was the Willow Run aircraft plant for Ford, a mile-long assembly line served by 1,600 machine tools and 7,500 jigs and fixtures. Construction began in April 1941. Sixteen months later, four-engine B-24 Liberator bombers began coming out before construction was complete. At peak production in 1944, a bomber rolled off every sixty-three minutes around the clock.[17] People still whistle at the sheer volume, but overall performance was far from outstanding. General Motors outproduced Ford by three times, and the War Department threatened to take over Ford's management of the effort.[18]

Then peace broke out. Organizations resumed normal levels of contentiousness and infighting. The whiz kids Henry Ford II brought in to resurrect Ford came to symbolize the postwar approach to management—young, educated, analytical—the first wave of MBA types to splash financial analysis on the old managers' black cigars. Not only at Ford, but at most large companies, numerical reporting displaced hunches. In the plants, Taylorism was increasingly interpreted as producing high efficiency ratios and favorable accounting variances.

Like earlier generations, the new breed rising to the top was obsessed with growth, but in more quantified form. They ate numbers and managed by analytical inquisition. Extraordinary CEOs such as Harold Geneen of ITT could thereby monitor the performance of business units across a far-flung empire.

Exhilarating while it lasts, virgin manufacturing growth is physical—new mines, new plants, new products, congested docks, daring schedule ramp-ups, and people training others as fast as they can so they can move on. However, growth by acquisition—the numerical run-ups that created conglomerates—had less potential for the same kind of operational satisfaction. Neither virgin growth nor the creation of economy of scale, so it had less potential for the same kind of operational satisfaction.

Virgin growth like Silicon Valley start-ups still created excitement. The space race stirred spirits as deeply as any run-up in American history. The goal was focused, the challenge intense. Anyone remotely involved knew they were contributing to history. But by the 1970s the original wave of industrial growth in the United States had long since crested. Judging by the phrase "Rust Belt," much of the enthusiasm for it had also ebbed.

Mass production is a legacy from a time when expansion and abundance seemingly had no limit. Taylorist concepts for running large organizations supported the confidence in growth and laissez-faire capitalism that became popular during the twentieth century. Now a shrinking world and the information wave are beginning to make Taylorism obsolete. Some Taylorist concepts are:

- Separate functional hierarchies.
- Conviction that management rationality is superior.
- Staff specialists solving technical problems alone.
- Measuring performance by "scientific" standards (which rapidly evolved into accounting budgets and variances, and financial control).
- Belief in independent economic units operating at arm's length and frequently using confrontational methods.
- Belief that more is almost always better.

For example, Taylorist engineers designed processes; others merely ran them. Control jibed nicely with an absentee owner's concept of manufacturing, stewardship: high efficiency, everything abuzz, maximizing salable output, every invested dollar ostensibly maximizing return. But Taylorist concepts, now embedded deep in the American psyche, became increasingly dysfunctional. Minds were tuned to *control* of a money machine, not *improvement* of its functions and processes.

Alternative approaches were discussed all through the mass-production era. In 1920 a methods study engineer named Allan Mogensen sensed fear in workers he time-studied (to set standards). He believed that he could teach anyone to improve his work methods and essentially set standards himself. In 1933, he created Work Simplification, a practical course to show workers how to work smarter, not harder, but few people under fifty have heard of Work Simplification today.

In 1988, Mogensen summed up his seventy-two years of living with Taylorism. Asked what he thought was the major problem of American industry, he replied, "It is the same now as the first day I went to work in 1916. The managers think they can control the company in every detail, and the workers are only a bunch of ungrateful wretches."[19]

Mass production and Taylorism left us a legacy stretching back over a hundred years. Despite its glorious past, this legacy is increasingly seen as having many shortcomings. Among them:

1. Difficulty accepting the importance of multiple dimensions of performance (customer satisfaction, quality, flexibility, safety, environmental protection, and so on).
2. Managing for results rather than leading people and managing processes.
3. Believing an enterprise is in inert assets rather than people.
4. Acceptance of performance meeting minimal quality standards.
5. Overreliance on specialized staffs and chains of command, now colorfully described by such phases as the "pigeon roost phenomenon" (droppings from higher levels cascade on those immediately below).
6. Regarding other companies in the same supply chain as competitors.

Worse, the system is growth dependent. When the growth goes out of it, the soul leaves too. Perhaps all that is left is the frantic stock pumping and deal making of the 1980s—trying to create the illusion of growth even if nothing much is happening.

The Rise of Lean Manufacturing

After World War II the Japanese were determined to regain world respect by becoming an economic power. The most successful model to study was the American manufacturing machine that had run over them. Japanese manufacturing was fired by the "hungry spirit"—the clear, simple goal of catching up. The results of their determination are now grist for thousands of management seminars the world over.

Spirit was a major factor in the Japanese miracle. The best Japanese graduates jumped into manufacturing. Public policies promoted saving. Men took pride in working incredible hours so that the Mitsubishis and Sumitomos might grow. In 1957, as John Kenneth Galbraith pronounced "the production problem solved" in the West, the Japanese considered manufacturing improvement a national duty.[20] But that was not all. The Japanese began a new movement.

Japanese manufacturers aggressively combined the best practices from around the world and improved on them. The teachings of W. Edwards Deming, Joseph Juran, Peter Drucker, and other Americans in Japan are now a well-known story. The Japanese also knew how to learn. They observed others and tried new ideas as soon as possible, using the method known as the Deming Circle to improve on past practice and accumulate know-how very quickly.

Western Taylorist assumptions were befuddled by Total Quality Management, just-in-time manufacturing, employee involvement, and close cooperation with suppliers—all people-intensive processes—often clothed in the customs of a long-isolated Asian culture. But the transition for Japanese manufacturers was not easy either. They often had to invoke various strains of Japanese tradition for new practices to be accepted. Today, while leading Japanese companies are busy pushing onward, some still do not accept TQM or JIT.

Seminars on quality, just-in-time, benchmarking, total preventive maintenance, employee involvement, and so on are popular not only in the established manufacturing companies, but in the newly emerging ones as well—from Malaysia to South Africa. In fact, "manufacturing excellence" thinking may catch on quicker if it does not have to contend with an old history of contrary practices. The extent to which the concepts are accepted (if not practiced) in the United States can be seen by comparing the tables of contents of business publications, from *Business Week* to the *Harvard Business Review*, over the past ten years.

Almost everyone has had the same hang-ups learning from the Japanese as the Japanese did learning from everyone else. For example, to accept Japanese practices, Americans must often recall nearly forgotten examples of Henry Ford's early version of JIT or Allan Mogensen's form of employee involvement. Coming up with a catchy name is often important. Americans have begun to refer to manufacturing excellence as "lean manufacturing," as described in the popular book *The Machine That Changed the World.*[21]

Despite the popularity of Japan bashing, national pride is only a minor snag. The major mind blocks occur because lean manufacturing runs counter to the Taylorist legacy, both in Japan and elsewhere. Lean manufacturing contradicts the basic idea that if a business belongs exclusively to its owners, to do with as they please, all employees should do their direct bidding. Lean manufacturing also challenges the notion of every business independently trying to maximize its own profit.

The intent—the soul of lean manufacturing—is quality growth. That is, the objective is to flat-out beat the competition in operating capability and customer satisfaction. Accomplishing this takes great cooperation among all parties to simultaneously decrease cost, eliminate waste, improve quality (eliminate scrap and defects, plus improve customer satisfaction with reliability, durability, service, and so on), and increase the speed of response to external changes. Such objectives are more demanding than simply making a consistent profit. Attaining them is impossible if the few direct the many in great detail in a centrally controlled, Taylorist-managed company.

The ideas are simple. The practice is difficult. Most organizations improve quality and reduce lead times by removing the waste from the flow of work. Very few have progressed to Toyota-level proficiency, using a uniform load schedule with calculated work-cycle times ("takt times") to coordinate regular improvement cycles throughout all operations. Without it, the potential of the system is still not realized.

In fact, the mind-set of Taylorism blocks a deep understanding of lean manufacturing. Almost all of us who have been Taylorists (including the author) at first want to understand it by grafting some new techniques onto our cumulative prior experience. Most of the grafts don't take. For example, popular speeches today often feature testimony describing five or ten years' personal progress toward a profound appreciation that all the techniques of TQM really add up to constant attention to customer satisfaction.

Two features of lean manufacturing differentiate it from Taylorism. One is that it motivates average working people to improve the performance of almost anything in the workplace. Improvement takes place because workers take responsibility. Second, lean manufacturing focuses on customers, not owners.

Until now the gut-level motivation for lean manufacturing as practiced almost everywhere, including Japan, has been quality growth—which is still growth. Usually the ultimate business objective is either to maximize market share or to maximize profits through superior operations and aggressive marketing. Participants in improvement processes more willingly accept the challenges if they clearly foresee sharing in growth. Thus practiced, lean manufacturing is only mass production done more efficiently.

If job loss is greatly feared, keeping a job may be sufficient reward. Suppose that with lean manufacturing, a company doubles productivity in a short time. Only through aggressive growth can it employ all the excess people; otherwise it is faced with tough decisions. For example, Omark Industries (now Blount, Inc.) was one of the first American companies to fully embrace lean manufacturing. Before long it had to decide which plants to keep open because it already had such a high share of the chain saw blade market that it was unable to significantly increase sales.

The basics of lean manufacturing depend on the capabilities of both managers and workers, and especially on their attitudes. Therefore, they can be practiced anywhere in the world. Lean manufacturing is only a training regimen for advanced twenty-first–century enterprises.

The New Challenge: Holistic Remanufacturing

While Americans in the 1980s worried about regaining a competitive edge, a feeling of unease began creeping into Japan, too. Top graduates began to avoid factory apprenticeships because the work was associated with the three Ds: Dirty, Dangerous, and Difficult. Although by 1992 disgust with Japanese financial scandals counterbalanced the three Ds, the young had delivered a message: Daily work had to become less of an ordeal.

In addition, mass markets were fragmenting. Labor-intensive work was outsourced, and factories hired more foreign workers. Environmental concerns became more intense. Leading Japanese manufacturers figured that within a decade Japan would import most mass-produced, low-cost goods from newer industrial countries. Their future was giving customers exactly what they want in a very short time.[22]

Toyota-style lean manufacturing is human-integrated manufacturing independent of computers. Elegance is achieved through simplicity—by eliminating all unnecessary steps so that no move is wasted. Watching a well-developed process is the industrial equivalent of watching a ballet. Because the graceful overall effect is achieved by cumulatively increasing skills for years, it appears to be much easier than it actually is.

Now we are beginning the computer age, but we haven't learned to use a computer gracefully yet. The ubiquitous machine hasn't contributed much to improve dancing, but that may come. The marvels of biofeedback, graphical choreography, virtual reality, and other computer-assisted preparation may still revolutionize dance.

In business, it is very tempting to use a computer to complicate life—as when airfare rates become incomprehensible—instead of simplifying it, but a computer is an incomparable tool. In an information-age enterprise, control systems—information, sensors, programming, and human responsibility—become the critical factors. For example, boilers are no longer stoked; programmed burners regulate burning as part of an overall system that controls removal of pollutants from the exhaust. This wave has only begun.

The new wave needs a new form of enterprise. Companies cannot preach teamwork between customers, employees, and suppliers while making key decisions that maximize only the interests of each separate set of owners. We need a more challenging, holistic view of the purposes of enterprise, something beyond balancing the conflicts between fiduciary duties (for profitability), customer satisfaction, purifying the environment, and the like. Self-interest will not disappear, but it's clear that a business system built on the premise that every operating entity functions strictly in its own interest cannot cope with holistic considerations.

Signs of the Times

In old industrial economies, the markets for established goods are maturing while the growth potential for those markets is very high elsewhere. In the United States, most of the middle-class population is already saturated with cars, TVs, refrigerators, and so on.

Accompanying this maturation process is the fragmentation of markets into niches. In the food business, so many new products (or at least new packages) appear that retailers are hard pressed to manage the churn, and consumers cannot react to them. Numerous models of VCRs—all programmed slightly differently—are available to record programs from more channels than any individual has the time or diversity of taste to enjoy. Even the number of auto models is so large that buyers must restrict their search to a few. Customers should be able to obtain exactly what they want or need with less time and waste. One forecast is that customers will participate more in the creation of goods and services they consume. Taking such responsibility treats life as an organism that occupies a point in a materials transfer flow chart halfway between a shopping mall and a dump.

Environmental concerns continue to mount. Some issues are only disguises for other political agendas, but the overall crisis is genuine. As environmentalists outgrow attention-getting polemics, "sustainable manufacturing" as a practical matter seems destined to grow in importance. Environmental control of a full cycle of material use will require business to organize for cooperation as well as competition.

A New Form of Enterprise

The new form of business must be more open than it is today. For many reasons, information that once was tightly controlled must be shared within an operation, and often with the whole world. First, the public simply requires more disclosure. For example, they want to know the ingredients of a can of food even when the terms are poorly understood. They want to see data indicating the reliability or history of similar products. They want to know what is being dumped in the ground, air, and water.

Second, working to the standards of world-class quality requires employees to take a great deal of responsibility and work closely together. As company after company has found, world-class performance begins with world-class trust. Trust begins when the in-house secrets are extremely limited and managers stop being bottlenecks of information flow. Visibility systems make it easy to know the status of projects and work flows. Most company information, including costs, is simply available to whoever needs to use it in their work.

Third, when suppliers and customers are truly partners, they want to know a great deal about products, services, and operations. In fact, they may expect to see the actual cost figures—a no-no of business-as-usual. In fact, the kind of organization needed is likely to be a full birth-to-death supply cycle. If various companies do not combine into a formal organization, they will at a minimum have a binding relationship with an organization that oversees the full cycle. (A full birth-to-death cycle is more extensive than either a supply chain or a marketing channel.)

This kind of business demands more cooperation than it would under conditions of wide-open growth. A great deal of work must be done to find practical ways to ensure this cooperation.

Likewise, the definition of a competitor needs refinement. A competitor is not an enemy. A competitor simply offers an alternative to the same customers using a different set of players in a full birth-to-death cycle of material use, and using a different improvement process. For the fastest innovation, competitors should steal ideas from each other. (The fastest rates of technical progress have occurred during times of stress—as during wartime or the space race—when companies were motivated to work together as never before.) Customers, suppliers, or other departments serving the same customers are *not* competitors, but collaborators.

A related issue is standardization of hardware, software, measurement systems, and so on. In the nineteenth century, the railroads first used different gauges of track and different methods of coupling cars. A nationwide rail system was impossible until railroads developed standard hardware and standard systems to exchange cars and divide freight payments.

Similar issues demand attention in various industries today. The computer business is nearing the same status as railroads in the nineteenth century. If the machines cannot easily talk to each other, their value is limited. A familiar example of the problem is the proliferation of different telephone companies and carriers since the breakup of AT&T. Making a long-distance call from a strange phone is an exercise in decoding the local access formula.

In Search of a New Soul

The global rise of industrial growth, computerization, the practice of lean manufacturing (or lean operations), and environmental problems are each momentous enough to cause major shifts. Taken together, they point toward the need for twenty-first–century enterprise to have new soul. Jockeying for growth and profit, challenging as it may be, is no longer sufficient. The soul of the new wave is growth in the quality of life.

The soul of an enterprise is a shared feeling that its objectives are worth sacrifice by those who work in it and by the society it serves. A company motivated by growth and profitability alone may attract its stakeholders by splitting the take. An enterprise with a broader purpose needs other attractions for its stakeholders. It needs a different soul.

When the railroads of the United States stopped expanding and coasted along as a service business, they eventually began to decline. The system did not know how to create excellence without the promise of growth. That defect in the system must be overcome.

Finding the spirit, or soul, of this movement is a formidable task. Big emotional consequences accompany even small changes in organizational practice, such as giving working-level employees operating responsibility once reserved for managers. Managers have difficulty letting go and not all workers are eager to assume responsibility. Human trust comes hard despite much gushing of words like *quality*, *responsibility*, and *dignity*.

Other new philosophers are more optimistic. For example, Christopher Lasch advocates a society in which the code of "self-interest" is replaced by "civic virtue."[23] Michael Vlahos projects that within two decades a feeling of "unity through civic virtue" will prevail over a "patchwork quilt" of narrow ethic, economic, and religious interests.[24] Gurus from Lester Thurow to Tom Peters all proclaim that a different management course must be taken. Peter Drucker suggests that companies guide their affairs by "maximizing the wealth-producing capacity of the enterprise" rather than maximizing short-term profits.[25] (Finding a self-proclaimed short-termer is impossible; any action can be self-justified as contributing to long-term welfare.)

No single would-be prophet's vision constitutes a social movement, but this sea change is more than a one-person splash. Behavioral and social changes occur when people are drawn to them in their own interest—or for survival. Seen from almost any perspective, the information age on "spaceship Earth" must draw us all into new dimensions of human performance.

The new wave demands near perfection in operating performance. Computers are precise machines. Environmental protection is a zero-defect, fail-safe game. Ultimate quality is a do-it-right-the-first-time-every-time ideal, a standard by which almost all operations still fall short. Rapid problem solving is a disciplined activity that requires innovative thinking. By contrast, the ideal of business-as-usual thinking has been to create profit margins so robust that they leave plenty of slack for waste and error in actual operations—so that they make easy money.

This rigor calls for a different spirit as part of the soul of this new form of enterprise. Perhaps it could be called the spirit of inquiry, a continuous quest to somehow make things better. Better is not necessarily bigger or more profitable. Better is reliable transportation, instant communication anywhere, a low crime rate, recycled polymers indistinguishable in use from virgin material, and so on—and enough new challenges to prevent active people from "going to seed." A spirit of inquiry is a lifelong interest in learning how to do something new.

But a spirit of inquiry is only part of the general motivation to improve the quality of life. Overall economic growth loses meaning. Although improving the quality of life is a broad and mushy concept, it is no more vague than maximizing long-run profit. Any such philosophical themes remain vague until they come to life in a specific enterprise.

Quality of life, the soul of the new era, depends on a more holistic view of progress, a new concept of business, and a broader scope of enterprise performance. Each enterprise is a network of people; its soul is the tie that binds them together. A new spirit of enterprise seems within reach, but it requires self-discipline, and so must be achieved by popular will.

A new soul is emerging, not because people are altruistic, but because without it we cannot deal with the new circumstances: environmental protection, computerization, limited growth, demanding customers, and so forth. *The new soul will prevail only if enterprises functioning in a new way can both exceed the economic performance of the old one and cope with broader challenges.*

NOTES

1. Thomas F. O'Boyle and Joan E. Rigdon, "As Economy Falters, Even the Affluent Are Fearful and Cautious," *The Wall Street Journal*, 24 December 1991.

2. Estimate from NMTBA, Association for Manufacturing Technology (formerly National Machine Tool Builders Association). Around six hundred companies are left. Some listed as builders are really just distributors. Just the change in name conveys a brief message on the "paradigm shift" in the equipment business.

3. A typical report on zero growth is "What Happened to the American Dream?" *Business Week*, 19 August 1991, 80–85.

4. Figures from *Wards Automotive Yearbook* and the U.S. Department of Commerce.

5. Estimates on vehicle stocks from the Motor Vehicle Manufacturers Association and the Federal Highway Administration show discrepancies, but they do not substantially change the conclusion.

6. Alex Groner, *The History of American Business and Industry* (New York: The American Heritage Publishing Co. [McGraw-Hill], 1972), p. 275.

7. Alvin Toffler, *The Third Wave* (New York: William Morrow, 1980).

8. Daniel Bell, *The Coming of Post-Industrial Society* (New York: Basic Books, 1973).

9. Laurence F. Gross, "Building on Success: Lowell Mill Construction and Its Results," *The Journal of the Society for Industrial Archaeology*, 14, no. 2 (1988): 23–34.

10. Alfred D. Chandler, *The Visible Hand* (Cambridge, MA: Belknap Press, Harvard U., 1977).

11. Robert L. Heilbroner, "Epitaph for the Steel Master," *Great Stories of American Businessmen* (New York: American Heritage Publishing Co. [McGraw-Hill], 1972), pp. 248–59. (Originally appeared in *American Heritage Magazine*, August 1960.)

12. Sudhir Kakar, *Frederick Taylor: A Study of Personality and Innovation* (Cambridge, MA: MIT Press, 1970), pp. 92–93.

13. David A. Hounshell, *From the American System to Mass Production* (Baltimore: Johns Hopkins University Press, 1984), p. 106.

14. Daniel Nelson, *Managers and Workers* (Madison: The University of Wisconsin Press, 1975), pp. 101–21.

15. Daniel Nelson, *Taylor and Scientific Management* (Madison: University of Wisconsin Press, 1980), p. 113.

16. Ibid., p. 320.

17. From records kept in Public Relations at the Willow Run plant, now owned by General Motors (and which is scheduled to be closed).

18. Robert Lacey, *Ford: The Men and the Machine* (New York: Ballantine Books, 1986), p. 412.

19. Personal conversation with Allan Mogensen.

20. John K. Galbraith, *The Affluent Society* (Boston: Houghton Mifflin, 1958).

21. Daniel T. Jones, Daniel Roos, and James P. Womack, *The Machine That Changed the World* (New York: HarperCollins, 1990).

22. *Manufacturing 21 Report*, Japan Machinery Federation and Waseda University, published by the Association for Manufacturing Excellence, Wheeling, Illinois, 1990.

23. Christopher Lasch, *The True and Only Heaven* (New York: Norton, 1991).

24. Michael Vlahos, "Culture and Foreign Policy," *Foreign Policy* 82 (Spring 1991): 59–78.

25. Peter Drucker, "Reckoning with the Pension Fund Revolution," *Harvard Business Review* 69, no. 2 (March–April 1991): 106–14.

2

BEYOND THE ACRONYMS– THE THREE-DAY CAR

THE HALF-LIFE OF A BUZZWORD ISN'T WHAT IT USED TO BE. EARLY IN THE twentieth century "scientific management" was part of a small trickle of management catchphrases. By the 1980s that trickle had swelled into a river of aphorisms and pronunciamentos so deep, and moving so fast, that professors and consultants who work full-time to keep up no sooner learn one of them than others of their number declare the phrase passé.

"Acronyms" (systems or techniques dubbed by acronyms such as MRP, CIM, TQM, JIT, TPM, or TEI,) are a useful core competence for management consulting; they're definable on an invoice. Creative consultants invent their own, or at least give them catchy names. Acronyms appeal to rationality. With the right technology, the right system, the right incentives—or even the right behavioral tweaks— surely customers will be pleased and competitors outclassed. An acronym is an enlightened whiz kid's logical sequel to the legacy of Taylorism.

As expounded by their enthusiasts, some acronyms are *the* revolution. Most go through initial rollout, then trial, then media deflation as critics note that the results of adopting PDQ stop somewhere short of nirvana.

At their worst, acronyms become "silver bullets" promulgated by consultants desperate for billings and sold to managers seeking quick solutions. Usually the results are fad solutions typified by:

- A consultant in XXX finds the market switching to YYY. Writes proposals based on XXX, but dressed up with a few YYY ideas in YYY terminology.
- Manager bones up on YYY and hires the consultant. Figures that "installing" YYY might be a quick hit leading to promotion in a year or two. The consultant, manager, and others learn together. Successful or not, the manager moves on in two years. End of YYY. Next manager wants to try ZZZ.
- After enough of this has gone on, the media become tired of it. All the cult followers have tried YYY and maybe ZZZ. It's time to go back to the basics with AAA again.

Although it's easy to be cynical, successful acronyms leave behind evidence of their passing. Something changes permanently, and for the better. All the participants learn something of value. So long as they are not complete illusions or shams, acronyms stir improvement. Everybody has to call a new practice something and define specifically what to do just to communicate. It is easy for the literati to belittle the simple explanations needed when people must learn steps one through ten of how to *do* something.

The number of acronyms is now dizzying. They add to the complexities of taxes, foreign currency hedging, environmental pressures, and regulations. Meanwhile competitive pressures demand downsizing and simplified organization. Managers look for help from two sources: computer systems and consultants.

Some managers think computer systems will allow them to cope with complexity. Others cannot cope with the computer systems themselves and seek a consultant, or perhaps a separate company, just to handle their computing requirements (like EDS did for GM).

Consultants have proliferated on every subject from environmental control to media relations. By 1989, over forty thousand full-time professionals could be counted in management consulting alone. That count is probably short by half. Professors and other part-timers add to the total. Ninety percent of management-consulting companies are less than thirty years old. The largest ones grew 10–30 percent annually until the 1990–91 recession.[1] A century earlier, only a handful of consultants was needed to catalyze the rise of Taylorism.

The reasons for the growth of consulting are simple. Companies increasingly cannot afford to carry full-time the expertise they need to run themselves. Conditions are changing rapidly at the same time competitive pressures intensify. Even the largest companies have cut back. For example, in 1990 General Electric disbanded most of its corporate internal consulting staff.

As a consequence, many formerly closed corporate enclaves are evolving into open-system operations, substantially influenced by external experts. In fact some companies have increasing difficulty distinguishing full-time employees, temporary employees, consultants, employees of suppliers—and even employees of customers. Something more momentous is taking place than "cycling through the acronyms."

The changes sweeping manufacturing are summarized in buzzphrases. Now we have lean manufacturing, time-based competition, learning organizations, and others—all extensions of the basic concepts of JIT, TQM, DFM and other acronyms, and all overlapping in definition. All require the leadership of top management, a sign that merely learning the techniques is insufficient.

Followers of acronym creep will recognize the paradigm comparisons in Figure 2-1 as a compilation of the philosophical changes needed to practice most of the current acronyms. American managers during the 1980s made a bigger leap than they realize—in ideals, if not always in actual accomplishment.

NEW ENTERPRISE, NEW SOUL

Attaching new acronyms and buzzphrases to an old mind-set creates a patchwork of thought and practice. In part, this is inescapable because people cannot make the transition from one kind of world to another without fumbling with a complicated mix of the two. However, we need a simpler system of thought to describe where we are headed.

FIGURE 2-1

EVERYTHING ISN'T THE WAY IT USED TO BE

Mass Production Business-as-Usual	*Lean Manufacturing Paradigms of the "Acronyms"*
Economy of scale (Bigger is better) (Mass production) (Production pushed out to the customers)	Economy of time (Quicker is better) (Make only what is wanted) (Customers "moved" into the operations)
Assets are things	Assets are people
Profit is #1 (Sell the maximum of whatever the customer will accept)	Customer satisfaction is #1 (Quality is a religion)
Owners, managers, and staff are thinkers separated from doers	Doers are thinkers; and thinkers are doers
Organizations controlled by hierarchies; functional departments separated	Weak hierarchies; organize based on teamwork; numerous cross-functional teams.
Suppliers kept at arm's length, and contracted by bid and negotiation	Suppliers are partners, integrated into many customer operations
Performance measurement for control (financially dominated)	Performance measurement for improvement (broader measures)

Perhaps companies as we have thought of them are becoming incomplete as operating organizations capable of carrying out the world's work. Not even vertically integrated giants accomplish their purposes by themselves. They function by grace of a network that some call a virtual company. I prefer the term "enterprise."

An enterprise is a network of *people*—employees, service representatives, agents, consortia members, consultants, advisors, suppliers, dealers, and even customers. Today, that network is often called a "supply chain," a phrase that too often connotes only first- or second-tier suppliers of materials. That meaning is far too narrow.

In an enterprise, a network of partners work with each other to serve the same customer. Each partner hopes that the others work toward a similar vision using a similar improvement process. (An improvement process is one of those stepwise approaches to improvement that have become well known in organizations rigorously working on quality.) A competitor is an enterprise offering customers alternatives and engaged in different improvement processes.

Another company or another person working in an enterprise may also be a member of other enterprises. Therefore, as we now think of the network, the company or person might be a competitor, a supplier, and a customer all at the same time. Motorola and IBM already have that relationship. So do each of the Big Three automakers.

Company boundaries as we now recognize them are determined by ownership. That definition is becoming less useful. Boundaries are now determined by the common customers the enterprise serves and by the common participants engaged in the process of serving them.

An enterprise is bound together by the needs of the same or similar customers, and ideally, by dedication to the same goals and visions for improving service to them. Legal creations may allocate money and liabilities, but the ultimate responsibility for an enterprise belongs to the linkages of people who carry out its work.

No individual can know all the enterprise partners two or three connections removed from the core operations (like the laundry service to a tooling supplier). Mapping the outer limit in detail would not be worth the effort. For actual performance purposes, it's more important to understand the primary flows of information and operations than it is to comprehend the legal personae of the various participants.

In North America, Honda is an example of an early-stage enterprise. Legally, Honda consists of several subsidiaries. Many suppliers are sole sources and partners in operations, and Honda also wants its dealers to be partners in understanding and serving the customer. Honda operations are a web of tightly knit activities directed to three markets: automotive, motorcycle, and power equipment.

In the United States, Xerox Business Products and Systems Group has begun to resemble an enterprise by concentrating on several copier market segments. Many other companies that are "reducing their supplier base" and "forming alliances" are migrating toward enterprise relationships.

However, the enterprise relationships inside current organizational boundaries are as important as those outside. Companies are organized with separation of powers more for managerial or ownership control than for customer service. Despite a big push toward team building, nearly all companies have schisms between functional departments. At its worst, this internecine warfare is more intense than the battles with competitors. Enterprise building has just begun.

The Soul of the Enterprise

"Soul" has often been used to express a common ethnic spirit among black Americans, a common appreciation of their music, history, feelings, and mores. "Soul" implies basic gut-level emotions—the stuff at the core of life. More generally, "kindred souls" suggests an intangible but unifying belief motivating a large number of otherwise diverse people.

From the European viewpoint, the soul of the Renaissance was growth through intellectual enlightenment. The soul of the age of exploration (or colonization) was geographic expansion, and the soul of the Industrial Revolution was growth through technical progress. (Both of the latter were easily transformed into desire for wealth.) The soul of the information wave is growth in the quality of life, a more complex vision than in prior ages. It may not be as easily subverted into wealth accumulation, but since normal human behavior seeks distinctive status, no soul or system is incorruptible.

The soul of enterprise is the unifying commitment of its collaborators to customer service, excellence in operations (such as environmental protection), and an allegiance to a common process of improvement. It transcends petty differences. The soul of an enterprise has counterparts in the reasons participants take pride in the Metropolitan Opera or Notre Dame football. One can divide the soul of enterprise into three kinds of motivation, somewhat like Scrooge's ghosts of Christmas:

Soul of the Past	Reputation. Tradition. Heritage. Pride. Brand allegiance. Goodwill.
Soul of the Present	Commitment. Obligation. Concern. Responsibility to customers, internal and external, and to other stakeholders in the enterprise.
Soul of the Future	A motivating vision of what could be, including laurels for accomplishment and specters of doom.

Great leaders exhort by using all three "souls." For example, Lincoln's Gettysburg Address flows from past to present to future in one oratorical sweep. Although Lincoln referred to a concept of government still relatively new, the United States was a tangible entity. Creating the same stir over a less tangible enterprise is impossible as long as the idea remains an ethereal vision with no name and an ill-defined form.

An enterprise business structure is now possible because computer and communications technologies allow it. However, the enterprise is only a technician's dream unless the motivation for it is stronger than technical adventure. Technology creates enthusiasm but not a cause many will die for.

An enterprise form of business will emerge only when it becomes obvious that we need it to achieve the high operating proficiencies that will simultaneously create a reasonable quality of life and preserve a sustainable environment. Quality of life and a sustainable environment are not the same as maximum profit or even maximum wealth. They cannot be completely expressed as dollars.

Motivation to reach for goals imperfectly translatable to dollars depends on the fine arts of leadership and persuasion. Great business leaders have long exercised this kind of persuasion, from JCPenney's "The customer is always right" to Robert Galvin exhorting Motorola to make customer satisfaction its supreme goal through "six-stigma" (error rates of 3.4 or less per million opportunities).

A well-stated vision promises laurels for accomplishment: customers pleased, market share saved or increased, jobs saved, more interesting work. An antithetical vision paints a specter of doom: customers lost, pay cut, jobs lost, plants or offices closed, living areas turned uninhabitable.

Open-System Enterprise

In computing vernacular, an open system enables communication between all kinds of hardware and software. Despite their peculiarities, the machines can communicate in a common language instead of gibberish. Implied is that each machine can read information from anywhere that is not security coded. In an open system, new generations of hardware and software can digest old programs and data, so systems can evolve without start-from-scratch relearning, like suddenly switching from English to Chinese.

Open-system enterprise is analogous to open computing systems in three respects. First, people may enter, make contributions, and leave. Virtually all companies operating in the United States are somewhat open in this sense. They define how employees and contractors enter and leave and the obligations and benefits incurred.

Second, open information is the rule and not the exception. Anyone can gain access to basic operating information, including competitors. In general, only competitive product-development information and private personnel records are kept restricted.

The third is a pursuit of facts, and a predisposition to base our actions on them. We all interpret observations to fit our prior theories and experience. No one wants to be embarrassed or criticized (no pilot wants to admit that pilot error, even if it was within procedure, led to a crash). This requires enormous self-discipline of human nature.

An open-system enterprise presumes social discipline. A continuous improvement process requires people to take both personal and cooperative responsibility. To many, "discipline" suggests military close-order drill, but social discipline in an enterprise implies discipline in individual thought rather than in taking orders.

The phrase "taking ownership" is commonly used to mean taking responsibility. A capitalist presumption is that that owners take responsibility for service, efficiency, and improvement, but that does not always happen. Corporate chieftans such as Charles Keating, Jr., who became the symbol of savings and loan scandals, are publicized mostly for defrauding investors. More common is the absentee owner, public or private, focused exclusively on earnings and having little interest in the business's customers or operations. The assumption is that professional managers will assume that responsibility—subject to controls designed to maximize ROI.

Investor leadership is not intrinsically inspirational. A cash flow projection may be vital, but it has no soul. Operations striving for ultimate performance make many more demands on the whole nature of man.

Why Open-System Enterprise Must Be Different

The legal and tax systems of the United States presume stand-alone companies, operating at arm's length, dedicated to making a profit and serving a social purpose to obtain it. "Arm's length" means telling the other party nothing. However, responsible industry leaders have always worked together a great deal, particularly in times of public need.

The general assumption is that risk, responsibility, and reward belong disproportionately to owners and managers, the movers and shakers to whom others "report." They are responsible to the other stakeholders; it's their job to satisfy customers, repay bankers, and pay employees. In an open-system enterprise, many of the other stakeholders (employees, suppliers, and even customers) must take substantial operating responsibility. As the information waves rolls over us, the performance level expected of enterprise requires distributing responsibility more broadly.

An open-system enterprise serves a socially useful purpose by serving direct customers and the general public—and making a profit—for everyone, not just the owners. In fact, to sustain its share of social overhead (taxes, retirement, benefits, and contributions), enterprises need to have high margins. To accomplish these goals, individuals in an enterprise must feel a high level of responsibility. The difference between that high level of responsibility and business-as-usual reflects the difference between "institutional" attitudes and decentralized but networked "entrepreneurial" attitudes.

The Economics 101 theory of the firm—a set of behavioral assumptions with the juice squeezed out—holds that owners are entitled to run a business in their self-interest because their money is at risk. A company is a possession that can be bought and sold. Competing companies operating in their owners' self-interest will maximize wealth—overall growth—through that mysterious force, the invisible hand of market forces. Free markets will prevent any firm from perpetuating an unfair advantage.[2]

In practice "lemonade-stand economics" works as long as stand-alone, self-interest manufacturers can accomplish society's needs. But over the last century, things became complicated as simple entrepreneurships grew into publicly owned, multidivisional, mass-production Goliaths run by professional managers.[3]

Now the system stands to become impossibly complicated unless it is rethought. Performance depends as much on the development of human capital—people collectively developing themselves—as on the use of investment capital. The old control relationship is not the same. Figure 2-2 compares enterprise thinking and business-as-usual thinking.

WHERE ARE WE GOING?

With all the acronyms and buzzwords, it's a struggle to avoid being cast adrift in a sea of hype. Scenarios of the future would help set a direction. In fact, visions of this type are increasingly important. When a future direction is not quite as one dimensional as "heading west," a vision is an important guide to help everyone find the same path.

Beyond lean manufacturing et al., where are we going? The major features saturating future scenarios are:

- The rise of the information wave: Pervasive use of computers and electronics with data instantly communicated almost anywhere and having applications still difficult to grasp.
- Rigorous operating performance requirements: All the acronyms are nothing but a base from which this new level of performance can start.
- Open-system information: Open in the sense that everyone participating in an operational system has high visibility of objectives, data, and status. Much more is involved than compatible computers and interactive software.

FIGURE 2-2

THEMES OF THE
NEW SOUL OF THE ENTERPRISE

Open-system enterprise assumes all the "paradigm shifts"
in Figure 2–1, plus other mind-set inversions, as suggested below:

Industrial Wave: *Business-as-Usual*	*Information Wave:* *Open-System Enterprise*
Goal is growth	Goal is quality of life
Profit-driven (Profit as a reward)	Performance-driven (Profit as a tax)
Owner-controlled companies	Customer-guided enterprises
Companies are defined as inert assets	Companies and enterprises are defined as people
Product cost drives operations	Holistic performance drives operations
Control by the managers	Responsibility a duty of everyone (including customers)
Education for the elite: training for workers (maybe)	Training and education a necessity for all
Fortress companies	Open systems; porous boundaries
Information access restricted; exclusion a means of control	Open systems; few restrictions
Environmental protection considered a drag on growth	Environmental protection is part of the quality of life (zero-discharge manufacturing at lower cost is the ideal)

• Distributed, interactive organizations: A radically different
form of business organization with much smaller operating
units, each focused on its own process but linked by communications. Much more decentralization of responsibility. Probably, control over material used through an entire cycle of its
use: birth-to-death-to-reuse.

- Common human operating systems: Compatibility in problem-solving approaches. Common operating-performance measures. High standards of performance systemwide.
- Ability to serve customers with products or service tailored just for them.
- Highly flexible (or agile) systems in engineering, production, and support operations: Blurring of distinctions between functions of a business as conceived today. Ability to routinely discover, develop, and deploy more complex technology than ever before.
- Environmentally sustainable operations: Zero-discharge manufacturing.
- Dominance of the need to develop people—human capital—not only as "workers" but as customers.
- Creation of high-value-added, high-margin enterprises capable of sustaining a high social overhead.
- Much more emphasis on quality of life as a goal. Recognition that high margins are necessary to create and sustain it.
- Guidance by visions, especially during periods of tough transition.

Escaping the Imperial Court

A new form of enterprise is not assured, of course. We are unable to use the technology we have at hand today, so the major challenges are not technical. They are human, and they are tough.

Consider just one human problem—a limited perspective of the world. All of us see the world from different specialized backgrounds. This condition cannot be escaped. Mentally, we all live at the center of our own universe, but simply recognizing this fact helps promote a common vision.

As long as people could simply exist in their own little community, their own little company, or in their own little part of a big company, they could believe their own experience to be much more unique than it actually was. Such myopia is analogous to geographic perception. Most ancient people drawing a man believed their own locale was the center of the universe, a trait called ethnocentrism. For centuries the ancient Chinese believed that the world literally centered on the imperial court, as in Figure 2-3.

FIGURE 2-3

WORLD VIEW OF THE CHINESE CIRCA 500 B.C.

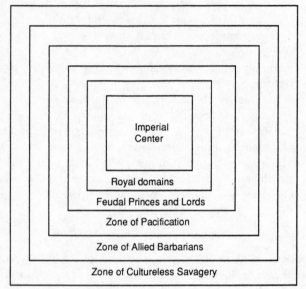

North

West

East

Imperial Center

Royal domains

Feudal Princes and Lords

Zone of Pacification

Zone of Allied Barbarians

Zone of Cultureless Savagery

South

The Chinese ethnocentric view of the world differed from that of other people only in its particulars. Ancient civilizations had little concept of the existence of others. The concept of Europeans discovering America and other regions of the world is a story of the gradual expansion of an ethnocentric view, but the view remained ethnocentric. Ethnocentric views obviously remain a worldwide phenomenon and an obstacle to peace locally and globally.

SOURCE: *From Yi-Fu Tuan,* Topophilia *(Englewood Cliffs, NJ: Prentice-Hall, 1974), p. 38.*

Advocates hyping a new acronym frequently invoke Copernicus's discovery that the earth rotates around the sun rather than being the center around which the universe moves. This old story has been cited by the advancing army of paradigm shifters so often that it has become trite. Nonetheless, it remains important.

Advances in transportation and communications allow us to see that we are only one small part of a whole, but incompletely, and then only if we are willing. That is, pumping rivers of information anywhere in the world does not completely erase our view of ourselves as the center of our own universe.

Mentally escaping the imperial court at the center of our own experience is important because participants in an open-system enterprise need to have an overview of it. None can understand it all in detail, but each can figure out how to access the detail needed. Design engineers sometimes call this ability having systems-thinking in addition to a technical specialty. A broad outlook is necessary to discharge responsibility within an open-system enterprise.

Our vision of the future is constructed by projecting the evolution of our limited mental map or updating a version of our past experience—mentally going "back to the future," like generals who prepare to fight the last war. We can construct a different kind of enterprise no faster than we can map out a larger mental territory. It's a fundamental change in mental mapping to go from picturing a fortress company at the center of an infinite world to being a participant in one part of a large but finite world.[4]

THE CHALLENGES OF
TWENTY-FIRST-CENTURY VISIONS

A vision can never be a precise forecast. No two people ever "see" a vision exactly the same way. It can, however, provide a rough guideline to future development. If consistently evoked for guidance, visions become drivers of major change.

A vision is not a pipe dream. It is tested for feasibility. Well done, a vision represents a multiple set of goals. If we keep working on the various pieces long enough and try to keep the pieces cohesive (the objective of the vision), eventually we should make progress in some form. Undoubtedly, the condition attained will not be like the original scenarios.

Technical visions have in the past few decades been called technological forecasts. Their track record has not been outstanding. Most projections made by scientists and engineers overestimate the acceptance of technical change by the public or underestimate the costs of achievement.

Social projections of an ideal society are called utopias, after Thomas More's work by that name. Utopias do not enjoy a great reputation for accuracy either, and some make no pretense of being anything but fiction.

So why make such projections? Because we do not know how to otherwise stimulate people to join in devising a plan for where the future should go. Because without a rough guide we all go in different directions. Many of our present problems promise to be the kind that are insolvable by individual persons, companies, or even governments working on their own, and no one should pretend that agreeing on the most minimal of collaborative actions is easy.

The scenarios to be presented are technically tame. Some of the technology they projected has already come to pass. The most severe of the human challenges they present are to our business and organizational thinking.

General Projections

Holistic remanufacturing, or agile manufacturing, comes in three versions: one from the Agile Manufacturing Enterprise Forum, and a U.S. group that coined the term "agile"; an earlier version from Japan; and some modifications by the author.

"Agility" is a rigorous interpretation of the term "flexibility" in manufacturing: Deliver what the customer wants, including design changes, when wanted, where wanted, at reasonable cost, with no quality glitches and no environmental degradation. At a ridiculous extreme, agility is meeting any need for change instantly. It's a twenty-first–century ideal for manufacturing excellence—if such a different milieu can still be called "manufacturing."

Scenarios bring this vision to life. Many scenarios have been proposed. They began with the Japanese Manufacturing 21 Project (reported in the *Manufacturing 21 Report*).[5] Later, the Agile Manufacturing Enterprise Forum crystalized four scenarios in its 1991 projection of twenty-first–century manufacturing.[6]

Some of the general projections common to the scenarios of both groups are include the following.

Fragmentation of Mass Media.   During most of the twentieth century the mass media dominated in both print and broadcast forms. The big newspapers and major TV networks are already giving way to a myriad of information sources. As soon as TV viewers can connect on-line through their household instruments, it will be a different media world. Phenomena such as computer bulletin boards already presage what will come. The importance: Mass media make mass markets. Fragmented media make niche markets. Interactive media will make individual markets.

Prosumers.   "Prosumers" are consumers who are involved in the design or production of the products or services they use. In the information age, they may interact with producers on-line as well as in person. Prosumers blur the distinction between a service business and manufacturing as we have known it.[7]

The End of Market Expansion.   Mass markets have been based on cheap transportation and cheap distribution. Now, however, the costs of distribution usually exceed those of production. In addition, there is a limit to the physical volume of goods that each individual can use, store, and maintain—or that can be recycled for reuse. In the future, information networks should simplify direct delivery from producer to consumer with much less need for middleman services. (United Parcel Service and Federal Express operations combined with computer shopping are 1992 examples.)

Software over Hardware.   By the twenty-first century, computers and sensors will be integrated into every kind of product, making the functioning of the product incomplete without the software. In some cases, the purpose of hardware is only to enable software to function. Software will become the dominant feature of a total service package in which the hardware plays only a role. Furthermore, some software can be customized by the user. Some of it (like home appliances with fuzzy logic programming) will adapt the hardware to the user's needs without the user being conscious of it.

Mass Production to the NICs.   As the information wave advances, routine mass production using stable technology will shift to the newly industrializing (NICs). Today, competition for mass markets is very intense. Soon, advanced economies will obtain standard products from NICs while protecting technical skills or manufacturing capabilities they consider vital to their self-interest. Still longer-term, a significant fraction of advanced production will be individualized remanufacturing for prosumers.

Remanufacturing.   Considerable production is apt to shift to retrofitting, remanufacturing, and recycling. Retrofitting simply upgrades an old product with add-ons. Remanufacturing is rebuilding an old product, but often to a higher quality level than when it was new and with added features. Recycling presumes reducing all materials to their separate raw states and refabricating them into completely different designs or products. (Environmentalists have popularized recycling, but retrofitting or remanufacturing usually uses even less energy.)

Product Tracking.   "Smart chips" buried in virtually every durable good will track product history. They might even diagnose problems for owners or service technicians or be used for individual marketing—suggesting that a different package or feature would be more suitable. For instance, the chip in a self-adjusting vacuum cleaner might record that it works at the top of its power range more than 30 percent of the time, indicating that a heavier-duty unit might work better. Because of product tracking, companies that now think of themselves as manufacturers will find that a major part of their business is after-sales service, seeking to better match their offering to a customer's needs.

Zero-Discharge Manufacturing.   The American team of the Agile Manufacturing Enterprise Forum boldly advocated the ultimate in going green—a goal of zero emissions and zero effluents—which would be pursued with the vigor of the moon race by at least certain kinds of industry (particularly specialty chemicals and heavy industry). At the same time, industry should increase its energy efficiency. The energy and material savings would pay for the huge capital expenditure.

Virtual Companies.   This concept is almost identical to open-system enterprise, described earlier. Where a market opportunity is sensed, a "virtual company" can be quickly assembled to seize it. A virtual company would be populated by people from various base companies. Much of the work would take place long-distance, using "plug compatible" systems. When its purpose is exhausted, the virtual company would disband.

Factory America Network (FAN, or FANit).   The Agile Manufacturing Enterprise Forum proposed a huge network of databases—an electronic map of industrial America, including cross-indexed references to process types and capabilities, engineering experience, materials handling, programming capabilities, software and hardware catalogs, and so on. The value of a totally comprehensive system of this type has been questioned. However, any operation participating in an enterprise would have to be a participant in the databases vital to that enterprise.

The four scenarios that follow were devised by the Agile Manufacturing Enterprise Forum. The ASICs scenario and the "three-day car" are takeoffs on two very similar scenarios by the Japanese Manufacturing 21 team. But the scenario that captures the most attention is the "three-day car." Automotive manufacturing integrates many technologies, and everyone can relate to cars. The industry is big, old, and traditional, so this scenario starkly contrasts the new with the old.

UltraComm

An UltraComm is the ultimate multimedia communications instrument, a combination of computer, cellular telephone, and television. By early next century, UltraComms will be everywhere—in business, homes, and cars—and used to communicate with almost anyone in the civilized world. They will be as common as telephones are in the 1980s, and we will wonder how we ever got along without them.

However, UltraComm instruments are useless without a huge network of UltraComm databases. For instance, firefighters and police officers on a run could call up a map routing them to the scene, then another map of the building they are about to enter, and perhaps information on the contents of the building. Many of the maps would be accessible to private citizens. UltraComm is *the* ultimate worldwide open system.

The UltraComm instrument is manufactured by a virtual company, or open-system enterprise, operating largely through computer networks. The same enterprise creates and maintains some of the databases. No company alone possesses the hardware, software, and information services necessary to make up UltraComm in total, so a virtual company, described as an "electronic mosaic" of about sixty companies, sustains it. The UltraComm central staff tracks activities, records contributions by each of the members, and disburses revenue to them. The manufacturing side of UltraComm is a hardware support system for the information services. Final assembly plants (which also upgrade and remanufacture) are located all over the world. Various suppliers send modules to the assembly plants for final configuration.

Many UltraComm instruments are custom designed for specific users. The modular design allows an UltraComm to be upgraded or downgraded to whatever capabilities its owner desires and can afford. A history chip in each one tracks usage, maintenance, and condition. An almost limitless number of configurations can be built to order in a fast-flow process. Quality is designed in, and most manufacturing processes are studied and improved until the mean time between failures of UltraComm instruments is decades. Each network of suppliers and final assembly plants can accept an order, credit-check it, validate it, and quickly schedule the correct set of modules to meet at final assembly. (Lead time is not specified, but implied to be short—days—or hours.) If a customer request can be met by a different software or different board, one of the suppliers in the UltraComm network ships direct to the customer.

Application-Specific Integrated Circuit (ASICs)

By the late 1990s, the cost of a plant to make 64–256 megabit DRAMS will rise to $1 billion or more. The investment for a billion-bit chip is even higher. By 2000 the economics of miniaturizing computer power will favor optical memories and optoelectronic circuitry. They will make possible hybrid computers combining parallel, sequential, and neural-net structures having performance capabilities a thousand times better than in 1990. Almost everyone can see that within a decade or two, further additions to raw computing power will have less value than creating applications of interest.

That condition will lead to powerful, ubiquitous "smart chips." These will create the performance features customers want in any product: vehicles, communication products, appliances, credit cards, toys, or even furniture. The important feature of any chip to a customer is what it will do. That is, the hardware is only a carrier for the desired software capability, and the business will evolve into providing "software solutions."

Imagine U.S. ASICs, a company in the business of marketing application-specific integrated circuits. On a 1990s balance sheet, its most important asset is its production facilities. Actually, U.S. ASIC's most important asset is its chip design software, available from ASICnet.

U.S. ASICs files contain generic chip specifications, processing histories, ASIC device simulators, processing statistics, for U.S. ASICs plants worldwide, order-status information, and so on. The files are designed to attract customers. They are as useful to U.S. ASICs as the SABRE reservation system is to American Airlines. U.S. ASICs operations, like those of an airline, provide a service to customers.

The heart of the software is ASIC design packages. Customers can lease a package and design chips themselves, if they are able. If not, U.S. ASICs will train their engineers in the use of the package. Chips designed with U.S. ASICs software will probably be downloaded for production to U.S. ASICs plants, but some customers produce their own, and occasionally a customer will have the chip built in a competitor's plant. (That can be done with open-system computing.)

Exposing the design software would seem to invite pirating. This result is unlikely because nonexperts will pay a premium to obtain the latest software and advice in tough cases. (Similarly, when a medical problem becomes serious, it also stops being a do-it-yourself project.)

The intrinsic nature of U.S. ASICs requires operating in an open-system environment worldwide. Plants can be built almost anywhere, and software is transportable with the speed of light. The spread of the ASICnet will rapidly diffuse high-tech capability around the globe, although for some time ability to access and use the latest ASIC technology will remain a sign of information wave status. (One goal in both the American and the Japanese scenarios was to keep advanced manufacturing in the home country. However, the scenarios themselves, particularly ASICs, show the futility of that aspiration.)

Chemicals Without Muss or Fuss

The chemical industry has been at the forefront of the movement toward green manufacturing. The lion's share of industrial waste and emissions comes from generating energy and processing chemicals, including foodstuffs. From all the scientific and public criticism (not all of it well founded, of course) in the 1980s, the major chemical companies got the message to "go green." The chemical industry decreased its energy use 30 percent between 1975 and 1990, for instance.

So far, the industry has reduced the environmental side effects of established manufacturing practices. But that's not nearly enough. Major chemical companies should publicly declare their intention to achieve zero-discharge manufacturing during the next ten years and call for public support in doing it. Public commitments are harder to back down from. The direction of the industry—downsizing—will aid the effort.

Economy of scale for producing commodity chemicals has not disappeared, but the new direction takes away much of its advantage, and for specialty chemicals, small is the way to go. Several factors are combining to shrink process sizes. The major ones are electronics and software. Supercomputer simulations already predict the characteristics of molecules and reactions with much less time and mess than laboratory experiments. It is the coming way to perform chemical research. Simulating production scale reactions saves more time and cost. Transferring processes directly from lab to production eliminates pilot plant tests and other stages of scale-up.

Intelligent process control, sensing, and sampling dramatically improve processing flexibility. The increased ability to sense exactly what is occurring in chemical-unit operations leads to better yields, lower unit costs, and shorter lead times. These advantages can be gained in any size plant, but smaller equipment responds quicker and can be used more flexibly.

Take, for instance, polymerization of ethylene into different molecular weights of polyethylene. The composition of ethylene gas entering a reaction varies, depending on the oil stock it came from and distillation variability at a refinery. In the bad old days, polymerization conditions were set hit-or-miss on a target grade. On-target polyethylene was sold to particular customers; off-target was held until somebody wanted that grade, or it was sold at discount. One had to overproduce to be sure of getting enough of the tougher-to-make target grades.

Now, however, the ability to produce what is wanted when it is wanted confers the enormous advantages in quality, cost, and environmental control. It also improves the economics of small plants. Smaller plants avoid the expense of overproduction. If they are located close to customers, or on customer sites, transport costs are also slashed. Furthermore, the most economical way to stop accidents during transportation is to use the chemicals without shipping them anywhere. Finally, producers at plants on the customers' sites can better understand how customers use their products.

As an example of how a small speciality chemical plant might operate, Toyo Engineering Corporation of Tokyo built a small modular-design, pipeless chemical plant for batch processing. Instead of piping "stuff" from various storage tanks into reactors, a robot transporter carries the reactor to different stations—to get another shot of reagent, hook up to an agitator, or be heated. Coupling and uncoupling is automatic and unattended, and monitored by as many fail-safe devices as possible. If anything does go wrong, the robot, not an operator, sniffs the fumes and absorbs the spills.

A ChemNet database will assist with residual problems. Buyers for the by-products and wastes can be identified. ChemNet's files will describe hazardous materials and how to handle them. In addition, shipping in returnable containers, already a widespread practice, stops many chemicals from going to rest in unwanted places—like landfills.

Running small, decentralized plants will require a more knowledgeable work force, educated and experienced in every position. Manager-worker class wars are inconsistent with the level of responsibility expected of every worker in the new-style plants. Many companies have already begun a different system of production using self-directed work teams. Longer run, the descendent of that new system must cement trust between people.

The Three-Day Car

This scenario is presented first from the Japanese viewpoint. They lead in the transition to this new world in autos. By 2001, the Japanese auto industry expects to have four major bases of production: Japan, North America, Europe, and the newly industrializing countries (NICs). Annual unit production in Japan will have declined by 20 percent or more. To offset the loss of volume revenue, higher-priced models must be produced domestically.

Like the United States, a mature Japan cannot compete against low-cost areas making "econobox" cars. In the 1990s, the domestic industry must learn how to profitably build higher-value, special-niche models selling fewer than twenty thousand units over a lifetime. The Mazda Miata is an example of one step in this strategic direction. The three-day car comes later.

Changes in the North American market will affect the speed of changes in the automotive production system in Japan. Overall, the North American market is expected to be nearly flat, growing by 1 percent or less per year, assuming that the price of oil stabilizes (but not necessarily at a low level). Companies will stage a dogfight for the high end of this market (sports/luxury models, which, along with the pickup trucks, gained market share in the past decade).

By 2001, electric vehicles will be made commercially, but not for large segments of the market, and solar cars will be about where gasoline-powered ones were a century earlier. Despite environmental pressure, the internal combustion engine will probably have several more reprieves before disappearing. The potential for more efficient conversion of fuel energy to motion is still considerable, and so is the potential for alternative fuels such as LPG. Clean exhaust and vehicular fuel efficiency will remain high on the list of customer demands.

The degree of success of Japanese transplant manufacturing is critical to manufacturing changes in Japan itself. Japanese manufacturers expect to level out auto production in North America at 2.5–3.0 million vehicles per year. The plan has long been to add supply plants and to link up with American suppliers until local content tops 80 percent to both decrease trade deficits and hedge against currency fluctuations. Exports to North America will drop to about five hundred thousand vehicles per year. Most of these will be high-performance or luxury cars.

If the exchange rate stays above 120¥ to the dollar, exports to the United States will decrease slowly. If it sinks below 100¥, exports will drop rapidly.

Combining both homeland-built and transplant-built vehicles, the total number of Japanese nameplate cars sold in the United States will remain a nearly constant percent of the market. The new threat to both Americans and the Japanese in the North American market could well be imports from NICs, which could rise to between one and two million units by 2001, depending on the trade policies of the U.S. government.

NIC nameplates will take the entry-level market from both Japanese and Big Three companies. A percentage of Japanese transplant production will be sold as American nameplates, and both Japanese companies and the Big Three will sell NIC entry-level imports under their own labels. One or more Japanese car companies could move their headquarters to the United States. (Honda is the most-rumored possibility.)

For a decade or two, transplants in North America will continue to mass produce midscale vehicles. Production strategy will be to implement factory automation along with productivity and equality improvements so that the quality of cars is equal to those built in Japan at a competitive price. The most advanced processes will not start in the transplants.

While the auto makers stagnate in the established industrial economies (how many more cars can we use?), they could boom in some of the developing countries. However, near-term, rapid growth will be confined to pockets of the People's Republic of China, the former Soviet Union, and Eastern Europe. Most of this developing world market will be for mass-produced econoboxes, but affluent "third-worlders" will be a significant market for upscale cars.

Sometime in the 1990s South Korea will probably replace Japan as the major exporter (in units) to North America. Taiwan, Malaysia, and other NICs moving to automotive production may also try to establish marketing beachheads in North America. Japanese companies having joint relations with NIC auto companies will mass-produce a limited number of inexpensive basic models exportable to a worldwide market, including Japan. Procurement strategy will again aim for high local content, focusing on the quality of parts.

The Japanese domestic car market will continue to expand by 1.5 percent per year—but might top out because of traffic congestion. If current forces continue, imports from established countries will capture 5–10 percent of this market, about 1 percent from the United States and the rest from Europe. Most of these will be upscale cars unique to Japan. The major shift will be in small cars imported from the NICs.

About half of the Japanese domestic market will fragment into many small niches. The other half will be supplied from domestic production of basic transportation nameplates selling twenty thousand to a hundred thousand units per year, much as now. The fragmented half will consist of numerous different models produced in quantities of less than twenty thousand per year. A small but significant number of customers will desire cars to be tailored to their individual requirements—extensive customization.

Serving the niche and custom markets is the most difficult challenge. If niche and custom markets can be dominated and a fair share of the basic car market retained, the Japanese domestic auto industry will remain healthy. So can the American one.

Flexibility: A First Step for the 1990s

An intermediate strategy is vital because we cannot instantly transform to the wild world of the future. Today, not a decade from now, challenge number 1 is to break dependence on economy of scale in *production*—big lots and long runs. Go for niche markets. Internationally, "economy of scale" is in marketing, common processes, and common systems, and the nature of these functions will begin changing significantly from the way we know them today. Worldwide name recognition promotes marketing, but people will want a car unique to them—if they can afford it.

Properly used, a common information system for product and process development in every production base in the world should stop engineers in both product and process development from "reinventing the wheel." Any production base should be able to quickly modify any design for its target customers and start building it—if its personnel, equipment, tooling, and processes have been developed for flexibility.[8]

Challenge number 2 is to create a system to produce vehicles in low volumes at reasonable cost. Manufacturing excellence is a great start, but to take advantage of it, the time and cost of new model development and start-up must be drastically cut. This is now the number one priority of the Japanese auto industry. Product and process design must occur in parallel. Tooling and equipment conversion time and expense must be reduced by *about an order of magnitude.*

For this intermediate system to be financially sound, many new models must make a profit on ten to twenty thousand cars in their lifetime. Development cost can beheld down by reusing old ideas and modifying them to new needs. Certification of power plants and tooling for body parts are the most expensive development costs.

Intelligent Body Systems

The Nissan Intelligent Body System, already in use, is an opening move in reducing new body costs. The basic idea is to design flexible body handling and metal fabrication equipment so that equipment within a given size range needs no modification for new body shapes. Tooling remains as the major new-model expense. The objective in a stamping shop is die changes in five minutes or less (on monster dies) for small lot sizes. Then, flexible equipment in a body shop should weld any sequence of body styles without any time for changeover. That is possible if equipment can accommodate any configuration within its working space.

Other car companies are known to be working on their own version of the Intelligent Body System. Implementation is made easier by the convergence of body shapes. The need for a low wind drag coefficient restricts the envelope in which all body shapes can be differentiated.

In addition, assembly lines are designed and manned by highly skilled, adaptable workers who can trade off work among themselves within team-operated line stations. A large number of detailed practices, including the ability to reposition equipment and materials either manually or automatically, allow workers to assemble multiple models intermingled in sequence at varying rates. At the same time, with less focus on rock-bottom cost, the Japanese companies are investing in equipment (and continuous improvement) to make the work easier on the worker. More variety results in high mental alertness and less physical stress. But this is 1990s intermediate strategy, not a three-day car for the twenty-first century.

The Manufacturing 21 "Three-Day Car"

If one wants to offer truly customized cars to a segment of the market, unit-body construction has limitations, no matter how intelligent the system to design and build it. To break through these limitations, the Japanese Manufacturing 21 team considered many different concepts to achieve several challenging objectives:

1. Challenge number 3: Deliver a car with custom features very quickly—within three days after the order is placed. Today, delivery takes about three days if the order is expedited through the system. (Ten days or so is a more normal Japanese domestic customer lead time.)
2. Challenge number 4: Further downsize the scale of production operations. Build clusters of small plants, with suppliers feeding a miniassembly plant, all near the customers to cut the transport traffic, expense, and time.
3. Challenge number 5: Allow the same components to be configured many different ways in assembly.
4. Challenge number 6: Create work stimulating to the people doing it.

All of these challenges can be met by a modularly designed car. Fabricate and assemble each module in a space that's small compared with today's plants. Final assembly would also require little space. This cannot be done with unit-body designs because large parts must be fabricated on big machines, welded together in a large body shop, painted as a unit, and then have hundreds or thousands of parts attached to them. The space necessary to do this can be compressed only so far.

Cars designed in structural modules could be subassembled in different locations, then brought together for final assembly and attachment of the body panels. The external shape of the completed body is thereby partly independent of the form of the structural framework. (This design concept is one step beyond that of the Saturn and the Pontiac Fiero, in which body panels fasten to an underbody framework. The extra step, building the underbody in modules so a big plant is not required, is similar to a twenty-eight-module production concept once proposed by Chrysler.) A design truly ingenious in dimensional stability and modular interconnects could even be assembled in a dealer shop.

Easy assembly (and disassembly) without high-precision parts should be possible through smart design that allows dimensional variations to be easily compensated. However, if parts are to be reused or remanufactured a number of times, perhaps some will require high-tech materials, but they'll be formable using down-to-earth budgets.

Whatever the final result of technical changes to designs and production processes, the key factors are the development of suppliers and the acceptance of customers. If large subassemblies are fabricated and assembled prior to final assembly, the supply network must change. The modules are either made by the car company itself or by very capable suppliers working very closely with the car company. The high-tech demands and the degree of coordination required suggest that the suppliers need to be high-tech partners with each other as well as with the customer company.

This concept also presumes that many features of a car are electronically achieved. For example, on a few models the ride of a suspension can now be adjusted by the driver.

Ordering a Three-Day Car

This car would not be ordered off a dealer lot. Instead of taking a spin around the block, the customer might view displays or demonstrators, then enter a simulator. Inside this "flight trainer" he can position controls in different locations and replicate different rides and responses—a form of virtual reality. The set of preferences checked would be stored and converted to design requirements for the order.

From the simulator, the customer can sit down at a design work station, possibly with help from an advisor (futurespeak for a salesperson). The work station would be a CAD-type program linked to the production and design system. Using the station the customer can check the physical appearance of the car inside and out. With a 3-D screen, the visualization may be close to reality. The system will permit selection only of feasible or safe designs or option combinations.

The three-day car will be exclusively made to order—no dealer inventory. By today's system, American Big three dealer stocks normally range from sixty to ninety days of sales, which cover the normal lead time for a factory order of six to seven weeks plus order cycle time. In Japan today, similar lead times to receive a factory-ordered car range from three to twenty-one days, so the average domestic dealer stocks twenty to thirty days' worth of cars, which covers his lead time for replenishment (about a week for the sales order cycle plus about ten to twenty days from order to receipt, using a pessimistic forecast).

Cars built in modules would probably require more expensive materials. Without an easy pay plan, this concept might initially appeal only to the affluent. Over time it should become accepted by everyone, not just car buffs. One can anticipate prosumers having different levels of trust in their own judgment on features. Many might simply want to have a car that suits them with minimum time on their part evaluating complex alternatives. The total design-to-delivery time must be short, though from the customer's viewpoint how short is debatable. However, custom-built cars eliminate the need for dealer stock, so that savings alone would help offset the higher cost, and for customers of modest means, payments for a long-life vehicle could be spread over a long period.

Challenge number 7, crucial to success, is cultivating *automotive prosumers* to participate in their own service or order fulfillment with computer assistance—a high-tech version of a "do-it-yourselfer." Prosumer-friendly design software will first be used to select a combination of body structure, drivetrain components, and suspension components that have been tested for safety and performance. A number of creature-comfort features can be custom designed, depending on how much the customer wants to pay. The seat contour can be custom profiled, the car's lighting system designed as the customer likes, and the instrument panel layout modified to suit personal preferences (easily done if it just consists of repositioning images on screens). Within limits, prosumers might even modify the shape of body panels (want your monogram stamped in the door?), design their own trim, and "imagineer" sound systems to use their own tastes. Of course, features that are electronically controlled can be modified by a different PC board or different software, possibly without visiting the dealer.

Challenge number 8 is creating an ordering system that will instantly check the combination of requests by the customer for safety and feasibility, then convert it directly to production instructions. As soon as an order is generated and checked, it will be transmitted to the cluster of factories that will build it. *Lead time to delivery: three days.* That is where the three-day car got its name.

This story in various forms has circulated in Detroit for some time. A popular version of it has a three-day car achieved if the line-up of vehicles in an assembly plant's schedule is no more than a three-day sequence. That's far short of the idea.

Engineering, Production, and Delivery

Data requirements are huge. Suppose a custom-designed vehicle is damaged. To make the replacement parts, it would be necessary to secure the vehicle's CAD/CAM record (or escort memory) and transmit it to the proper plants. Challenge number 9 is assembling these unbelievably large masses of data for use and controlling their flow. Central control might create a choke point. Sending only "macro instructions" to locations that maintain the detailed data is the simple way to do it. For example, the detailed bills of material, test data, and instructions for a fuel system need to be kept only at a supplier location.

Learning the human discipline to operate such a system seems as daunting as generating the data and software. Distributed data also requires distributed control coordinated throughout the network. (The Japanese refer to both the software and "humanware" aspects of this as a "holonic" system.)

After an order is entered, it is transmitted from the dealership to the cluster of plants (car company plus supplier plants) selected to build the order based on distance and backlog. Orders would flow to the plants individually, not in groups, as they do in 1993. One can imagine that some order requests would not automatically process on the design software or translate into CAM instructions at the plants and kick out for immediate engineering attention. Some orders would require discussion with people building various modules of the car. One can anticipate that the connoisseurs among auto prosumers would relish participation in this form of "car talk."

As soon as the assembly plant has sequenced an incoming order, the sequence and relevant data, including necessary CAM instructions, is transmitted to all supply plants. (Imagine an elegant database organization for this.) Each plant keeps very little in the way of parts inventory that is not designated for an actual order, but fabricating plants might need to have the correct raw material on hand to start an order. All this planning needs to sequence jobs through two or more tiers of suppliers (easier if everyone can work in lot sizes of one in any sequence). With no backlog, fabrication work could begin almost immediately after an order is validated.

Each cluster of plants operates its quick-change, adaptive equipment nearly around the clock. Some equipment self-repairs its own minor faults, so no long daily downtime periods are required. System maintenance downtime takes a few hours once a week, similar to the periods now required for large computers. Once activated, many cells can operate "in the dark" for prolonged periods without attention.

An order begun in fabrication passes to module assembly and then to final assembly in vehicle identification number (VIN) sequence. Sequence control moves material where needed when needed. Processes in any plant can check the sequence and status of orders in assembly plants or in other fabrication plants as necessary. From any point in the system, news of a really serious glitch can be quickly transmitted throughout the system so that orders can be resequenced if necessary, but that is rarely done.

Challenge number 10 is production control by the computer synchronization of the whole system, so that material, tools, tests, and data march in unison through the network of supply areas into final assembly. Though similar to the "broadcast" system now used by auto companies to bring such items as seats to assembly in proper sequence, the system is neither material requirements planning (MRP) nor a pull system. It can work only if all the items to be marched are "designed for marching."

Though some parts for repair and retrofitting may be made by off-line facilities, a portion of the main system's production time is regularly set aside to make parts. Many customers of modularly designed cars will surely want to change their features or add "new releases" (like software) to existing cars. They might install the easy ones themselves. Service agreements must contain clauses on retrofitting.

By day three, the order should be ready to ship. Since the order is usually built by a cluster of plants close to the customer, the car should arrive at the dealership within a day. Some customers may come to the plants to pick up the cars themselves and even to watch them being assembled.

The production and engineering concepts for the three-day car simply assume that Total Quality and the fail-safing of operations are at maturity. The system will choke unless defect rates on complex cars and processes are infinitesimal. (Japanese refer to this as "Zero Defects"—easily confused with an earlier phase of our development in North America.)

The synchronization of a distributed system—assembly, feeders, suppliers, dealers, planning centers, maintenance, service centers—carries JIT concepts to a new level. Everything—CAD/CAM systems, product specifications, vehicle performance data, customer credit information—must be able to link. Nothing like it exists today, although databases and data communications could grow into this state.

The Agile Manufacturing Version

In the summer of 1991, the Agile Manufacturing Enterprise Forum at the Iacocca Institute, Lehigh University, received a grant from the Department of Defense to create an American vision of twenty-first–century manufacturing. They adapted the Japanese scenario of the three-day car to the United States. One modification illustrated the Department of Defense as an institutional prosumer of military vehicles. An enhancement emphasized the modularity and interchangeability of many parts and subassemblies in the basic design. A customer's pet features, such as a custom-contoured seat, could simply be retained while much of the vehicle was reconfigured to a different purpose for its owner. This might be desired when the owner goes through a life change such as a growing family or retirement.

Another adaptation considered prosumer maintenance of a complex vehicle. Using one or more special service compartments, the owner could perform normal oil changes and other fluid additions while "dressed in a suit." Each vehicle's full history would be recorded and updated by an on-board "smart chip." The system would tell the owner when service is needed. Unless a malfunction were disastrous, the "limp in" design should prevent unfortunates from being stranded in some godforsaken locale.

The agile scenario also projected the future of "roadside service" to include electronic diagnosis. Any apparent malfunction not diagnosed by the vehicle itself could be recorded during vehicle operation for later play on a service center's diagnostic computer. Better yet, if digital data can be easily transmitted via UltraComm, a car can be diagnosed by the manufacturer's computers while it is still on the road.

The Agile Forum scenario also began to consider environmental implications. A totally instrumented car should be much less prone to drift out of environmentally safe operating conditions.

Finally, while the American version concentrated on technical requirements, it noted that a major challenge of bringing such a world to pass was human development: flat organizations, tight links between small operating units, and enterprise integration of relationships between people and between computers. Although the present trends toward team organization will strengthen, the Americans viewed future organizations more as a linking of entrepreneurial operating units.

The Plot Thickens

Both the American and the Japanese versions of the three-day car were devised by people with manufacturing experience. While no one can foretell any long-term scenario with precision, the concepts are not crackpot. The designers subjected their dreams to reality checks. The conclusion: The technology is at hand. The human will to change is more doubtful.

Reflection by the author on the implications of these changes leads to other possibilities. Any system resembling the three-day car changes the basic nature of the auto industry. Challenge number 11 is recognition by everyone involved that the basic mission of an auto company is to provide transportation *service* to its customers. Manufacturing as we have thought of it is only part of the means to do this. Although almost everyone who has brainstormed this issue in depth is committed to strengthening manufacturing, few like to admit that the scenarios do not revitalize Rust Belt industry according to the principles of conventional economic growth. The twenty-first century will not be like the twentieth, with factories absorbing millions of additional workers.

In fact, the big old mass-production companies will probably not survive in anything like their present form. For example, sharply reduced tooling costs will drastically change the production economics of behemoths like General Motors or even Toyota and reduce barriers to entering business. Smaller operating companies hooked to partners may enter the auto enterprise system. To see why, add a few more twists to the scenario.

The design of the three-day car envisions a mechanical frame that is really a platform for the electronics, software, and cosmetics (more like ships, aircraft, and computer frames). The cars may be equipped for "smart highways"—traffic advisories allowing drivers to avoid jams, and computer-controlled vehicles that allow dense parking in high-traffic flows. In addition, a current planning trend is to improve the connections between cars and other forms of transport—like planes, ships, and trains. That will surely become part of the intelligence network available to drivers of twenty-first–century "smartwagons."

Thus equipped, a car can be easily tracked. A car bristling with electronic sensors and transmitters will also deter thieves seeking to practice rapid disassembly on modular equipment. However, one can easily imagine civil libertarians revolting at the thought that police can constantly check their vehicles' whereabouts. Privacy issues will surely arise. (Will parking in lover's lane become a quaint twentieth-century custom?)

To continue lightening the mechanical platform, components should be made of more durable materials. For instance, precise, long-life bearing might be smaller than they are today but still more reliable. Interchangeable, retrofitable frame parts might have a working life longer than people do. That is not a growth scenario in the historic sense, though the replacement of the current stock of vehicles should provide a steady business. The 160 million cars now licensed for American roads will not pass out of existence quickly.

Long run, we may really have a case for remanufacturing rather than manufacturing as we have known it. Remanufacturing upgrades a product into a better-than-new condition. Then, cars would not be so much bought and sold as periodically taken to service centers for refurbishment and upgrade. Challenge number 12 is learning from remanufacturing.

Ecology could become a bigger driver of the scenario than the desire for ultimate transportation service. A car that can be remanufactured is "greener" than one that requires recycling of its base materials. If the electronic content changes the quickest, the ability to remanufacture or recycle PC boards will become a growing issue.

At the outset, a three-day car might be only for the affluent, but if the scenario becomes ecology-driven, it will evolve into a system for the average driver. If the car or its parts must be disposed of by its manufacturer (or service company), then owning a car begins to be less interesting. Long-term car leasing, already a tend, could avoid complications. On the other hand, long-term ownership combined with service contracts might be a way to make a superior vehicle affordable to the average person. (How about a twenty-year mortgage on your car?)

So What?

The advent of a new millennium leads to anticipation of more change than may actually occur, but the shape of changes now beginning casts the shadow of those to come. An assumption of the three-day car is that lean manufacturing and the acronyms that now define excellence are but the starting points for a different kind of manufacturing system, and perhaps a modified economic system.

The acronyms themselves should fade as their content becomes mainstream, but they will never be totally natural. Therefore inculcation of the attitudes that foster them must begin early in life. Challenge number 13, the biggest of all, is a redirection of ourselves and our human institutions. It begins with our approach to education (much belabored by industry leaders). We need a more rigorous approach to prepare for life in any world that resembles this and more intense development of people by the enterprises within which they work. We do not yet recognize that in an information age, the key to the use of all technology and all capital is ourselves, the human element.

Today, it is commonly said in the systems business that hardware has outrun software. Beyond that, software is years ahead of "humanware." The kind of world that is upon us is not beyond our imagination, but any version of the three-day car leads to the conclusion that achieving prosperity and a high quality of life in the future depends on us improving ourselves rather than hoping for more fortunate circumstances.

NOTES

1. "An Analysis of the Management Consulting Business in the United States Today," 1990 Edition, Kennedy Publications, Fitzwilliam, New Hampshire.
2. This "lassez-faire" version of the theory of the firm is short and simplistic, but reflects the self-interest doctrine that can be traced back through Adam Smith to Bernard de Mandeville's *The Fable of the Bees,* 1714.
3. A well-researched history of simple entrepreneurship evolving into complexity is Alfred D. Chandler, Jr., *The Visible Hand* (Harvard University Press, 1977).
4. See, for instance, the story of Tokai Rika in Robert W. Hall, *Zero Inventories* (Homewood, IL: Business One Irwin, 1983), pp. 284–94. Similar kinds of events have occurred at American companies such as Jacobs Vehicle Equipment Company, where a shop-floor transformation began with a one-week whirlwind known as "Five Days and Four Nights," sponsored by Productivity, Inc., Stamford, Connecticut.
5. Iwata, Makashima, Otani, et al., *Manufacturing 21 Report,* Research Report of the Association for Manufacturing Excellence, AME, 380 Palatine Road, Wheeling, Illinois, 1990.
6. Iacocca Institute, *21st Century Manufacturing Enterprise Strategy* (Bethlehem, PA: Lehigh University, Mohler Laboratory #200, 1991). In two volumes. The scenarios are in volume 1. (Also available from AME.)

7. Alvin Toffler originated the word "prosumer" in *The Third Wave* (New York: William Morrow, 1980).

8. R. W. Hall and J. Nakane, *Flexibility: Manufacturing Battlefield of the 90s*, Research Report of the Association for Manufacturing Excellence, 380 Palatine Road, Wheeling Illinois, 1990.

3

QUALITY GROWTH

In 1933, SHORTLY AFTER MOTOROLA WAS FOUNDED TO MANUFACTURE THE first car radio, company chronicles record the woeful tale of the Model 55, shipped with an underdesigned power supply. To compensate, the radio was wired directly to the battery, because a fuse made a loud buzz. Underpowered, the vibrator would first start to burn the transformer, then the wiring, and finally the vehicle itself. Motorola founder Paul Galvin was irked when engineers testing radios set his personal car on fire twice in one month. A Sioux City lawyer switched on a Model 55 in a car parked in his garage, incinerating car, garage, and half the house. Topping the ignominy: "A Model 55, installed in a hearse, set the vehicle on fire, and to the dismay of family and friends, who preferred a more conventional funeral, the hapless cadaver was cremated."[1]

Thus began the company that in 1988 was one of the first three winners of the Baldrige Award, and whose defect rates in virtually all operations now better those of the average company by perhaps a hundred times. "Six-sigma" quality is virtually its logo. Should anything comparable to the Model 55 disaster recur today, everyone involved would sink into a legal abyss, never to return, but in the 1930s any workable radio beat no radio. The engineer responsible for the Model 55 was not specifically identified, but some suspect that he lived, learned, and later became president of Motorola.

In 1971, when Boeing shepherded its first 747 jumbo jets into service, the company consumed the first eighteen months or so of the 747's life fixing little things. One oversight was a multihole shortfall in toilet capacity to serve the five hundred–plus passengers on long flights. Flyers subsequently recalled numerous creative moments of grace under pressure.

For delivery of Boeing's new 777 jumbo in 1995, "systems integration" and "service ready" are the maxims. Besides the technical exotica among its 1.8 million part numbers, the Boeing 777 team must tend to the little things that please both airlines and passengers. Should Boeing in 1995 rerun the 747's find-and-fix product launch of twenty-five years earlier, the airlines would start dropping orders, and the media would fan the stink.

Few executives will dispute that as products, processes, and customer service become more demanding, organizational performance that once exuded "can do" confidence slides into obsolescence. But it's easy to underestimate both the nature of the challenge and the far-reaching changes needed to meet it. Detractors of quality fixation fail to see that we must learn to do it *all*: innovate, make a profit, and have mistake-proof processes.

"Quality growth" is the seedbed of lean manufacturing and of the human performance needed beyond that in the twenty-first century. "Quality growth" can be understood in three senses: (1) expansion of personal understanding toward a *global vision* of quality performance; (2) growth in *quality processes* actually used, including different understandings of customers and suppliers; and (3) growth in *quality of life* as a new kind of economic objective.

Quality, in the sense of personal understanding, is a set of learned behaviors. Some can be described as technical skills; the rest, human skills—in leadership, in followership, and in collaborating with others. Behavior isn't knowledge; behavior is practice, which is far harder to acquire.

The continued advance of quality concepts depends on a steady advance in practice. Quality growth will succeed not because the philosophy is persuasive or people are suddenly overwhelmed with altruism but because it beats the old thinking at its own game—

economic growth—and in addition leads the transition to a new concept of progress.

EXPANDING TOWARD A
GLOBAL VISION OF QUALITY

A dictionary definition of quality will not help anyone comprehend the bafflegab now used by quality aficionados. Dictionaries define quality as the innate nature of a person or thing, as if it were an unchangeable characteristic. That is the concept in the inner court of the mind from which almost everyone begins to expand his or her quality perception. (See Figure 3-1.)

The implications of the word "total" attached to many descriptions of quality seldom register on superlative-weary readers. It suggests that quality improvement encompasses every aspect of an enterprise: market research, marketing, design, production, delivery, service, supply, support, and advisory functions. "Total" also takes in every aspect of individual and collective working performance, including that of the customers themselves. It's a different way to think about business. Most of us are unable to instantly saturate our brain cells with such comprehensive news.

When semantic barrages start to lose their bang, quality proponents must reload with fresh verbiage, but if actual practice does not keep up with the rhetoric, quality becomes just another tired word. One CEO, Ralph Stayer of Johnsonville Foods, refuses to use the term "quality" inside the company. Instead, the term "performance" used with modifiers communicates very similar ideas.

To expand quality perception, proponents compile many lists of the dimensions of both product and service quality, including aesthetics, perceived quality, and participation.[2] They also must usually adopt stepwise improvement processes such as the one described in Figure 3–2, encased in plastic and kept at the ready by "associates" (quality-speak meaning "empowered employees").

No prescribed pathway leads through the different zones of understanding in Figure 3–1. At first, quality is understood only as better materials and craftsmanship. Perhaps a group next warms to statisti-

FIGURE 3-1

EXPANDING TOWARD A
GLOBAL UNDERSTANDING OF QUALITY

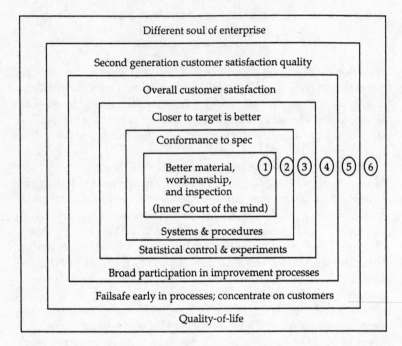

Circles denote zones of perception.

FIGURE 3-2

EXAMPLE OF A STEPWISE
IMPROVEMENT PROCESS

The Six Steps to Six Sigma (Motorola Inc.)

Step 1   Identify the product you create or the service you provide.

Step 2   Identify the customer(s) for your product or service, and determine what they consider important.

Step 3   Identify your needs (to provide product/service so that it satisfies the customer).

Step 4   Define the process for doing the work.

Step 5   Mistake-proof the process for doing the work.

Step 6   Ensure continuous improvement by six-sigma measuring, analyzing, and controlling the improved process.

Motorola itself uses several variations of six steps to six sigma in different kinds of work. Other companies have formally adopted similar four-to-nine-step improvement processes. The procedures are taught to associates (employees) by rote and by example. Then the stepwise procedure is promoted using pocket cards, displays, newsletters, etc. The serious use the methodology to structure the majority of corporate meetings on almost any subject. Promulgation of the stepwise improvement process is almost always accompanied by promoting at least two other companywide tenets: (1) a company mission statement; and (2) a statement of company policy or creed toward its associates. (An example is Hewlett-Packard's "HP Way.")

cal charting and design of experiments (Zone 3). Then they begin to see that those practices are of limited effect until everyone is focused on discovering customer needs and satisfying them. Today, many quality veterans, jaded from expanding their zones of enlightenment, regard customer satisfaction, Zone 4, as ultimately "being what it is all about."

But customer satisfaction is not always possible. Some customers, like a belligerent drunk or a frenzied two-year-old, cannot be satisfied. Occasionally a customer has criminal intent. Quality neoorthodoxy presumes that rational and consistent associates can discover ways to satisfy a higher percentage of customers, even if reasoning with them is nearly impossible, but that the energy might be better spent with more cooperative ones. In fact, a good customer is an improvement partner with the supplier (an idea that resembles Toffler's concept of a *prosumer*).

Zone 5 is a stage beyond most current thinking about customer satisfaction. It includes two key ideas. The first one is to preclude the possibility of ordinary defects at the earliest possible stage of their development. An example is to incorporate fail-safe checks and routines into CAD/CAM processes so that a designer cannot unintentionally leave a recessed surface difficult to machine, call for components that will perform marginally in the intended application (nonrobust design), or put lines in the wrong overlay.

The second idea Zone 5 suggests is the need to concentrate on preferences that customers may not understand themselves—something they don't realize they want until they experience it. Examples from old technology are basic copiers and facsimile machines. People had to try them before they could want them. A newer example is the lines of an automotive design. A few degrees' difference in the rake of a windshield or in the rounding of a surface makes a difference in customer acceptance, even if it is only to a small niche of customers. Another example is a chair that reconfigures to the person sitting in it.

Zone 5 is a major step toward the three-day car scenarios. Building fail-safe methodology into the information used for equipment and tooling has a significance similar to Henry Ford simplifying the design of the Model T so much that mass production became inevitable. Eliminating little idiosyncrasies and undocumented differences and removing steps from the part-creation process will allow truly interchangeable *tooling*, or perhaps fabrication of interchangeable parts without hard tooling (by fusing a stack of cut laminates, for example). It simplifies manufacturing and remanufacturing in the auto business, among others. In electronics, the function of an old printed circuit board can be replicated and enhanced by a new board designed into its place. This vista of a new era is about where mass production was in 1900.

In Zone 5 the basic thought process of "Total Quality" is extended to the information wave, recognizing that information systems create products and services. As these thought processes mature, they allow a still wider perspective of quality. Just pleasing an end customer is not sufficient. One must consider everyone in the complete life cycle of the product: assemblers, repair technicians, salvage workers, and even the general public (suppose the product contains toxic materials). Zone 5 represents opportunities to attack many old problems much more creatively.

Beyond "customer satisfaction" lies at least one more zone, dimly seen at first. Zone 6 invokes quality of life rather than growth as an economic motivation—a different soul of enterprise.

Quality of life is not about having more but having better. Defining *better* is much of what quality is all about. Better is an improvement on one dimension of performance without a trade-off elsewhere, like double the gas mileage with no penalties in space or comfort. Quality of life encompasses health, the environment, personal opportunities, and justice (including absence of crime). It's more than high-quality products.

Quality of life presupposes a society attuned to improvement processes. Today, industrial customers and suppliers sometimes become partners in an improvement process—a methodical, rational relationship to improve quality (and financial gain) to both parties. If improvement processes became a social norm for many individuals and institutions, improving our quality of life would not be so farfetched.

The journey toward this conclusion is different for each of us. Someone with a finance background will see it differently than an engineer will. The financially oriented may at first see quality only as earnings and question how anyone could lose money satisfying customers—but suppose just one major customer does not pay?[3] A design engineer may wonder how customers can be unhappy when a company obviously has the best-stepping motors in the world. But perhaps no one knows about them, or the design engineer's concept of an excellent motor is not what the customer wants.

Arriving at a common, global vision of quality will result from expanding the perception of many individuals, each starting from a different inner court. As the engineers, financial analysts, and others keep expanding their visions, they learn to locate their detailed concerns on a larger map of quality-of-life factors. Eventually, a significant fraction of the global population may partly overcome the "Tower of Babel effect" and use quality improvement processes on detailed local problems to help overcome global quality-of-life issues.

Information-Wave
Improvement Processes

W. Edwards Deming, one of the foremost proponents of managing by process and not for results, holds that managing any system, from ecosystems to tying shoes, is action based on prediction. When we predicted that ozone holes would become hazardous to life and that release of CFCs caused them, we devised CFC substitutes. If we predict that a slick, stiff shoelace will not stay tied, we get a crinkly, flexible one.[4]

Deming is known as a statistician, and statistics are always helpful in improvement processes when appropriately used, but mere use of statistics does not necessarily lead to accurate prediction of outcomes. For example, sales jobs are often "snowcased" in statistics; aspirin advertisements are one of the more prominent examples.

The statistics of quality are worthless unless they are used as part of a methodology for improvement. W. Edwards Deming, Walter Shewhart, Joseph Juran, and other pioneers of the quality movement all held the same belief: *The most effective use of people, energy, materials, space, and time, for whatever purpose, is achieved through actions taken as a result of a systematic method of learning about the processes of their use.*

Improvement processes are modeled on the scientific method of thought. Most people are exposed to the scientific method in about the sixth or seventh grade, but unless coached, few remain conscious of it, and most never learn to apply it to real-life, gray-area problems. The best-known version of the scientific method is the Deming Cycle:

plan, do, study, act. The cycle can be applied to almost any area of human concern, whether global or minuscule in scope (but it is not a replacement for the specialized research techniques of various scientific disciplines). Versions of the methodology are now taught to millions of people under names varying from "storyboard" to "continuous-improvement technique."

When such a process is used by all the people of an enterprise, it becomes a shared language—a common rationale that helps otherwise diverse people agree not only on facts but on what to do. Then individuals from a number of different areas of expertise can more readily define problems and agree on solutions. Once an individual's understanding reaches this stage, his perception has already traversed several zones.

Improvement processes, sometimes called learning processes, change human relationships. Status based on leverage becomes less important. Collaboration to agree on facts and follow-on action becomes much more significant. The difficult parts of the process are: (1) gaining the effective participation of large numbers of diverse people; and (2) actually making improvements and holding to them until an even better process change is agreed upon.

Whatever Deming's creative intentions were, his definition of management as predicting and controlling any kind of process is an information-wave concept. It shifts the primary focus of organizations from results (what will we gain) to processes (how do things *really* work and what will happen). Status shifts from the possessors of assets to the improvers of processes. Quality-scoffers doubt that so profound a social shift can endure, while quality-philes search for ways to disperse such improvement processes through as many detailed customer-supplier linkages as possible. These linkages are the basis for organizing open-system enterprises, and Deming's definition of management is the link that turns the quality-of-life vision into something that has a pragmatic chance.

GROWTH IN PRACTICING QUALITY PROCESSES

Company histories have frequently enshrined noble sentiments about quality, and businessmen such as Marshall Field and JC Penney always went overboard pleasing customers.[5] But quality performance has lacked methodology and a consistent definition. The development of consistent quality concepts and practices has occurred within the lifetime of the two living quality patriarchs, Deming and Juran.

In the 1920s statisticians began bringing a new perspective to agriculture and industry, combining science with practicality. Sir Ronald A. Fisher conceived the first experimental design for agriculture, breaking the scientific tradition of varying one factor at a time in controlled conditions. He analyzed experiments conducted in typical growing fields rather than in hothouses with carefully controlled temperature, humidity, soil, and so forth. Fisher's experiments included the effects of wind, insects, soil variability, and other factors that actually exist in farm fields.[6]

About the same time, Walter Shewhart of Bell Laboratories began using Western Electric plants as laboratories to study actual operating conditions. Experiments and applications expanded rapidly in the 1930s. Deming became Shewhart's student and then colleague, editing his second text in 1939.[7]

However, the statisticians were not marketers. As scientists, they thought proven logic and proven results would surely impress managements. Postwar campaigns to spread statistical process control flopped. Early texts had an engineering flavor, so the Taylorists relegated technical minutiae to their engineering functions. They called it quality control—a proper subject for guys wearing pocket protectors eating chicken at the Dew-Drop Inn.

Meanwhile, postwar Japanese industrialists were determined to carefully study whatever had just hit them. When Deming and other quality apostles came to proselytize, the Japanese began Nipponizing Western methods as never before. Deming in particular was miffed because American industrial chieftains did not see that systematic improvement was *their* responsibility. In Japan he charged presidents and CEOs with creating work environments where the grass-roots science of quality could thrive. Unaware of the American torpor, Japanese corporate leaders actually believed him.

Kaoru Ishikawa and others simplified statistical tools and repackaged improvement process thinking for workers. When Armand Feigenbaum (an American) originated the concept of Total Quality Control (TQC), the Japanese quickly seized on it, and by the late

1960s, the world's most prolific quality practitioners were becoming quality innovators, spewing forth new acronyms. By 1980, Cinderella wowed them at the economic ball.

The Japanese have always worked hard, and Japanese public policy has long promoted industrial growth, but the necessary changes in organizational attitudes were no easier for them than for anyone else. Quality improvement processes began in the late 1940s and early 1950s, a period of intense labor disputes and strikes few Westerners recall today.

Developing the human side of the improvement process was most important, but time consuming. When Komatsu, for example, began TQC in 1964, the company accepted modest results for the first four years while it repotted the corporate culture to accept it. As a result, experienced American manufacturers who have viewed Japanese operations firsthand estimate that the Japanese lead by about ten years in "TQC culture building."

The Search for the Japanese Mystique

As 1980s American companies contemplated what had hit them, sorting through the Japanese miracle became a fascination. Americans learned statistics from names like Ishikawa and Taguchi. Deming and Juran, plucked from obscurity, went on tour again. Americans scrambled to learn techniques such as Dorian Shainan's precontrol analysis, largely overlooked by the Japanese, in hopes of finding some kind of edge. Novices chasing techniques papered walls with control charts and hung acronym banners. Others initiated thousands of "empowered teams" without educating them in the methodology of improvement processes. But the will—the soul—for a high standard of performance materializes slowly.

The serious learned that technique wasn't enough; they had to stimulate people to control processes and manage by fact. They issued pocket cards showing missions, goals, and stepwise improvement-process lists. Some of the most effective promotions were presentations of improvement-process accomplishments by first-line workers. Although amateurish in appearance, these demonstrations were the real thing from real people.

From the outset, the new thinking challenged the old practices of Taylorism. Fail-safing and streamlining flows of work broke functional departments into process-flow teams. Responsibility dropped onto those doing the work, and companies shed middle layers of staff and supervision. Productivity and quality increased dramatically in U.S. manufacturing companies in the 1980s, but by 1992 many still floundered, wondering where they stood against world competition, how to execute what they knew, and what further changes were necessary.

Redefining Quality

Back when quality was considered only the function of a quality department, defining it was easier: conformance to specification. Anything that passed inspection was acceptable—until it failed in use. A quality department mostly performed police work; employees could ignore feedback unless they were in violation, and then they could try plea bargaining.

Defining quality as customer satisfaction sounds as if it relaxes standards. Instead, it shifts responsibility to each point of action, so everyone must think about what a customer wants. Processes for setting specifications themselves must be "right." Just passing inspection is not good enough.

If better performance is desired, why not just tighten the specifications limits? That prompts the expense of sorting more rejects or using tighter tolerance tooling without reviewing the real nature of the customer's need. Responsibility stays with the policemen.

Improvement thinking concentrates first on what is necessary to satisfy the customer, then on simplifying total processes, eliminating costly errors and defects wherever possible, and concentrating investment in areas where it counts. Performance that seemed impossible by specify-and-inspect systems starts to become routine, but it expands the responsibility of *everyone* in every position, including the customers. (A responsible customer assists with their suppliers' improvement processes.)

One of the more popular ways to classify customer-pleasing performance was introduced to the United States by Noritake Kano. Kano identifies four major categories of quality:

1. *Indifferent quality.* Garnish on the plates for a junior high school football banquet is probably not a high priority to the customers. At a plastics company, engineers worked for months to deepen the embossing for a decorative packaging film, only to learn that consumers did not notice the difference.

2. *Expected quality.* Window lifts on a car or cleanliness of a hotel room are simply expected; otherwise, most customers are displeased. Marketing researchers call these "knockout factors," and Kano calls them "must-be" quality. Safety features, such as reliable car brakes, are an extreme form of it.

3. *One-dimensional quality.* Features that customers like if they are present and miss if they are absent. Friendliness of waiters and delivery persons is often in this category. However, such features do not necessarily distinguish one competitor from another.

4. *Unexpected quality, or exciting quality.* Pleasant surprises create preferences for one competitor over another—selling points. Some, like a baby-sitting service at a supermarket or a detailed maintenance history of a used car, might add cost—but they pay off in reduced hassle time.

Ford separates these quality factors into two groups, "things gone wrong"—defects or errors—and "things gone right." The Taurus, introduced in the mid-1980s, logged its share of shop time with things gone wrong, but despite that, its design attracted buyers with things gone right.

These categories constitute four of the nine cells in Figure 3–3 (Kano's actual questionnaire designs are much more complex). Customer responses in some cells are inconsistent and hard to interpret. For example, people sometimes suspect that friendly service is a setup for a scam.

The Kano classification, or similar schemata, raises a question of *who* interprets what customers want. Questionnaires are answered by only a few people; the answers are interpreted by fewer still. Everyone cannot participate in formal market research. However, in the course of daily work, many people must try. A hotel night clerk must decide in some small way how to please everyone who asks for a room. So must the housekeeper who cleans a room.

Employees often assume that "management" has satisfactorily pre-

FIGURE 3—3

FOUR CLASSIFICATIONS OF QUALITY FROM KANO

EXAMPLE: REACTION TO FRIENDLY SERVICE FROM HOTEL DESK CLERK

IF SERVICE IS FRIENDLY:

IF SERVICE IS <u>NOT</u> FRIENDLY:	I LIKE IT	I DON'T LIKE IT	I'M INDIFFERENT OR DIDN'T NOTICE
I LIKE IT	⑥ Contradictory Nonsense?	⑤ Suspicious Responses	⑤ Suspicious
I DON'T LIKE IT	③ One-dimensional	⑥ Contradictory Nonsense?	② Expected Quality
I'M INDIFFERENT OR DIDN'T NOTICE	④ Unexpected Quality	⑤ Suspicious Responses	① Indifferent

This kind of tabulation is prepared by recording responses of the same person to two related questions, one assuming that a particular quality feature has been experienced, the second assuming that the same quality feature has *not* been experienced.

If the questionnaire is given to many people, a cross-tabulated check sheet can be developed and the frequencies of response statistically analyzed. The purpose is to determine which aspects of a product or service are important to customers, and in what way. Customers can be classified into different segments depending on their responses.

SOURCE: This classification system originated with Noritake Kano, published in *Better Designs in Half the Time*, by Bob King, GOAL/QPC, Methuen, Massachusetts, 1987. The original source cited is Noritake Kano, Nobohiru Seraku, Funio Takahashi, and Shiniji Tsuji, "Attractive Quality and Must-Be Quality," *Quality* 14, no. 2 (1984): 39–48.

defined a problem. For instance, if a sales vice president "thinks" aftermarket sales of spark plugs are sputtering because the package is dull, a designer is assigned to spiff up the container, and no one else is responsible for questioning whether that strikes at the root cause of low sales.

Different Kinds of Customers and Suppliers

In Figure 3-2 the second step of the improvement process was labeled "identify customer." Figure 3-4 shows four different categories of customers, and four more of suppliers. Identifying the primary external customer is useful. For example, several years ago Blount, Inc., realized that its product feedback on chain-saw blades came mostly from buyers, not from people who actually used the saws. Questioning the primary customers elicited complaints they did not believe at first. Tapes of the interviews had to be replayed at company meetings, but eventually the complaints led to major improvements. Now, checking product performance with primary customers is routine.

Refining how customers are classified is very helpful in tracing the total processes associated with products or services. Considering secondary customers or suppliers can help identify environmental issues, among other things. For instance, a transmission mechanic is an important secondary customer of a transmission manufacturer. How does this person dispose of used transmission fluid that may have heavy metals in it (as well as understand how to service the beast)?

The classifications are another horizon broadener that reminds us not to forget third-tier suppliers—or in reverse, the ultimate customer. Some years ago a GM auto line shut down, not because of GM or a direct supplier, but because a subcontractor that coated a part for the carburetor supplier made a change in its process that it thought was harmless. Mentally the supplier was just treating parts, not serving a specific process, and thought "parts is parts."

Not all customers and suppliers are equally important to a given process. Classifying customers and suppliers in a given service process is a starting point in sorting out who should be our *improvement collaborators* or who should be our partners in an open-enterprise arrangement.

FIGURE 3-4

DIFFERENT TYPES OF
CUSTOMERS AND SUPPLIERS

Types of Customers		*Types of Suppliers*	
External	Final recipient or *user* of product or service	*External*	Provider of product or service
Internal	Next person in the ongoing chain of operations, or next stage of process	*Internal*	Preceding person in the chain of operations, or the preceding stage of the process
Primary	Firsthand users experiencing the product or service	*Primary*	Persons performing the operations that directly provide the product or service
Secondary	Agents, dealers, service persons, sales clerks, etc. In the large sense, even includes the general public environmentally affected by the product or service.	*Secondary*	Second-tier and indirect suppliers

Customer-Supplier Links

The logic of different kinds of customers and suppliers can be carried to the point that we are concerned with the welfare and input of everyone else on earth. But we cannot humanly communicate with them all—not even with all our primary customers and suppliers in most cases. The communication between customer-supplier links must be very efficient.

Suppose Ford's North American Automotive Operations wants to simplify shipping procedures with suppliers and reduce error rates. Thousands of people across thousands of miles participate in that process. One human's perception cannot comprehend it all. However, relatively ordinary mortals do flowchart a version of such processes and write software for it—usually a big program impossible to debug completely. Human interaction with the system is also a source of variance in the process. Without a unifying vision, a thousand improvement collaborators will never reconcile their views, and without their participation, the human interaction with the system is never debugged. (Ford substantially simplified this process using flowcharting with a huge cross-company project team, but the company is still far short of using a simple JIT system.)

A symptom that another major process needed improvement appeared at an airline while ticket pricing was at its ultimate in complexity. In a single day I was given three different ticket prices for the same round-trip by three different agents of the same airline. Each agent averred the accuracy of a different price, the highest being more than double the lowest. Were the inconsistencies caused by software, complex pricing, agent skills, my mumbled requests, or other factors?

Speculating on the cause of this apparent problem is fun, but it's unproductive without data. Furthermore, unless counter agents stir awareness, management can remain ignorant of this kind of problem for a long time, especially if the direct cause is not software. And agents will avoid raising the issue if they believe management will only berate them for incompetence.

To participate in systems improvement, agents need a sense of the total system. Their work gives them wide experience with their company and industry, and they deal with customers firsthand. To be a greater force for improvement, they also need to understand a disciplined, common improvement process. Then they are more likely to agree how to define such a problem and what data to collect. In addition, it is helpful if the agents participate in cross-functional teams (with MIS specialists or others).

Of course, an airline designing a new reservation system can ask for input from counter agents, but only a few could participate significantly with a cross-functional team actually engaged in such a project. In the future, improvement processes will likely be divided into breakthrough projects assigned to cross-functional teams (or cross-enterprise teams in the case of big ones) and refinement projects undertaken by whatever group or individual sees the need and can proceed responsibly.

The refinement processes are just as important as the breakthrough projects. They make the difference between a "family" of associates, most of whom are intent on serving customers ever better, and a mass of employees who must just use the system as best they can. In concept, this approach is widely used today, but frequently with a good deal of awkwardness because the action-level associates either don't quite know how to go about it or do not feel truly empowered to do it. (They don't have access to cost data, or no one will tell them exactly how a software code works, and so on.)

In the Taylorist tradition, process development was for scientists, engineers, and other "experts." We are well on the way to a different tradition, one in which expanding and contracting teams and enterprises span the details of processes and cross the boundaries of organizations as we have known them.

It will take a major effort to surmount two traditions that currently stand in the way. One is the established status system based on ownership or hierarchical rank. The second is the basic assumptions of the business system: arm's-length negotiations, bid systems, decisions only by return on investment, and so forth. We need not have a bloody revolution; most of the alternative practices have a precedent in prior practice. But the change in the soul of the enterprise will most likely be a painful evolution.

The Evolution of Quality Performance Measurement

Until the Japanese instituted the Deming Prize in 1951, almost all quality prizes were for results, not process. The fastest horse won the race, and a jar of pickles judged tastiest was tagged with a blue ribbon. The checklist for the Deming Prize considers results but emphasizes quality practices and procedures. A winner that continues to improve its processes to serve the customer should be better in the future than it was at the time it received the award, which so far seems to have been a reasonable assumption, including the case of Florida Power & Light, the only American recipient. Accustomed to best-in-class awards for final results, not the process of getting there, the public has a difficult time understanding the Deming Prize, or its American offspring, the Baldrige Award.

Public response to the Baldrige Award will probably never equal the attention the Japanese gave to the Deming Prize twenty years ago. Winners then frequently enjoyed a 15–25 percent increase in domestic market share the following year. The marketing departments of companies sometimes goaded them to apply for the Deming, but the people on the operations side of the company took the brunt of preparation for it, frequently long days, seven days a week for months before the site inspection. Most of them could not bear the thought of having to go through it again, and suffered a letdown in energy and enthusiasm even if they won. Today, the public prestige of the Deming Prize is not quite what it was because so many companies have now won. The leading Japanese companies are on to more challenging visions—perhaps like those of Manufacturing 21.

The criteria of the Baldrige Award give more weight to customer satisfaction, but the examination still concentrates on processes. A winner is selected not because its products won a blue ribbon but because its processes to satisfy customers are considered to be excellent, with results evident. Most companies find great benefit just in performing a self-assessment by the Baldrige criteria, whether they submit an application or not. Those who figure that fielding a competitive entry is a matter of floating a little puffery around their usual practices are in for a jolt.

The winners—Motorola, Milliken, Xerox, et al.—went through an extended born-again experience before they could snag the Baldrige, and none of them is close to ultimate performance. In fact, the Wallace Company descended into receivership a year after winning in 1990. The Baldrige criteria do not include financial indicators. The omission makes no sense to investors whose concept of performance is ROI. (The European Quality Award, begun in 1992 and modeled after Baldrige, does include treatment of ownership and environmental protection as part of its criteria of overall excellence.) Newer criteria keep shifting toward a customer-guided enterprise.

The purposes of the Baldrige Award were to create national interest in quality and to trumpet role models for American companies. Another objective, not stated, is maintaining a current consensus defining quality performance. That alone is a worthwhile achievement. It has spawned a series of more comprehensive performance-assessment systems.

For example, the National Center for Manufacturing Sciences (NCMS) has created a self-assessment checklist of fourteen hundred items in fourteen categories, broader than the Baldrige criteria. (The Deming Prize uses a ten-item, two-page checklist.) Motorola's Quality Supplier Review document is based on the Baldrige but has more categories. These assessment lists are likely forerunners of tough, comprehensive performance appraisal systems for twenty-first–century open-system enterprise, and none of them yet places major emphasis on emissions and effluents.

Demanding measurement systems demand action. Mouthing the words and blubbering the sentiment are no substitutes for real changes.

Ultimate Manufacturing Quality

Meanwhile, back in the operations world, the objective is to make quality of systems and products a nonissue to the customer. People can only perform with excellence consistently if the methods they use prevent them from making mistakes. The most common names for this are "fail-safe" or "foolproof" (disliked by those using a system because it suggests that they are incompetent). The Japanese term is *poke-yoke*, which is coming into use worldwide.

Fail-safe methods have been routine for years in such activities as flying. Warning lights and alarm systems signal a pilot when all is not well. These systems are expensive, but they are one of the major reasons why airlines have such a good safety record.

Simple, inexpensive fail-safe methods are coming into greater use in factories and offices. An example is an assembly fixture that will not release a panel until all the screws that are supposed to be installed have penetrated the panel and made contact with the fixture.

Determining the cause of a quality problem is not the same as fixing it and certainly not the equivalent of making sure it won't happen again. With more and more complex products, fail-safe methods are becoming more and more essential. For example, screws skipped or jammed are a major quality problem in automation. One level of correction is to equip an automatic screwdriver so that if a screw is missing or jammed, the machine stops and the correction is made. A second level is to fail-safe the production of screws so that defectives never leave the supplier's factory. The third level, and best, is to eliminate screws in design, thus eliminating both the quality problem and all its associated expense.

Today, fail-safe mechanisms are becoming part of both manufacturing processes and other business procedures. (Word-processing software that provides prompts and backups is becoming an everyday example of fail-safe systems.) If a process is so poorly understood that no one knows how to equip machines to be fail-safe, the process is not yet ready for automation. As companies enter Zone 5 thinking (Figure 3–1), fail-safe systems should become so routine that systematically produced things-gone-wrong cease to be a significant factor in customer satisfaction. (New cars are never recalled for a workmanship defect and rarely for a design flaw.)

No Shirt, No Shoes, No Service

At the only blinker light in Stilesville, Indiana, a sign on Randy's Motors used-car lot reads "Quality is not expensive; it is priceless." Randy has joined the quality movement. Long the stereotype of sleaze, legitimate used-car dealers no longer just "sell cars." Disclosures and certifications now require more quality-improvement or "value-adding" service, and Randy wants to do better than meet the minimum requirements.

What does satisfaction with a used car mean, and to what kind of customer? A $30K low-mileage Lexus is expected to be flawless, but Randy's clientele are more into the Ford-versus-Chevy truck debates. For a few, a $100 Pinto—if Randy would sell it—will do if it runs without leaving a trail of yowling smoke alarms in its wake.

Randy likes cars with a known maintenance history so both he and a prospect can predict their performance. Without that, car trading is the direct descendant of the ancient rite of horse trading. Back when, everyone was obliged to know their horses, and traders pitted their judgments in a universal adult game. Cars have become too complicated for that; and the consequences of failure too high.

Used-car lots epitomize a free marketer's concept of quality; buyers weigh issues of reliability, speed, safety, and so on against their pocketbook and decide. Regulators prohibit sellers from deceiving buyers and putting junkers on the road. Environmentalists think that it was a mistake to build the road in the first place. Improvement processes are not on the mental map of any of them.

Quality begins by defining the market niche and its customers' needs. (No white tablecloths at Denny's, and don't expect Aunt Martha at Randy's if the decor is spittoons and pinups.) If customer preferences are inconsistent, the same actions cannot please them all, so seek "good customers"—meaning those Randy can figure out how to please.

Improvement processes start by culling out customers that can be pleased, starting with the sign, "No shirt, no shoes, no service." Randy's customers are not always right: The drunk who wants a test drive. The guy palming off a trade-in as mint, but his oil flows like goose droppings. The know-all who can cure his own engine for $50 if he had the time. Before Randy can concentrate on improvement processes with rational customers, he has to deal with irrational ones without wasting time: removing the drunk without a scene, calling the cheat's ruse with utmost courtesy, and telling the know-all to go ahead with his repair.

Randy's strategy is cultivating "good customers" so they will come back. Good customers assist the improvement process, investing a little of their own time to make Randy's service better. Even scribbling comment cards forces customers to think. (A counter at the local cafe is the site of Randy's "focus groups.") Lazy customers benefit from the efforts of his improvement collaborators.

The most respected used-car dealers do not "sell cars." In effect, they buy cars for customers and prepare them for use, guaranteeing satisfaction. That is a process that can be improved, and it starts with finding good customers. Once started, the improvement process can extend to such services as emissions certification, and Randy can consider secondary customers in addition to primary ones.

What of the future? Randy is several microchips short of high-tech. UltraComm and a retrofittable three-day car do not yet exist, but something like it is coming. Randy's approach to customers makes him a likely candidate to become part of an automotive service network, though he is not now a new-car dealer. As part of a network,

Randy would sell transportation satisfaction, not used cars. Will such a service improve Randy's economic fortunes? In the traditional sense, perhaps not; in the quality sense, yes.

Would customers go for it? Yes, provided on-line, retrofittable auto-service guarantees performance for moderate dollars (possibly by a service leasing agreement). Part of the service agreement is participation in improving the service. The uncooperative are stuck pitting their wits against lot salesmen.

Could an improvement process work for "low-credit, no-credit" customers? Certainly—if they are willing to be improvement collaborators. Whatever their pocketbook size, the most difficult customers have a win-lose mind-set, conniving and leveraging, doing unto others before they are done in themselves, and condemned to the bait-and-haggle weedlots of the economy. Don't forget that a huge percentage of the world's population cannot dream of so much as a $100 Pinto. Developing large numbers of people to participate in improvement processes is no small challenge.

GROWTH IN THE QUALITY OF LIFE

"Quality of life" is a phrase often used in reference to unfortunates who are starving, dying of a painful disease, or otherwise debilitated, and what might be done to help them enjoy the common pleasures of living along with the able-bodied portion of the population. It is frequently heard in hospices and nursing homes. Occasionally, it is used to describe living conditions near an environmental unpleasantness, like an ethyl amine plant (which has a smell like dead fish) or an outright hazard (open sewers). Quality of life therefore connotes something less than opulent material consumption: multiple mansions, gourmet dining, and a Jacuzzi in one's private jet. With a modicum of discipline, three cars are not necessarily preferable to two, nor is a big house with a wall-to-wall television better than a modest-sized dwelling. One can only drive one car at a time and be present in one room at a time. At some point the quantity of personal hardware exceeds the time available to use it and care for it. (For example, the utilization rates of personal pleasure boats are very low.)

Social scientists use quality of life to describe human health or relative living conditions in underprivileged regions. The World Bank's social indicators of development include mortality rates and investments in health and education. One of the more comprehensive definitions of quality of life is the twenty-four "fundamental social concerns" (shown in Figure 3–5) that evolved from meetings of the OECD ministers from 1970 to 1974. A 1970 U.N. group declared, "Growth is not an end in itself, but rather an instrument for creating better conditions of life," and proceeded to dash social concern upon a number of perceived evils of unplanned growth.[8]

Fewer than half the twenty-four points in Figure 3–5 encompass business and economic activity as we usually classify them. The rest describe social conditions and services, and the longest sublist outlines personal development. These fundamental social concerns were worded to be relatively culture-free, giving individuals great freedom to interpret their own quality of life. The list avoids prescription on controversial issues, such as public versus private ownership, but capitalists fixated on growth are inclined to dismiss it as one more example of sociological piddle-poop. The list is not widely quoted, but it is an indicator of what a broad spectrum of people might like from life. In one sense, the list was about fifteen years ahead of its time by emphasizing personal development and education as a prerequisite to a quality life.

In a broad sense then, quality of life suggests living to the fullest without great consumption of resources. A large part of the world's population is frugal of necessity. It's hard to imagine the whole world consuming energy and virgin materials at the rate of the United States in the twentieth century. Therefore, the quest is for a high quality of life through a high-tech, lean-manufacturing use of the resources obtainable, sustaining a standard of living much better than living on collard greens and rainwater.

Having a good quality of life also implies having choices. The wealthy have more options—collecting antique aircraft, vacations in Rio—but even poverty-stricken souls have likes and dislikes, though they can afford only simple likes. More assets confer more options, but so does ability to do more, which modifies the definition of wealth to be more consistent with the information wave. To most people, enjoyment of life depends on the ability to have a range of activities

FIGURE 3-5
QUALITY OF LIFE DEFINED AS
FUNDAMENTAL SOCIAL CONCERNS

A. **Health**
  1. The probability of health through all stages of the life cycle.
  2. Impact of health impairment on individuals.

B. **Individual Development**
  3. Acquisition by children of basic knowledge, skills and values for individual development and to function as citizens.
  4. Opportunities for continuing self-development and propensities to use them.
  5. Development and maintenance by individuals of the knowledge, skill, and flexibility to fulfill their economic potential and to integrate in the economic process.
  6. Individual satisfaction with processes of learning while engaged in them.
  7. Development and maintenance of cultural heritage as it contributes to the well being of various social groups.

C. **Quality of Working Life**
  8. Availability of gainful employment by those who desire it.
  9. Quality of working life (on the job).
  10. Individual satisfaction with the experience of working life.

D. **Time and Leisure**
  11. Availability of effective choices for the use of time.

E. **Command over Goods and Services**
  12. Personal command over goods and services.
  13. Number of individuals experiencing material deprivation.
  14. Equitable distribution of command over goods and services.
  15. Quality range of choice, and accessibility of public and private goods and services.
  16. Protection of individuals and families from economic hazards.

F. **Physical Environment**
  17. Housing conditions.
  18. Exposure to harmful or unpleasant pollutants.
  19. Benefits from the use and management of the environment.

(*continued*)

FIGURE 3-5 (cont.)

G. **Personal Safety and Justice**
    20. Violence, victimization and harassment of individuals.
    21. Fairness and humanity in the administration of justice.
    22. Confidence in the administration of justice.

H. **Social Opportunity**
    23. Degree of social inequality.
    24. Opportunity to participate in community life, institutions and decision making.

SOURCE: *This list has been summarized from Lars Andersson; and Lennart Levi;* Population, Environment, and Quality of Life, A *Report of the Swedish Royal Ministry for Foreign Affairs, Sweden, on the 1974 World Population Conference (United Nations), pp. 63–64.*

and experiences, and that depends on skills, not just the ability to consume materials. It always did.

Quality-of-life choices delightful to one individual are anathema to another, what with personal interests ranging from tatting lace to alligator wrestling. While the information wave entices us to establish a great many systems in common, an objective of economies, industries, and sometimes individual enterprises is to create as many individual options as possible using limited resources. The twenty-first–century scenarios point in the direction of the ultimate market segment being one person. Prosumerism is high-tech, do-it-yourself exercise of choices, and quality of life depends on personal and collective development for it.

Quality Growth in Governments and Services

The expansion of quality-improvement processes has quickly extended into schools, hospitals, and sometimes government agencies. While quality thinking is still a mystery in the majority of such institutions, the spread of the Deming definition of management (as prediction and control) is beginning to have a broad, diverse impact. Quality-improvement processes have infiltrated many school districts, numerous hospitals, the city of Madison, Wisconsin, and the 4950th

Test Wing at Wright-Patterson Air Force Base, among other military units.

Of these, the rise of quality-improvement processes in health care is indicative of a change in thinking that is beginning to directly affect the physical quality of life. Perhaps it is also an example of twenty-first–century prosumerism that will pursue quality of life in many different ways.

The rising spiral of health care costs is a front-burner issue in 1993. Blue Cross/Blue Shield has been General Motors' highest dollar-volume supplier for years, and the bill is not decreasing. Insurance companies themselves, in an effort to contain costs, designate lower-cost hospitals as preferred providers for different kinds of diagnoses and treatment. The reimbursement guidelines of the Medicare Diagnostic Review Group attempt to restrain costs. The unintended result is analogous to decades-old industrial control systems: the providers set budget guidelines and minimal quality standards and attempt to police the practitioners into compliance. The result is snowballing bureaucracy.

Everyone agrees that the health industry must learn how to achieve better value using less. To this end, many hospitals (and insurance companies) have now adopted some form of Total Quality Management, though efforts frequently stop with clerical, nursing, and support functions. In a few places the MDs themselves are learning to review their work by a Total Quality process. Two other influences may help this movement along: clinical pathways and health-active medical consumers.

Clinical pathways attempt to standardize the processes that patients go through when admitted to a hospital. Suppose a middle-aged woman is admitted with aspiration pneumonia. Orders: oral fluids every thirty minutes, intravenous antibiotics, oxygen, and respiratory treatments every four hours; expected stay about three days. That's the basic clinical pathway if everything goes right.[9]

But everything does not always go right. Quality people refer to it as "process variance." Busy nurses don't have time to offer fluids every thirty minutes. Aides rushing to help are unaware that the physician wants all output measured. In addition, a sputum specimen is desired before starting the antibiotic IV, but sniffing unhumidified oxygen makes the patient's secretions too thick to cough up easily, so the antibiotic is started twenty hours later than intended. In all, the stay lasts six days.

A clinical pathway is usually developed by a team led by a nurse with advice from a physician. Many physicians, but far from all, order standard protocols to treat particular diagnoses. The clinical pathway describes the key incidents, and their timing, that should occur if the patient is to complete the corrective action for a specific diagnosis on schedule. Thus, a clinical pathway becomes the basis for the treatment goals of the patient, the sequence of work to be done by the hospital staff, and the follow-up analyses of what went right or wrong so that everyone can help improve the process (amend the clinical pathway).

Clinical pathways also help allay patient and family fear of the unknown when treatment is begun. Informed of a clinical pathway at admission or after diagnosis, patients and their families can anticipate what should happen (provided they are in a condition to comprehend it). Then patients and their families establish goals for themselves and monitor their progress, good or bad. They can better assist a busy health care staff, plus more often than not the psychological effect is positive. They start to become health-active patients, or prosumer patients assisting with their own recovery, if they can.

Some physicians regard a clinical pathway as "cookbook medicine." Others recognize it as a way to focus both the patients and the staff on the treatment pattern of each individual. The physician's role then is to specify the deviations from the pathway that are necessary for each individual case. Deviations from pattern and the reasons for them must then be the core of patient reports when nurses change shift. Problems cannot so easily be passed from person to person without resolution. In hospitals, as in industrial job shops, patients (work orders) can easily pass from department to department, including physicians, for specialized attention without anyone concentrating on the patients' welfare.

Causes of variance from a clinical pathway become grist for the improvement of hospital and staff performance. Reasons for changing the clinical pathway are easier to understand—rather than a doctor leaving perplexed nurses to question new orders. The causes of variance from a clinical pathway are easier to document for third-party payers, too. Fewer pneumonia patients should leave a day early because nobody will pay. Most important, clinical pathways clarify an improvement process for health care by those who are closest to it, including the patient.

Health-active consumers eagerly seek health information—and sometimes misinformation—from wellness centers, dial-a-nurse, and yogis. As the amount of on-line health information of various kinds increases, an increasing percentage of consumers are expected to be health-active, perhaps 20–25 percent by the turn of the century.[10] Health-active patients, accustomed to taking health-maintenance actions on their own, insist on knowing treatment procedures and closely question health care professionals.

Authoritarian physicians are jolted by health-active patients who come to them having already checked medical databases and references. They seek a consultant, not a father figure, and they won't hesitate to get second and third opinions. They have their own notion of clinical pathways (varying from orthodox to mystic).

Physiological preventive maintenance and early detection, coupled with improvement processes, are likely bets to slow the rise of health care costs. However, they will not reverse the trend in the 1990s because of: (1) an aging population (half of all health care costs are in the last six months of life); (2) significant epidemiological diseases (such as AIDS); (3) extended consequences of dissipation (drugs, for example); and (4) the simple fact that health professionals have learned how to keep physical wrecks alive a long time.[11]

The health care industry as we know it cannot grow forever. Routine health care will gravitate to information systems, health clubs, advisory services, monitoring of vital signs by UltraComm from the patient's home, and so on. For the population capable of participating, quality of life will thereby improve. However, in a decade or two, advanced societies will also have to make bitter, divisive decisions on some tough issues: When should an artificially maintained life be discontinued, and who makes the decision?

Quality of Life as an Economic Challenge

Developing quality of life depends on improving us—on the expansion of quality living, which is something learned, not merely found or acquired. Not that there is anything wrong with having a bigger ranch in Texas or a taller skyscraper in New York, but as symbols, big-scale achievements do not mean what they once did. Being the world's biggest-tonnage steel producer is less impressive and less challenging than customizing the product so that customers can do exactly what they need with only the material available.

That's a change in incentive for many of the industrial regions of the world. Companies have always had a sentiment for giving customers what they want, but not a social mandate for it. The change from our historical motivation is subtle, but it's big.

During the agricultural wave, big expanses of rich ground were the source of wealth, and the path to prosperity was territorial expansion. When the industrial wave began, wealth sprang from access to minerals, materials, and energy and knowing how to use them. Mass production allowed materials to be churned into product ever faster. First-time buyers were seldom overly particular, and cash for goodies beat plowing with a mule. Hordes of well-paid production workers in the most vibrant industries—like automobiles or aircraft—could consume more material than the princes of yore.

After a time, material accumulated and mass transportation became cheap. Low cost, high productivity, and product quality became more advantageous to new producers than product innovation and proximity to raw material. The more proficient soon found themselves competitive in established markets while still engaged in considerable virgin growth at home.

Expansionary, virgin growth is the initial saturation of users with produced goods, primarily from virgin resources—timber, ore, and so on. Material consumption soared with the population explosion. As the world becomes mapped and probed, the need for limits at some point is obvious, but the issue is controversial because no one knows the exact points. Developing industrial regions adopt a growth mindset, but for them the feeling will be shorter-lived. There is only one world to expand into.

But quality-improvement processes and the information wave are sweeping over the world in advance of this doomsday scenario, and information-wave consumption is different. If no cost or environmental impediments existed, sooner or later many individuals would be saturated with the pure tonnage of hardware. Additional per capita use of energy and materials no longer results in an increased quality of life. (Driving twice as long each day in heavier traffic does not necessarily equate to enjoying it more, even if part of the driving were handled automatically.)

Quality of life questions the mind-set of per capita economic growth—meaning more energy and material use per person. To starving people, growth is an obvious addition to the quality of life. To the sated, it isn't.

The economic incentives of growth are well understood. Whenever the economy stalls, money pumps are primed so we can grow faster. A sign of a company in trouble is lagging sales. Among public companies, any stock that is not increasing in value is suspect. Business schools discuss how to improve a company's operations better only if "improvement" is intended to make that company grow faster. Turnaround management is exciting.

However, quality of life may or may not be achieved through conventional economic growth. Quality is making that which we know how to use better. A quality product is worthless if its owner does not know how to use it, and worse if the owner misuses it. (How many people can program a VCR?)

The saturated U.S. auto market shows signs of migrating into growth in quality of life rather than growth in unit sales. Despite protests that they don't make them like they used to, 1991 automobiles beat the 1971 versions in ride, mileage, durability—almost any criterion except price tag. Prices of the same models rose about 70 percent in constant dollars between 1971 and 1991.[12] About 10 percent of the cost of a fully loaded car is now electronics and software, and that figure is expected to rise.[13] For example, sound systems are creeping up buyers' priority lists of features that differentiate offerings. That suggests quality growth in product features. Other indicators: lower defect rates, faster customer-response times, higher recycle percentages, and so on.

An extreme example of a quality-of-life project would be a defect-free solar car that could compete with the amenities of the 1993 gasoline-powered models. (Even battery-powered ones lack enough zip for air-conditioning.) The nature of the challenge is intellectually understandable, but very different from setting a new land-speed record or building the Titanic. To anyone born with the urge to peel rubber, there's little intrinsic pizzazz.

Quality-of-life products will have long-life components, easily adapted to changing needs. Manufacturing and remanufacturing will be by high-yield, low-energy, low-waste methods. Quality of life is living with gusto, but with minimum waste of resources.

Unfortunately, it takes a disciplined, cooperative society to learn how to do that. That represents a drastically different kind of motivation, or soul.

The soul of the Taylorists has been growth—the exhilarating mindset of a fortress-mentality company expanding in a world without known limits. Growth has driven Europeans and their descendants since the Renaissance. First, scientific advance; then land; then gold; then raw materials; and a burgeoning population looking for something to do. Always the excuse of the exploiters (colonials thought of Westerners that way) was that they could gain more from the resources than the locals, thus increasing wealth for everybody. (The population explosion began with the Industrial Revolution in Europe, boomed around the world, and is now echoing back.)

Quality of life is achieved more by inward growth and expanding human capability—by mastering the science and the know-how to predict and control physical phenomena and to accomplish what we choose. A broader, deeper range of human abilities is necessary than merely learning how to use more resources, even when customers are satisfied with the results. Perhaps that's one reason why a tinge of religion coats the quality movements of today.

Inward growth begins by taking more responsibility for achieving it—more willpower and more demands on our social systems. The mental set is much different than if resources can be wasted willy-nilly and learning done the expensive way. Responsibility is missing from the OECD quality-of-life wish list in Figure 3–5, but quality of life is not going to just happen.

The inward part is the most difficult part of this journey; more than intellectual understanding is necessary. First, it is hard for owners and managers to appreciate that fail-safe prediction and control of processes demands much more of everyone than mere organization for control of resources (what most corporate systems are intended to do). Then, it is difficult to regard a business as its associates as well as its assets. Finally, it is hard to see that a company is not stand-alone, but a contributor to a customer-guided, multibusiness enterprise. Such an enterprise requires a more open, people-development kind of leadership than does obtaining control of a traditional company and driving it to commercial success.

NOTES

1. Harry Mark Petrakis, *The Founder's Touch* (New York: McGraw-Hill, 1965). (A history of Motorola).

2. Two of the more quoted lists can be found in David A. Garvin, "Competing on the Eight Dimensions of Quality," *Harvard Business Review*, 65, no. 6 (November–December 1987): 101–09; and in Figure 3–5 of Franco D'Egidio; *The Service Era* (Cambridge, MA: Productivity Press, 1990), p. 32. D'Egidio's book also introduced another popular quality expression, "moment of truth," meaning to do with grace whatever is necessary to please a troubled but reasonable customer at the right time.

3. For example, a critique of the Baldrige Award appeared in *The Economist*, July 30, 1991, p. 83. The writer could not understand how a company's quality process could amount to anything if its earnings were disappointing.

4. W. Edwards Deming, "A System of Profound Knowledge," *Actionline* (Automotive Industry Action Group 9, no. 8, (August 1990): 20–26.

5. A typical company history, and one that describes a long-term, patriarchal contrast with the investment mind-set of Boott Mill owners is: G. O. Robinson, *The Story of Greenwood Mills* (Greenwood, SC: privately printed, 1967).

6. George Box and Soren Bisgaard, "The Scientific Context of Quality Improvement," Report No. 25, Center for Quality and Productivity Improvement, University of Wisconsin, Madison, Wisconsin, 1987.

7. Walter A. Shewhart, *Statistical Methods from the Viewpoint of Quality Control*, ed. by W. Edwards Deming (Washington, D.C.: Graduate School, Department of Agriculture, 1939).

8. Reported by Lars Andersson and Lennart Levi, *Population, Environment, and Quality of Life*, a report by the Swedish Royal Ministry for Foreign Affairs on the 1974 World Population Conference (United Nations).

9. The story of clinical pathways is from James P. O'Donnell, a student and pharmacist at Community Hospital, Indianapolis, Indiana, where a clinical pathways program is in progress.

10. From the Health Strategy Group, as reported by Tom Ferguson, "Patient, Heal Thyself," *The Futurist* 26, no. 1 (January–February 1992): 9–13.

11. From a presentation by Dr. Brent James, Intermountain Health Care, Inc., at the 17th Partners in Business Productivity and Quality Seminar, Utah State University, Logan, Utah, May 7, 1992.

12. Estimates based on comparing sticker prices in *Wards Auto World* for three American nameplates little changed in market orientation over the twenty years: Mustang, Caprice, and Sedan DeVille. The auto companies claim the price rise is much lower. During the same period, Japanese price markups galloped even faster, helped considerably by virtual doubling of the dollar–yen exchange rate.

13. Separating the electronics cost from the rest of a system takes some digging. For example, electronics and software are enabling technology to be buried in many new features of automobiles, such as air bags and antilock brakes. A push is on to squeeze costs enough that luxury car features can be added to entry-level vehicles. See "Spectacular Growth Seen in Electronics World" (by Steve Plum, but no byline) *Wards Auto World*, August 1991, pp. 34–35.

4

CATCHING UP
WITH THE TIMES

AT THE BEGINNING OF EACH HOLIDAY SEASON, GREETING CARD COMPANIES overstock retail stores with cards to give customers a large selection. The return of surplus cards is wasteful, but it beats dissatisfied customers and lost sales. To reduce the waste, card companies such as Hallmark and American Greetings jumped into lean manufacturing. They cut setup times, formed cells, and organized pull-through systems. The added flexibility allowed them to quickly rerun popular cards for a season's closing rush and led to more effective distribution.

Next, the companies attacked the lead times to create fresh cards for each new season. If creative and graphics lead times for each new card line could be cut in half, with the corresponding work times for each line likewise halved, the company's card lines could be renewed twice as often. Or additional lines of cards could be promoted to cover more occasions (bosses' day, grandparents' day, and so forth).

These changes are stimulating the growth and profitability of the card business as it is currently conceived. Fresher card variety is presented to customers at lower cost, and with less excess stock at the end of each season. From a social view, if more people send prepared greetings to each other, we hope we are all a little happier. From the crass view of material flow, more trees are cut (although a high per-

centage of cards are now recyclable) so that people can ship senti-
mental bits of paper to each other, and part of the flow is siphoned off
and transformed into wages and profit.

How would the basic concept of the greetings business evolve in a
computer-literate world? First, customers select cards by computer—
perhaps with the help of a card-store clerk. Instead of keeping cards in
stock, a high percentage of them (not requiring complex printing
processes) would be downloaded from files and printed at the store.
Some of the files searched might be in distant locations.

A step beyond that, customers would view different pieces of artwork and lyrics on the screen and create their own cards to be printed
at the store. They might even create cards by computer at home but
mail them from stores with their signatures electronically transcribed.
Finally, if greetings were totally created, sent, and read electronically,
the need for paper, ink, and printers would be eliminated.

The technology for an electronic greetings business as described is
an extension of today's desktop publishing, but with more computing
power, wilder scenarios are easily concocted. The imaginative could
send their friends Disney-quality animated graphics to be played using a virtual reality setup or holographic imaging. But as always, the
bugaboo is anticipating customer reaction, especially that of compu-
terphobes.

The greetings business also illustrates two other critical points. One
is that all-electronic greetings remove much of the waste from all
parts of the business: no overstocking, no delays to create artwork or
lyrics, and no waste or errors in printing, packaging, and distribution
of cards. It's all gone.

Also gone is the business's conventional growth by converting more
natural resources into attractive form. The card is a convenient unit
to price to a customer. By contrast, artistic software is easily priced
only if it is securely represented by a disk or chip. If it is easily pirated,
the company's work is nearly worthless. Thus, an all-electronic greetings industry would depend on intellectual property values, which
basically boil down to finding an equitable way to reward people for
creatively using their time. Almost all solutions to such problems
require the observance of legal sanctions, such as patents, copyrights,
and licenses to practice.

The second point is the value of human time. A greeting is appreciated because it's the thought that counts, meaning that the sender took personal time to prepare it. An automatically processed, impersonal greeting is instantly discounted—no soul. If a new generation of children learns to draw pictures by computer, do-it-yourself valentines and birthday greetings by software may seem natural, but not today. Those who are accustomed to computers may still not wish to fumble with artistic software, or if they do, they have little confidence in their own taste. Proficiency as a high-tech prosumer covers a wide scope of skills and inclinations—perhaps a more imaginative version of becoming a Victorian-era lady or gentleman for those who had enough money.

The information wave is not about high-tech leaps. It is about people learning how to work and behave very differently from the past. The story of just-in-time manufacturing is part of that evolution.

THE MYSTERIES OF JIT

One of the most insidious misunderstandings about JIT is that the objective is merely to reduce inventory on the company's books. The real objective is to remove the waste—and costs. Inventory is only one kind of waste, but it happens to be an indicator of long materials lead times, which in turn suggests that many other kinds of waste lurk in places far removed from shops and warehouses. The Japanese consultant Shigeo Shingo identified seven wastes, like the seven sins, from the waste of overproduction to the waste of defects, but he missed at least one, the waste of inefficiently creating and using information.[1]

However, many companies believe that JIT is merely having the supplier hold the inventory, either off-site or on consignment. Changing the point at which title transfers simulates a JIT effect on the customer company's books, but waste still abounds. It may even increase. Should the shortfall of understanding be deep enough, a company will even build a special JIT warehouse for this purpose.[2]

Those who understand business through financial analysis may not see the benefits of JIT at first. At the extreme, they view a business as a limited-boundary, financial input-output mechanism generating a return on investment; it's something that can be bought and sold. In that mental model, cutting lead times does not immediately translate into gains except by reduction of inventory investment. But cutting operating lead times (operating wastes) improves the turnover ratios of many kinds of assets. A cost-time profile such as the one shown in Figure 4–1 has often helped managers to visualize the effect.

Understanding often comes slowly and stagnates quickly. Japanese, Americans, and JIT pioneers everywhere have frequently had to invoke samurai, Henry Ford, and other cultural icons to legitimize new thinking when the going got tough. Actually transforming operations for minimal waste is a learning experience not gained vicariously. A supervisor in the throes of transformation explained the difficulty nicely: "It's hard to stop doing what you're doing long enough to figure out how to do something different."

This difficulty explains why one of the major roles of top management is communicating a vision of where changes are going, but then most visions fade out too soon. Few American companies are beyond the first stage of lift-off with JIT (or whatever acronym they use) much less using time concepts to give business operations a different dimension. Projecting the implications of several just-in-time concepts helps to create that vision:

1. Time, rather than space, is the basis of twenty-first–century organization.
2. Learning is a time-based concept.
3. Eliminating wasted information may eliminate the ultimate waste.
4. Decreasing lead-times-to-change increases flexibility and responsiveness.
5. Decreasing routine lead times without adding resources signifies the elimination of waste.

THE TIME-BASED ORGANIZATION

New approaches to organizational design are based more on time—the communication patterns and human relationships that should shift over time. Time concepts describe organizations differently.

FIGURE 4-1
COST-TIME PROFILES AT WESTINGHOUSE

Simplified profiles of process to enter and engineer orders for apparatus sold to utilities. Time shrank from twenty-two days to one day; cost shrank by 50 percent.

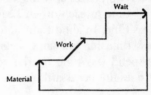

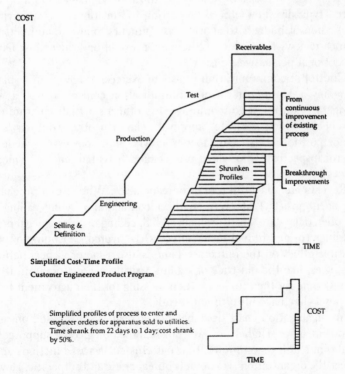

Simplified Cost-Time Profile

Customer Engineered Product Program

Simplified profiles of process to enter and engineer orders for apparatus sold to utilities. Time shrank from 22 days to 1 day; cost shrank by 50%.

SOURCE: *Courtesy of Nicola C. Sirianni, Westinghouse Productivity and Quality Center, Pittsburgh, Pennsylvania.*

They lead to different kinds of organizational relationships from those prescribed by fixed-position functional hierarchies.

When time is used to describe "power" and other organizational relationships, they are seen differently. For example, a leader takes action that precedes or causes actions taken by others. (A "dreamer's" vision never precedes anything else.) Human relationships are investments of time in each other. Learning takes time; efficient learning takes less time. In almost any activity those who are proficient often take less time for the same accomplishment, but not always. (Par golfers spend less time on the course than duffers, but a virtuoso pianist does not necessarily consume less-than-average time playing a piece.)

Power is control over resources or rewards. The powerful can speed or delay the proposals of others. Organization charts—seldom up to date—typically show official "reporting to" relationships, signifying possession of budgets to allocate, assignments to award, and performance reviews to conduct. Otherwise, a would-be leader must have exceptional persuasive skills.

Control of communication is also an exercise of power. In a small company a common form of communication control, as well as of budgetary control, is to require the top officer's actual signature on all checks, which institutes approval delays. In other contexts, superior position accrues to supervisors who alone possess a schedule or to inspectors who alone understand pass-fail criteria (more delays).

Reviews are a favorite tool of bureaucracies. Whenever a purchasing agent insists that every engineer contact him before calling a supplier, delays are "institutionalized." Speeding or slowing legal proceedings (or any formal review process) is favored depending on its possible effect on the outcome. Time is also a factor in negotiating strategies, like the old trick of stalling visiting negotiators until it is almost time for them to leave, then pressing for their agreement to a proposal they have little time to study.

An organization chart describes power relationships based on positions in space. Higher or lower boxes show how people supposedly relate, but unless communication patterns cut across functions and levels, the organization is extremely bureaucratic and autocratic. However, everyone generally understands "where they are" because it's easy to see. (The time-based indicators of power are who waits on whom, who delays, and who expedites.)

An organization chart is a symbol of timeless relationships that do not exist in fact. Henry Ford, who understood the value of reduced lead times in production better than other industrialists of his time, thought of his company, his designs, his factories, and his system as timeless assets, like land. His was a semifeudal concept of organization. His realm once established, he need not continue changing, but ever after his goal was to defend it from attack, both from without and within.

After 1920 Henry organized and manipulated to stay in control, not for further improvement. He delayed both the six-cylinder engine and the V-8. Despising the annual model changes instigated by Chevrolet, he maintained veto power over them. Henry conceived organization in terms of space and position: his position was the high turret in a fortress company, with everyone else in subordinate positions—not unlike the ancient Chinese concept of the world as zones extending from the imperial court.

Considerable energy has been expended to circumvent large bureaucracies. Classic project organization creates smaller functional organizations, or teams, to focus on specific projects or programs—an improvement until the projects become large. In matrix organizations individuals simultaneously belong to one or more project organizations as well as functional departments, which often fosters conflict in the power relationships. However, both project management and matrix management are intended to cut communication and decision times.

Regardless of any formal organizational structure, most of us must set priorities and allocate our time among a number of concurrent responsibilities. When we do, we think like members of time-based organizations. Organization charts clarify the "power relationships" but seldom the communication linkages.

The conclusions from all this: (1) "power" is fundamental to almost any human organization or relationship; (2) establishing a time-based organization to greatly reduce delays and lead times cannot be done without rethinking power relationships; and (3) shifting to a time-based organization is not a restructuring. A spatial diagram will probably still show a few major power relationships, and those might be restructured. The rest is a process of developing people so that communication is unimpeded and responsibilities are understood with minimum delays for review, approval, or coordination.

Why We Need Open-System Enterprise

Maintaining trust between people is the number one factor in time-based organization. Trust is confidence in other people, confidence that they can and will do what they say. Bidding and negotiating from positions of mutual ignorance is extremely time-consuming. Nudge almost anyone involved in lean manufacturing, and they will say that building trust between people is the key.

An activity that takes a high level of trust is payment systems. These also take time. Delays caused by tollgating—stopping processes to determine cost or to receive payment—are often ignored because they are the feeding processes of business. (What percentage of your shopping time is at checkout?)

Delays occur primarily to prevent cheating and to cover credit arrangements—meaning delays of payment. Credit arrangements, by which some organizations in an economic food chain "carry" others, are complicated by large inventories, long process lead times, and financial float (inventory of dollars covering the lead time to process transactions). To make payment systems less time-consuming, costs, prices, and credit arrangements need to be simple and open.

Suppose we lived in a perfect JIT world of nearly instant processing of material, near zero stocks, and electronic funds transfer without delays. Companies would then have nearly negligible receivables, payables, and inventories, as shown by the imaginary manufacturing company statements in Figure 4–2. The elimination of receivables, payables, and inventory would raise profit and ROI considerably—if no competitors were doing the same. But that won't happen.

A single company cannot do this by itself. The simplification of business arrangements that would minimize tollgating is possible only if each participant's current business status is openly known. That is, each company's operating proficiency, books, and credit status are open to all participants who wish to know. That is crucial to open-system enterprise.

An open system in this sense is anathema to any company that can

FIGURE 4-2
HYPOTHETICAL
FINANCIAL STATEMENTS SHOWING
EFFECTS OF TIME COMPRESSION

	Rust-Belt Manufacturing	*Instant-Action Manufacturing*
Income		
Sales	100	100
Cost of goods sold	70	60
Gross margin	30	40
Selling and administration	20	20
Interest	5	2
Net before tax	5	18
Balance Sheet		
ASSETS		
Cash	15	10
Accounts receivable	20	0
Inventory	20	5
Plant and equity	40	40
Other	5	5
Total assets	100	60
LIABILITIES AND EQUITY		
Accounts payable	15	0
Debt	45	20
Equity	40	40
	100	100

These statements are intended to give a quick illustration of the potential of "profile-shrinking" on financial position. Inventory is greatly reduced and both receivables and payables are virtually wiped out by electronic funds transfers with no delay. The streamlining generally reduces costs, too, so cost of goods sold is reduced. Whether sales prices would stay high enough to fatten profit is questionable. If competition is doing the same customers expect price reductions.

find a pot of gold all by itself ("maximize short-term profits" in economics lingo). For example, tobacco companies are not interested in open disclosure of *everything*. Warren Buffet has been quoted as describing the business in this way: "It [a pack of cigarettes] costs a penny to make, sell it for a dollar, it's addictive, and there's fantastic brand loyalty."[3] Any company that believes that it could do something like that, even for a short time, with a monopoly on a billion-bit memory chip will likewise hold information as tightly as possible.

Only when they become convinced that El Dorado is a mirage are companies interested in open-system sharing—only when they become convinced that quality of life for them as well as their customers is through superb, fail-safe processes, products, and services. Then the need to perfect quality and cut lead times becomes more apparent, and existing operating organizations cannot do that all by themselves. Organizations will become more like extended networks that shift over time but that must communicate responsibilities and hold groups and individuals accountable. The only way to shorten the trust-building time required before people work openly with each other is by making open information the norm.

Different Senses of Time

Myopia is considered by many to be a chronic disease of American managers in publicly held companies. The one condition analysts almost always cite is the damaging affects of "quarterly financial reports" on long-term business investment and development.

One symptom of the short-term perspective should be called NIN (Need It Now—obviously related to Sin). The lion's share of public investment is done by professional fund managers, who are judged on quarterly and annual earnings. Rightly or wrongly, the heads of established publicly held companies therefore believe that fund managers expect them to lay the yellow brick road on schedule with quarter after quarter of growth in returns. However, improvements built by investing in people may take years to hit the bottom line. Human development lead times and cash cow milking cycles do not coincide.

The Council on Competitiveness commissioned Michael Porter of Harvard Business School to research whether short-term thinking is a real phenomenon, and if so, what causes it. Porter concluded that fixation on profitability by investors does lead to bias to improve short-term cash flow. This bias leads to underinvesting in the intangibles of long-term development and to excessive contentiousness between "stakeholders" who should work together. Concentration on near-term issues crowds out the development of long-term vision.[4]

General Electric illustrates the problem. GE promotes a program it calls Work Out to develop continuous improvement at operating levels, and the company has received its share of press for tightening operations. However, unless a business is number one or number two in market share, GE prefers to sell it. GE will not squander money on mediocre financial performers or piddle with niche markets. The policy is a hit with investors, but militates against long-term, come-from-behind improvement processes and risky start-ups. It also does not fit with participation in anything like an open-system enterprise.

The Floating Crap Game

Time-based organization is a cohesive set of working teams having the same goals. Some, but not all, are "self-directed"; some even self-organize and self-terminate. An individual's exact position may not be easily defined, but if the organization is effective, the person's responsibilities should be clear. Academicians often speak not of their position but of "what I'm into now." That phrase implies a time-based concept of work, one independent of organization, as if responsibilities and results did not need to be coordinated.

This type of organization is roughly similar to "floating crap games," the dice games played in streets and alleys. Players come and players go, and when the cops get close, everyone scatters. They soon meet again at a new spot and resume play. Street characters in the know probably sense where the game has moved, but when asked they give a straight answer only to someone they trust. However, dice games are simple to organize compared to the teamwork required of people engaged in technical derring-do. There, a team must rely more on schedules and responsibility charts, like those that have been developed over the years for project management.

Communication for improvement not only simplifies processes but also simplifies communication patterns, and with them the form of organization. Communications links among customers and suppliers can be documented by "sociograms," that is, process relationship diagrams based on the time people spend with each team. These establish the actual working organization and define how it changes through time.

The actual organization thus continually evolves as missions and needs change. Many teams or organizations will be chartered for specific missions, go through an enterprise history, and disband. Charles Savage calls such organizations virtual teams or virtual companies, a reference to the swapping of memory space in virtual-memory computers. Teams may be partly free-association organizations, but some kind of power system will surely be present to track performance and responsibility.[5] The Lehigh "agile" manufacturing scenario (in Chapter 2) adopted Savage's "virtual company" to define the coalition and collaboration of persons in distant locations communicating by an advanced version of today's computer bulletin board.

MIT faculty, notably Peter Senge, have coupled these ideas with learning processes and refer to the time-based organization as a "learning organization."[6] In other words, a time-based organization creates learning time for its members. For example, the rotation of leadership roles among members of a self-directed work team gives each member of the team an opportunity for cross-training. However, without clear direction, such an organization is confusing. The "learning organization" seems to depend on several factors:

1. A strong set of expected behaviors through a working culture or code.
2. Unified visions or objectives—taking time to be sure that everyone is pointed in the same direction. (Experience with hierarchical command leads executives to ignore this.)
3. A strong sense of responsibility. (This implies the need for a power system, not necessarily a person, to confer rewards and sanctions for performance.)
4. A common improvement process using universally understood language and logic *in practice* (knowing how to learn).
5. A consistent system of performance measurement.
6. Regular planning and improvement cycles—learning cycles—to stimulate improvement.

LEARNING IS A TIME-BASED CONCEPT

The compression of learning time challenges human capacity, and one of the fastest ways for the enthusiastic has always been do-it-yourself. For example, tinkering with cars was a do-it-yourself education for youngsters until autos became complex. Now, middle-aged men buy old cars just for nostalgic wrench twirling, and self-taught computer sophisticates specify the modules for their own personal computer, assembling and testing the things themselves. They interact with suppliers in a learning *process*, not just a purchase.

Learning is not complete until demonstrated by accomplishment. One can "learn" golf by watching a tape but never swing a club. Business learning is therefore indistinguishable from the improvement of performance—improving on at least one dimension of performance without losing on any others—a continuous-improvement process. Continuous improvement is learning; improving faster is more efficient learning.

Learning consumes human time. Quality of life cannot improve any faster than people can learn how to perform better; otherwise, the technology of the few outruns the appreciation of the many.

Variance in time is a stimulus, and being aware of a deviation from a desired state stimulates corrective action. On a grand scale, being in a state that is far removed from some desired one is the reason leaders of time-based organizations must emphasize the gap between a vision of the future and current reality. On a small scale, if a part being machined is drifting off dimension, it is time to make a correction.

Human awareness of variances to be fixed is deadened if people do no more than work incessantly to the rhythm of an assembly line. Software routines extend this regularity to higher orders of complexity, but the result is still soul-deadening. People tethered to system menus are connected to reality only through prescribed images and numbers. They become system zombies, segregated from real customers or real products and therefore denied the opportunity to learn from the real thing.[7]

Some learning is by rote, as with multiplication tables. Original learning, however, is a discovery process: structuring the unstructured; discovering something orderly in chaos; making the irregular and unpredictable into something as regular as clockwork. Fast learners must be unfettered—free to experience reality and free to experiment with it. Unfortunately, learning is retarded when communications are controlled. Stimulating open communication presumes that everyone will take responsibility and that they will readily learn and improve. That does not happen unless people know how to collectively learn.

The "real JIT" on the shop floor is learning fast by doing: size up a work area, formulate a plan, move the equipment overnight (if it is not too big), and operate in a different cell configuration by next morning. If it doesn't work well, do it again. Many Japanese companies introduced JIT by do-it-now blitzkrieg, and American companies are starting to do the same. After the moves, everyone should be closer to their internal customers and suppliers, and learning accelerates. Errors are caught sooner. Corrections occur faster. Less labor is wasted. New problems are anticipated quicker. Less computer planning is required.

Another objective is consistency of performance. The same result time after time is important for any production, but of particular value for items such as rubber parts for which consistent blends and time-temperature profiles give standard results. Consistent performance varies little in either lead times or in work-cycle times. Fluctuating work-cycle times (an out-of-control pattern) signify that plenty is left to learn. Perhaps operators can discover more fail-safe methods or simpler methods of work.

However, once achieved, utterly consistent work is utterly boring. Stimulated workers can squeeze out more waste while maintaining consistency, but finally, low-variance, low-waste processes should be automated. They are dehumanizing, but cheap to automate.

Improvement Cycles

Visitors to well-done JIT factories are usually amazed by the simplicity. It doesn't just happen. It's grown by a carefully cultivated learning process, and learning processes are stimulated by regular long-cycle deadlines, like school semesters and project deadlines.

An improvement cycle is a learning cycle. Organizations such as Toyota that practice regular improvement-process cycles do not necessarily show better performance cycle after cycle. The extending of Toyota product lines and logistics lines over the past decade has taken a toll on Toyota lead times, for instance. But as in golf, unless one practices improvement regularly, the game becomes much worse.

Model years in the auto industry are design-improvement cycles, but most cars change drastically only on a major redesign cycle of five to ten years, or even longer. Design cycles in televisions, appliances, cellular telephones, and other products are opportunities for improvement cycles on the total service processes associated with the products. Obviously, the opportunities are sometimes missed.

Proponents of time-based competition note that competitors with shorter design cycles will loop back faster in marketing dogfights and soon be in position for the kill. Less noted is that a habit of disciplined improvement cycles of many lengths and on all kinds of processes throughout a total organization conditions it for the dogfight.[8]

Organizations with regular improvement cycles are like athletes with regular training. They do not always win, but they have a greater chance of it. Time-based competition is more and better improvement processes, by more people, on faster cycles.

Cumulative Learning

Cumulative learning is associated with continuity of learning. Learning new habits presumes unlearning old ones. Maintaining an improvement process presumes building on old accomplishments. Every doctoral candidate is expected to complete a survey of past accomplishment so that a new dissertation will add to a body of knowledge. However, that presumes that the prior body of knowledge has not been seriously questioned. Breakthroughs usually reject earlier notions in some way; Henry Ford in his heyday sometimes did not promote experienced people because someone new would try an old flop again from a different angle, and the second time it might work.

A saying at Honda is that one must "break old habits; even the good habits." That describes a culture of continuous improvement. The human side of it begins with acceptance of constant change and an understanding of where practice has been and where it is going.

Continuous improvement is continuous revolution. Even with brains on full alert, the rate of learning (and relearning) is still limited. Nothing can go faster than people themselves can progress, and it helps not to go backward. One company that had successfully started cell manufacturing reverted to departmentalized production—at increased cost—because new management did not understand. They even believed economic order quantities were a marvelous new concept.

Hiring employees only for eight hours of work per day places no value on their cumulative learning. Investment in associates (employees) includes paid instructional time, and they invest time in themselves. To switch on their brains, an enterprise must engage their interest and their trust. Learning philosophy and adages takes months. Learning how to improve quality with cross-functional teams takes years and is still only a start. Cumulative learning is a lifetime experience.

Cumulative improvement also takes two kinds of human development: (1) understanding parts of a process in detail; and (2) understanding how the process fits with the rest of the world in general. Many talented technicians have failed to contribute because they did not appreciate point two. Development of a true learning organization depends on every member of it basically understanding its scope and environment. That is, everyone should be developed as a generalist as well as a specialist.[9]

INFORMATION IS THE ULTIMATE WASTE

In an information age the biggest waste is information. When products are designed by computer and the production instructions are downloaded to machines by computer (called CAD/CAM), a shop floor is only the physical manifestation of a mass of information. The same is true of publishing, flying by wire, space launches, and television production.

Public communication is such a hit-or-miss endeavor that information waste is seldom recognized. Of all the books, magazines, and newspapers printed, how many are purchased? Of those purchased, how many are read? If an advertisement in one is noticed, is it remembered? When seminar announcements are mailed, a response rate of 1 percent or more is considered quite good. The rest are landfill feed. The print media have become a conduit to sort, transport, and recycle material.

The same can be said of television and radio, except the waste is not so visible. Thirty-four channels come to my television. I can watch only one at a time, and then often when less than fully alert. How many radio stations can be received is unknown, but the cost of transporting signals is so low that a minuscule hit ratio is acceptable.

Today, however, the waste of competing for attention in an information-saturated environment seems to be more the human kind. The more disruptive processes, like junk mail and autodial telemarketing, push information on recipients. The friendlier ones (TV) at least have an off button.

In computer-integrated manufacturing, the bulk of the physical waste is first represented by information. Most of it is encrypted in computer chips, but crucial elements of communication may simply be person-to-person—a decision to change a schedule, for instance. Much of the waste is of human time as well as of machine time, occurring in offices as well as shops.

In an information age, one objective is to avoid the generation of information waste as early in the process as possible. A second objective is to shorten all the feedback loops. That begins with product and process design. Therefore, a product designed with fewer parts of lesser complexity takes less information. Achieving that end today is one aim of another acronym, design for manufacturing (DFM). A simple, compact production process requires less information to manage than a complex, widely scattered one. Robust processes are those in which small deviations make little difference, and almost by definition, those take less information than finicky ones. The moral: It may be the information age, but keeping operations simple will still pay off handsomely. Simplifying product designs as much as possible has a huge payoff.

Information simplification is a major reason for decreasing the number of suppliers. Having a hundred suppliers in a hundred locations allows more communication in more detail with fewer people using a simpler system than managing a thousand suppliers in a thousand locations. The logistics are simpler. Interaction on product and process design is simpler. Solving quality problems is simpler. Transactions are simpler.

The most verbally bludgeoned areas of information overkill are in accounting, materials transactions, and legal proceedings. In factories, the transaction load has been referred to as "the hidden factory."[10] While the visible factory builds product, the hidden one builds transactional information. In a complex, sprawling, big-batch factory, an elaborate control system is needed. Waste begets waste.

Poor quality also generates information waste. First, quality errors are likely to have originated from an information error in product specification (or its interpretation) order transmittal, order entry, or elsewhere. Second, while accountants sometimes grouse about the amount of information needed for quality documentation, it takes much less information to operate processes that are in control than those out of control, or on the verge of it.

In the teaching of JIT, a favorite exercise is operating a simple factory and comparing "push-flow" systems with "pull-flow" systems, and the pull system wins every time. A few of these exercises move to another stage, where participants dump a few special orders into the fast-flow factory and watch the response. The production rate slows while they communicate how to handle the simplest of order-spec changes. The lesson is that one of the most important aspects of JIT is how to handle routine communication without delay—how to eliminate wasted information. Once a factory can respond to changes without a hiccup, it can easily best competitors who require huge amounts of information, checking and rechecking to do the same thing.

However, the standardization of information flows and formats has potential that is frequently unseen until circumstances force it. That is the equivalent of using a common language in place of many. For example, use of a common bar code and data sets by producers, shippers, and retailers presently allows great simplification (and automation) of material replenishment direct to retail shelves. Eventually the system may bypass the retail stop to go straight to the consumer.

The beginning of such a system is Quick Response—producers managing the finished inventory all the way to the retail shelf if they can. The producers should also respond to style changes quicker. Major retailers favor Quick Response as long as it decreases their investment and increases their sales. If it promises to circumvent both middlemen and stores, opposition will rise.

However, we now catch only a glimmer of the potential for using information—computer-based systems—to greatly simplify manufacturing and business processes in general. With enough ingenuity, we may be able to simplify or eliminate many kinds of "hard" tooling as we know it today. Precise designs with simple fasteners might also eliminate many hand tools and hand fitting. Such designs might make remanufacturing more the norm than original manufacturing. However, we are still plowing the same old ruts, devising software to do better what we have always done, rather than approaching the most basic work in a greatly different way. It's a slow evolution because we can't learn how to work in a radically different way without actually doing it.

REDUCING TIMES-TO-CHANGE

The most easily understood strategic advantage of time-based competition is beating competitors to market with newer or better products. If Honda or Mazda can field a new model in twenty-four months while everyone else takes four to five years to piece together their newest brainstorms, the avant-garde will beat a path to Honda and Mazda. In addition, Honda and Mazda are learning faster. They go through at least two new-model learning experiences to every one for their competitors.

The American automotive companies were able to get away with passing the development baton between large functional departments for far too long—back when the penalty of long development times could easily be paid by the advantages of long-run production. Aerospace companies long had to form cross-functional skunk works teams whenever the job had to be done in short order. Now, the methods for reducing new-product lead times are becoming much more prevalent.

An organization cannot regularly launch new models and products with short lead times unless geared for it throughout all operations—including those with suppliers. Short lead times become a way of life. New-model introductions are routine.

Routine new-model introduction has long been a way of life among the Japanese motorcycle manufacturers. Ten years ago, during the now famous new-model war between Yamaha and Honda, each of the motorcycle manufacturers regularly replenished 5 percent or so of the models in its lineup every month in a pre-CAD/CAM environment. Engineering development had a target date. The tooling shops that made new tooling regularly worked extra shifts, and the companies analyzed the engineering-to-tooling processes both to avoid the introduction of errors and to wring the wasted steps out.

Trials of new tooling on production equipment were regularly added to the daily production schedules. This was possible because both the equipment and the tooling had been designed for fast setup times. If all the tooling worked, the new model was added to next month's schedule; if not, it was deferred. Similar kinds of programs were also pressed at the key suppliers' shops. Rapidly responding to markets and executing design changes became a way of life. It was marvelous until the motorcycle market saturated.

Reducing the time to bring new models or even new technology to market is a matter of streamlining the processes by which it happens, making change as routine as possible. It's a major step beyond mass production, like the JIT exercise of making paper airplanes. If the participants study the communication pattern needed to quickly adapt their production process to different dimensions, colors, or markings, the result is variety to the customer with very little penalty in production capacity—high variety at mass-production prices.

The production of Model Ts was classic mass production because the throughput times of materials were short, but the variety was limited. Common sense tells us we should expect a trade-off; more variety should cost more, assuming that setup times are significant in length. Early in the mass-production wave, that was true. A mass-production engine-transfer line would have to be virtually rebuilt to machine a different size engine block.

By contrast, machinery designed or modified for fast setup times has the flexibility to handle a variety of sizes and shapes one right after another. For instance, Komatsu machines a family of engine blocks on one flexible transfer line in lot sizes of one. Any increase in machine cycle time per block is insignificant. Today, the ideal is customer flexibility from a fast-flow process—a major extension of what Chevrolet did to Ford in the 1920s.

Flexibility generally connotes the ability to adapt to new conditions or requirements—the ability to accommodate each customer's wants. But flexibility is of limited value unless it can be done quickly. The reduction of operating lead times in all kinds of operations confers increased *flexibility* in many senses: (1) response to customer requests for specials or changes; (2) ability to quickly increase or decrease overall production levels; (3) quickly making big adjustments in production mix; and (4) having a short *time-to-market*, from concept to completion of new models, or even new technology. Each of these capabilities confers strategic advantages in the 1990s business climate. They are the precursor to the capabilities that a computer-driven twenty-first–century should make possible, but if we are unable to master the disciplines that enable 1990s flexibility, we may not be able to master twenty-first–century technology either.[11]

Lead Times and Cycle Times

Today, the reduction of learning times is often interpreted to mean reduction only of lead times to develop new models of a similar product. Drastically cutting development times starts by simplifying processes; for example, reducing the total number of parts used, reducing the number of new parts to design, and designing those that remain to an existing process. Some parts are designed by suppliers. Interactive CAD/CAM using teams of customers and suppliers is more sophisticated, but it first requires compatible systems. Then one can begin to minimize human error.

Streamlining development time may only offset the increasing complexity of some products, and thus make them possible. For instance, design engineers working by the methods of thirty years ago would not live long enough to finish a Boeing 777.

The terms *cycle time* and *lead time* are now used interchangeably. For working purposes, definitions need to be more precise. Lead time is elapsed time of operations that may never occur again. Cycle time is the time between recurring events. Lead time, or project duration, to bring out a new model is not the same as cycle time, or time between new-model introductions, as illustrated in Figure 4–3.

Reducing lead times for new models is possible only by using development resources more effectively. It is done by flowcharting processes and taking out the waste, much as in production or clerical

FIGURE 4-3
PRODUCT-DEVELOPMENT
LEAD TIMES AND
CYCLE TIMES

CASE A: DEVELOPMENT LEAD TIME LONGER THAN SALES LIFE

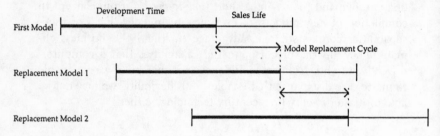

CASE B: DEVELOPMENT TIME SHORTER THAN SALES LIFE

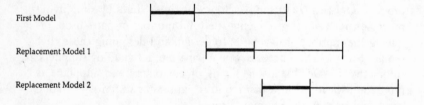

Note that in Case A, development of a third-version model must begin before market feedback is available on the first version. Case B bases new-model conception on feedback from the latest version. Model replacement cycles are therefore often constrained by the length of developmental lead times.

operations, although professionals sometimes do not want to admit that waste also exists in their work. It sounds simple. It is simple— simple as par golf. The only tough part is overcoming ourselves.

Suppose a food-can manufacturer wants to shorten and simplify the process of entering an order for a new can. If the new can is only a new configuration of materials that have been used before, there are no delays for testing or obtaining approval from the Food and Drug Administration. Although printed cans are not extraordinarily complex, an order for a new can is often tied to customer's marketing campaigns, so communication about them is frequently urgent and edgy. Consequently, field sales and the customer service department handle nearly all the communication, since they are in the best position to understand the customer's overall situation and needs.

Customer service is also the major bottleneck in the process, as can be seen in Figures 4–4A and 4–5A. Both figures were derived from the order-entry process of a major can company. Figure 4–4A, often called a relationship diagram, maps the players in the order-entry process. In a sense it reveals the complete network of internal customers and suppliers. Players who identify only their internal customers and suppliers one or two links removed have a useful insight, but they do not see a very big picture and may still remain ignorant of the nature of the external customer.

The dashed line in Figure 4–4A represents the boundary of players in the process who are known by a person in accounting—his immediate internal customers and suppliers. Until collectively constructing the diagram, some players in the network may be virtually unknown. A major function of the relationship diagram is discovering all the players in the process. Without input from most of them, construction of a complex flowchart (Figure 4–5A) is not as accurate, and the existing process is not completely understood. A real diagram may cover the wall of a large room.

A relationship diagram and a flow diagram together reveal a total process to *everyone*. Conventional wisdom is that only top managers or seasoned veterans are in a position to have such an overview. They really aren't because no one person can stay current comprehending all the detail. Creating and maintaining such diagrams is one step toward an open-system enterprise. (Similar flow diagrams are a bedrock tool to identify quality problems in a process.)

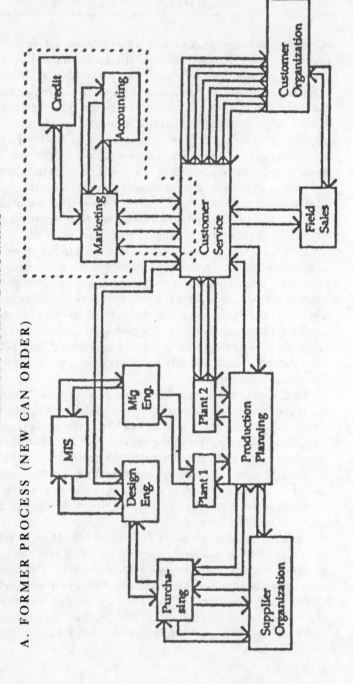

FIGURE 4-4

RELATIONSHIP DIAGRAMS

A. FORMER PROCESS (NEW CAN ORDER)

B. "TARGET" PROCESS

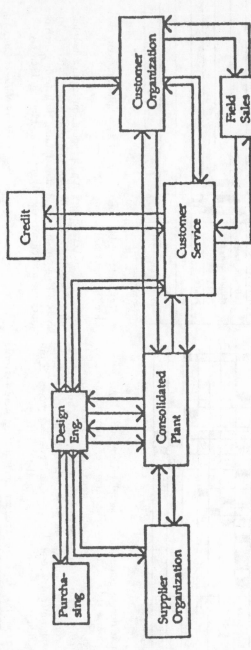

Both the A and B diagrams simplify the complexity of a real process in a big organization. However, B is much simpler than A, and neither attempts to define the relationships inside the customer or supplier organizations. Simplification entails considerable organizational change into a "process flow organization" along with a broadening of the responsibilities of many individuals. The effect is tumultuous even when those affected see the reasons for it. The diagram shows all the "customer-supplier relationships."

SOURCE: *Relationship mapping has been greatly developed by Geary Rummler. The example is based on a real one from American National Can Company given by Robert K. Hall.*

FIGURE 4-5
TIME-FLOW DIAGRAM

A. FORMER PROCESS (NEW CAN ORDER)

| Customer Organization |
| Field Samples |
| Marketing |
| Accounting |
| Credit |
| MIS |
| Customer Service |
| Design Engineering |
| Manufacturing Eng. |
| Plant 1 |
| Plant 2 |
| Production Planning |
| Purchasing |
| Supplier Organization |

Time, Weeks → 1 2 3 4 5 6

B. "TARGET" PROCESS

| Customer Organization |
| Field Samples |
| Marketing |
| Accounting |
| Credit |
| MIS |
| Customer Service |
| Design Engineering |
| Manufacturing Eng. |
| Plant 1 |
| Plant 2 |
| Production Planning |
| Purchasing |
| Supplier Organization |

Time, Weeks → 1 2 3 4 5 6

These flow diagrams are also simpler than reality. However, the B process reduces a six-week average lead time to about one week. Some orders take much longer than others. Sources of variance in time-to-process include telephone tag and rechecking communication. All the loop-back communications chatter by customer service at the center of the former process is impossible to meaningfully capture on the flow diagram.

As a tool, flowcharts are varied and ancient. They were a favorite tool of Frank and Lillian Gilbreth, the work study pioneers of the early twentieth century, for instance. However, only when reduc-tion of lead time becomes important do people commonly combine the chart with a time scale.

Key to new success: groups of people contributing to a flowchart, identifying themselves the process in which they interact. Analysts asking questions and diagramming their findings remove from the participants the insight created by self-discovery.

SOURCE: *The example is taken from American National Can Company; courtesy Robert K. Hall.*

Simplifying the new-can order process removes numerous complications that add to lead time and to the possibility of error, but it forces major changes in the players and in their roles. All must broaden their perspective and their responsibilities. Who should talk directly with the customer is only one "turf dispute." The natural instinct of a customer-service representative is to distrust others who would have to grow into a new role sharing that responsibility ("gotta coach another nerd engineer!").

Few people object to eliminating obvious redundancies or doing in parallel operations that were previously done in sequence. Rather, they object to eliminating provisions for contingencies, hesitate to broaden responsibilities, and fear that fewer people will be needed.

Another example from Figure 4–4B is contact with suppliers directly by the design engineer handling the order. If a particular supplier usually underprices new technical requirements, then jacks up the price later, buyers fear that an inexperienced engineer will "cost the company money" (and screw up the buyers' performance ratings). Marvelous as it sounds, simplifying entails cross-functional learning, teamwork, and development of not just trust, but confidence, both inside and outside the company. And handling relatively routine new-can orders is less complex than developing a new car—or an Ultra-Comm—or the mind-blowing scenario of designing the can at the customer's location by software, then downloading it to the plant. A very different form of organization with a different soul is needed for this challenge.

FIRING UP
THE AFTERBURNER
ON FUNDAMENTAL JIT

Most Western companies that today claim to be executing JIT have at best reached only the first stage of development. They reduce setup times, group operations into cells, form teams, reduce floor space, and initiate a pull system of production control. Production areas have items categorized and organized, and basic information is generally visible to operators. However, if the company is multilocation, personnel at several locations lag, adopting few initiatives but many excuses: methods sound Japanese, no one explained how, great ideas, lousy execution, don't trust 'em, and so on. The firm is caught between one world and another, so progress stalls.

Turning on the afterburner comes from two undervalued, often misunderstood activities: (1) visibility systems; and (2) scheduling improvement cycles.

Visibility Systems

Visibility is unspoken and often unwritten *human* communication; it is important to a well-run shop or office. It does not depend on computers, but it can employ them. Visibility reduces the time and energy of human communication, including the time needed to correct misunderstood communication. The reason visibility is not well understood is that visibility is communication from anyone to *everyone*—everyone who will pay attention.

Visibility is not top-down communication. It's not bottom-up communication, or even person-to-person. It's open to anyone, or at least anyone with access to a building or area where visibility is practiced.

One example of visibility is a 3-D model of a complex building placed by construction companies where everyone can easily see it. Such models lack detail, but they give anyone a perspective of how his or her effort fits into the whole without having to ask stupid questions. The model's value is so obvious that it is easily overlooked.

Improving visibility is one objective of JIT manufacturing. Many features of a JIT system create visibility in both offices and plants: Work standards and instructions are located to be easily found. Key ones are often "hung out to dry." Schedules are prominently posted so *everyone* can plan ahead. Many visibility cues are part of fail-safe quality systems: A light signals if a machining process starts drift. Date stickers or lights tripped by use cycle counters remind us it's time for preventive maintenance.

Visibility systems organize layouts not just for minimum material handling but to make operations that must be coordinated visible to each other. The ideal of a well-done office or shop floor is to make the work and the flows so evident that the layout itself is its own flow diagram and its own relationship diagram.

Those familiar with a work layout can read the status of the company from the positions of tools, material, or activity. Anyone who can directly see the next operation can easily serve it, especially if a set of visual cues is arranged for prompting. If the next operation is not in sight, kanban cards returned from each point where material is used create visibility of its requirements (like a smoke signals saying to send more). Cards arranged in informative displays help to interpret the situation.

Visibility enables a shop floor or an office to come as close as possible to managing itself. That is, daily work requirements, priorities, and problems are so self-evident that little or no operation supervision is required. Sometimes, managers are impressed that visibility allows *them* to see the status of their shop floor at a glance. However, the crucial factor is that *anyone* can see the status of the shop floor at a glance, and the system should stay in control all by itself.

However, self-operation is not the most important function of visibility. Suggesting improvement ideas is. Operations laden with visibility cues are self-represented flowcharts that almost self-suggest how they may be further improved.

Visibility systems are simple, minimalist human systems. To transfer megabytes of data, use computers. To transfer important cues and clues to people, use visibility systems and minimize clutter. (Breaking through the clutter is the problem of a good television ad.) Visibility systems grow where needed, like building sidewalks where paths are worn in the grass. In this way a visibility system is a noncomputerized communication system for a "virtual company."

"Electronic kanban" eliminates the time to return a card to its source. However, little symbols displayed on a computer screen are not visible to many people, so they lose impact. They are less effective at stimulating further process improvements. Perhaps workers also do not feel the same "ownership" as they would had they created the system themselves.

The next challenge is building visibility in the same sense into a computer integrated manufacturing (CIM) factory and distributed network using the principles employed on shop floors and manual offices. So far no one has satisfactorily done this. The information system driving the CIM factory is not a universal language leaving easily interpreted clues. The ideal system has been called an *autono-*

mous dispersed system. Each module of the system (a machine, a transporter, an accounting routine) should be capable of functioning on its own, but send and receive from almost all other modules. Then, like a factory visibility system, a sudden change will be almost instantly transmitted and the system will start determining how to respond to it—just as when a schedule change is posted on a department wall and all workers start planning what they must do to adjust to it.[12]

In the end, much of the crucial communication of an advanced open-enterprise system may be a human visibility system with computers transmitting simple prompts. However, information transmitted by computer may replace the shipment of hardware. (Instead of shipping a part, ship the instructions for making a part.)

Much communications time is waste. Both today and in the future, the superior organization will minimize the total information and human communication time needed to add value. Each of us has only a limited amount of time and limited perceptual capacity to communicate and process information. The key is continuously improving the visibility to humans of a computer-integrated system so that the system is also human integrated. That's what a visibility system accomplishes in a noncomputer environment.

Scheduling Improvement Cycles

At its heart, the Toyota system schedules and promotes learning cycles. Almost everyone first begins to understand the Toyota system as a set of techniques, defined in Toyota language: quality circles, kanban, and so on. Almost everyone experiences the same initial oversight, thinking that if they merely adopt a few of the techniques, they understand. Then the persistent ones start realizing that it is Toyota's use of people and the system of continuous improvement that counts, so they begin to chase that. Finally, as that begins to wear thin, they wonder how Toyota maintains a high level of improvement year after year.

Improvement cycles, or learning cycles, are simply built into the expectations and the schedules of the company. Improvement is everyone's job from day one. The most basic improvement cycles correspond to the major monthly schedule changes. Toyota is a repetitive manufacturer, so schedules show quantities per day or per shift. They also state the time lapse between the need for each part if parts are used at the rate planned. That's an important idea called *takt time.*

Instinct is to think of rate of production: how many cars per hour, how many parts per hour. However, detailed planning and execution centers on takt time, the time allowed to make each part if production keeps up with part use.

Using takt time, experienced operators can determine how to organize their work and lay out their areas for next month's production. Their complete work cycle, on average, must fit into the time window allowed by takt time. All operators should plan in detail how to work within the time allowed, revising their own work methods to achieve minimum waste and fail-safe quality. Since most work is done in teams, much of the work planning is done in groups, and it can be done in coordination with internal customers and suppliers in the same process. The workers become their own industrial engineers.

If takt times increase (production slows), work must be reapportioned, and fewer workers are needed. They shift elsewhere. If takt times decrease (faster production), more workers must transfer from offices, maintenance, or elsewhere.

The basic Toyota production system differs fundamentally from Taylorism because all experienced workers, aided by supervisors and staff if necessary, plan their own work. In the Taylorist system, staff plans; workers work. Taylorist managers, distrustful of workers, are at first appalled that workers should, in effect, write their own standards. In the Toyota system the workers have detailed current knowledge about their work area that is impossible to communicate or keep updated by staff personnel.

The workers' planning processes are coordinated by everyone having the same planning cycles, which are really regular improvement cycles. Schedules usually change takt time once a month, occasionally more often in nervous markets. Every month workers replan all tasks to fit within the new allowed time. When they do, they incorporate improvement ideas accumulated during the past period that could not be implemented immediately. Furthermore, other improvement cycles key on the monthly change too; tooling trials, machine changes, and so forth.

Operations at the work-station level are replanned far more frequently in the Toyota system. More important, the dispersed nature of both detailed planning and improvement processes means that improvement cycles—with regular deadlines—are a regular part of everyone's job, individually and collectively. Plants operating by the Taylorist system in many cases set work standards that went unchanged for decades. Faced with the Toyota system, they are sitting ducks.

While the Toyota system concentrated originally on production, the basic concepts were soon applied to all functions of the enterprise. For example, sales planning is done on a monthly cycle corresponding to the production-schedule cycle. Improvement ideas to spur sales or customer service can be incorporated on a regular basis, too. The outwardly directed improvement cycles may be even more effective than those in production. An outwardly directed cycle is a monthly or quarterly improvement plan to consistently make changes where it counts—where it is noticed by the customer.

The entire Japanese domestic auto industry schedules regular improvement cycles, though some organizations like Toyota and its lead suppliers take better advantage of them than others. Sales plans for all the car companies are normally complete about the thirteenth of each month for the following month. These are incorporated in production planning at midmonth. By about the twenty-second next month's production plan has been translated into production schedules (and takt times) for all first-tier suppliers, so an auto supplier has fresh input from all major customers to replan its own work. A customer on a different planning cycle is not going to screw up the plan by dropping something down in the middle of it. The Japanese industry may have almost stumbled into a regular learning cycle for total enterprises without fully appreciating its potential.

That's how many Japanese auto-assembly plants learned to build a wide variety of vehicles on the same line. The workers over time cumulatively learned how to organize the equipment and the team coordination for it until they could vary assembly speeds about ± 15 percent from a midpoint, and the network of suppliers learned to supply the lines JIT in response. Similar processes were used to decrease the cost and lead times of tooling. No other auto enterprises in the world achieved such effective, low-cost flexibility in the 1980s, nor have work forces been so well positioned to make a run for the three-day car.

SPEAKING OF TIME

That Americans have not matured in using time as part of improvement processes is evidenced by loosely using the term "cycle time" to mean almost any kind of elapsed time associated with operations. Those who become serious about time-based improvement cycles need more precise descriptions. Some definitions:

Lead time: Duration—the elapsed time from beginning to end of a process that may or may not be repeated, such as the lead time to construct a building. Lead time, once upon a year, before the fuzzing of "cycle time" to also mean lead time, inferred only *duration* of a process.

Throughput time: One kind of lead time, the time for material (or something else) to progress from one defined point to another in a process.

Cycle time: The time between recurring events: time between completing units on an assembly line; time between completing parts on a machine; or time between replanning schedules. Cycle times with little variance, like machine cycle time, are clear in meaning. Cycle times with huge variance, like the times between the introduction of new products, lead to sloppy use of the phrase.

Cycle time—time between occurrences—may or may not be the same as the duration, or lead time, of the process generating the occurrences. In the absence of commonly understood terms, clear communication requires the use of time-line graphs.

Takt time: The time between completion of units or parts, determined by dividing the total work time available during a schedule period by the number of items needed.

Work cycle: The time between completing a repetitive operation on one part, or actually finishing any other repetitive

(continued)

Speaking of Time (*cont.*)

task. The difference between takt time, or work time allowed, and work-cycle time is idle time. However, *work cycle* is occasionally used in a more aggregate sense. Suppose that a capital equipment shop on average completes two standard machines and one custom-engineered one every two weeks. That output then constitutes its standard two-week *work cycle*. By engaging in corresponding two-week improvement cycles, it may over time reduce the variance in the cycle and eventually reduce the length of this cycle—or redefine it into one that is more productive. (Usually an initial objective is just to cut excess material handling and unnecessary dithering over machine specifications.)

Planning cycle: Time lapse between replanning work. Some cycles are major and some are minor. All usually correspond to calendar divisions.

Learning cycles or Improvement cycles: Everyone is familiar with the school examples: class hours, program modules, and semesters. However, very few companies prompt improvement processes in regular cycles as does Toyota. However, as everyone knows, learning progresses faster on a repeating cycle. Few people improve as quickly in the absence of a regular stimulus.

NOTES

1. Shigeo Shingo, *Study of the Toyota Production System from an Industrial Engineering Viewpoint* (Tokyo: Japan Management Association, 1981).
2. The first American writers on JIT manufacturing a decade ago briefly debated whether the practices coming from Japan should be called "just-in-time." The phrase itself does not stand alone as an explanation. It calls attention to the delivery of material just before the time it is needed. Anyone who pursues the concept no further is left wondering how such a silly idea could ever produce large reductions in cost. Casual readers interpret

"just-in-time" to mean only one thought out of thousands that are implied.

3. "The Tobacco Trade," *The Economist*, 16 May 1992, 21.

4. Michael E. Porter, "Capital Disadvantage: America's Failing Capital Investment System," *Harvard Business Review* 70, no. 5 (September–October, 1992): 65–82.

5. Charles M. Savage, *5th Generation Management* (Bedford, MA: Digital Press, 1990). Savage proposes that "associates" belong to multiple task teams. Some may be assigned tasks, and some may simply find that their activities include them in the process. The organization thus evolves over time and some of the teams are never explictly defined, so that Savage calls them virtual teams, an analogy to virtual memory in a computer.

6. Peter M. Senge, *The Fifth Discipline* (New York: Doubleday/Currency, 1990).

7. Jeremy Rifken, *Time Wars* (New York: Henry Holt, 1987), p. 155. Rifken decries computer culture as empty of content, a world of want-to-be pilots flying simulators, but never the real thing.

8. George Stalk, Jr., and Thomas M. Houk, *Competing against Time* (New York: Free Press, 1990). The fighter pilot analogy starts on p. 180, referring to the OODA loop (Observe, Orient, Decide, Act). Top-gun pilots quickly size up the situation and preempt the moves of their opponent. The similarity of the OODA loop to the PDCA Deming Cycle for improvement processes is remarkable.

9. Senge makes quite a point of this in *The Fifth Discipline*. The better Japanese companies—Toyota, Toshiba, NEC, and so on—all take pains early in each employee's career to make sure that he or she understands the company's history, traditions, and overall situation.

10. J. G. Miller and Thomas E. Vollmann, "The Hidden Factory," *Harvard Business Review* 63, no. 5 (September–October, 1985): 141–50.

11. The consequences of the improved flexibility of Japanese auto plants compared to American are well presented in James P. Womack, Daniel T. Jones, and Daniel Roos, *The Machine That Changed the World* (New York: HarperCollins, 1990). A little more detail on the achievement of flexibility is in Robert W. Hall and Jinichiro Nakane, *Flexibility, Battlefield of the 90s*. Research Report of the Association for Manufacturing Excellence, Wheeling, Illinois, 1990. See particularly the auto case comparison.

12. Makashima Iwata, et al., *Manufacturing 21 Report: The Future of Japanese Manufacturing*. Research Report by the Association for Manufacturing Excellence, Wheeling, Illinois, 1990.

5

REVERSE UTOPIA: ENVIRONMENTALISM

TWO DRUMS HAND-LABELED AS CHLORINATED BIPHENYL SOMETHING-OR-OTHER sat in the gloom of the old storage building. Bill and Joe had no idea what the stuff was or where it came from. Nothing like it appeared on the last printout of storage contents before the building had been closed five years ago.

Bill and Joe knew that the trash company hauling away the boards and blocks and clutter would not touch the drums. They also knew that they had to have the premises clean for a crew to start remodeling them for offices by the next morning. They also vaguely knew that laws, records, and paperwork on disposal of "chemical stuff" might chew up most of their cleanup time.

At lunch they phoned a hazardous waste disposal company in the yellow pages and asked a general question about the procedure. Sure enough, if the contents of a container were uncertain, they had to be identified before final disposal, and in advance no one could say how long that might take or how much it might cost. Bill and Joe dared not mention it to the safety officer back at the plant. He got bent out of shape over fly spray in the lunch room.

Joe's brother-in-law solved the problem. He came by in a pickup to haul away a few blocks to line his flowerbed (the blocks were headed for the dump anyway), and Joe mentioned the drums. "No problem," said brother-in-law. He had handled such things before, so he'd take care of it in return for the blocks. The drums disappeared on his truck.

The next weekend at church Joe asked brother-in-law where the goop went. "It doesn't exist anymore," was the response, "so there's no problem."

Curious, Joe asked a guy who worked with his brother-in-law about his modus operandi for chemical disposal. "He gets rid of all our dinky stuff. You know, leftover die lubricant, a can of cutting oil, bug spray—that kinda thing. Dumps it all in one barrel. Loads the barrel on the truck and heads for the desert. Lays the barrel down on the tailgate, uncaps it, and drives away. In fifteen or twenty minutes nobody knows where the stuff went. He's always driving around with something in his truck, so nobody pays any attention."

This story is hearsay as told by Joe. It has the ring of truth, though it can't be verified. The companies described are small, so no one in them is an expert on environmental issues. The story also illustrates many of the issues of going green:

- We're dealing with unknowns. So many questions have no definitive answers that it is easy to be either paranoid or blasé.
- Issues come up by surprise. They often distract us from accomplishing other objectives.
- Neither workers nor managers are antienvironment in sentiment, but their systems don't encourage dealing with such problems.
- Economics seems to pressure us to defer a problem or get rid of it as expeditiously as possible—to take the easy way out. But if operations are guided by quality (prediction and control) and learning cycles, many issues are preventable. (Why was material left unused so that someone stored it, unrecorded, in poorly marked containers to begin with? Maybe the "chlorinated whatever" was never actually needed at all!)
- Prevention is the best cure. Prevention deals with problems yet unknown, but it takes a different mind-set and a shift in the business system—a new soul of enterprise.

GROWTH-VERSUS-GREEN DEBATES

The public is more aware of environmental issues than productivity or quality issues. Polls of adults during the 1980s show that over 80 percent of Americans agree that environmental requirements cannot be too high and improvements must be made regardless of cost.[1] That's the same public that is upset by job losses and that will drive ten miles to save $1 on a sack of groceries. Clearly they "want somebody to do something," but action is stymied because of growth-versus-green issues.

Sewage fees are at record highs, trash disposal costs a bundle, and some agency is always checking whether too much ozone is hanging around the earth's surface, while we design CFCs out of freezers because ozone won't hang around in the polar stratosphere, where it is supposed to be. The staunchest probusiness publications no longer pooh-pooh the issues. They just argue that hazards are not as serious as alleged and that cures cost too much. The system depends on growth and doesn't know how to function without it.

The major process industries—those that account for the lion's share of effluents and emissions—began cleaning up their act years ago and are probably furthest along in reconciling environmental protection with the need to make a profit. As a result, visible problems are reduced in most heavy industrial areas; the air is clearer and the rivers cleaner.

However, companies hard-pressed to avoid moving a plant to Mexico—like Joe's company—are still in a denial phase. Environmental protection is only one of their many pains. Unless they have personally felt public heat, few managers sense how little they are trusted to be environmentally responsible. Once burned, avoiding further publicity and harassment is a negative motivator, but beyond a warm fuzzy feeling, few see any positive incentives to go green.

The ecological buzzphrase for improving everyone's quality of life, while maintaining the carrying capacity of the earth, is "sustainable development." But any owner or manager inured to dog-eat-dog capitalist competition is naturally wary of betting the company on "sustainable development." First, he or she must internally reconcile the growth-versus-green arguments—two opposing visions of what constitutes a better life, much less how to achieve it.

GROWTH: THE INDUSTRIAL-WAVE UTOPIA

A utopia pictures its author's vision of an ideal society. Utopian thinking seems to be coming back into style. Corporate chiefs today are being urged to crank up at least a vision, if not a utopia, to give their floundering associates something to go for.

Most full-blown utopias have quickly sunk from sight, but a few have been highly influential. For example, Sir John Harrington's *Oceana* influenced the writing of the Declaration of Independence. Early in the twentieth century, utopian fiction such as the old Tom Swift series imparted a sense of unquestioning confidence that the advance of technology would make the world a better place. Essay-type utopias pictured the abolition of hunger and pain and trumpeted the view that science and industry could best any tribulation nature could visit upon mankind. Most of today's senior management grew up on this kind of literature.[2]

As the benefits of science and industry spread around the world, the utopian dream became encapsulated in numbers, GNP and GNP per capita, or GDP (gross domestic product). Economic growth statistics documented the improvement in the quality of life. Anyone older than a baby boomer remembers when advancement meant displacing hopeless squalor in the far corners of the earth with the benefits of modern living.

People *do* live longer as well as better in countries with a higher GNP per capita, as shown in Figure 5-1. Historical evidence to support the benefits of "growth"—to some point—is formidable. Better living increases life span, and one of the first requisites of a quality life is being alive longer to enjoy it.

Almost from its beginning, a continuously higher standard of living became expected in the United States. That's what people came here for. During the twentieth century an auto became a necessity and is now regarded as almost a birthright. With nature subdued, most people expected to live longer and enjoy it more—to participate in some version of quality of life.

FIGURE 5-1

LIFE EXPECTANCY AT BIRTH (1980–1985) BY GROSS NATIONAL PRODUCT PER CAPITA, 1983

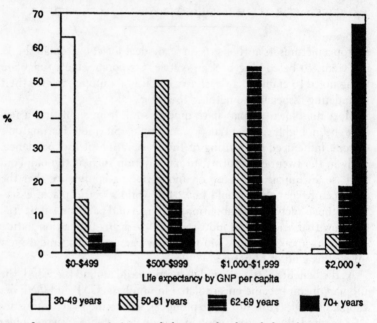

In very poor societies people have neither knowledge of preventive health care nor access to corrective health care, and great difficulty escaping squalid conditions. The great breakthrough seems to be attaining the knowledge and ability to control the conditions of one's own living environment.

SOURCE: *From* World Population Trends and Policies, 1987 Monitoring Report, *Population Studies No. 103 (New York: Department of International Economic and Social Affairs, United Nations), p. 152.*

However, some environmentalists now decrying the evils of industry like to romanticize peasant living. With modern knowledge, folkways are more tolerable, but pictures of bedraggled Southern sharecroppers (and their counterparts elsewhere in the world) are seldom used to attract tourists.

In the good old days, a close-up, personal exposure to nature was unhealthy. Prehistoric life spans were exceedingly short. Existence resembled the Malthusian vision of many ecologists today.[3] By the beginning of the Industrial Revolution, life expectancy had doubled to about thirty years. Then, in industrial societies it rose steadily and rapidly, as shown in Figure 5-2. So did world population, zooming from 2.5 billion to 5.3 billion in forty years. Projections of twenty-first–century population loft on up to 8–11 billion before leveling off.

Most demographers cite the major causes of improved life expectancy as better nutrition (including the "green revolution" at midcentury), improved sanitation, and more effective medical care. As sanitation improved, those not subject to constant dysentery lived longer and enjoyed it more. Visitors from industrial societies to preindustrial locations have simultaneously been charmed by the romance of their culture and struck by the abysmal lack of sanitation. Consider a journal entry from a turn-of-the-century visit to that Shangri-la, Tibet: "Everything in the place is coated and grimed with filth. In the middle of the street, between two banks of filth and offal, runs a stinking channel. . . . In it horns and bones of every beast eaten or not eaten by the Tibetans. The stench is fearful."[4]

Better housing decreased stress and infections. Medical advances virtually eliminated plague, smallpox, and other diseases, so now people die from ailments few of their ancestors lived long enough to get. Life expectancies are still increasing even in poor regions, and most people prefer to die prematurely of "pollution" in this new world at age sixty than expire by an "unknown" natural cause by age thirty. In the most advanced countries life expectancy is pushing eighty years of age.

Consequently, industrially developed areas want to stay that way. Undeveloped areas usually seek economic growth, meaning the benefits of advanced agriculture and industry, whether manufacturing itself is encouraged or not. The benefits of economic growth, including virgin industrial growth, have been so obvious that wanting to stop it seems like wanting to revert to the plagues and perils of old. By this view, Malthusian ecologists aren't just party poopers; they would condemn our children to the horrors of antiquity from which we have so recently escaped.

FIGURE 5-2

LIFE SPAN IN INDUSTRIAL
REGIONS THROUGHOUT HISTORY

Era	Estimated Expectation of Life at Age Zero
Millions of years ago	15 years
1800	30 years
1900	50 years
1980	70 (male), 77.5 (female)

Estimates of life expectancy in prehistoric times are subject to considerable margins of error. Data in industrial countries since 1800 is relatively accurate. That there has been about a forty-five-year increase in expected life span since 1800 is not disputed.

The population explosion began with increased life expectancy in Europe. In the nineteenth century the European population grew beyond the then-existent capacity of the land to feed it. While many other factors influenced world events, Europeans had the technology to expand both themselves and their technology itself throughout the world, thus starting a population-explosion almost everywhere.

Until the nineteenth century male life expectancy exceeded female. In ancient times, the difference may have been considerable, though this is nearly impossible to prove. Before sterile conditions at childbirth became common, the high risks of childbirth to mothers, plus high infant mortality, required most women to hazard the experience as often as they dared. Consequently, women throughout the ages were consigned to domesticity and perpetuating the species. One of the striking characteristics of the increase in longevity has been the reversal of male-female differences, leading to upheavals in female roles–and the population of nursing homes to be largely female.

SOURCE: *Data and background from Barnet N. Berin, George J. Stolnitz, and Aaron Tenenbein, "Mortality Trends of Males and Females over the Ages,"* Society of Actuaries Transactions 41 (1989): 9–31.

Reverse Utopia: Environmentalism

The proponents of growth have now become victims of their own success. More people require more resources, but there is only one earth. In country after country—like Nigeria, where it is hard to estimate the population within twenty-five million persons—most problems with quality of life, from housing to AIDS, can be connected to the burgeoning numbers of people.

A limit will come, but no one knows where. Years back, economists studied the explosion of people on Taiwan after the 1949 exodus from mainland China. They joked that if the 1950s population growth rate had continued indefinitely, the universe would eventually have seen a ball of Taiwanese the size of the solar system expanding at the speed of light!

Science plus the effectiveness of mass production in turning materials into product has wrought new problems—and new fears from more knowledgeable worriers armed with ever more sensitive instruments. By late in the twentieth century, ecologists projected gloom-and-doom scenarios that might be called reverse utopias. Rachel Carson's *Silent Spring* in 1962 was one of the first.[5] The moral: Reform the cycles of material use on the planet or be condemned to ecological hell.

Some evils are visible. Burning dumps and dripping goo make good photo opportunities. Few people want to experience the sights, smells, and property-value decays of a nearby landfill. Visible problems have received attention. Invisible ones remain in the denial stage a little longer, as shown in Figure 5-3, but without correction, sensible people can see dire consequences from them, too.

However, as bad as environmental degradation may be in the United States and other advanced industrial countries, it is more serious elsewhere. For instance, the highest sulfur dioxide emissions per capita in the world are in eastern Germany, Poland, and Czechoslovakia. Mexico City is working to correct an air pollution level more severe than any in the United States. Thailand is struggling to keep environmental controls apace with rapid industrialization.[6] After three decades of growth, the standard of living of about forty of the world's poorest countries fell during the 1980s, probably because their resources were unable to keep up with burgeoning populations. Two

FIGURE 5-3

A. EMISSIONS OF SELECTED POLLUTANTS IN THE UNITED STATES, 1950–1987

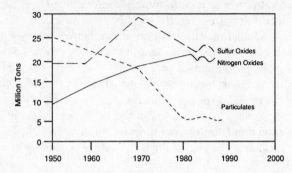

SOURCE: *Hilary French*, Worldwatch Paper No. 94, Worldwatch Institute, January 1990, p. 9.

B. CARBON EMISSIONS FROM FOSSIL FUELS, 1950–1989

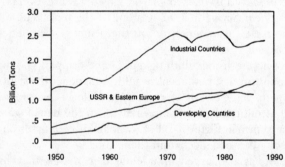

Deforestation burning adds another 1.5–2.0 billion tons to the 6 billion tons from fossil fuels in 1989. In the last one hundred years, atmospheric concentration of carbon dioxide has increased 25 percent and is increasing by 0.5 percent a year. Methane concentration has doubled, and is increasing by 0.9 percent per year.

SOURCES: Worldwatch Paper No. 101, *December 1990, citing Oak Ridge National Laboratories as the original source of the graph. And* New York Times, *11 April 1991, A12 citing "Policy on Greenhouse Warming" by the National Academy of Sciences.*

centuries ago, smoke in primitive huts was not exactly a pristine environment, but mankind was then incapable of burning all the firewood in the world.[7]

However, for most industrial managers, a continuing problem is separating serious issues from talk-show flak. For example, environmental zealots see a bogeyman in every trace of something that might be construed as a carcinogen. An example of unnecessary uproar was the CBS "Sixty Minutes" broadcast on Alar, the spray used on apples and other fruit. People eat far more natural carcinogens *in* an apple than they consume in the residue *on* the apple. Carcinogens are all around, identifying one is often tenuous, and they cannot all be avoided. The flap over a very minor environmental risk caused a reluctant Food and Drug Administration to ban the use of Alar.[8]

The media has little in the way of a system to rate the seriousness of environmental issues except that old standby, plumping stories that attract listeners or readers (a form of growth incentive). Consequently, the public's perception of risk differs from that of experts. The comparison of public perceptions versus expert ratings in Figure 5-4 covers only direct risk to human health, not other environmental risks. Just keeping definitions straight is the first step in avoiding misunderstanding.

Some of the most vehement growth-versus-green wars simplify and polarize tough issues. An Oregon bumper sticker reads "Save a logger; shoot an owl," meaning to put loggers back to work in forests declared off-limits because they are the habitat of the Rocky Mountain spotted owl, an endangered species. Many such wars occur because of continued virgin development—the cutting and mining of virgin natural resources to make product or just to clear land. Companies with relatively benign operations face delays when trying to start up a new plant on a green field site in any area that has previously experienced environmental unpleasantness. Environmental groups and apprehensive neighbors drag out the hearings and procedures.

"Sustainable development" attempts to reconcile growth versus green, but as long as people are restricted to business systems and performance measures intended to convert natural resources to product as fast as possible, they cannot internally resolve the conflicts. Finding new land or hitting a new strike has been a major route to

FIGURE 5-4

CLASSIFICATION OF
SELECTED ENVIRONMENTAL RISKS

Hazard	Usual Scope	EPA, Direct Risk to Human Health	Risk as Perceived by Public	Time Lag for Many Effects
Industrial accidents	Individual, Small group	Not rated	Not rated	Immediate
Work-site chemical exposure	Work site	High	High	Cumulative, years
Hazardous waste sites	Area	Medium to low	High	Cumulative, years
Indoor air pollution	Building	High	Low	Days to years
Acid rain	Regional concentration, globally detectable	High	Medium to low	Years
Carbon emissions	Global	Low	Low	Decades

The public appears to be more concerned about involuntary risks than voluntary ones. Publicized risks or those close at hand cause more concern than uncertain issues or problems that are geographically remote. (A dump down the road generates more excitement than acid rain.) A dramatic catastrophe, like an oil tanker breaking open, however low the probability, stirs protests. Hardly a thought is given to indoor air pollution from poor air circulation in tightly constructed buildings, a potential source of long-term, cumulative illnesses.

SOURCES: *The EPA risk assessments in the third and fourth columns were taken originally from Frederick Allen, U.S. Environmental Protection Agency, based on the EPA report, "Unfinished Problems: A Comparative Assessment of Environmental Problems." A panel of EPA senior professionals experienced with many different hazards combined their knowledge into an overall assessment. Four years later, their judgments may have changed. The public assessments came from polls of the Roper Organization, December 1987 and December 1988. These ratings were first contrasted by Elaine Labach in* Target *6, no. 4 (Winter 1990): 12.*

prosperity, if not riches. It was never easy. One had to be a risk taker, and people staked claims to arid desert as well as lush plains. However, a land-rush mentality coupled with a resource growth concept of economics works only as long as the natural wealth holds out.

One has only to observe the behavior of those who have struck gold or oil to see the problem. Having found their personal El Dorado, many want to build monuments to their own existence. A good description of the problem is the old Texas phrase, "Spending it like there ain't no tomorrow," which also is the consumer's role in keeping the economy moving. Unfortunately, tomorrow is arriving quickly.

ECOLOGICAL ROULETTE: RISKS AND UNKNOWNS

Someone takes a risk if he or she can predict possible outcomes but is not in full control of a process, as with stock investments or weather forecasts. Unknowns are by definition not predictable. Risks can be quantified, just as weather forecasters assess the probability of rain tomorrow. Completely unprecedented experiences "zing in out of the blue," or at least, they are a concern before they become a known risk. For example, radium in oil found in some locations has recently been discovered to emit significant radiation in storage tanks and other facilities. The seriousness of this hazard is not yet known.[9]

Uncertainty is further defined as the anticipation of occurrences for which cause-and-effect relationships have never been established. The risks of living on a dung heap are unknown if no one has ever observed any evidence connecting poor health with the heap.

Visible pollution could never be denied, but whether it represented a significant risk was at first strongly doubted. After debate, the first American environmental legislation a century ago concerned sanitation and filthy waterways. Action to reduce visible air pollution began at midcentury. Reduction of particulate emissions since then can be seen in Figure 5-3A. Over time people have grown willing to accept the existence of invisible risks. Radon in houses is an example.

Many environmental problems are measurable only with the right instruments in the right place, and they can be analyzed only by isolating their effects from a great deal of statistical noise. Worse, the consequences are unknown. Such was the detective work that determined that ozone holes in the atmosphere existed and that CFCs were a major cause. Extra UV radiation causing skin cancer is predictable but relatively minor. The effects on all flora and fauna are unknowable, but they could have relatively major consequences. For example, could extra ultraviolet radiation damage oceanic phytoplankton, basic to the food chain? There is no way to lab-test every possibility.

The King Kong unknown of environmental ogres is global warming. Scientists agree only that the atmospheric carbon dioxide level is increasing, and that without drastic changes, it will continue to increase. Global warming's near-term direct risk to human health is low (see Figure 5-4), but indirect effects are unknown. Atmospheric models have suggested scenarios from little change, to dense clouds drenching lush vegetation, to New Orleans under the sea and the American Midwest a desert of bleached bones. However, it is still possible that a threat exists that is more serious than CO_2 or one of the better-known greenhouse gases.

Cautious environmentalists wish to avoid unknowns and so prefer human activity that disturbs the environment as little as possible. The more confident discount unknowns, sometimes to an extreme. For instance, after the accidental release of methyl isocyanate in Bhopal, India, a number of Union Carbide engineers still refused to believe that it was lethal after hearing reports of bodies in the streets.

Chemical exposure is an example of unknown hazards. Of seventy-thousand or so chemicals in common use, about fifty thousand are listed as potential risks by the EPA. Risks are not clearly mapped because toxicological studies have been performed on only ten thousand or so, and as the investigation of PCB and other chemicals shows, studies may not lead to rapid, definitive conclusions.[10]

The complexities of exposure add to uncertainty. For instance, vitamin A is essential to human health in small doses but toxic in large ones. Allergic reactions vary by individual, and many causes are never pinpointed. Other biological processes are just as impenetrable. Substances not now clearly understood will occasionally turn out to have unintended consequences. And the danger does not have to be real; the public just has to fear that it is.

People want action to control understood risks, particularly if the risks are taken involuntarily. On the other hand, being thrown by a horse is an understood occupational hazard of rodeo riders, and the same people will applaud them for taking the risks. Publicized unknowns may or may not create fear.

A company often runs as much risk to its reputation by how it handles incidents as by the actual public danger itself. The public may forgive a company for lacking scientific omniscience but not for *appearing* unconcerned or callous. The fallout from reacting poorly to media-blown adversity can be severe, as with Exxon and the Exxon Valdez or Dow-Corning with silicone implants.[11] Westinghouse's problems with PCBs show that public opprobrium can run high when the nature of a hazard is feared (see box, page 150) even if the hazard is unproven.

The commercial and legal system does not encourage public candor, explanations, or apologies. No one wants to blurt revelations that might later be entered into evidence. However, keeping secret the research and problem solving on suspected hazards not only limits the brainpower directed to them, but a jury might later construe it as a cover-up. A key factor in the landmark decision against Johns-Manville, for instance, was that the company deliberately withheld knowledge of asbestosis from workers.[12] Legal logic is designed to build a case either for or against a presumed culprit, and it prefers to address ongoing problems through the rearview mirror of legal precedent. It does not build trust in open-system problem solving.

Very soon we need a system of business that does not constantly force everyone to reconcile growth-versus-green issues. Too many solutions—such as adding a $1 per gallon gasoline tax to force fuel economy—are trade-offs couched only in terms of traditional economic scarcity. The economics of a closed-system, limited-resource "spaceship" are different. We need more fresh, novel, holistic reviews of basic issues. Why do people want to live a long distance from their work? Why do we want to heat a large space when we only occupy one small area at a time? What is the basic function of a package?

Action will have to be based on projections that never fully relieve uncertainty. That suggests a concept of management as learning cycles to better predict and control unknowns, and beyond that, nothing less than systematically changing underlying business motivations and assumptions.

WESTINGHOUSE, PCBs, AND THE LEGALITIES OF UNKNOWN HAZARDS

PCBs were used as fire retardants and coolants in large electrical capacitors and transformers from the 1930s until their use was discontinued in 1979. Suspicions that long-term exposure to PCBs might be hazardous date back to at least 1947, but evidence was not conclusive, and opinions were mixed. PCBs degrade slowly. Like many other chemicals, they build up in tissues. A number of Japanese who ate rice oil contaminated with PCBs became ill and suffered longterm aftereffects, but subsequent reviews of the case pointed to a chemical other than PCBs as the culprit. The mechanism by which PCBs may cause cancer or lead to birth defects is still unknown, and no study has established unarguable evidence that they do.

Experiments with rats showed that those regularly ingesting PCBs with a high percentage of chlorine developed liver cancers in old age. Those fed PCBs with lower chlorine content showed no difference. Extending the results of animal toxicity tests to humans has increasingly been criticized as potentially misleading.

Linkages of PCBs to cancer may be tenuous, but once publicized they rouse suspicion and generate fear. In 1983 Westinghouse signed a consent decree with the city of Bloomington, Indiana, to pay for a very costly cleanup of PCBs in landfills. Westinghouse has since sold the plant to Asea-Brown-Boveri, but its liability for cleanup continues. No one wants the final resting place of PCBs to be located near them, and the effectiveness of the cleanup is still in dispute. Workers are suing, and the legal morass surrounding the case—and all its environmental uncertainties—continues to deepen.

Meantime the plant now uses zinc oxide in making a new product. The state limits the discharge of zinc metal into sewers to fifty parts per billion because zinc kills the bacteria that catalyze sewage decomposition. Zinc oxide is harmless to the bacteria and anything else so far as anyone knows, but the state mandates atomic absorption as the test for zinc in discharged waste, and that test cannot distinguish between Zn and ZnO. The new owners are not yet ready to consider it, but the expense of zero-discharge manufacturing may be preferable to anticipating how to deal with the next environmental ogre, whether real or only imagined.

SOURCE: *Based in part on Michael Schoeder, "Did Westinghouse Keep Mum on PCBs?"* Business Week, 12 Aug. 1991, 68–71; *and Philip H. Abelson, "Excessive Fear of PCBs,"* Science 253 (26 July 1991): 361.

That's utopian enough, but without general recognition of everyone's common dependence on a world ecology, we will not force such a big challenge upon ourselves. The new system is an extension of the movements toward quality, time-based operations, open-system enterprise, and all the rest.

CLOSED-LOOP, ZERO-DISCHARGE MATERIALS-USE CYCLES

Global scenarios of future environmental scarcity take two extremes: utopia and reverse utopia. In all likelihood, some of both extremes will occur. The reverse utopian theme is that resource scarcity takes care of environmental problems (overpopulation) as it always has: the have-nots die of disease and malnutrition while the haves hunker down in high-tech enclaves and ignore them—and perhaps kill them if they get too uppity and aggressive.

The primitive utopia theme of low-tech environmentalists is little better. Everybody-a-compost-specialist is not likely to work much better than reverse utopia in a world with ten billion people rather than one billion.

The utopian theme is that a high fraction of the world's population will adopt high-tech, high-cooperation solutions to resource scarcity. They will learn to live very comfortably in a low-energy world with closed-loop material use. At least in polls, the public in almost all the advanced industrial countries expresses the conviction that environmental problems demand action. Whether they yet are persuaded enough to discipline their personal habits is less certain, but momentum continues to build. As it does, the notion of managing closed-loop cycles of material use becomes less farfetched. The conventional business system is heavily biased toward labor productivity (taking the easy way out) and will need modification.

Such a shift will promote zero-discharge manufacturing, but manufacturing is only part of a full closed loop of material use. The ideal should be minimal discharge (effluents and emissions) throughout a complete material-use cycle, including its service life. A material-use cycle is either (1) dirt-to-dirt (mining to disposal), or (2) reuse, of which there are various kinds (see Figure 5-5). If in addition a cycle is "closed loop," the implication is that material is not lost or contaminated.

For complex products, a "pure" form of any type of reuse cycle is unlikely. Some parts would be remanufactured, some recycled, and a few perhaps made of virgin material. In time, the remanufacturing processes should improve their ratio of materials reused without modification—no machining or meltdown, for example, and perhaps no degreasing with petroleum-based solvents.

While we may never literally achieve closed-loop material-use cycles, this approach is a good start toward minimizing unknown environmental dangers as well as understood ones. Closed-loop material cycles will seem very costly at first. Present methods of thinking and working may never get us there. Quality-improvement processes, lead-time compression, open-system process information, and organizations that span material-use cycles are promising changes in our work life that may do it.

However, nothing is quite as simple as it seems. Comparing the

FIGURE 5-5

DEFINITIONS OF MATERIAL-USE CYCLES

Material-Use Cycle:	The complete flow diagram of material used by man, including natural processes as well as man-made ones. For example, a recycled aluminum drink can is describable starting at any point on the cycle. In simplified form: use to disposal container to aluminum furnace to rolling mill to can machine to filling machine to distribution to reuse.
Dirt-to-Dirt Cycle:	A material-use cycle that begins with natural materials and ends with disposal in ground, air, or water. If a can made from virgin aluminum is sent to a landfill, it follows a dirt-to-dirt cycle.
Reuse Cycle:	A material-use cycle in which material returns to its same application. The recycled can is one example of a reuse cycle.
Rebuilding:	A product, such as an engine, that is restored to its original condition, or something near it. Some parts can be recovered; some must be replaced. The more parts that can be recovered, in general, the higher the efficiency of rebuild.
Remanufacturing:	A product is restored to better-than-original condition, but without parts being reduced to raw materials. Its durability, reliability, economy, and features are usually improved; in addition, it may be more benign to the environment.
Recycling:	A product or its parts are reduced to raw material and reformulated and refabricated.

overall environmental impacts of two different material-use cycles is not easy. The famous comparisons of Styrofoam versus paper cups found experts disagreeing because they both have pluses and minuses. Perhaps they could have gone further than rate which of two existing alternatives was "least worst," but rating environment impact and risk is still in its infancy. What could be done to make a container use less of everything and discharge nothing? In fact, what is the purpose of the container?

Chapter 4 told the story of reducing the order-entry process for a new food can to its barest minimum. The next stage after designing the can by software—or perhaps several stages before that—is questioning why the can is needed at all. For example, Japanese food manufacturers are starting to switch from metal food containers to coated paper and plastic film containers. These are slightly more expensive, but lighter and less difficult for landfill disposal. (Japan has a severe solid-waste disposal problem; a can costs around $0.63 to dispose of after use.)[13] But this "solution" is still just a small green improvement on a dirt-to-dirt cycle.

A better solution is cheap, reusable containers that preserve portions of food until time for serving. The preservation part is vital. It is amazing how many stories of shortage and famine (Ethiopia, Russia, the Sahel) feature simultaneous waste and spoilage of huge amounts of foodstuffs. Such containers will call for changes in buying and consumption habits, but they might be paid for if containers were also reordering mechanisms. One of the ultimate systems of retail-level, computerized Quick Response replenishment features containers that "reorder" themselves. The full powers of collaborative human ingenuity have yet to be focused on this problem and many others like it.

An example of future thinking is the new electronic light bulb, or E-lamp, designed to consume one fourth the energy of incandescent bulbs and last ten to twenty times longer. They will also cost $20, so the cash-strapped won't make the initial outlay. But now suppose the development can go one step further, and the lamp can be made recyclable or remanufacturable. Then the E-lamp is never discarded but turned in for a new one. The manufacturer becomes a remanufacturer in the service business. Perhaps lamps can be rented, not sold. (That was the financial stroke that turned the Xerox machine from a curiosity into a commercial sensation.)

THE CASE FOR
REMANUFACTURING AND RECYCLING

The effects of global warming may still be up in the air, but disposal of solid waste is already an acute operating problem that is expected to quickly become much worse. About 80 percent of waste is carted off to landfills, and landfills are becoming scarce. Since trash volumes continue to increase, disposal problems affect almost everyone. There is no easy solution.

A popular view is that plastics in landfills are a major problem because they do not decompose. Unfortunately, neither does almost anything else, including paper. Plastic is about 12 percent by volume; paper is 55 percent by volume, and it has doubled in the past twenty years. Much of it is discharged from computers, copiers, and telephone book presses. The paperless society is still a distant vision.[14] Unfortunately, *everything* buried deep away from oxygen, not just plastic, is preserved as if in King Tut's tomb.

Alternatives such as dumping at sea or exporting trash to Africa are under increasing attack. Higher-tech solutions also have drawbacks. Superincinerators have come under fire for spewing mercury over the landscape, much of it from dry cell batteries included with the flammables. Smoke scrubbers seemed to work on almost everything but mercury, and the ubiquitous dry cell has become another redesign and recycle problem.

High-pressure compaction enables refuse encased in concrete to be used as a construction base—with the hope that some ugly toxin does not ooze through a crack—but now NIMBYs (Not-In-My-Backyard protesters) do not want to live on top of squashed trash any more than buried refuse. For a time the Japanese sited new buildings on compacted refuse landfills in Tokyo Bay until nearby residents protested, some violently.[15]

The shortage of landfills is not the result of lack of space. In the last five years, the number of landfills permitted in the United States has dropped by about half and will continue dropping. For example, the permit for a huge Los Angeles landfill sought by Browning-Ferris has been held up so authorities can restudy soil porosity.[16] To most people a nearby "dump" creates visions of toxic leachates, nauseous smells—or rats, so landfills are being "NIMBYed" out of existence.

The more adamant NIMBYs are determined to become NOPEs (Not On Planet Earth). While national and international environmentalist organizations have become more willing to compromise with industry, local groups have not. Local efforts are coordinated by the Citizen's Clearinghouse on Hazardous Waste (CCHW) and the National Toxics Campaign (NTC). As soon as any local group gets wind of a new dump site, these groups are ready to support any opposition effort. Lois Gibbs, executive director of CCHW, claims that no new toxic waste sites have opened in the United States since 1978.

The squeeze is on disposal of "benign" solid waste as well as hazardous waste. Eventually, the solution has to be discarding very little waste—minimizing dirt-to-dirt material-use cycles that have characterized the industrial wave. Rebuilding will become popular. A great deal of manufacturing will become remanufacturing, particularly if existing stocks can be imaginatively modified to make them easy to remanufacture. Recycling should become more viable. Moreover, the full cycles of material use must be "under control"; this means that there must be near-zero leakage from a closed-loop system.

However, this probably will still not happen in the absence of further incentives to force manufacturing away from dirt-to-dirt cycles and toward remanufacturing with closed-loop materials-use cycles. Sooner or later public policy will likely opt for taxation of the kind that has been heaped on coal mines—heavy severance taxes or reclamation taxes.

ORGANIZATIONS SPANNING
THE MATERIAL-USE CYCLE

As long as environmental protection is everyone's problem, it is no one's responsibility. The first step is for those who design and operate processes to take responsibility for environmental protection, and this comes atop other responsibilities for customer satisfaction and productivity now being assumed. That is, an enterprise working with its customers and suppliers is responsible for a complete cycle of material use.

Finding substitutes for CFCs has been a more tractable problem than many others, although some now suspect that the substitutes will also have an ugly long-term effect. CFCs are made by relatively few companies, so responsibility for replacement can be pinpointed. The appearance of a northern ozone hole earlier than predicted accelerated replacement. Responsibility for cleaning CFCs from old refrigerators scrapped or now in use is harder to pinpoint, but not if it were assigned to the refrigerator manufacturers. Naturally, they would have to be paid a premium for taking on this responsibility at first, else the same old economics apply.

One of the major problems of managing closed-loop cycles of material use today is that a single organization is seldom responsible for the full cycle. The company that makes the container is not responsible for filling it, nor for using it, nor for disposing of it. The cycle becomes a marketing or economics problem rather than a systemic problem.

The way to overcome this problem is by defining responsibilities for the cycle, that is, by making a specific chain of people responsible for a cycle of material use. Suppose the can company, the food company, the transport company, the food retailer, or a combination of them all were responsible for the disposal or reuse of the container. You make it; you find a place to dispose of it. Defining such responsibility would force all the self-interested parties to cooperate. As long as each company is looking for its own lowest-cost solution, it has no reason to even recognize the full-material use cycle.

Legalities are beginning to stimulate that kind of responsibility. For example, Germany has mandated that 80 percent of all packaging waste must be recycled by 1995. The effect on package designs by anyone doing business in Germany is considerable. The threat of similar legislation for cars is driving German automakers to design cars to rebuild or recycle.[17]

Responsibility for a full material-use cycle is a powerful incentive for open-system enterprise, probably the strongest one imaginable. The various parties in such an enterprise also have a strong incentive to share information with each other. The sharing begins with the design of products and processes.

Design for Material Reuse Cycles

Environmental product design begins by eliminating environmentally troublesome materials. For instance, plated-metal parts are "designed out" to eliminate the potential hazards of plating, or the metal is coated in other ways. Paint and coating formulas now rarely use mercury fungicides or lead. Whenever possible, water-based paints eliminate the evaporation of organic solvents. The best way to handle hazardous waste is to have none.

Design for disassembly (DFD) promotes remanufacturing and recycling. A well-publicized DFD automobile is BMW's Z1 sportster. It uses pop-on, pop-off fasteners and thermoplastic parts, which can be recycled, in place of thermosets, which cannot. By contrast, the low recycle value of Japanese auto design and lower scrap-iron prices have recently driven Japanese "car cannibalizers" out of business.[18]

BMW's Z1 design extends the basic concept of the Pontiac Fiero and Saturn. These cars' underbodies have detachable plastic panels. A Saturn rammed by a pickup truck recently demonstrated an advantage of the design for repair. The body panels were removed, the underframe straightened, and the same panels remounted. The owner could not tell the difference.

Having a large number of parts obviously adds time to both assembly and disassembly. Well-established methods of design for assembly that reduce part counts may also aid disassembly—if fasteners are removable. Complex fasteners are a pain. One idea of the NCR Corporation's design engineering, for instance, is "No screws; no glue; no adjustments." Screws not only take time to install, but defective ones jam automated assembly equipment, then freeze when installed and refuse to peaceably disassemble.

In addition, using a number of diverse materials creates problems, both in production and in . . . er . . . reproduction. The more materials used, the harder to take them apart, and the more work to sort them.

Today's limits and trade-offs are challenges for the future. Now a high-density printed circuit board is not a DFD candidate, and tires may be recapped but not recycled. Modern tires are composites of different polymer compounds formulated for wear and performance in a given application. Composite frame parts increase strength-to-weight ratios, very important for lighter, more fuel-efficient cars—especially solar-powered ones. But composites designed to bind together for performance do not easily come apart for recycling. Much better to design items such as PC boards and tires for remanufacturing.

The marketing side of DFD presents an interesting opportunity. Initially, the concept may attract "green" buyers, but longer run, a return deposit on durables such as cars and computers would not have the same effect as with a soft-drink bottle. It does not even get the same response for an aluminum can. Instead, DFD represents another step in a manufacturing company becoming more like a service company. Do not sell a product. Sell a service. Combining DFD with modular design will let buyers periodically upgrade the purchase, much as they now buy newer versions of software. Don't like the color of your car? Trade it for a new skin. Want an upgraded computerized map in it? Push-pull, click-click.

DFD modular design presents possibilities for service by interchanging modules. In fact, if the original manufacturers do not compete with excellent service, one can easily imagine knock-off shops stealing it from them. That leads back to the environmental aspect of DFD: how to have social control of the dirt-to-dirt cycle of use.

The basic concept is simple. Do not sell product. Sell a service *process* with products embedded in the service. In effect, lease products and charge for their use. Once customers sign on for service, they must return a product or module to get something else. If they want to sign on with a competitor, they return product. Provisions can be made for damage. Losses would be a serious matter, but resolvable.

The economics of this make no sense as long as materials, energy, and disposal are cheap. If these are expensive, then enterprises that are superior at managing total dirt-to-use-to-dirt recycling processes with customers will be able to beat the costs of competitors using throwaway methods. The system should encourage maximum service competition with a minimum of Big Brother regulation. Real competition to improve the processes, however, depends on open-system information.

This trend is a high-tech version of remanufacturing. The economic precedent is from third-world countries where skills existed to repair and rebuild, but resources to manufacture from scratch were lacking. For example, Lima, Peru, for many years had a thriving network of garages to rebuild old American cars. Vehicles ran many times their normal scrap-out mileage in the United States. Since the same economics prevailed with other products, very little solid refuse ever made it to a landfill.[19]

To execute environmental design well, the open-systems organization also needs open information. That begins with sharing process information and design ideas for DFD, but it goes further.

Open-System Information

Open-system information is essential for many environmental purposes. For example, chemical companies are increasingly reluctant to sell to customers who will not return containers or reveal how material is used. Knowingly selling hazardous materials to sloppy operations is a legal risk. If the company's drums are found in an uncontrolled dump, they may willy-nilly bear the cost of cleanup. One of the easiest ways to avoid this is to require the return of the empty container before issuance of a full one. That happens to be very close to the idea of a JIT kanban system. In addition, the seller provides a service by advising the customer on secure methods of handling and use and by assisting the customer to make those methods fail-safe.

To operate this way both customer and supplier must know something about each other's operations. Secrecy is very limited. However, companies are starting to become much more interested in sharing information anyway.

Stimulated by the quality movement and by time-based competition, one of the hottest current management topics is "benchmarking." It is the comparison of various operating measures and practices with others doing similar things in the hope of learning from any operation found to be better, wherever it may be located. Properly used, benchmarking is part of the search and study steps of improvement processes—part of the process of finding and recognizing opportunities for improvement.

The Malcolm Baldrige National Quality Award stimulated interest in benchmarking by asking companies whether they knew how they stood against competitors and "world-class" operations. Now, divisions and plants of large companies regularly compare *operations* with each other on a far broader set of measures and practices than merely sales or profit margins. That's internal benchmarking, and it's a start.

Finding best-in-class operations by any organization in any location is a step beyond that. Most companies today start benchmarking without being organized to do much more than go on a "fishing expedition," but hopefully they will learn.

Significant to both quality improvement and environmental improvement is that companies are openly sharing the details of methods and operations. A decade ago, only financial ratios were compared. Comparing operations encourages much more mutual improvement than merely reporting financial summary data. It is the beginning of open-system information. A consortium of larger electronic companies has been instructing the total industry how to clean printed circuit boards without using CFCs. Companies regularly benchmark how to label materials to meet EPA requirements. Just as important as meeting the EPA requirements is the use of standard labeling and language. That in itself reduces the chances of accidents and errors.

In 1986 the Superfund Amendments and Reauthorization Act (SARA) required companies to disclose emissions levels of about three hundred chemicals. The reports feed into the EPA's Toxic Release Inventory database. From it anyone can learn, for instance, how much sulfur dioxide the steel plants along Lake Michigan release.

However, the process of gathering the data and the ability to make comparisons has stimulated companies themselves to review the losses in their material balances and find better ways to staunch releases. A plant or company that does not compare well has incentive to move up on the list. Furthermore, since the information is known and improvement processes are in progress, there is nothing to hide. Dow Chemical Company, for example, encourages plant managers to meet with community groups and discuss the company's progress.[20]

Open-system information encourages process-improvement competition. That is one of the most beneficial forms of competition, because everybody wins: customers, employees—all the stakeholders plus the environment. In addition, and almost by surprise, SARA represents one of the best forms of regulation. It stimulates environmental improvement consortia to exchange performance measures and techniques by those responsible for doing the work. Open information among competitors encourages all of them to infinitely improve, in contrast to know-it-all regulatory requirements setting up minimum standards and trusting in compliance by inspection.

The Limits of Regulations

The quality movement today has made corrective action a familiar story. Turnaround goes through phases similar to those needed for the ecological ones: discovery, denial, acceptance, and finally pursuit of improvement processes everywhere. However, most environmental correction today consists of regulation rather than improvement processes. Unfortunately, regulatory compliance is patterned after Taylorism. Experts prescribe; operators conform—or pretend to.

Most end-of-pipe regulations set up minimum performance requirements or required procedures, often addressing one pollutant or issue at a time. Periodically they are tightened, creating games of regulatory roulette. Should a company risk a currently "noncompetitive overinvestment" in scrubbers or filters in anticipation of stricter interpretations later? Compliance cost about 17 percent of industry's total capital investment in 1988 and seems destined to grow substantially.

The concept and administration of the Superfund to clean up dumps has been a lesson in regulatory how-not-to, almost from its inception. Of four thousand or so hazardous waste sites identified, fewer than fifty have been cleaned up. Legal processes flow slower than the contaminants can ooze. Years or decades pass as the government decides which parties are the guiltiest and assigns payment. The processes encourage the same attitudes toward responsibility as patrimony suits. So far as is known, no one has constructed a time-flow diagram of a Superfund cleanup, but the value-added time in the process must be a minuscule fraction of the total. EPA is making changes to speed the resolution of cases.[21]

However, only extremists are so utopian as to believe regulations are unnecessary. People cannot police themselves. Through negligence or ignorance, some will pour formaldehyde down a sewer or open a dry cleaner knowing nothing of carbon tetrachloride. Even those with an exemplary record may slight the tending of emissions scrubbers if pressed to please a customer. Regulatory vigilance builds public trust that a minimum level of competence and honesty is practiced—in most cases. But regulations did not prevent the Exxon *Valdez* spill.

Regulations are a contentious, minimalist approach. Genuine enthusiasm is necessary to eliminate the need for hazardous materials or the conditions that allow losses of them, much less maximize all customers' sustainable quality of life.

Open-system regulations will help to materialize a new soul in enterprise. Make environmental improvement part of the competition between enterprises. Let companies advertise what percentage of their product is rebuilt or recycled. Definitional complications will doubtless be a source of controversy, but if customers are "green-minded" at all, the source of inspiration shifts from compliance to competitive pride.

Put BTU ratings on containers so users can see how much energy (and by implication, carbon budget) was used to make that can, bottle, bag—or bowling ball. Ideas similar to the mile-per-gallon ratings for automobiles all have comparison problems, but no more than for food labeling or product-safety warnings.

In fact, environmental concerns (and quality-of-life considerations) should broaden the measurements publicly used to rate companies beyond financial and economic indicators. GNP, sales, margins, and profits direct attention to growth, suggesting growth in resource use. Weights, full-process-cycle energy ratings, material-loss percentages (and warranty returns), rebuild percentages, and the like, all suggest conservation of resources.

Evaluation of process economics would rely more on direct matter-based and energy-based measures of process efficiency and less on cost measures derived from transactions, but costs cannot be escaped as a way to estimate aggregate resource use. Wherever a full process cycle can be flowcharted, the basis also exists to cost the process cycle rather than just part of it. Life-cycle costing is an old concept actually used only for aircraft and heavy trucks. Few consumers so far compare cars on life-cycle cost or lifetime cost per mile.

Finally, regulations do little to encourage enterprises to push the state of the art—to discover the unknowns in their processes. The new soul of enterprise tries to anticipate and control problems. Regulations, almost by definition, awkwardly police phenomena that have already stirred protest.[22]

Discovering the Unknowns in a Process

Lifting environmental impact statements for a fossil-fuel power plant would be good exercise for Arnold Schwartzenegger. Weighty reviews, broad in scope and highly detailed, seemingly probe every possible ramification: Will construction unearth Indian artifacts? How much does the building weigh?

Yet jokes about impact statements abound. Expensive and time-consuming, ponderous to read, and loaded with arguable assumptions, impact statements exemplify regulations trying to deal with unknowns.

Linkages between impact statement intentions, construction plans, and finished reality have gaps. Experts plan. Nonexperts carry out the plan—maybe. Experience shows that plant and equipment construction in many details "as built" differ significantly from "per drawing." What operators actually do is seldom exactly what others think they are doing.

Carefully preplanning operations is commendable. More important is improving the environmental performance of operations as they are actually run. If one can design products for remanufacturing, many remaining effluent and emission problems would be losses of material from the cycle, whether in tons or in molecular quantities.

Suppose we wish to evaluate the environmental impact of using aluminum beverage cans, from bauxite to disposal, including recycle loops. A simple, summarized flowchart is easy. Detailing one with the involvement of those doing the work at multiple locations, plus some consumers of cans, is monumental.

Doing a material-balance analysis on subparts of the process adds to knowledge. Chemists and engineers have long used material balances. Taking inventory and reconciling are business forms of material balance. Lack of precise measurements often makes the accuracy questionable, but the principle is that what comes out of a process should theoretically equal what goes in. However, even allowing for inaccurate measurement, there are usually unexplained losses.

A smaller-scale material balance might check presses used to print aluminum cans. The losses go down the drain, into the air, into scrap, or are still stuck to the equipment. Most operations simply have a loss allowance, with speculative explanations such as evaporation, leakage, trim, setup, or scrap. Just trying to discover what causes unknown loss suggests actions to stop "easy-case" losses. Others are much more challenging.

If losses are environmentally significant, the incentive to find them is not cost-driven. However, discovering and correcting the detailed reasons for material loss has a benefit similar to that of finding and correcting every possible quality problem. Operations, as performed, become thoroughly understood and in control. Discovering the detailed unknowns is not possible without the help of those doing the work.

Material losses are a common form of unknown. Occupational health, customer health, and effects on surroundings present a different class of unknowns. As is well known, discovering process-cycle unknowns is greatly aided if the process is small and visible. Doing an environmental impact analysis on a closed cycle of production and consumption, while challenging, sounds much more feasible than if materials come from everywhere and no one knows where outgoing material comes to rest. By the same logic, predicting and controlling the total process sounds much more feasible if it is a closed-cycle system that ordinary humans can "get their hands around."

This adds up to a high-tech, high-skill version of the "small-is-beautiful" hypothesis. The original argument was that technology should be kept within local skills and environmental conditions. (For example, don't introduce irrigation pumps if no one can keep them running.) Everybody should just tend to his or her own field.[23]

The high-tech version is economy of process control. The economics of coal and oil are economies of scale—bigger is better. Electronics is economy by miniaturization, and telecommunications turns the world into a small place. With global communication, a material-use cycle may extend around the world but remain human in scope. That is, the responsible parties can flowchart the whole loop and plug the leaks.

If energy is limited, it seems almost too sensible to forecast that we will exchange information everywhere but move material short distances—especially the "heavy stuff." Once it has been removed from the ground for use, we will remanufacture it close to where it is used.

MANUFACTURING EXCELLENCE
LEADS TO ENVIRONMENTAL EXCELLENCE

Many of the ideas and practices needed to make closed-loop material-use cycles a reality are already in existence. Just-in-time production was born in poverty. Its original purpose was to minimize Toyota's waste of resources. Compacting operations into a small space avoided the need for new plants, for example, and short material-movement distances saved energy.

During the oil shortage of 1973–74, Toyota's JIT practices included running equipment to make only what was needed, when needed, and shutting down idle machines whenever feasible. The incentive was conservation of limited oil stocks, as well as cost.

One of the simplest ways to control hazardous materials is by another JIT idea—returnable containers. Instead of the user disposing of the material, the containers with any excess are returned to sender. A low inventory also helps. A big help maintaining control of hazardous materials is not having much to control. Even bigger is a clear chain of customer-supplier responsibility throughout the circuit of its use.

Preventive maintenance is another environment-friendly "excellence" practice. It saves downtime, saves energy, and prevents emissions and effluents. Like automobiles, production equipment runs more efficiently when properly maintained. Process-control equipment and pollution-control equipment themselves must be maintained to work properly.

A good deal of plant maintenance time is spent on roofs. A flat factory roof is not only leak-prone, and thus a potential quality problem, but is usually end-of-pipe for emissions into the atmosphere and often the start-of-pipe for air coming in. Flat roofs are often laden with equipment so that maintenance workers are assigned full time to the roof.

One of the simplest correlates of both safety and pollution control in a plant is cleanliness and orderliness—basic tenets of workplace simplification usually initiated in the early stages of "going JIT." (The five steps of workplace simplification in brief: [1.] simplification; [2.] everything in place; [3.] cleanliness; [4.] full participation; and [5.] discipline.) The most dangerous workplaces for both safety and environmental damage are rife with spills and sloppy labeling.

Intensive quality improvement supports environmental control and safety. Spills, releases, and physical injuries are nearly all accidents, and by definition, an accident is unanticipated. One of the major thrusts of Total Quality Management is better prediction and control of all kinds of operations, thus working out mysteries and eliminating surprises. For example, when Davidson Rubber began to involve employees in working on quality problems and starting JIT practices, lost-time accidents dropped from forty-four one year to none the next.[24] Flowcharts, Pareto analyses, and cause-and-effect diagrams used on quality problems can also be used to address safety problems.

FIGURE 5-6

ENVIRONMENTAL BENEFITS OF "MANUFACTURING EXCELLENCE" PRACTICES

Practice	*Example*
Flow-diagram methods to overview and improve total processes	Can make sure that environmental (as well as other) waste is eliminated from a total process rather than shifted to another point in it.
Returnable containers	Almost no cardboard is now discarded by the Saturn Plant (auto), or many other plants. Returning containers costs fuel and time, but so does hauling new, used, and recycled cardboard.
	Ashland Chemical has empty chemical drums sent back. Saves drums and saves waste disposal by customers.
Minimum inventory	The less material, the less hazard. Methyl isocyanate is an intermediate. Technically, it could be used immediately.
JIT, order only for immediate use	Overages must be stored. Eliminate disposal or return of unused material.
Fail-safe methods, a major principle of doing it right the first time	Fewer defects mean less scrap to discard, less rework energy, less energy correcting field problems, and higher reliability products (slightly longer life).
Reducing plant floor space	Saves on materials of construction, energy to heat, material handling energy, wasted real estate, etc.
Cell manufacturing	Less material handling, fewer defects, less inventory.
Design for manufacturing	This usually results in fewer parts, and often simpler ones. Translates to less material and energy use as well as less cost to the customer.

Environmental accidents are unanticipated for many reasons, but often because of failure to extend "manufacturing excellence" to environmental control.

NOTES

1. From *New York Times*/CBS polls taken from 1981–89 as reported in *Scientific American*, September 1989.
2. Sir Thomas More wrote the original *Utopia* about five hundred years ago. Until the twentieth century, More and most subsequent utopians idealized eliminating the evils of greed. Then they began to treat feminism and science-fiction themes. A good summary of the classic utopian literature is Joyce Oramel Hertzler, *The History of Utopian Thought* (New York: Cooper Square Publishers, 1965). A modern utopia that reverts to greed-bashing is Gordon Rattray Taylor, *Rethink* (New York: E. P. Dutton, 1973).
3. Barnet N. Berin, George J. Stolnitz, and Aaron Tenebein, "Mortality Trends of Males and Females over the Ages," *Society of Actuaries Transactions* 41 (1989): 9–32.
4. From the *New York Review of Books*, 20 December 1990, 58.
5. Rachel Carson, *Silent Spring* (Boston: Houghton-Mifflin, 1962).
6. "Dirty Stories," *The Economist*, 1 February 1991, 51.
7. Lester R. Brown, *State of the World, 1992* (Washington, D.C.: The Worldwatch Institute, 1992), p. 176. (Originally from World Bank data.)
8. Tests for carcinogenicity based on massive doses have become increasingly questioned and controversial. So has the assumption that an environment can be made totally carcinogen-free. See, for example, the editorial in *Science*, 27 July 1991, 361, or the review in *The Economist*, 21 September 1991, 103.
9. Keith Schneider, "Radiation Danger Found in Oil Fields across Nation," *New York Times*, 3, December 1990, 1.
10. Original source: O. Kharbanda and E. Stallworthy, *Waste Management: toward a More Sustainable Society* (Westport, CT: Auburn House, 1990).
11. Baraby J. Feder, "P.R. Mistakes Seen in Breast-Implant Case," *New York Times*, 29 January 1992, C1.
12. David Kotelchuck, "Asbestos, the Funeral Dress of Kings—and Others" in *Dying for Work*, ed. David Rosner and Gerald Markowitz (Bloomington: Indiana University Press, 1989): 192.
13. *The Japan Letter*, The Asia Letter Group, 1 March 1992, no. 443, 4.

14. William J. Rathje, "Rubbish," *The Atlantic*, December 1989, 99–106.
15. Satoru Nagoya, "Dumped on Ward's Assembly Protests Garbage Situation," *The Japan Times Weekly International Edition*, 9–15 September 1991, 7.
16. Jeff Bailey, "Browning-Ferris Denied Permit on Garbage Site," *The Wall Street Journal*, 13 August 1991, A4.
17. "A Wall of Waste," *The Economist*, 30 November 1991, 73
18. Bruce Nussbaum and John Templeton, "Built to Last—Until It's Time to Take It Apart," *Business Week*, 17 September 1990, 102–06, and "Disposable Cars Clutter Suburbs," *Japan Times Weekly International Edition*, 18–24 March 1991, 20.
19. Richard N. Farmer, *Farmer's Law: Junk in a World of Affluence* (New York: Stein & Day, 1973).
20. Art Kleiner, "What Does It Mean to Be Green?" *Harvard Business Review* 69, no. 4 (July–August 1991), 38–47.
21. "Why Superfund Doesn't Work," *Waste Age*, 22, no. 4 April 1991, 73.
22. For example, the long history of occupational health is marked by uncertainty, never knowing whether one is looking at the right problem, seeing a psychological effect or a physical one, interpreting data too conservatively, or reading too much into it. All too often, investigations and the information have been slowed by denial reactions—that something cannot really be wrong. See *Dying for Work*, ed. David Rosner and Gerald Markowitz.
23. E. F. Schumaker, *Small Is Beautiful* (New York: Harper & Row, 1973).
24. Charlene Adair and Ed Dawkins, "Davidson Instrument Panel Division—Textron," *Target* 3, no. 4 (Winter 1987): 31–32.

6

THE HIGH-TECH
RAT RACE

AMONG MY MEMORIES OF WORKING IN A GUN AND LOCK SHOP IN 1955 ARE LEG-
endary tales of the seventy-five-year-old owner, extraordinary of skill
and brusque of temperament. One of his most common repair jobs was
straightening the barrels of automatic shotguns, which were easily bent
by dropping them or even by pressure while cleaning them. Trueing a
barrel without doing further damage generally took time; it had to be
checked in a lathe, maybe heated and retempered, and the gunsmith
had to select just the right device and force to leverage the deviations.

One morning one of the local landed gentry stopped in with a slightly
bowed shotgun in hand. He had to have it straightened that day, for
that evening he was leaving on a hunting trip with associates of great
social and business importance. Old Ed told the man to just wait a
minute as he popped the barrel off, spun it in his hands, and eyed it.

In the shop was a wooden post covered with padded canvas. Ed
rapped the barrel across the post. Eyed it some more. Marked another
spot. Whacked again. About a half-dozen whacks later he held a
straight barrel.

"That'll be ten bucks," announced Ed. "Ten bucks!" snorted the
patrician. "I'm not paying ten dollars for a five-minute job."

"Took me sixty years to learn how to do that," said Ed. As the
would-be hunter opened his mouth to argue the point, Ed reinforced

his position on intellectual capital by rapping the barrel across the post again. The gentleman prepaid to observe Ed's final whack.

Dr. H. K. Dale, a renowned sugar chemist in the early twentieth century, loved research. Virtually his only concern for intellectual capital was whether someone would pay to let him keep compiling it. When he was in his eighties, he still stopped to chat with freshmen students doing cookbook lab exercises on his way to and from his own college lab, where he was still active. One day the students overheard his conversation with a friend:

"What's so interesting about freshman students?"

"Looking for researchers to talk to," Dale replied.

"What do you look for?"

"Kids that have to try their own twist on an experiment and can't wait to get back to the lab in the morning to see how it turned out."

"What about their intellectual capability?"

"Not worth a damn if their heart and soul isn't in it."

Ed and Dr. Dale are both long dead. In life they were probably separated by little difference in net worth but a big difference in attitude. Ed was secretive; Dale was open. Ed regarded any trick he learned as a trade secret for bargaining leverage (and as a come-on to win a beer now and then). His knowledge belonged to him. Dale talked openly but had difficulty finding people intrinsically interested in sugar chemistry unless some phenomenon promised big-time results.

The difference between these two men is still with us. A company that wants to protect its intellectual capital puts up walls to extract the appropriate fee for expertise that leaves its enclosure. However, the scope of the research and development process is expanding, and companies are finding that the economy of scale of R&D is too large for one company to handle easily. Along with quality, time compression, and ecology, R&D is one more reason why business institutions must become more cooperative.

INCENTIVES TO INNOVATE

One's concept of innovation is reflected in whether one thinks like Ed or Dr. Dale, but neither had a very broad concept of innovation.

Innovation is a process, not a product. For example, the innovation of xerography was more than Chester Carlson tinkering for a decade in his basement. Success took design refinement (by Battelle Institute, among other parties), capital, distribution, service—and charging by the copy rather than selling machines.

In fact, circumstances that enable a technical concept to become an established practice may not come together until decades after the technical concept is born. The best-known inventors, like Edison, Ford, and Lear, have been unabashed popularizers and promoters as well as persistent, diligent, and ingenious. A monumental innovation such as the automobile is a social movement as much as a machine. Without roads, oil, a service network, and licensing—and as it turned out, the absence of a general patent that would have delayed the advent of mass production—the car might have remained an aristocrat's toy. But when the time was ripe, the machine began suggesting its own uses, as is now happening with computers.

Innovation is not a product. It's a process, and a group process at that. The customer is part of the group. Innovations like application-specific integrated circuits (ASIC) or the three-day car will be social and systems developments in which products are only a part. In addition, an innovation process is now expected to be a nearly perfect experience from the beginning of full deployment. No more nuclear power plants without a clear plan to store or recover spent fuel rods, for instance.

All of us, including technical entrepreneurs, understand some parts of an innovation process much more clearly than others. Often, "my part" is considered the center of the process. The limited perspectives of various participants in an innovative process is a sometimes fatal disease. For example, a small research institute recently broke apart because its directors did not understand it the same way. The academic directors thought it should be a source of research funds, the business directors thought it should be a source of profitable spin-off ideas, and the government directors thought it should be a source of new jobs. None of the concepts of a fully deployed innovation process were very comprehensive.

Suppose an inventor has a bright idea for remanufacturable lawn furniture. Designing the furniture itself is as much a matter of taste as technology, and probably not patentable. Coming up with exactly the right kinds of materials is a systems problem. Possibly the chairs will be leased, not owned, so organizing the distribution and recovery system for chairs is not a one-company enterprise. Would this concept have any intellectual capital? If so, who should own it? A system design is virtually nonpatentable, and numerous participants contribute in ways both large and small. Today's business practices are awkward when they try to cope with this situation.

Intellectual Capital

Intellectual capital is any know-how that can be sold—composing symphonies, erasing tattoos . . . straightening gun barrels. Ed the gunsmith marketed his self-taught intellectual capital with the instincts of a consultant, sometimes using a technical patois, other times a fulsome repertoire of profanities. But he always tried to avoid giving away any "secrets" that would risk making a competitor out of either an employee or a customer—never The Great Communicator explaining "real how-to."

Intellectual capital descended from the basic concept of the corporation, itself beginning as a mechanism to financially promote exploration. Explorers risking life and limb had to be financially supported for a long time before finding anything to return, if they ever did. Corporations enabled many people to financially share those risks and rewards. Still today, the venturesome consider only those who risk personal money to be serious players in business.

Eventually, rewards for invention or artistry came to be regarded as analogous to each individual deserving an exclusive return from the patch of ground he hunted, tilled, mined, or drilled. With mass production, inventors could multiply their ideas into riches. After mass media arrived, artists could also multiply their creations into wealth. Bach, Mozart, et al. were simply supported by patrons, but financial supporters of later artists figured they had a chance to get a cut of a big future income.

Simplistically, intellectual capital is any method to recompense creative people and their supporters. Some people believe intellectual capital should reward smart, persistent risk takers (Ed's idea); others that it only needs to maintain support for well-directed research (Dale's idea). In any case, intellectual capital is the basic social arrangement whereby those who successfully contribute to innovation are recognized.

American rewards for intellectual capital tend to dramatize originality or creativity. An idea without a unique feature cannot command premium recognition for exclusivity. The only value of a nonoriginal idea lies in the elegance with which it can be executed. The downside of the concept of intellectual capital is that it almost automatically leads to rejection of "nonproprietary" ideas—the not-invented-here (NIH) syndrome.

American scientists and engineers are thoroughly steeped in a system of rewards and recognition for originality. The Japanese are not. With little recognition for creativity, an idea from anywhere is examined more critically for its ease and simplicity in practice. When pressed, Americans can acquire this habit, too. Probably the most publicized recent example is Motorola's "Bandit Project" to design and produce pagers, so named because project members were encouraged to shamelessly steal ideas from anywhere. Without incentives to borrow ideas, many creative engineers are too inhibited by NIH reactions to piece together simple, elegant, robust designs.

The patent system has seldom been effective in protecting overall designs or systems concepts rather than bits and pieces of technical ingenuity. For example, a company named Zelco patented an "itty-bitty" reading lamp design and sued seventy-two competitors with infringement. The legal wrangling sapped the little company, and it was forced to compete on distribution, price, quality, and service rather than sit on intellectual capital. Defending the uniqueness of a lamp design quickly turns fine legal minds to mush, particularly if the real innovation is in the total process.[1]

The American patent system is based on first-to-discover (like a land claim), but the process allows an idea's originator to keep it under wraps longer while he or she negotiates a piece of the action among the parties contributing to an innovation. Most foreign systems, including Japan's, are based on first-to-file. They are easier to administer, but the Japanese one in particular is administered very slowly and with built-in disclosure rules that pressure applicants to cross-license. Applicants seldom expect to retain exclusive rights. The Japanese are more conscious that a basic idea or a working demonstration is only one step toward commercial acceptance of a fully developed, debugged innovation. If a technical concept has obvious promise, better to have several companies developing it at once. (The wisdom of organizing multiple alternative development paths has been observed within individual American companies, too. Union Carbide has been one.)

Americans regard the Japanese system as unfair, but it accomplishes its purpose—quickly pushing technical ideas to fruition, whether they are domestic or foreign in origin. The innovative instincts of Japanese and Americans are mirrored by their patent systems. Americans demand exclusivity if they are inventors, but bemoan NIH resistance of others to whom they try to "sell" a new idea. The Japanese have few hang-ups about taking ideas from anywhere, but they struggle to induce individuals to be more "creative."[2]

Allocating the returns from a systems innovation in which many people have contributed is more complex than assigning the royalties from a mining claim. Contribution values are fuzzier than percentages of claims owned.

Ideas themselves are a dime a dozen. Ideas have value only when they are refined and combined through a process of innovation into real products and services. A broad innovation, like the new communication system suggested by the UltraComm scenario, is really a combination of many smaller innovations, some of which depend on the learning ability of the customers themselves.

A major issue is how to persuade customers to fund the continuance of R&D, innovative processes, and the education of people, including themselves. The overall system must pay for itself. "High-tech, open-system, sustainable manufacturing"—whatever we choose to call such a system of innovation—must be financially supported.

The traditional American way to fund development resembles staking a mining claim. Venture capitalists and high-flyer investors assess their risks by questioning market acceptance and the ability of an aspiring management to perform. Both are difficult to judge until a company has some form of track record.

"Bridge money" spans the time from start-up to first market acceptance and a track record begins. Inventor-entrepreneurs typically find themselves dealing away their future earnings to attract bridge money partners. Every new stage in financing leads to more dilemmas about earnings dilution and control—how to cut the pie and which investors have a say. The process is driven by the prospect of growth leveraged by claims on intellectual capital. While many factors are involved in the evolution of any specific company, eventually the only way to give many investors the payout they want is by going public—by selling the company.

On the other hand, customers seeking the lowest price avoid an R&D or quality premium. They are the market for pirates and knock-offs (not all of which are second-rate quality). Requiring payment to recover R&D plus give a fat return to risk takers is at the heart of old arguments on patent protection and on generic versus brand-name drugs, for instance. The higher price pays for "the system"; customers will pay it if they see the value. An old version of "paying for a system" is Sears exchanging damaged Craftsman wrenches for new ones, no questions asked.

A newer example of buying a system is paying for premium-priced, supported software versus pirated disks for $5 a throw. The difference to the user is quality, instructional assistance, and backup in case of a glitch. Once stung by a pirated system, many people will pay a premium for supported software, but they're paying for the service, not the writing of the software. This inclination is deeply under-stood—and feared—in the computer world. Open-system hardware and software quickly become "commodity packages" that command no margin. That is, customers are unwilling to pay for the R&D necessary to upgrade the system.

"Intellectual capital" suggests the maintenance of incentives for technical advancement—premium pricing of products and services to fund research and to recover developmental costs. More important, each organization's concept of intellectual capital strongly influences its willingness to cooperate in creative work.

A possessive attitude to intellectual capital fosters distrust between partners in research consortia, in customer-supplied partnerships or even between different departments of the same company. The busi-ness system favors protection of intellectual capital, not the sharing of it. Whenever companies try to form joint agreements on almost any research issue, their lawyers work feverishly to protect their clients' intellectual capital.

High-Tech Rat Races

Many small manufacturing businesses depend on milking some bit of intellectual capital, such as how to form a sharper cutting edge on diamond than anyone else in the world, how to focus a high-pressure fluid stream with a finer resolution, or how to formulate a high-temperature magnetic laminate. Technical entrepreneurs seek comfortable little monopolies. Since a patent has value only if its owner has the will and money to fight infringements, a great deal of intellectual capital is undisclosed know-how, sometimes difficult to describe, such as the actual blending processes and heat cycles that successfully laminate multiple polymers into a composite tire.

This system is becoming tired. The assumption supporting it is that companies can sell secret technologies to each other at arm's length, each charging what its corner on a small bit of intellectual capital is worth. However, optimal designs are not created that way. Technical know-how from many areas must meld together if a complex design is going to work, and particularly if it is going to be leading edge, low-cost, remanufacturable, and pleasing to the customer all at the same time. The big manufacturing achievements during World War II occurred in no small part because companies for a few short years shared intellectual capital and know-how as never before—or since.

After many generations of technological advance, marveling over it is more subdued. Questioning of side effects (as opposed to ignorant fear) is more severe. Expectations of performance are higher. Technology reduced to practice has to *work* very well the first time. Innovation has become more a rat race for survival than a glorious quest for a technical El Dorado.

For instance, a new auto model must meet expectations the "first time out of the box," and many process changes are unseen by the buyer. For example, General Motors' development of the Saturn is a substantially new process for the American industry, as well as a new car. Saturn was a "green field" start-up of a different "affordable" car design in a plant having many departures from prior practice in car building and work-force cooperation. Many of the people had not worked together before. And it was undertaken in a fiercely competitive, mature market of buyers now expecting "perfect" results. A historian looking back is apt to conclude that in its way, Saturn will have been every bit as challenging as Henry Ford's venture early in the century, whether it is successful or not.

Several of Saturn's innovations have attracted little attention. One is its scuff-resistant, polymeric body panels that can sometimes be run over by a truck and put back on the car without noticeable damage. Instead, much of the media's attention has focused on whether Saturn will "make it." A major factor in success is adroitly (and truthfully) explaining bobbles to the press. (One of the more significant miscues was an off-spec engine coolant from Texaco that caused GM to recall hundreds of vehicles.)

In the computer industry new tweaks of technology seem to be a daily occurrence, but product unreliability, software incompatibility, late delivery, or overpromised marketing have been the downfall of more than one erstwhile computer tycoon. Companies run on high-tech treadmills, keeping up just to keep from falling off.

For instance, the long-term revenue outlook for computer disk drives is nearly flat, not a scenario attractive to growth capital, but projections of available megabytes continue to soar. To survive, competitors must keep up with the pack by increasing storage density, decreasing disk sizes, using them in tandem, and so on. Beyond that is the breakthrough possibility that bubble memories, crystals, or something else will make disk drives obsolete. The value of a bit of intellectual capital is transitory. The business has for several years been drifting toward high-tech commodity status.[3]

Both the UltraComm and the ASIC scenarios of Chapter 2 project the maturity of electronic miniaturization. Megabyte memory chips today require Class 1 clean rooms (no more than one dust particle per cubic foot). The challenge is daunting. A seated person doing light work emits one million particles per minute. Defect rates are measured in parts per billion (not million). During the 1990s the world benchmark may stretch to parts per trillion (equivalent to about one second every 318 centuries).[4]

If this rat race continues, IC production will have to take place in outer space. Further mass production of miniature ICs will be questioned, just as hypersonic airliners and artificial hearts have been questioned. Even if new materials open up a new miniaturization frontier, standard memory will become a "commodity business." Those conditions set up the twenty-first-century ASICs scenario: IC design and manufacturing becoming a worldwide service business centered on design software for customer-designed chips, but they will not stop the rat race to enhance chips and the chip-making process.[5]

The ASICs scenario also suggests the direction of many kinds of future technical development. The goal of fewer technical races will be for an edge in intellectual capital (which translates to growth of independent companies and overall economic growth). More will be quests for overall process control. The situation is analogous to teenage basketball players discovering that when each player tries to maximize scoring, the result is seldom a winning combination.

Old industries now need rapid innovation and reorganization to survive. For example, Eastman Kodak's strategy once was to "give away" cameras to create demand for its high-margin film business. However, electronic images (as on VCR tapes) are now rapidly improving in sharpness. Electronic digitized images can be stored and manipulated by computer, so a customer (prosumer) can do much more than simply take pictures. They can creatively combine them, enhance them, or otherwise modify them while sitting at a terminal. Unfortunately, the leaders in this technology are Canon and Sony.

Kodak is betting the business on a hybrid technology, the Photo CD System, anticipating that it has about ten years before electronic imaging and printing is fully competitive with film. It will be a ten-year period of intense change from chemical expertise to electronics expertise. Also, it's largely a replacement-market strategy, not a virgin-growth strategy—a high-tech rat race. Furthermore, the new appeal to the customer will be different. Kodak, if it survives, may be a very different organization than it is today. Changing itself is more difficult than changing its technology.[6]

Our Limits Are Ourselves

Street cars that can now cruise at 150 miles per hour are mostly fuel guzzlers with unused capability. A driver can go that fast only on deserted autobahns and interstates. If economical solar rollers could miraculously hit similar speeds, Aunt Irma could not toodle from home to mall at 150 miles per hour without a control system comparable to that of bullet trains and considerable modification of real estate to build controlled-access racetracks. Public meetings on the issues conjure visions of technology-assessment disputes being argued before several generations of Supreme Court justices.

Were we able to make supercomputers the size of credit cards, embed them in everything, and let them communicate worldwide, we wouldn't know what to do with the capability. We are as lost as an eighteenth-century ship captain would be contemplating how to manage a rock concert. Human-oriented systems challenge the total nature of man more than pure technical achievements do.

Aircraft and air-system design has long contended with high-tech issues of human control. An F-15 fighter could perform maneuvers with much higher G-forces if it was not occupied by a fragile human pilot. A programmed airliner can fly virtually untouched from one airport to another, provided it is correctly programmed and nothing changes. Will pilots stay alert and intervene if something goes wrong? If an unmanned cruise missile can fly five hundred miles and disappear down the doorway of a bunker, why cannot it be programmed to deliver intercity packages from building to building without airports? The negatives focus on the lack of reliability of such craft and the programming of their flights. On the other hand, flight simulators allow pilots to practice handling emergency conditions that no one wants to replicate in actual flight, and bar codes allow delivery of huge volumes of packages door-to-door overnight. The direction of technical development today is substantially guided by human limitations.

Consumer electronics developments perplex customers choking on technobabble. Uncle Harry cannot program his microwave and is baffled by computers. The willingness of people to adapt and their ability to learn has always been a limitation. For instance, early auto drivers sometimes caused a traffic hazard by swinging far left before turning right, a habit left over from driving a horse and wagon.

Electronic "smart houses" are possible today. Home-management software can automatically update warranty and service records, pay service providers, and update "help" files on multiple computer systems, appliance systems, entertainment systems, security systems, and home-environment systems—if Uncle Harry can deal with it.

Simplified product designs allow ordinary mortals to learn devices without special training courses. Who wants to read a manual before trying to program a new digital phone-management system? (It isn't just an answering machine anymore.) Learning may be aided by "fuzzy logic" controls that automatically adjust to user preferences and idiosyncrasies: for example, camcorders that compensate for a shaky hand, and heating/cooling controls that replicate temperature adjustments previously made by the user whenever either indoor or outdoor environments have changed. Fuzzy logic is already built into many Japanese consumer products and will soon appear in some American-built ones.[7]

Simplification is necessary to maintain an environment customers and employees can tolerate. For example, offering choices to customers is an advantage unless they are irritated by it, like having to look through a ten-page menu when all they want is a burger and fries immediately.

Product variety and new offerings marketed through major chain stores are limited by the ability of retailers and customers to adjust. Revising store-shelf layouts more than once a quarter is expensive and confusing to shoppers. Companies like Procter & Gamble rotate new-product introductions in cycles determined by market reaction. Very few people care to spend much time deciding what soap to use, so a product can be well-researched and well-designed but still flop if it cannot gain attention in the clutter. The ultimate limit to the rate of change is us.

One solution to these limitations may be "prosumer options." These would allow customers to personally revise products to their own needs. For example, instead of selecting a laundry detergent off the shelf, let your friendly soap company's software service formulate one to suit your machine, your cleaning requirement, and the method of wash water disposal or recycling. If the washing machine also has self-adapting fuzzy logic built in, the software programs might "fight each other," so the laundry system must be coordinated between soap and washer companies. Otherwise, customers will be tempted to return to a bar of Fels-Naptha and a washboard.[8]

An automobile is certainly a product to which most buyers give more thought than most, but how many customers want to spend their time detailing the features of a totally different car? Japanese manufacturers found that the existence of option packages greatly assisted auto purchasers to make a selection from a plethora of choices.[9] If the idea is to catch on, it seems reasonable that many customers would prefer to upgrade a car with which they already have experience than to design one they have never actually driven—even though they can try it in a simulator.

We are limited by ourselves. High-tech industry is concerned that without improved education, it will not have competent workers. Without improved education, it may not have competent customers either. A fast track of disconnected change cannot be comprehended, much less accepted. Technical change increasingly requires offering services and systems, not just products, but one of the difficulties is financing such a system.

PAYING FOR THE INNOVATION PROCESS

Vigorous proponents of private industry praise the virtues of tough competition, assuming that it will promote rapid technical progress. It's an inconsistent position unless customers are willing to pay for the R&D. They're willing to pay if the company maintains a temporary monopoly through patents, trade secrets, and keeping new products under wraps. The fear is that without the secrecy, customers will refuse to pay for research and improvement processes—refuse to invest in the future.

By contrast, science is ideally an open system. Scientists verifying a claim of cold fusion in a bottle ultimately reduce theory to facts. However, the open nature of science is sometimes endangered by competition for funds and recognition.

Price-competitive companies cannot afford "unproductive" R&D. Since World War II, American steel companies evolved into spending much less on R&D and improvements than the Japanese. One of the fears of breaking up AT&T has been that eventually it will no longer be able to fund the Bell Laboratories. National Power, a recently privatized British utility, until recently supported a five-hundred person laboratory that studied acid rain, greenhouse gases, discharge of hot water into waterways, superconductivity, and energy conservation. Now the laboratory is being closed, a victim of electricity price competition—or so it appears to critics of the closing.[10]

Retail-level price pressures, part of the historical war to control marketing channels, also have an effect. Appliances sold through power retailers start to have the same margins as groceries. As brand-name margins erode on "commodity boxes," manufacturers try to offset the erosion with extra features. (One reason Motorola sold Quasar television to Matsushita in 1974 is that, anticipating the rise of power retailing, it opted to drop a business in which margins would not support R&D.)

In the computer business, to IBM's discomfort, clone makers have demonstrated how to turn hardware into "commodity boxes." Since a major differentiating feature is available software, a common adage in the business is to market software and "toss in" the supporting hardware at cost. That leads to financial analysts judging whether a company is stuck with hardware margins (rock bottom) or can command software margins (nicely padded while packages are new and in demand).[11]

Software margins must recover the big cost of writing and testing software, and perhaps the hardware that goes with it. Since piracy undercuts the investment in intellectual capital, control of piracy is one way to sustain a high margin long enough to repay the development cost. When lone companies must pay for the R&D, they typically retain control of a marketing channel or product-use cycle. Drug companies do this through the legal system. A company like Harley-Davidson has to do it through a strong dealer network and intense customer loyalty.

Companies that truly implement the "acronyms" like TQM, JIT, and employee involvement (some just use the words) build up intellectual capital in their work force, including those primarily charged with product and process development. One result is less waste in the total new-product introduction process. For a time these leaders may enjoy margins higher than competitors, but as these practices spread, the same old issues return.

Sharing the R&D Risk and Expense

The direction of technology, high-tech rat races, and environmental concerns are pushing companies toward more sharing of R&D risks and results. No thinking company wants to be left totally outside any fast-breaking development that may be overtaking its industry, nor does it want to risk betting wrong with the limited funds it alone can put into R&D. NIH has become an increasingly expensive attitude when a total system innovation has to work nearly flawlessly from the beginning. Intellectual capital is increasingly worth little as a stand-alone when innovations must fit into a total system.

The "answer" to the dilemma is more acceptance by industry of open-system research and information (a more scientific attitude) coupled with closed-cycle development and control of products and services, as was suggested for environmental reasons in Chapter 5. Research consortia and more open exchanges between companies have become much more popular in the past decade.

New lean-margin, open-system computer companies, such as Sun Microsystems and Compaq, rely on suppliers to support product development and later to produce their systems. This approach has many precedents. Semitrailer truck manufacturers are basically assemblers that have operated in this way for decades, pushing much R&D to suppliers. Thin margins in construction have long pushed that industry's expensive R&D onto construction equipment and materials suppliers.

What has been missing is a sense of system development and the spirit of an open system. The traditions of intellectual capital and fortress companies hinder cooperation and, consequently, learning how to promote appropriate cooperation and excellence in executing it.

Consortia

Manufacturing companies were never able to develop all their technology themselves. For instance, studies of Du Pont's and other companies' new products decades ago showed that the majority of them originated from ideas or developments outside the company.[12] Companies have long cross-licensed research findings or otherwise "horse-traded" bits of technology.

However, research consortia (as opposed to joint ventures) between companies are relatively new. The best known today are Sematech, the National Center for Manufacturing Sciences (NCMS), and Microelectronics and Computer Technology Corporation (MCC). All began in the mid-1980s. Results are just beginning to appear.

All three began as research organizations. While technical research remains their major thrust, they have also initiated research and cooperation on management methods. Sematech is organizing a set of training centers for suppliers to the electronics industry, and NCMS is promulgating a self-assessment program, "Achieving Manufacturing Excellence." The consortia, and before them numerous technology-transfer organizations, quickly began to see that management issues were a major cause of slow technical innovation.

Companies participating in consortia have several common dilemmas. One is whether to commit top technical talent to consortia projects or to internal work on which the title to intellectual capital is exclusive. Another is the fear that competitors or near-competitors will learn about the company's new product and process developments, so discussion is limited to precompetitive technology. Another is how fast to rotate representatives on consortia projects. High turnover leads to difficulty sustaining long-range consortium direction and momentum.

People from different companies must get to know each other. Suppliers, competitors, customers and noncorporate organizations provide a mix of people who come from different organizational cultures. It takes time for a work group to gel.

Distrust between competing companies is always a problem. In addition, some consortia participants distrust consultants, government employees, or even any research that is government funded. Their instinct is to learn as much as possible from others without giving away anything important. Those who are minimally active risk not recognizing research that competitors are eager to run with.

Despite the problems, American manufacturers are much more open with each other than they were only ten years ago. However, access to research is only the start of new products and processes. Rapid, "fail-safe" innovation takes not only creativity but integration of ideas from everywhere into the best overall package. The race goes not to those who try to sit on intellectual capital but to the swiftest and surest at taking new concepts to market.

High-Pressure Research

A great deal of research consumed by corporations begins in universities and institutes. Corporate managers sometimes believe that the academic world is Sleepy Hollow compared to their own milieus. Not so. Pressures are intense, and if consortia and management-by-fact become commonplace, some of the problems of academic research will be seen in commercial organizations. The current malaise within academic systems suggests problems that will arise among presumably cooperative research ventures and open-system research networks. No system is perfect.

In universities, intense pressure to show results (publish or perish) and to obtain funding spins both positive and negative, injecting emotion into management-by-fact fields. The imaginative sell breakthrough ideas to funding sources, but timid souls prefer projects sure to be favored by established reviewers.

Big-time competition for funds stresses the scientific ethic of letting the facts prevail. This side of the rationale for academic tenure is rarely instinctive to nonacademics. When jobs and funding are on the line, occasionally someone succumbs to the temptation to falsify results.[13]

Fraud cases from federally funded research invite political and legal adventuring. For instance, an attention-getting federal research fraud suit in California was brought by J. Thomas Condie of the University of Utah, who challenged data published by Dr. John L. Ninnemann, then at the University of California at San Diego. A review panel at San Diego upheld Dr. Ninnemann. A panel at Utah found no intentional falsification. Condie was forced to resign from the University of Utah. He says that another panel four years later agreed that the data were false.

Almost everyone fears that dumping legalities on such disputes is not the way to resolve them. However, Condie's lawyer, himself a scientist, says that no other resource will clean up the old boys' networks. He thinks universities should police research more strictly themselves; that is, they should strengthen institutional customs and ethics so that facts prevail in reviews.[14]

The review process is made more painful when outside control exercised by funding sources has other "strings" that jeopardize funding.

Federal agencies inconsistently check such things as procedures for handling hazardous waste, use of test animals, or records intended to deter fraud. Procurement regulations do not fit one-of-a-kind research requirements. Annual budget changes muddy long-term direction.

Though sleepy news to the public, the escalating distrust between scientists and funding agencies caused the editor of *Science* to call for Congress and the agencies to engage in "soul-searching."[15] They should. The basic ethos of scientific fact seeking is not money-motivated, though scientists have long had to solicit various kinds of patrons.

The accomplishments of American defense R&D, still heavily funded and once the leading edge in the world, now trail those of commercial R&D in many areas.[16] Some of the reasons they've fallen behind are lack of open communication, slowness of product development, ability to accept high-cost solutions, and encumbrance by requirements such as full traceability accounting of material on each contract. Where laxity occurs, the temptation is to add controls, but controls do not create trust. The trust is necessary for open communication and agreement on facts.

Private funding doesn't always lend itself to trust building either. Spin-offs from institutes and universities have filled Boston's Highway 128 and Silicon Valley companies. The ease of moving between these institutions has long been a major driver of technical start-ups. Academics with a pecuniary relationship with a private company are called "dual-rose" researchers. A survey of biotechnology departments showed that universities spawning the most start-ups—MIT, Stanford, and a handful of other leading names—also have the highest percentages of dual-role professors. About half the members of the National Academy of Sciences are believed to be dual-role.

The positive effects of dual-role researchers on research funding and time-to-market are highly praised. But what of the "negatives"?[17] The one that comes up the most is conflict of interest. Will dual-role scientists readily accept contrary evidence if financial confidence in a relationship company may be shaken as a result? Will they submit hot findings to peer review? Will they tilt their interests toward applied rather than basic research? Do they not capitalize on others' work by participating in peer reviews or by simply being in an exchange network (often worldwide electronic mail these days)? That is, when big monetary rewards for intellectual capital come to be a normal expectation, possessiveness begins to creep in and exchanges of information are guarded. At the extreme, if an accountant tried to measure the intellectual capital, he or she would try to attribute a future value to almost any data set exchanged.

However, easy exchanges of people and information have been the major force propelling rapid technological learning. About forty American universities or their institutes have industrial liaison programs. Donors (including consortia) wired into research have a running start on anything worth development. Universities that do not have working liaisons with companies have been reluctant to do so, in part because faculty have had difficulty accepting dual-role relationships. The reluctance itself prevents the researchers from better understanding "real needs" for their work. Breakthroughs occur where communication and excitement have transcended the objections, and often the researchers overestimate the value of their own work, not appreciating that it is only the first step in a full process of innovation.[18]

Recently, Japanese participation in liaison programs has stirred fears that spin-offs might not stay on American soil. For instance, Nihon University in Tokyo bought a clone of MIT's Media Lab for $10 million. Among other things, the Media Lab is a leader in the development of high-definition television. Most Japanese high-tech research is applied, therefore done under wraps by Japanese companies. The fear is that the arrangement will give Japanese companies a clear window into the Media Lab, but the window into Japan through the Tokyo lab will be fogged over. In the Japanese case, distrust is hard to displace because of language differences, cultural differences, and Japan's long history of appropriating ideas from the West (and often improving on them).

MIT's defense basically is that while its labs may have been an American resource during the early days of the cold war, they have undergone a transition to being a world resource. They need to collaborate around the world and engage foreign talent in the labs themselves. Funding is attracted from around the world, too.

The distinguishing characteristic of an advanced economy is that it builds common intellectual capital and sustains know-how in many fields of endeavor. Otherwise, it is not really advanced. Therefore, the system of commerce must be operated to pay the overhead necessary to maintain technological know-how. One issue is collectively having enough control of full cycles of material use to maintain quality improvement and environmental security—which implies extracting the funding necessary to pay for continuing R&D.

A pressing need is to modify the structure and ethos of working across the various kinds of institutions that have been necessary to technological change. Where the barriers to exchange have been few, advancements of almost any kind deemed useful have been forthcoming. Where the institutions (and individuals) hunker, each in its own corner, development of physical products is impeded. More than physical product innovation is necessary in the future. Innovations must fit within a system and include services as well as product.

CUTTING THE TIME TO INNOVATE[19]

A system to generate product change comparable to the three-day car is outlined in Figures 6-1 and 6-2. Current practice stops well short of that, but ability to quickly launch new products allows a contemporary company to be limited only by its customers' abilities to absorb change, rather than being unaware of their changing needs or unable to react to them.

The basic principle of the "ideal system" in Figures 6-1 and 6-2 is to minimize the feedback time to correct errors in designs, processes, and customer acceptance. The same principle runs through many of today's best practices in rapid product/process introduction that have been identified by a number of studies:

This ideal represents an excruciating challenge, but if no one ever starts experimenting to achieve it, nothing will happen. Henry Ford did not promote mass production merely by philosophizing about it.

1. Small, Dedicatetd, Experienced, Cross-Functional, Empowered Teams

It has become almost gospel to have multifunctional teams for "concurrent engineering." (These would be better named as concurrent product introduction teams. Engineering is only part of the total

FIGURE 6-1

SUMMARY: IDEALS OF COMBINING PRODUCT AND PROCESS DESIGN

The ideal product/process system achieves these service objectives:

Any product (in infinite variations), for
Any customer (in the segment of customers chosen to serve), at
Any location (within the geographic area served), in
Any volume (including lot sizes of one), and including
Any service (if the product/process system is a seamless extension of field operations, then everything is really a service), at
Any time (instantaneously if possible).

The ideal product/process system also achieves these objectives:

Environmental sustainability
Responsiveness to technological change
Economy (creates high margins at prices customers are willing to pay)

The principle is to minimize the feedback time to correct errors in designs, processes, and customer acceptance.

---

product introduction process.) Multifunctional, multicompany teams are the start of "virtual company" operations and reflect the fact that innovation is a total enterprise effort.

Technical competence and some experience on a team are vital, but so is a common bond among the members. Facilitators or even "social" meetings can help to coalesce inexperienced or immature teams, preferably early in the project.

Smaller "skunk works" teams located together perform better. The more people, and the more they are scattered, the more time and trouble in communicating, and the more difficult to really know others in the team. Geographic distance can be spanned electronically for many purposes, but emotional co-location is essential. Add critical customer and supplier personnel to the teams, and encourage contact

FIGURE 6-2

THE IDEAL PRODUCT/PROCESS DESIGN SERVICE SYSTEM

Product Design	*Product Creation Process*
Flexibility—unique to user	Design transmitted direct to work station
Adaptable while in use	Flexibility—any configuration possible within work space
	Set up times contained within work cycles
	Manufacturing and system technology is "migratable"
Designed for upgrade/retrofit	System is developed for remanufacturing as well as manufacturing
Durable/designed for remanufacturing	
Reliable/fault tolerant	Fail-safe features—nearly error free processes throughout
Maintainable/self-diagnosis features	
Safety in design	Improvement processes and improvement cycles "built-in"
Security systems built-in	
Zero discharge, zero residuals	Zero discharge, zero residuals

with customers and suppliers. (This is the beginning of "total material-use cycle process" teams.)

Retain key members on project teams through product launch. Pulling key people early causes delays for relearning and rebonding, and if the degree of technical adventure is limited, projects are more likely to remain on schedule. They may even be expedited. Better to have people concentrate on a project, finish it fast, and move on, than overcommitted to several projects at once and behind on all of them.

2. Bet Only on Known Technology for Product Development

Counting on a future technical breakthrough is betting on the discovery of unknowns. If every technical aspect has at least been proved in principle, the task is to make it work and integrate it into the product or process. That is challenge enough. More product introductions with less technical stretch in each is a much safer bet. Troubleshooting is problem solving rather than research.

Freeze designs and specifications. If a hot possibility occurs during development, save it for the next "model." Sony saves breakthroughs or new ideas from one project and carries them over into the next. Microsoft starts work on the next version of a software package before the one under development is released.

Freezing design requirements reduces the temptation to solve design problems by relaxing performance specifications. It eliminates excuses for missing schedule. It reduces reasons for needing engineering changes and winding up with an "as built" configuration substantially different from the original drawings.

3. Use Established Parts and Processes

For example, Black & Decker designs new appliances around common motor sizes. A short expression for this is "Design new products, not new parts." Design to an established, fast-flow production process, or develop the production and transport processes at the same time as the product (concurrent engineering). If the technical reach is limited, a new-product introduction can more likely be planned and scheduled almost as a routine activity.

4. Common Vision and Visibility

Consistent objectives throughout a project boost morale and simplify planning and communication, but changes always occur. Team members should be close enough to the customer to understand why objectives change, if they change. Leadership, sometimes political in nature, has the task of keeping objectives from being frivolously derailed. Senior managers restrain themselves from micromanaging. If they sustain the vision and promote an excellent process, they have done their job. Better to remind everyone that they are "launching the most efficient CFC-free refrigerator ever built" than grumble, "Another day, another corrosion test to run."

Excellent projects are almost self-controlled through visibility systems that allow a project to almost "run itself." Co-located teams are more easily managed with visibility systems, but if that is impossible, "war rooms" create a locus of activity that conveys the same feeling. Copious charts show everyone where the project stands. Drawings, conceptual mock-ups, or even prototypes on display illustrate where the project is going—and generate enthusiasm. Self-posted personnel boards show where everyone is. Meeting times and locations are posted. One of the most common Japanese practices is open access to drawing files, so anyone can easily determine which drawings are the latest revisions. An elaborate computerized version of the same idea in the Boeing 777 project allows anyone to regularly check how his or her piece of a complex design fits into the whole.

5. Define the Product Thoroughly

In detail, research the requirements of both primary and secondary customers. Translate these requirements into detailed design and process requirements. Quality Function Deployment (QFD) is now the most widely used methodology for doing this. *Everyone* needs to understand customer requirements, not just a market research department.

The hard part is not the QFD methodology. So far, American experience with QFD has been that human attitudes and organizational turf battles are impediments to satisfactory use. Addressing customer needs objectively, without second-guessing, takes dedication to managing by fact and experience asking the right questions. Oregon Cutting Chain, General Electric, and other companies have all found that QFD requires much more time in the up-front conceptual stage of a project in order to avoid later backtracking, amendments, and delays. Keeping the faith during this period is crucial because money is being spent with no results to show.

In this early stage, basic objectives may need rethinking. For example, have we defined the real users of the product? Do those customers' needs form a consistent set or do we need to redefine segments of the market?

Understanding customer requirements in detail is an easily underestimated challenge. Baldrige Quality Award examiners report that this is a weak point common to all applicants, and that even the winners are far from meeting it as well as they would like.

6. Robust Design

The classic example of robust design is Genichi Taguchi's original case of the Ina Tile Company. Since the tile were susceptible to stress-cracking from temperature changes in the kiln, the initial countermeasure was to carefully control the kiln heat, which was very expensive. Later, engineers found that a cheap additive made the tile much more resistant to heat stress, so no changes to the kiln were necessary.

An even earlier example of a design robust in use was the DC-3 airplane, long known as easy to fly, stable in many conditions, and adaptable to many kinds of service. Many are still flying, decades after production stopped. By contrast, the B-26 Marauder was briefly infamous as an unforgiving, cantankerous beast with a short, accident-marred service history. The team that designed the DC-3 fashioned every part of it with consideration for the whole rather than integrating a number of separately designed modules.

In the Ina Tile case, the problem was resolved after a statistical experiment. Today, experimental designs lead to robust designs with much less testing than decades ago, but the products are also more complex. In the DC-3 case, robust design began with simple, stable design objectives. Then the design was executed to incorporate big "margins" and "safety factors" so equipment could survive "worst-case" combinations of parts, abuses in operation, and conditions of use.

Robust design has now come to include many design "acronyms": design for assembly, design for manufacturability, design for disassembly, design for remanufacturing, design for maintenance, and others. Design for easy assembly is mostly a matter of considering numbers of parts and part geometry. Improvements beyond that depend on software features, systems fit, materials science, and fundamental chemistry.

All these "design fors" emphasize the need for broad integration of design considerations. The need to integrate electronics and control systems is obvious, but the mechanical counterpart is a concept called "power density," or the ability to transmit a greater force or absorb more stress by a smaller and smaller piece of material.[20] That capability is a function of the purity of the material, the treatment of its surface, the precision of its fabrication (or machining), its geometry, and the overall design of a mechanism. Integrated application of "power density" allows mechanical performance improvements an order of magnitude or more over 1950s concepts, often with fewer fabrication steps and therefore at lower cost. In vehicular design alone it promotes:

- Much lighter vehicles with big payloads and high fuel efficiencies.
- Smaller, streamlined vehicles with more interior space.
- Smaller brakes, quieter power trains, and smoother performance.

Young design engineers still often consider their work to only be introducing new technology. However, robust design must now consider many conflicting requriements in form, fit, and function. Design engineering seems to be reverting to a highly integrative human activity practiced by experienced masters.

7. Time as the Driving Measurement

Time must be the major measurement driving project teams. Once a product is defined, set firm time milestones. The time goal may be beyond control of the team, for example, making an industry show date or beating the release of a competing product.

Map, flowchart, and streamline the process. Many projects have a schedule and budget, but the process "just happens." The up-front time used to conceptualize a product and the overall process helps keep a project from degenerating into change-and-expedite at the end.

Pay special attention to improving critical path processes. For example, tooling time is one reason why Japanese auto companies' concept-to-market time is faster than their competitors'. Japanese tools are team-designed and team-built, sometimes on multiple shifts, using fabrication processes that have been studied to eliminate waste. American tools and dies are often individually designed, and then built by only one craftsman. (The best approach is eliminating the need for as many tools and dies as possible.)

It also saves time and corrections if tool builders, whether part of the same organization or supplier partners, are part of a design team from the beginning. That is, the use of time reduction as a guiding measurement stimulates most of the other practices advocated.

8. Use of Flexible Processes

Designing by computer, then transferring instructions straight to tooling or production (CAD/CAM) is a process that lends itself to easy revision of prior designs, but learning the software takes time, and using it well takes discipline. Another problem is systems integration so that every piece of software can communicate with the others.

One of the most complex CAD/CAM systems is Boeing's software for the 777 program. It takes six to nine months to learn, but it allows designers to try different ideas, many from Boeing customers, and integrates them into an extremely complex design. (Boeing's time from concept to rollout is not reduced, but the 777 must be much more service-ready at rollout than any previous model.)

Flexible production processes have always aided flexibility in product development, beginning by saving development time and money. If a transfer line is built special for one design engine, a major equipment project must be financed if the design configuration is changed.

American auto plants once retooled and substantially reequipped for new models. The new investment could be justified only by the expected volume of a new model (engineers could justify the big expenditures for automation). All that is changing rapidly. Now, automation must be flexible, meaning easily adaptable to design changes or volume changes.

Build prototypes on production equipment. With less technical adventure, the new-model introduction process can have extra steps taken out, and the ability to make changes is increased because the phenomena being dealt with are better understood.

The strategy is to experiment with new equipment on old products—one set of unknowns at a time. Then design new models to established processes, which is feasible except when a technical change is radical. The strategy is to evolve by many small steps, quickly taken. It beats long downtimes to gestate special new production systems. Meantime, the evolutionists are selling product.

9. End-of-Project Learning

Each project should be a learning experience not only for the team but for other teams as well. While cross-fertilization of ideas does not have to wait until project end, the key idea is to set aside time to objectively reexamine a project's history. Ideas that once failed may work a second time under different conditions—such as starting with higher-purity material. In fact, progress often depends on trying promising ideas from the past that failed. All too often humans don't really know the reasons for past failures or selectively recall them.

More and more lessons learned suggest that development organizations must end the illusion of intellectual self-sufficiency. The new demands of technology are forcing us to cooperate even when we are reluctant.

NOTES

1. Bruce Nussbaum, "For Noel Zeller, Good Design Is Just the Beginning," *Business Week*, 5 November 1990, 104–08.
2. Drew Poulin, "Long Delays Beset Inventors at Overtaxed Patent Office," *The Japan Times Weekly International Edition*, 27 August 1990, 1.
3. Earl W. Hildebrandt, "Supply Management in Minnesota," *Target* 5, no. 1 (Spring 1989): 22–29.
4. Bill Brunkhardt, "MOS 11 Facility and People Set the Standard for Manufacturing Innovation," *Tower Voice* (August 1991) 7. (Motorola employee newsletter).
5. *Manufacturing 21 Report*, Association for Manufacturing Excellence Research Report, 1990. Also the *21st Century Manufacturing Enterprise Strat-*

egy, Iacocca Institute, Lehigh University, Bethlehem, Pennsylvania, vol. 1, November 1991.

6. John Holusha, "American Snapshot, the Next Generation," *New York Times*, 7 June, 1992 3-1.

7. One of the best popular press articles on this subject is Robert Neff, and Bruce Nussbaum, "I Can't Work This Thing!" *Business Week*, 29 April, 1991, 58–66.

8. The concept of a "prosumer" is a major theme of the Japanese Manufacturing 21 scenarios. The basic concept was first described by Alvin Toffler in *The Third Wave* (New York: William Morrow, 1980).

9. Robert W. Hall and Jinichiro Nakane, *Flexibility: Manufacturing Battlefield of the 90s*, Research Report, Association for Manufacturing Excellence, Wheeling, Illinois, 1990, p. 106. Option packages were first promoted by Japanese auto companies to promote customer acceptance rather than make production life easier, as is usually believed by American car manufacturers.

10. "The Perils of Privatization," *Nature*, 8 August 1991, 460.

11. The concept of hardware and software margins was picked up from Russell Redenbaugh in his newsletter, "IBM, Apple, and the PCs," March 15, 1989, copyright by Cooke and Bieler, Philadelphia.

12. John Jewkes, David Sawers, and Richard Stillerman, *The Sources of Invention*, 2nd ed. (New York: W.W. Norton, 1969).

13. This problem is not new. Historical review of scientific research frequently indicates that data were fudged or fabricated.

14. Katherine Bishop, "U.S. Backs Researcher in Suing Ex-Colleague Over Accuracy of Data," *New York Times*, February 6, 1991, B-7.

15. Philip H. Abelson, "Federal Impediments to Scientific Research," *Science*, 8 February 1991, 605.

16. This was generally acknowledged by attendees at a Hudston Institute conference, "An Agenda for Leadership in Technology and Manufacturing," March 19, 1991.

17. James E. Ennis, Sheldon Krimsky, and Robert Weissman, "Academic-Corporate Ties in Biotechnolocy," *Science, Technology and Human Values* 16, no 3 (Summer 1991): 275–87.

18. Almost any conversation with entrepreneurs who have dealt with academic spin-offs produces a story about an academic who sends an invoice after the most minor of consultations.

19. This synopsis was derived from the work of Stephen Wheelwright, Kim Clark, and Takashiro Fujimoto; Harvard University; Joseph Blackburn, Vanderbilt University; Roger Schmenner and John Muth, Indiana University; Steven R. Rosenthal, Boston University; and Clement Wilson, University of Tennessee. Several concepts were obtained from presenters at the Time-to-

Market Seminar sponsored by the Association for Manufacturing Excellence in Seattle, Washington, April 16–17, 1991. In particular, the organization of points was adapted from an extensive survey on this subject conducted by the General Electric Company and presented at that seminar by Gerard Hock.

20. Robert L. Liebensperger, "Power Density: Product Design for the 21st Century," *International Journal for Technology Management*, 1991, pp. 216–24. (Special Publication on the Role of Technology in Corporate Policy).

7

THE OPEN SYSTEM—
LEARNING TO BE
A NONSELLER

THE ASSOCIATION FOR MANUFACTURING EXCELLENCE HAS BEEN NOTED FOR holding one-and-a-half-day workshops at host-company facilities. During the first half-day the host explains its improvement process and its goals. The second half-day, visitors tour the working areas and talk with workers. The third half-day is a continuous-improvement session. Visitors share how they are tackling the same situations as their host. Both individually and in groups, they offer ideas to the host for further improvement. Over time the focus of the workshops has shifted from techniques to the human relationships that allow new practices to be successful.

The success of a workshop depends on establishing an open dialogue. The host has the right to exclude direct competitors. The host work force may not tell everything, but they come close. It is impossible to coordinate a deceptive pitch in detail in an open visit through a host facility.

If a workshop host's work force is enthusiastic, its members immediately generate an open attitude among the visitors. Visitors begin to share their shortcomings—their secrets—with others present. If the same people attend several times and begin to trust each other, they open up a great deal more. Simple as the experience is, it is the beginning of an open system.

Only two workshops out of a hundred or more have been complete "busts." Both times, the host's marketing department took control of the meeting to present its company in the best light. People began walking out rather than listen to a sales pitch. By its very nature, a sales presentation in such a setting is an act of distrust. The people doing the work might not disguise the business's shortcomings, so management doesn't trust them. The hearers are not trusted. They might abuse any knowledge of shortcomings to scare away potential customers, or worse.

By contrast, an operations facility with nothing to hide may become a marketing tool in itself if prospects are taken to the working areas. If workers in shops and offices simply explain how they handle the customer order they are working on at the time, that is often enough to clinch a deal. Williams Technologies is only one of a number of companies that have let the facts and their workers do the selling. In contrast to a sales pitch, an open system depends on visible evidence, verifiable facts, and the opportunity to directly check many processes.

The Quest for the Open System

The quest for an open computer system began as soon as communication between computers became possible, but commercial traditions are based on closed human systems. In open-system computing, machines and software should interact in a network just as telephones do, but both the technical problems and the human problems are more challenging.

Most telephones in the world can now be connected, but the parties on each end may not understand each other. Human integration is as important as integrating computer networks. An open human system has several connotations: Anyone in the system can communicate with anyone else, and visibility systems are the norm. Structures, roles, and status systems are not rigid, although they also cannot be amorphous, lest all activity turn to chaos. The criteria and opportunities for entering and leaving the system are known; it's not a secret society. Access to information is minimally restricted. Just as important, information to assist idea generation or performance improvement is assiduously gathered and disseminated.

THE CONSEQUENCES OF CLOSED SYSTEMS

While none of us can be omniscient, the consequences of choosing to be aware of only a small fraction of the world is self-enforced ignorance. Believing that we are the center of knowledge makes us like the ancient Chinese, who believed that the farther distant from the imperial court a thing was, the more barbaric it was. It's a condition of limited perception, not a limitation of native brainpower, a distinction made famous in a different context by Joel Barker's popularization of scientific paradigms.[1]

A number of observations common to almost anyone with experience in the manufacturing world illustrates the point. Competent engineers have started a company, but they paid little heed to cash-flow projections and found themselves unable to borrow as sales took off. Robot enthusiasts have believed that a highly automated plant must be "better" in some sense, although casual observation showed that manual operations were equal in quality and used fewer people and far less equipment. (GM, IBM, and several other large companies provided the world with examples of this during the 1980s.) Sears believed that rewarding service writers at its car-repair stores on the basis of parts sold would boost sales, but management never believed complaints of overcharging until California regulators began to shut down stores.

Beginning about 1980, many Americans began looking for the reasons behind Japanese economic success, so that now almost everyone is a Japan expert of sorts. Most observers began by believing that the Japanese advantages must be confined to a few phenomena.

In the early 1980s, financiers toured Japanese factories but failed to grasp the significance of much of what was before their own eyes. Seeing few robots and very simple equipment, they concluded that the advantages must be sweatshop labor—or quality circles—or "unfair" trade practices. A decade later, observers began to conclude that the advantage started with development of children and continued into many different detailed practices. (No observer can grasp the scope and impact of a system crafted over a lifetime in a single short visit.)

Even today, experts fail to see the interdependencies in the total Japanese manufacturing system. For example, some concentrate only on fast prototyping because it contributes to fast product introduction and is therefore strategic. However, rapid new-product deployment is impossible without a shop-floor system amenable to it, a highly observant cadre studying customers, a system for cultivating highly capable people to work as a team, and on and on.

Failing to see is, in many ways, failing to share. Sharing is learning not to sell. That's contrary to most formulas for success, which teach that everyone must sell themselves, always.

"Selling" is not the same as marketing. Marketing is carefully finding the right used car to suit a customer whose needs you have carefully studied. Selling is pressuring a customer to buy any used car of unknown pedigree. Selling does not need to be deceptive, but to many people, the term has come to have that connotation. Marketing continues to build trust; one-shot "selling" doesn't.

Learning to participate in improvement processes is inseparable from learning to trust other people—not all of them, but some of them. Learning to base actions on data is as much derived from having trusted sources of data as on learning the processes.

Having to "sell" in a scientific field wastes scientific talent and money. Defining such waste is literally impossible, but it certainly impedes open discussion. For example, a behind-the-scenes battle has been raging since 1989 over the orthodoxy that AIDS is exclusively caused by the HIV virus. An anonymous federally funded AIDS researcher has been quoted as saying, "I'd bet my professional reputation that something more than HIV is involved in this disease, but I wouldn't bet my grants, my ability to work."[2]

If such problems exist in scientific fields, many times more problems must exist for people under commercial time pressure to decide what customers do or do not want. That's executive decision. Seemingly, time and funding so often curtail the study of an issue that it is easy to simply lapse into not seeking data at all—to be deluded that the decision maker is at the center of the universe. In turn, the various factions to a dispute seek to control the information that reaches a presumed decision maker, just as courtesans once controlled access to the emperor of China. Trying to open a human system is not a new problem, nor has it been successfully overcome, even in scientific fields where we like to think that "pursuit of truth" is the supreme ideal. An open system is a supreme human challenge. Nothing suggests that it will ever be a human achievement to take for granted.

Learning to place trust in someone else takes time. We must see evidence of their performance. Attempts to shortcut the trust-building process fly in the face of human nature. Combat troops thrown together for the first time have to gain confidence in each other even if they are all seasoned veterans. Only in very unusual circumstances will people "bare their souls" to strangers.

The High Cost of Distrust

A flap over the drug Clozaril includes several points about trust, open systems, and control of a cycle of material use (as in Chapter 5). Clozaril treats symptoms of schizophrenia more effectively than older drugs and with fewer side effects—except that about 2 percent of its recipients risk fatal destruction of their white blood cells. Therein lies the flap.

Clozaril originated at Case Western Reserve University but is produced and marketed under a three-year contract by Sandoz Pharmaceutical. Sandoz initially required all patients to use a contracted laboratory to have their blood tested weekly, claiming that its lab's test process was fail-safe. Without it, they cannot be sure that patients are properly monitored. Clozaril itself is estimated to cost $2,000 per year, compared to about $600 per year for older drugs. The test service adds about $7,000 per year. Most users cannot pay $9,000 a year, and neither will the government, so only a small percentage of schizophrenia cases are treated.

Interestingly, Sandoz distributed the drug in Europe through national health care systems without requiring use of the test service. It claims that high-stakes litigation is less likely there if a slipup occurs (for example, a patient is not monitored closely or a false test result occurs).

Naturally, American physicians and hospitals were upset. A white cell count costs only $10. Sandoz rejected plans for physicians to send in test results in return for another week's dosage, fearing that the consequences of even a few false test results from independent labs would leave Sandoz exposed to high liability anyway. Physicians and hospitals fear that Sandoz wants to take away their control of patient monitoring—monopolistic, they say, meaning that the $7,000 lab charge is beyond what is needed to assure control of the process. The effect on physicians' fees was not mentioned.[3]

In time, every state in the union joined in a federal lawsuit on behalf of their state-funded medical programs. Sandoz settled amid denunciations that their approach was intolerable. Although the legal heat emitted little enlightenment, the case suggests several problems with trust, open systems, control of product-use cycles, and the offering of a total service:

1. The quality of an overall service, not just a product, must be assured.
2. Fear of regulations and legalities assure only a minimum level of competence. It does not build trust in excellent performance.
3. Regulation promotes control, but control does not promote open communication or improvement processes.
4. Sandoz's price covered intellectual capital—and then some, perhaps—but it mostly covered an extremely high cost of distrust.
5. The objection to control of a total service cycle is lack of open entry—fear that a "monopoly" will become both inept and unfair.

The case would have been more interesting had two companies been licensed to make and market Clozaril. Then, two competing service cycles could have been established, and they might even have learned from each other. The pricing would probably still have been high enough to pay for R&D. However, most drug companies would think that is crazy, for most new drugs are marketed as exclusive monopolies, the risks hang heavy, and the soul of those enterprises is confined by the need to compensate risks with a high ROI.

Although drugs are a somewhat unique product, and Clozaril presents a unique risk, the situation still illustrates the problems when companies attempt to control service cycles. Those that have closely controlled their service generally have not had partners in the process. For example, when IBM went into personal computers, designing the machine was not as big a challenge as the change from personal contact service to impersonal sales through third parties. Dragged more and more into open-system computing, the company has not figured out how to retain the service supremacy for which it has long been noted.

There are many reasons for control of service cycles: increased environmental concerns, stiff performance requirements, and high customer expectations. Control of service in an open system requires a basic shift in thinking—from defensive postures to aggressively working with partners to overcome the problems. That is a different soul of enterprise.

Why Cooperate in an Open System

The reasons to cooperate continue to increase. One is the risk and expense of research. Environmental need-to-know situations with products or on work sites is another. Lack of worker flexibility has become an obvious impediment not only to efficient shop-floor operations but in offices and elsewhere. For example, inadequately prepared associates taking orders from customers can be a disaster—one reason why companies with poorly trained employees do not trust them.

Transactions across boundaries add waste and cost; they promote isolation, not communication. To promote expertise, one organization (or formal company) concentrates on the functional characteristics of electronic circuit design, another on the chemistry of printed circuit boards, and so on. Boundaries promote specialization but inhibit integration of effort and concentration on the end customer. Smooth integration across boundaries requires opening systems through cross-functional teams, using common visibility systems—and not least—sharing a common "vision."

A common set of codes or regulations—same air control system, same standards for homogenized milk, same telephone communication codes—are a start toward an open system. Common communication standards are very helpful, but if adopted with a regulatory mentality, they result only in minimal compliance and minimal disclosure. Regulations force only those below a minimal standard to improve performance. The major reason for an open system is very fast improvement to performance levels well above a minimum tolerated. Open systems promote rapid learning.

Limits to an Open System

The virtues of open-system organization cannot be promoted lightly, for the consequences of some kinds of full disclosure hang heavy. By wiping someone's arrest record clean, a judge removes a stigma. So does erasing evidence of a shaky history from someone's credit file. Disregarding a student's prior failures gives him or her an opportunity to start over. Official forgetfulness of a working associate's past errors is often an action co-workers should take. Very few of us want to be branded for life by one or two indiscretions.

The United States in particular has a long history of giving many people a new opportunity. Tolerating telemarketers, ticket scalpers, and punk rockers is part of that legacy. Selling themselves a new chance in life has been the way most people tugged at their own bootstraps. That new chance often means selling a service never before performed or a product not yet made. At some point almost every innovation requires selling people an idea they have never before tried.

In the popular view, selling "a pig in a poke" is part of free-market economics. Learning processes, improvement processes, or management by fact are not generally considered in free-market theory. Unfortunately, the need for high-performance service and manufacturing requires some modification of existing practices and expectations. The excesses of overselling have been suppressed (not stopped) by regulation. Virtually all high-performance business is regulated by licensing and inspection. Not just anyone can operate an airline or manufacture heart pacemakers, but regulation does not stimulate striving for ultimate performance. The highest-performance, highest innovation-rate (not just idea-rate) business requires the utmost in human organization, and that requires some form of open-system arrangement.

At the same time, everyone cannot suddenly convert to an open-system approach. Some will never be able to do it. Those that can will have to migrate into it. However, public policy must recognize the twenty-first–century requirements for high-performance service and industry.

LEARNING ORGANIZATIONS
AND LEARNING COMPETITION

Both Peter Senge and W. Edwards Deming decry management by control. Deming seems rather extreme about it at times. After all, without a modicum of budgetary discipline, for instance, most organizations contemplate a short existence. However, even when keeping budgets, a controller can either keep every subgroup's numbers relatively secret from each other or manage budgets as an open document. Anyone can view anyone else's numerical targets—and their success in meeting them.

It's not as easy as it sounds. Production managers pinching every penny will naturally resent promotion money being "blown" by marketers. The easy way out is not to disclose how much marketing is spending. The existence of an open system presumes the existence of open minds—that most people have a nonparochial view of the business and of their industry. It's the development of the nonparochial view that is tough, but that development begins with relatively open information.

Fast, effective improvement is perhaps the foremost reason for open systems across all kinds of human boundaries. The pursuit of improvement processes requires trust between parties to find the root causes of problems and deal with them, and the pursuit of a problem should not be limited in scope. The "learning organization" movement recognizes that people working in any position need to deal directly and simply with problems. This too sounds much easier to do than it is.

Senge's original description of a learning organization cross-pollinated continuous improvement practices with systems theory. Learning begins with a shared vision—not the same as a vision statement written by the CEO. A vision is a shared process of examining over and over what we really want to achieve. Otherwise, individuals interpret a vision statement however they choose.

Another characteristic of the learning organization is that it tests existing methods. This is the first stage or two of problem seeking as described by most stepwise improvement processes (Chapter 3). The emotional part is questioning existing patterns of thought.

A third characteristic is a systems viewpoint. That is a nonparochial view coupled with systems sense—analyzing interactions and processes rather than being driven by events—learning to examine what is happening rather than searching for the guilty (and being a hero fixing one crisis after another).

Boundary issues complicate problem solving because every little group acts in its own narrow self-interest. Each maximizes blame shifting and minimizes problem solving. The author's experience is that people in overcontrolled, narrowly bounded organizations spend their entire working lives circling essentially the same issues, nagging each other, and seldom resolving anything. After a time, they never intend to resolve anything. The disputation process itself becomes the substance of life. Often they give up, simply referring to a "a cruel market" or to "the unchangeable nature of the beast."

Take the example of an engine remanufacturer. First, if the oil is not drained before shipment from a junkyard stripper, leakage during shipment starts arguments, some with the shipper, some with the EPA. The history of the engine is unknown, so it may not be suitable for remanufacture. If the remanufactured engine is sold back to a dealer, how and where it is installed are unknown, so only the most limited assurances can be given about its performance. (Customers have complained of failure after only two months—of nonstop use in a dusty foundry with no record of either air-filter or oil-filter changes.)

Engine remanufacturers must keep up with the original manufacturer's (OEM's) changes in specification, but why should an OEM trust a competitor with its latest bill of material on an old engine? When push comes to shove, is the OEM legally liable if an engine remanufactured by a third party undergoes a catastrophic failure? Furthermore, a remanufactured engine may carry a stronger warranty and have features (probably electronic) not on the original, so it may compete with new engines for some applications. Usually, the OEMs release information reluctantly.

Contrast that situation with Williams Technologies, a remanufacturer of transmissions in subcontracting partnership with OEM manufacturers such as GM Powertrain. Williams identifies the causes of failure of old GM transmissions it receives. GM not only advises Williams of new revisions on transmission configuration but assists with quality problems and with managing cores (old transmissions to be remanufactured). And the collaboration can be much improved.

These situations illustrate the paradox of open-system competition. A competitor represents an alternative to customers, but a competitor is not a no-holds-barred enemy. In fact, many competitors *must* share technical information and adhere to common standards. The consequences of not cooperating with a competent competitor are unpleasant, though not as severe as revealing marketing plans to them. If a remanufactured engine or transmission fails because the OEM failed to disclose a known critical wear factor on a part, with whom will the customer be most angry?

Real competition is in execution of service to the customer. Just as in athletic games, one can see what opponents are doing but must execute well enough to beat them, or at least keep up with them. If the ethos of competition as superior execution prevails over the ethos of competition using secret practices (hoarding of intellectual capital), an open system will also prevail. All the competitors learn from each other, thereby strengthening all the competitors as a whole. At some point, competitors may all intellectually understand what to do. They cannot all learn to do it equally well, just as athletic teams cannot all perform equally well. When everyone is progressing rapidly, they steal ideas from each other (sometimes without admitting it) as madly and rapidly as possible.

In production areas a common experience has been finding people who have not seen any plant except their own in twenty years. They may read professional and trade publications and attend shows, but without actually seeing and experiencing how other people approach a similar business, they can be embarrassingly oblivious to simple work practices common elsewhere: how to position tools, how to move heavy loads, or how to lay out a cell.

An open system is certainly not devoid of politics or human emotions. The scientific arena is one of the most open human work environments, but speeding scientific learning is sometimes a harsh process. An interesting scientific incident from the 1970s illustrates this.

Professor Joseph Weber of the University of Maryland published in respected journals of physics the results of a series of experiments that seemed to substantiate the existence of high fluxes of "gravitational radiation"—extremely weak waves similar to light or electromagnetic radiation. These waves may result from changes in the length of a very heavy bar caused by differential gravitational attraction between its parts, detectable by extremely sensitive sensors and a highly efficient signal amplifier. However, such experiments are always subject to considerable error. Arguments between different experimenters centered on the minutiae of apparatus setups and analytical processes.

Weber seemed to be convincing many colleagues of the existence of higher-than-expected gravitational radiation. Scoffers in the scientific community circulated informal critiques withheld from the official journals. Squabbling camps used the evidence as ammunition in logical forays loosed on each other. Finally, a doubting colleague learned from one of Weber's computer programmers that his analysis program contained mistakes. Nobody wanted to censure a prominent scientist publicly, and the colleague feared that if he debunked Weber without using any experimental results of his own, his views would not be accepted. So he ran a small experiment to obtain some negative results in order to legitimize a direct attack on Weber. The debunkers explained that they did not want the arguments to drag on for twenty years.[4]

Unlearning is the harsh part of any learning process. Position and prestige are at risk. Giving up cherished beliefs and old habits is having to choke on one's own ego. Yet that is exactly what most of us in manufacturing have to do today. Learning from each other creates a social setting in which unlearning is sometimes brutal, but if others around are going through the same emotions, it is easier to tolerate.

A learning attitude is probably the most important attribute of a quick study. Quickly giving up old practices upon seeing someone else with better ones is the mark of a person to whom performance is more important than position. Lack of a learning attitude, rather than mental rigidities resulting from age, is probably why substantial change too often must wait for a few funerals.

The intellectual counterpart to the Chinese belief that the world centered on the imperial court is the belief that learning consists of what we have learned. It is a professional hazard to professors and consultants who make their living by dispensing wisdom to others. A learning experience very often is accompanied by backing away from a position previously argued in public. Too many retractions are bad for the professional reputation.

A vested interest in "intellectual capital" is one reason why consultants (and perhaps faculty members) have a hard time reforming according to their own managerial advice. Difficulties are too easy to blame on inept clients, and defensive reasoning comes naturally. Many highly capable, previously successful senior managers in other types of companies also have the same emotional blocks.[5]

The toughest part of learning anywhere is creating the setting in which it can happen. Any group of trusted souls who can commiserate their pain and embarrassment with this kind of learning process will accelerate actual change. Rapid learning consists of big changes accompanied by elation, frequently followed by having one's nose rubbed in a humbling experience. The proper attitude is one of always being a student, never a guru—never having found the "center of the earth."

Benchmarking

One of the most popular versions of open-system learning today is called *benchmarking*, a term coined by Xerox for a process it began in the early 1980s. It's usually explained with one of those four- or five-step charts. So many people have suddenly become benchmarking experts that defining the practice has become a challenge. After interviewing many different companies to find a common definition, Michael Spendolini proposed the following: "Benchmarking is a continuous, systematic process for evaluating the products, services and work processes of organizations that are recognized as representing best practices *for the purpose of organizational improvement*."[6] (Italics added.)

Some people confuse benchmarking with competitive or strategic analysis—doing a strengths-weaknesses-threats-opportunities review. Others confuse it with reverse engineering—doing a tear-down analysis of competitive products. The best benchmarking is followed by *action* to make operating practices better. Much of it is conducted by those who do the work. They must be convinced that someone, somewhere, does a better job. They must be moved to match or exceed performance seen elsewhere. That is, effective benchmarking is see-do learning.

Benchmarking is part of an improvement process. A company should first have an internal improvement process before undertaking benchmarking forays (as contrasted with learning visits to top companies done mostly for shock effect). Comparing measurements is important, but not nearly as important as improvement of attitudes and operations.

Here are some examples of benchmarking process comparisons: how to improve stockroom inventory record accuracy to 99.9 percent; how to avoid mutilage in auto assembly (inadvertent scratches or dents caused by workers themselves); how to reduce the setup time on a gear hobber; how to reduce the time to close the accounting books at a fabrication plant.

These seem to be simple undertakings. So why do experienced lecturers on benchmarking spend so much time explaining what benchmarking is not rather than what it is? Reasons begin with benchmarking teams not being prepared—not having an improvement process and therefore little performance data or methodology to share with prospective partners. Some are not sufficiently focused. For example, the group that wanted to benchmark the accuracy of inventory data had spent little time considering whether their stockroom was needed at all. The group interested in the gear hobber consisted of two engineers who had never set up their own machine, so they did not ask questions critical to a setup worker.

The Japanese have long performed their own versions of benchmarking, although they never called it by that name. The first trip to a plant or other facility may just be a scouting trip to build friendships and see if something there is of interest. Suppose the scouts are attracted to a foundry pouring line that is instrumented to predict its own maintenance needs. On the second trip, three or more people may visit. Each has a specific assignment: an item of data to obtain, a few questions to ask. The team will ask the same questions of anyone they meet, not relying on just one response. After the visit they attempt to put the picture together. If a key part is missing, they ask to return. Finally, they will attempt to adapt and replicate the system seen in their own context—to DO something with it. Because of the not-invented-here syndrome, an American team is more apt to pooh-pooh another company's processes or try to top them before fully understanding what they are doing.

A second of many benchmarking failings is not recognizing it as a two-way street. At a minimum, a team on a visit should bring data.

Better, they should invite their host to send a team to their operations. When it's well done, benchmarking is a mutual learning and improvement process. It depends on a relatively open environment. It also depends on cultivating the right attitude for rapid learning and improvement.

One of the better exercises that a new benchmarking group can undertake is to examine and copy a successful version of a specific improvement process itself. The term "benchmarking" implies that methods and techniques are being learned or exchanged. However, the key to successful exchange is learning how to learn—acquiring the open frame of mind to teach others and to rapidly use knowledge that we gain from them.

Precise comparisons of operating performance measurements mean little, but open knowledge of roughly comparable standard measurements will stimulate improvement. A printed circuit-board shop with a defect rate of fewer than ten parts per million will currently be pestered with requests for benchmarking visits. In the future, open knowledge of such data in a network of manufacturing partners will help give them confidence in each other.

At its best, benchmarking is only part of a mutual improvement compact between partners. In fact, even the best American companies are still far short of having vigorous, organized programs of exchange that push everyone to improve as rapidly as possible. Many are acquiring the technical potential to operate according to a twenty-first–century vision. Few are yet acquiring the human potential.

CHARACTERISTICS OF AN OPEN SYSTEM

Open Computing Systems

In an open computing system, all the machines can talk to each other—somehow. Machines may use the same bit-level codes or achieve compatibility though more complex translations, such as a full seven-level architecture connection as described by the open system for interconnection (OSI) model of the International Standards Organization (ISO). Those who are not deeply immersed in computers quickly lose interest in the details by which machines communicate, but the strategic implications of connectivity are enormous.

As computers tend toward the UltraComm vision, most of them should become as compatible as telephones, but computers in 1992 are still far from that state. Computing companies are being dragged willy-nilly into telecommunications-type compatibility.

Any computing company interested in maximizing its profit potential still covets proprietary machines and proprietary software for a particular application (like an advanced Computer-Aided Design package). If a company could force an entire market segment to use its products, it could leverage its intellectual capital nicely. Beyond that, the ultimate intellectual capital monopoly would be a computer that could read everyone else's software but spew out code utterly unintelligible to any foreign machine. That strategic position was the ideal of a much fatter, preclone IBM.

A proprietary computer system is a closed system. Anyone wanting to use the computer or software must deal with the originator. In a totally open computer system:

1. Equipment is compatible.
2. Software is compatible.
3. Equipment and software are migratable. That is, as computer systems are upgraded, old data and application programs can be revised to be read and used at low cost.

The technical challenges of creating open systems are immense. Just a few of the challenges are maintaining coupling between data structures and procedures, maintaining documentation, and discipline in software maintenance. A programmer's rule of thumb is that after 1980s' software has been revised several times, the patching over so degrades it and the documentation is so complex that a new package had just as well be written.

One approach is to henceforth develop software with characteristics better suited to compatibility and migratability. One promising approach, not yet totally proved, is object-oriented programming (OOP). OOP achieves a new level in user-friendliness and has many useful characteristics such as self-documentation. But it hogs memory and processor capacities. However, if hardware capabilities increase another order of magnitude, the primary consideration will shift to effectiveness of applications use rather than efficiency of hardware use. Something like OOP should come to pass.

Despite the incompatibility of much hardware, most experts in 1991 asserted that in manufacturing applications, hardware capabilities were "two years or more" ahead of software.[7] More than that, Americans were coming off a time when computers had been prominently misused in manufacturing. Companies had constructed complex material requirements planning (MRP) systems before simplifying the processes they were supposed to plan and control. Companies that had totally automated manufacturing floors had learned that they needed to pay more attention to fundamentals first. The standard caution to manufacturing engineers was: simplify, integrate, then automate—both on shop floors and in supporting systems.

Automating the Past

As Thailand was beginning its industrial boom in the early 1980s, a building materials company decided it was time to computerize. After due study the company purchased an IBM mainframe because it could rely on Big Blue to make it work. It hired experienced programmers from India to write software that worked.

The programmers did as the managers bade them, flow-diagramming and coding existing business processes just as the users described them. After the usual debugging flapdoodle, computer-generated documents began replacing handwritten versions.

In due course, management began to note that the computer and its associated activity cost much more, but none of the converted operations seemed easier, simpler, or less expensive. Some concluded that only companies in advanced industrial regions were rich enough to afford computers. Few could think that they had to change their concept of business operations.[8]

Our state of development in the United States today makes it obvious that the people of the Thai company wanted to automate their past experience—minimally disturb familiar thought patterns, status systems, and business relationships—and minimize known risk. However, not so many years ago, this thinking was common in American companies, too, and in many ways it still is. People that have used computers for decades still are substantially influenced by engineering and business practices of the past. Creating new systems and bringing them to acceptance among the business community as a whole is a big social-improvement process. The chances of success are higher by realizing that new technology applied to old thinking does not advance much from the past. Unfortunately, when these changes are discussed in detail, they seem trivial, so changes are not pushed vigorously.

The challenge of creating a new form of business and manufacturing is enormous. We seem determined to use computers to complicate rather than simplify. The history of materials requirements planning illustrates the problem. In the 1960s bullpens of human planners approximated future requirements for thousands of parts, then expedited assembly shortages. In the 1970s, computers allowed planners to time-phase future parts requirements much more precisely—if the forecasts and on-hand data were any good. Sloppy data transactions undermined MRP until its importance was recognized. Soon, technical presentations on MRP were augmented by discussions on training and human change. Clerical accuracy and working to plan takes a different mind-set than wing-and-a-prayer expediting.

The second generation of MRP systems connected production planning and control with accounting, order entry, and other systems. However, the effort only automated the management of manufacturing processes that took place much as they had in the past. Japanese competitors drove home the lesson that basic manufacturing concepts also had to change. A scow with a computer on board will not win a race with a yacht.

Computer applications in equipment and elsewhere broadened to become the concept of computer integrated manufacturing (CIM). The Society of Manufacturing Engineers first diagramed CIM as a wheel having a hub of systems architecture that integrated manufacturing functions much as they had always been done. Now, the diagram is starting to be called a computer-integrated *enterprise* wheel, but the diagram still assumes CIM in companies organized much as at present. A two-dimensional diagram is probably inadequate to convey the concept.

In consumer banking, computing at first automated the green eyeshade—check proofing and statement printing. Credit-card processing, ATMs, and automated telephone response units soon followed. Competition prompted financial institutions to complicate their computer-powered services. Instead of a checking account and a savings account, an individual can now have a dozen or more different kinds of accounts, each including daily interest, fees per transaction, and automatic payments and receipts until the reports run beyond the capacity of individuals to track what is happening to them.

The well-connected can now perform many financial transactions from a home terminal using networks crafted to thwart hackers. In the system, each of us is now represented by clumps of data constantly jiggered by transactions. Too seldom asked is how many transactions are utter waste. The human side of such an open system is far more challenging than software and data highways.

As computers came to be linked by telecommunications, companies began developing electronic data interchange (EDI). The acronym generally refers to interchange of logistics or financial data rather than CAD/CAM data (design information). Ideally, computer systems should talk directly to each other without anyone rekeying data. That happens in far fewer than half of all cases thus far, so EDI accomplishes little more than fax machines. Old systems that began separately do not migrate into compatible form very quickly, even when the users intend to marry them.

Unfortunately, the human problems exceed those of computer systems. Many EDI users still think that their company is the center of the universe and therefore all other systems can become compatible with *theirs*. More than computer codes must match. Bar codes (or codes read from smart chips in more advanced cases) must be compatible. The auto industry and several others use Code 39 as a standard, but the retail bar code is UPC. Beyond that, transaction sets, data-field sizes, formats—and item identification numbers—must be compatible.

For example, GM's number for a radiator cap is not the same as its suppliers' numbers for the same cap, so numbers need to be translated to communicate between the systems, and the translator has to be updated with each engineering change. If GM has three different suppliers for the same cap, there are three translators to update. And then there are the potential suppliers of radiator caps for the aftermarket. The long rows of cross-referenced parts manuals in auto-parts stores were part translators in paper form rather than by computer?[9] There has to be a simpler way to identify a radiator cap for a 1984 Olds Cutlass Supreme. Despite all the problems, the number of registered EDI users has nearly doubled each year since 1987.[10]

The problems of transmitting design data are similar. A half dozen or so CAD/CAM software packages are in popular use. Moving data from one system to another takes relatively expensive conversion software at best, and then one is always concerned whether some little fluke in the conversion will introduce an error.

The use and transmission of CAD/CAM software (sometimes called Technical Data Interchange [TDI]) is now creating data accuracy issues somewhat like those in the early days of MRP. A survey of Michigan tool-and-die shops revealed a variety of problems in the CAD data received from customers. In 51 percent of cases the tool-and-die shop had to "fix" the data. In 25 percent of cases the tool-and-die shop *had to completely re-create the data set*. Possibilities for error are high. One cause of these problems is system incompatibility. A second is designer error. The designer shows a line in the wrong overlay of a computer drawing, for instance. The human eye may not pick up the error, and if the computer drawing is used directly to create cutting-machine instructions, a very expensive mistake is created. These problems alone were estimated to add about 25 percent to the lead time to build tooling, and tooling is almost always on the critical path of new-product development.[11]

Of course, one approach—not pleasant to tool-and-die builders—is to minimize the amount of tooling to be built. A second is to find inherently simpler and less-expensive ways to create tooling. A third is to find fast, fail-safe ways to build current concept tooling, putting more emphasis on practices to improve data communication and data integrity. (An engineer can dimension a drawing such that it is technically correct, but the data are so poorly presented that the interpreter, whether man or machine, can easily be misled.) Changing some companies' reward systems would help. Paying designers for the number of drawings produced does not encourage them to communicate in any fashion.

The problems of trying to create Computer Integrated Manufacturing are now becoming much better appreciated. Many of them are human in origin. Proprietary systems are devised so that each company can maximize its own profit potential. The operating systems for new hardware keep changing, so applications programming must be altered in response. So much application programmer time must be expended in patchwork to keep the system integrated that programmers have little time to thoroughly learn the phenomena their program is supposed to address. Often, different software suppliers, wary of losing a tidbit of intellectual capital, must be dragged into the same room by a customer and forced to collaborate in making their systems compatible. Customer manufacturing engineers resent being "shown up" by suppliers. Production personnel kept out of the process during its gestation are furious when a half-debugged system is thrust on them. Education gets short shrift in the budgets.[12]

The practical job of bringing twenty-first–century manufacturing visions into reality consists of human integration. Many of the issues are detailed, nitty-gritty human miscommunications and system incompatibilities. Congress cannot pass a bill and make them go away. Thousands of individuals have to give up a small part of their uniqueness in order to communicate.

Global thinkers seldom want to dwell on such thoughts. Devising the strategy for a lone company seems global enough, and if a good strategy is well promoted, surely growth will follow. By contrast, fast-trackers seldom consider assignment to an industry standards committee as a plum. But in the end, the rules for future business competition and the media for future problem solving will be established by working out the detailed ways in which humans communicate using computers and the ways computers communicate by themselves.

An open-system ethos and organization seems a bit strange, but a great deal of collaboration has taken place in many industries for years. Competitors are rivals only for the attentions of the same customers. Their collaboration is bounded only by the narrowest considerations for rival customer service. For example, a number of engineers from customer airlines are on the project development team for the new Boeing 777. The only information withheld is the cabin configuration of each airline's orders, which would tip off rivals about the kind of service the airline plans in the future. All other information is essential to a top-performance, safe airline service.

Finally, in truly open-system enterprise, everything is not broadcast, but a great deal of information is accessible to anyone who needs it, or sometimes who just wants it. For instance, pay is not a secret, including pay of top officers. Neither are margins, prices, profits, product failures, or performance reviews. Often such data is kept under wraps on the grounds that exposing it creates more problems than management has time to deal with. Not least, the bottom line is a matter of general knowledge, and hopefully, of general concern.

OPEN-SYSTEM ENTERPRISE
AND THE NATURE OF COMPETITION

An enterprise is a coalition of individuals and groups that serve the same customers and manage the same cycle of material use. It might or might not be one company as we think of it today. An open system within such an enterprise signifies a different spirit. When companies consider themselves to be independent fortresses and each competes to grab as much bounty as it can, they stunt the notion of an open system. Only when the concept of competition implies superior performance to customers rather than greater resource use do open systems make sense.

If competitors use contrasting learning processes, each trying to improve quality of life using limited resources, they become more like rival schools than rival land barons—contentious, but not mortal enemies. Trying to achieve more with less takes more finesse and cooperation than trying to maximize possessions and expand control. Maximizing customer satisfaction is consistent with maximizing growth and profit if resources are expanding. If resources are limited, maximizing customer satisfaction requires collaboration with many partners to expand and extend know-how as much as possible. This shift is a nonlinear philosophic change.

For example, consider the nature of the operations to service a fleet of remanufacturable cars for fussy customers compared with Henry Ford's goal of selling a car to every American household. Ford's vision in its day stimulated a new kind of design and migration to a different concept of manufacturing—and toward different manufacturing-centered economic institutions to carry it out. Now the three-day, remanufacturable car and visions like it are equally daunting. A different kind of motivation, a new process-centered mentality, and an open system of process partners are needed to migrate toward that vision. The enormity of this transformation is signified by the current lack of words to describe something never before undertaken.

The technology changes are not difficult to comprehend. The motivation, the process changes, and the open-system network are a much bigger challenge.

Why Have Open-System Enterprise?

Few people dispute that we should have computer-integrated enterprise, but they envisioned it as current companies linked by computer. ("Enterprise integration" is currently a stock consulting phrase meaning to make a given company's islands of software communicate with each other.) A better question is whether we should have human enterprise integrated in a different way. If so, how?

Opponents of human enterprise integration argue that diversity is good for us and integrating into one great system stifles it. A quick romp through philosophy produces many rationales for that position. Here are some of the main ones:

1. First, independent entrepreneurs are diverse individuals who find solutions to many problems by working outside an industry system rather than being confined by it—sort of an economic and scientific biodiversity theory. Integrated systems would make it very difficult to introduce major change from outside.

2. A related argument suggests that integrated systems are not compatible with democratic government. Large numbers of people or organizations all tuned to the same channels might not be sufficiently independent of mind to have independent views or to vigorously promulgate them. (Similar arguments have been made about mass media networks.)

3. A collaborative approach to life is thought not to generate much human energy or motivation. True enthusiasm and excellence comes from competing "to grab the brass ring," not from having an

exclusive franchise or having to follow the same standard system. The same arguments are made about working for utilities or public schools. (This argument is based on the presumption of control mechanisms and lack of improvement processes that encourage creativity. Those suppressed go outside such a system.)

4. Finally, a supposition is that integrated enterprise simply would not give mavericks enough slack. Unless an individual is free to express himself in his own way, he is stunted. The very essence of a great painting, or even a cute cartoon, is that an individual must be free to represent his impressions, feelings, and positions in his own way or his unique contribution will never be known to anyone else. (However, mere self-expression goes nowhere in attempts to execute an innovation that is really a social process.)

Integrated enterprises should compete with each other. The form of organization will change, and the nature of competition will change, but it may be no less stimulating than freebooter competition for growth in resource use. In fact, the complexity of the new kind of competition should tax the whole nature of man more than the old. By far the biggest challenge of developing open-system enterprise is finding new forms of human organization. Computers only allow a different form of human integration.

A worldwide network of machines blasting digits at each other through fiber-optic hoses is technically an integrated system, but it may not be effective at all, just as early attempts at integrated automation were blunders. A great deal of human integration need not depend on computers at all. In both offices and factories, line-of-sight visibility methods have already proved to be excellent ways to communicate and to stimulate problem solving. Computer communication systems must be tools that humans use that are complementary to us.

Migration to this new form of enterprise will be difficult because the vision of it is still a shimmer in the distance, but clearly the toughest migration will be by people, not computers. The evolution of practices may take twists not seen today—especially not by productivity-conscious manufacturing managers functioning by the mass-production paradigm, or even the lean-manufacturing one.

For example, the objective of a delivery system may be to create more customer satisfaction in the spending of *their* time. Service in which the customers are participants hints that the social part of doing business may turn out to be very important. How many computer-literate retail bank customers will walk past an ATM just to be able to talk to a real person during a transaction? In the three-day car scenario, would the business turn on joyrides in simulators, complete with clubs and mock races in high-tech adult video arcades? The clubs themselves and the data from them could turn out to be the backbone of the business.

Some kinds of service defy much direct productivity improvement. Reading to a child is one of those. Doing the same thing by automatic means is no longer the same thing. The value to the "customer" is in who performs the service, how it is done, and the actual time taken.

In an open-system enterprise economy, much of the competition is based on service. Service process *delivery* can be radically improved by attacking waste, just as in manufacturing. However, if the core value-adding experience is social time, that time cannot be reduced by much and still satisfy customers. A higher-quality service experience is not the same as high-productivity service delivery.

In fact, one can make a case that as an open-system economy develops, resource waste will be reduced, but productivity improvement will hit a plateau. Suppose a great deal of work is done automatically, but most of the residual is one-on-one customer contact required by the human psyche or human learning. Improvement of human-contact productivity would probably be secondary to improving satisfaction with the service.

All these changes are nonlinear jumps in thinking. Just revising a production operation into a cell may reduce inventory an order of magnitude, and if quality problems are vigorously attacked, defect rates may decline just as dramatically.[13] Those kinds of changes are just preparation for takeoff into an open-system enterprise world.

We must migrate to a different kind of thinking to determine how life can be improved with resource use reduced at the same time. Usually, people must begin experiencing order-of-magnitude changes in a few activities before they can imagine radically different processes. That is, the mental sets slowly evolve through a series of problems until a fast-flow process is achieved. We are limited by our own speed of mental and experiential migration.

The stimulus for such a change is seldom just an abstract concept. Very few people have the tenacity to turn an abstract concept into something practical, even after a very powerful vision is presented. The new world must be built one step at a time. The difficult change is us, and the best we can hope for is rapid migration. Open systems are necessary to build trust. Holding back information is one of the major symbols of distrust.

NOTES

1. Joel Barker, "The Business of Paradigms," video distributed by Charthouse Clearing Corp. Barnesville, Minnesota.

2. Elinor Burket, "HIV: Is It a Dead End?" Knight-Ridder Newspapers, published in Sunday supplements on Sunday 20 January, 1991.

3. Lisa M. Kreiger, "Drug Comforts Schizophrenics—If They Can Afford It," *The Indianapolis Star*, 9 December, 1990, F-8. Reporting of the Clozaril case ran from the *Science News*, May 26, 1990, 137, no. 21, 334, until the lawsuits were settled per the *New York Times*, September 4, 1992, C-3.

4. H. M. Collins, *Changing Order* (Beverly Hills, CA: Sage Publications, 1985), pp. 79–111.

5. Chris Argyris, "Teaching Smart People How to Learn," *Harvard Business Review* 69, no. 3 (May–June 1991): 99–109.

6. Michael J. Spendolini, *The Benchmarking Book* (New York: AMACOM, 1992), p. 9.

7. From statements made by various experts at a conference, "An Integrated Approach to American Leadership in Science, Industry, and Trade," Hudson Institute, Indianapolis, Indiana, March 1, 1991.

8. From a personal story in a term paper by a Thai student who wished to remain anonymous and keep the company name anonymous.

9. Within the auto industry most of the progress toward EDI has been achieved through the various committees of the Automotive Industry Action Group. 26200 Lahser Road, Southfield, Michigan 48034

10. According to EDI Yellow Pages International, Dallas, Texas.

11. "CAD/CAM Data Problems and Costs in the Tool-and-Die Industry," Industrial Technology Institute and the Detroit Chapter of the National Tooling and Machining Association, Ann Arbor, Michigan, March 12, 1991.

12. *Flexible Assembly Systems: Insights Based on Experience*, one of the Blue Book Series by the Society of Manufacturing Engineers, Dearborn, Michigan, 1990.
13. The term "nonlinear" change applied to process thinking was originated by James Swartz. His concepts are detailed in *Innovative Business Systems*, forthcoming from Productivity Press, Cambridge, Massachusetts.

8

ASSOCIATES OF THE WORLD, ARISE!

OVER A CENTURY HAS PASSED SINCE KARL MARX AND FRIEDRICH ENGLES penned *The Communist Manifesto,* with its famous line "Workers of the world, unite." The Communist vision powerfully influenced the twentieth century, but it flopped because in practice, and often in spite of themselves, capitalists better stimulated worker responsibility. The Communists could not conceive of work as service—as something other than making use of natural resources by politically controllable means.

Both Communists and capitalists have difficulty accepting employees as managers responsible for the enterprise around them. Oblivious to the dead hand of state control, Marxists loved to point out that capitalist companies guided by the invisible hand of the market are internally organized first for control, then efficiency. The question seldom raised is, what kind of organization is designed for ultimate efficiency—then for control?

A challenge more formidable than either Adam Smith or Karl Marx dreamed is upon us: improving quality of life without explosive growth in overall resource use. Such a world is not possible without individuals motivated to exercise more foresight and responsibility than at present.

The level of responsibility must exceed that found by people who really work only of necessity. Simplistically, people are thought to work for money. Certainly no one works long without it, except in volunteer jobs, but few people possessed of a work ethic show up just for a paycheck. If the work does not fully engage them, they divert their primary interests and energies elsewhere.

Despite contrary evidence from the Hawthorne studies onward, many managers' practicing theory of human motivation remains you-work-I-pay. Harry Levinson called this carrot-and-stick philosophy of motivation "the jackass fallacy." When asked what was between the carrot and the stick, executives most often imagined a jackass.[1] That is, if subordinates are presumed to be controllable by reward and punishment, they are visualized in a jackass position. However, regarded as peers, subordinates are suddenly seen as having more complex motivations. An eye opener is loading more responsibility onto first-line supervisors and operative workers and moving them from jackass relationships into work teams—often called self-directed work teams.

Many managements today understand the advantage of responsibility at the operating level but cannot move beyond the acronym stage of empowerment. Calling everyone an associate symbolizes the sentiment, even if control is still detailed and autocratic. Self-directed work teams exist in name but not in spirit. When many managers have more than a hundred "direct reports," the shift may be sold as a way to eliminate cost and complexity by "outplacing" several layers of middle management and staff.

The more serious change is from top-down reward and recognition systems to more horizontal ones. They begin when managers listen to internal customers when evaluating subordinate performance. Organizational roles shift toward cross-functional organizations. Career paths in flat organizations hop across a checkerboard rather than climb a ladder. New forms of organization are becoming more participative, although the number of Chapter 11 filings suggest that the discipline of the capitalist system is as strong as ever.

This movement is the start of open-system enterprise. (Or network entrepreneurship, team capitalism, associate enterprise, or whatever name imparts the appropriate pizzazz.) The first steps toward this system are not perfect. The system will never be anyone's utopia. No system of human organization can be perfect. All it must do is be more effective for its time. In due course, if current experimentation continues, a better system should evolve.

The Trouble with Silos, Chimneys, and Pigeon Roosts

As the need for high-performance operations becomes apparent, most managers see that a hierarchical form of organizational control is inadequate. The inadequacies of hierarchies have in recent years been popularized by many colorful phrases: the functional silo syndrome (tall structures filled with smelly silage and separated by long distances), chimneys (similar connotation), the pigeon-roost phenomenon (droppings from each tier fall on all those below), and others usually reserved for multi-beer commiserating. Hierarchies have been found inadequate for several reasons:

1. Hierarchies tend to form around functions. Functional specialization encourages expertise in depth, but it hinders cross-functional communication and filters upward communication.

2. Hierarchies slow communications and decisions. Anyone disgusted with slow decision speed refers to hierarchies as bureaucracies encumbered with "buck passing" and other ills. Empowerment moves service decisions and improvement processes to low levels for fast improvement and fast response to customers. (Any multistage decision process has the same effect whether it is in a hierarchy or not.)

3. Hierarchies are centralized. That is, decision making is remote from problems and distant from customers. (This problem can also occur without a hierarchy.)

4. Parts of a hierarchy can easily be more interested in their own welfare than that of the total organization—or its stakeholders.

Despite the criticisms, hierarchies are a natural, effective form of organization for many reasons: Everyone cannot be a committee of the whole. Everyone cannot be responsible for everything. Everyone cannot talk about everything. Outsiders want to know who to talk to (get action by talking to the boss). Rank, status, and pay are easily compared, so that fairness (or lack of it) is definable. Functional specialists can jump from one company to another without having to learn the total business. (Purchasing paint on a quote-and-bid system is a transferable expertise.)

Simple hierarchies are formed by everything from ant colonies to elephant herds. Gather a group of strangers around any common purpose, and in short order one or more elected leaders will be conducting a meeting. Complete absence of organizational form leaves responsibilities so vague that nothing happens—or a disaster happens. Before universally condemning the hierarchical form of organizational control, it is well to remember that a major difference between a highly disciplined army and a mob has been the effectiveness of a hierarchical command structure.

The objectives of eliminating or (most likely) weakening a hierarchy are (1) to give broad responsibility to those doing the work; (2) to increase horizontal coordination; (3) to give everyone responsibility for improvement and stimulate improvement processes among workers; and (4) to prevent functional departments or subgroups from thinking of themselves as a permanent establishment and thus resisting change or interaction.

Americans sometimes believe that Japanese do not have a strong hierarchical system. That's not true. Most companies have clearly identified hierarchical distinctions, a rank system much like the military. Some manufacturing plants even have insignias of rank. Despite a movement toward meritocratic pay and promotion in the past decade, seniors still receive considerable deference.

To cut through their functional hierarchies, the Japanese have used visibility systems, cross-functional teams, rotational assignments, and informal networks. Despite huge problems, an advantage is the expectation that almost any work group is expected to function as a team and not bring disgrace upon its supervisor. Japanese organization has been very effective during the postwar period, but their organizations and many of their institutions were designed for rapid catch-up growth. That system must also migrate to something different.

Westerners, too, have used many mechanisms to circumvent hierarchies: project management, product management, task forces, matrix management, committees, liaisons, and so on, all with a history of do's and don'ts from experience. So why does anyone now want to push further?

1. Because our new challenges are more human than technical. Computer networks enable teamwork around the globe if old hierarchies and distrust do not get in the way. (Perhaps co-located

teams perform better because everyone better understands what was *not* communicated as well as what was. Physical presence is a full-sensory experience, and opportunities for social interaction increase.)

2. Because improving a total service process or a total cycle of material use affects a chain of activities geographically scattered and rarely under the same hierarchy.

3. Because improvement processes for time compression, customer satisfaction, and environmental protection typically require collaboration rather than interfunctional or supplier-customer competition. In a hierarchy, individuals are motivated to improve only a narrow slice of a process, not the whole. If a vision of long-run performance encompasses only one function, or only one company, sooner or later improvement processes decay.

4. But primarily because fast-learning, high-performance operations must now be organized around processes (which may be geographically dispersed) that flow and evolve, rather than being based on static functions. We should prevent people from constructing organizations based on analogies of space and position—building organizational monuments—rather than having an organization crafted to operate changing processes—and that changes with them. (That's not the same as destroying every vestige of hierarchy.)

These changes are not just a little twist to make existing institutions more competitive. They constitute a fundamentally different concept of how much of the world's work should be done. The future belongs to those who can frequently reorganize high-morale teams around the needs of changing processes.

Champions of empowerment can for a time motivate people to work outside a company's hierarchical culture, but champions can be lost to retirements, sale of the company, or the simple fading of a crisis. Before corporate veterans climb on a bandwagon, they check whether the wheels might fall off. Converting business institutions to open-system enterprise takes more than one-man charisma in a single company.

Letting Go

Developing an able, responsible, enthused work force is fundamental to any version of open-system enterprise. It is probably the most difficult step. Owners and general managers today are usually frustrated when they try to empower a work force. The key word is *trust*. Even the language used to describe the problem reveals how difficult it is to span the trust gap. An expression I've heard more than once is, "They have to really feel they are empowered" (somewhat self-contradictory).

Many companies are still in the acronym stage of empowerment—using a training system or reward formula without actually letting go of anything. The emotional experience is much like raising teenagers. They cannot be warned about all the mistakes they might make, and management cannot take over every time they screw up. Workers that take responsibility must learn how to do it themselves. It's hard for managers and staff to keep their hands off when subordinates make obvious mistakes, but the more successful companies know that doing so is a matter of developing people.

Paul Rimington and Chuck Brewer, co-owners of Diemasters Manufacturing, discovered that "fake empowerment" did not work. They could not insist that subordinates be empowered. They could not make it naturally evolve from a training program. Finally, their staff asked them to sign a contract to let the associates run the company, and each time the owners interfered, they would be fined $100. The owners accepted, and several infractions later, the associates began to feel that they really were trusted, and still, their transition has only begun.[2]

Trust building also takes an open system. In a capitalist system, that includes confidence in where the money goes. Many workers don't expect to get a cut of "the real money." Owners who took big risks deserve that. They resent being deceived, or being underpaid (hard to define sometimes), when owners and managers are rolling in money.

Job security is another key issue. Occasionally, managers toy with the idea of guaranteeing jobs, usually because they think the Japanese do that. However, corporate officers and owners cannot literally guarantee others' job security when they cannot guarantee their own. They can share both rewards and hardships when they come. (That's what the Japanese practices also boil down to.) They can encourage skill building and teamwork that make people more employable elsewhere if worse comes to worst and try to help people make a transition if a blow comes.

Many companies contract outplacement services to help associates if their work disappears. More than that is needed to build trust. When Hasbro purchased the old Parker Brothers plant that for decades had made the Monopoly board game, it discovered that the plant could probably never be run at a profit. It had to close. Instead of merely hiring an outplacement service, Hasbro invited prospective new employers to come to the plant to see the workers demonstrate their skills for themselves. That's going the extra mile, but it is necessary to build trust in remaining associates.

Trust is not a guarantee. Nothing in this world is guaranteed. Trust is built by "telling it like it is" and sharing both good times and bad.

The case of Weirton Steel exemplifies the difficulty and the depth of feeling involved in trust building. Weirton is much reduced in size from its former self. Only part of the operation was in good enough condition to remain viable in a 1984 employee buyout through an employee stock ownership plan. Workers accepted a pay cut and six-year wage freeze.

But not everything went right. Steel production is over capacity worldwide, and Weirton had to simultaneously cut costs and improve quality. Weirton also had to invest heavily in modernization to continue being competitive. The capital came from reduced employee profit sharing plus outside investors. A new rolling mill went $18 million over budget. A computer room fire cost another $10 million. The capacity lost during downtime hurt. Dividends were eliminated, an income loss to all workers as well as to the outside stockholders. Though productivity improved, the market didn't, and to further conserve cash, some workers were laid off.

However, some workers believed that ownership meant that they had bought their job—were guaranteed a job. The union elected a new president on a platform of not further sacrificing jobs to maximize profit for outside shareholders. An investment manager grumbled that Weirton was being run for the employees instead of the stockholders. Old battle lines all too common in a shrinking industry blew a great deal of the trust that had built up over six years. (The stakeholders did not see themselves as fairly sharing the misery.) The accounts of the case do not suggest that a well-developed improvement process was helping Weirton survive.

Possessing certificates of ownership does not break anyone's old activity patterns or points of view. Feelings run high over fairness of who takes a hit. Other employee-owned companies have also had layoffs and other employee-owners have struck against themselves, so to speak.[3]

This kind of situation tries the soul of enterprise. Productivity improvements without growth make outplacements inevitable. Creating and sustaining the morale necessary to form new kinds of business relationships in a nongrowth market is a grossly underestimated challenge in companies more financially sound than Weirton. No owner or manager can do better than handle both windfalls and failures as openly and fairly as possible.

The issue of job security—and trust—was resoundingly the number one issue in a 1990–91 survey of workers in six plants, all geniunely striving for employee involvement and "continuous improvement." Without considering management execution, about 64 percent of the workers agreed with the philosophies of Total Quality, continuous improvement, and so on. However, they were less sure of their own management's commitment and handling of these initiatives. Two of the six plants had recently had layoffs, and responses there were more negative. At all plants, most workers believed that no matter how committed they were to teamwork, continuous improvement, and so forth, jobs would continue to disappear, probably to countries with lower wage rates.[4]

Two points from this survey are worthy of note. First, in the absence of any firm attack on basic reasons for outsourcing, and since many of the basic practices of lean manufacturing can be well executed anywhere, the surveyed workers have reason to fear job disappearance. Second, recognition and positive reinforcement by management is more difficult than most imagine. In a crunch, quality can still be sacrificed to output. Workers seldom hear about customer satisfaction, or lack of it. They feel powerless when suppliers send parts or materials that are marginal.

These findings are from plants that are recognized as among the best. There was little difference in the responses of union and non-union plants. Older employees were less trustful than younger, possibly because they had "seen it all." A comment from a veteran worker (not part of the survey, with his own business on the side) illustrates the feeling: "For years, I kept machines running for them, and they told me nothing. Now they want to play team ball, but they still don't tell me much. Deep down, you know if the numbers sneeze they could move it all to Mexico. I just want to retire and forget about it."

Reconstituting manufacturing enterprise in a flat-growth market depends on human sharing of risk—something more than severance plans. That aspect was captured in a phrase used by Art Carter, Sr., a public accountant who served mostly minority businesses in areas not promoted for tourism. "He'll walk the alley with you" is how Art described someone he fully trusted.

Separation of stalwart contributors from an enterprise is part of the process of renewal, whether people have been classified as blue collar or white—as if that were still important. It is how it is done that counts. In an open system almost everyone will understand the need for separation. Recognition of people and respect for their accomplishments is as important for people who leave as for those who remain. When a high-morale unit breaks up, the experience is marked by one or more events—insider ceremonies. They will likely have a party. Afterward, they may hold reunions.

Much is now being written and spoken about the kind of leadership required to create the high-respect, high-performance, high-recognition environment in which open-system enterprise can thrive. No company, or derivation of a company is yet engaging in the kind of cross-boundary, virtual company activities envisioned by open-system enterprise. When such achievements become regular, a number of people will have learned how to exercise the kind of leadership that in the past we have considered extraordinary.[5]

Recognition

What causes someone with little expectation of great wealth to spend extra time, energy, and imagination in his or her work? Recognition. All that most people will ever gain from anything extraordinary they accomplish in their life is sincere recognition by someone who really knows what was done. The recognition can even be backhanded. For instance, the accolade "Cheatin' SOB" was once accepted as the highest form of respect among fellow mechanics all trying to qualify a race car at the Indianapolis Motor Speedway under rules that sometimes bordered on the arcane.

Most workers can no more imagine having a condo on the Riviera or retiring in Palm Springs than they can imagine personally taking a moonwalk. But everyone likes recognition, the difference between being human and being a computer. Some recognition is only flattery, as when a clerk compliments your taste in colors, unaware that you are color blind. However, the humblest genuine recognition is part of any organization's soul.

For instance, underground mines have never been kind to one's health, and decades ago conditions were harsh. From 1907 to 1912, 23 percent of all coal miner deaths were from accidents, not counting incapacitating accidents and illness from back lung.[6] Miners said that no one could pay them enough to go down a black hole, but they took pride in going down anyway, though virtually the only recognition was from fellow miners and their families. This mutual recognition made the United Mine Workers into the ideal of union solidarity in the first half of the twentieth century. In such circumstances workers starved for recognition provided it for themselves. Mine owners who could not see beyond cost per ton could never figure it out.

In the 1980s, managers seeking to empower employees discovered the power of recognition. Suggestion programs were better greased by personal recognition than by payouts, particularly if cash awards were high enough to cause jealousy. Improvement processes progressed better when contributors were recognized than when they were only paid bonuses. Managers began to recognize the obvious; recognition was more influential than pay plans.

That expectations and recognition are the foundation of work culture is readily seen in noncommercial occupations. No golden chains keep people in teaching, public health, or police work (unless they are on the take). They stay because society occasionally signals its respect for them. That is recognition.

Recognition is more than employee-of-the-month pins, dinners, and prime parking spots. Recognition is personal time taken to show respect for others' performance and improvement—acknowledgement that people have (or have not) dedicated themselves. Symbols associated with genuine recognition are meaningful; perfunctory rituals are not. (All merit badge associates will receive their pins from the appropriate representative at the Tuesday luncheons.) A worker at

General Motors Pontiac Division expressed it perfectly: "I don't want a lot of bosh; just give a damn."

Not all the recognition need come from management. For instance, when fabrication workers give engineers a "slick toad award" (no warts) for presenting them new tooling that needs no corrective adjustments, the recognition is "the real thing," although to outsiders the ritual may be as meaningless as initiation into the Mystic Order of the Sea. Even better is recognition that someone is "making history"—accomplishing something never done before.

The heart of an acronym called Performance Management is systematic recognition. Its basic concept is reinforcing behavior or performance that made things go right, rather than giving negative feedback on things gone wrong. Reprimands are seldom necessary for the 95 percent of people honestly trying. The approach guides improvement processes through people rather than through supervisory concentration on events and activities. It depends on increasing the skills and responsibilities of those doing the work.[7]

At the Tennessee Eastman Company, a huge chemical company headquartered in Kingsport, Tennessee, Performance Management is the foundation of quality-improvement processes and preventive-maintenance practices. It has made a complete change in the premises of management. Eight years ago, supervisory practice was to check on errors and problems, often with sharp questioning and a search for the guilty, then order corrective action. Managers and supervisors concentrated on immediate operations.

Now, the processes have been "turned over" to the work force. Performance measurement is on the processes themselves, and improvement is a team effort. No one pretends that Tennessee Eastman has reached a state of perfection, but the spirit of the place is quite different, and performance has vastly improved by almost any measure used. The difference is that management today improves the work force, and the work force improves the processes—and satisfies the customers.

Most important is giving recognition where it is due. Normal human behavior is accepting credit for achievements not entirely our own—easy to do when others honestly believe that the cat pawing a mouse is the same one that pounced on it. The normal assumption of hierarchical management makes this temptation difficult to resist.

In interviews during the Gulf War, Gen. Norman Schwartzkopf frequently referred to the team effort of the *allied* forces there—all of them from all countries, and not just their brass—but the media naturally hounded the quotable commander, ready to capture any General Patton bombast if it appeared. Attention to leaders thus tempts runaway ego, well recognized as a hazard to publicized champions. Maintaining the conditions in which everyone receives deserved recognition is a much more time-consuming leadership task than is generally recognized.

Pay plans that focus only on individual contributions can also wreck recognition and teamwork. Group pay plans are an important way to support teamwork, but they are not as important as recognition of team contribution.

Picking Up

Once the atmosphere is created, most workers will begin to assume more responsibility, but to perform well they need preparation. The best companies have always recognized that an excellent work force of any kind is always well educated and well trained. Work teams also need to impose discipline. Among factory workers, one of the first issues when assuming more responsibility is the system for fairly assessing and disciplining attendance, for example.

Personnel issues such as attendance always seem to be swathed in legalities about work hours, overtime rates, documented notices, and so on. Therefore, personnel departments are loathe to let work groups themselves enforce policies lest they get the company in legal entanglements because of inconsistencies. However, with training, attention, and a suitable overall policy, ordinary people can assume these responsibilities. A simple point system for attendance seems to be easily enforceable, and co-workers are apt to be more discerning about attendance than a staffer removed from the scene. Staff personnel become advisors. Yes, the "amateurs" may make mistakes, but so do overworked professionals. After acclimation, work groups begin to assume much of their own administration.

Selection of people to become associates in this kind of organization is another tricky responsibility. Fairness requires adherence to a number of laws and company fair-hiring practices, so again the personnel professionals and the lawyers may be squeamish. However, a number of self-directed work teams do make the selection of new hires to join them.

Much the same can be said of estimating costs. Assuming that workers have a good, basic education—often uncertain if new hires are not well screened—nonprofessionals again can do a credible job of estimating the costs of proposals, provided they have had basic training in the cost system. The accountant becomes an advisor.

"Picking up" is a process of the work force learning to work in teams, performing a number of basic tasks for themselves. Small work groups therefore start to become small business units in themselves. A well-coached team can "run the business" in their little corner of it. An aggressive team can even become entrepreneurial—come up with ideas that lead to new business. In addition, if people learn to assume considerable responsibility in various kinds of work groups, after a time it is no trick to assemble a competent, cross-functional, cross-company team to address difficult challenges—to figure out, for example, how to organize a variety of modules and components so that almost any customer-selected filing cabinet configuration can be built and shipped in two days. The development of these kinds of capabilities is the basic building block of the open-system enterprise.

Pay and Reward Systems

Certainly profit sharing, gainsharing, and widely distributed bonus payments are more likely to support teamwork than bonuses only to corporate officers. The number of Fortune 1000 companies with workers covered by gainsharing plans increased from 26 percent to 40 percent between 1987 and 1990.[8] Without question, monetary motivation is alive and well.

Individual performance payment systems do not contribute to teamwork. The most obvious of these are output-based individual incentive plans. Most work groups, however, recognize that a modicum of teamwork is necessary if each member is to maximize his or her individual gain. For instance, piece-rate workers at Jantzen readily cooperated in a quality-improvement program when they recognized that doing so would likely increase individual earnings. However, their basic goal is still to maximize individual output that conforms to specification rather than be broadly concerned with customers, internal or external, or make only what is wanted when it is wanted. It is a short-term, unbalanced reward system.

Various payment plans all have data to prove why they are successful, but usually using a limited set of criteria. Piece rates do increase individual output. However, not much is said about indirect labor, customer satisfaction, and so on.

A balanced reward system is more attuned to teamwork, broad perception, a long-term outlook, and performance achievements that at first look impossible. To displace a system that inhibited people from working in cells and paying attention to what customers really need, a number of companies like Stanadyne Diesel Systems spent several years doing a "buyout" of individual incentives. That is, everyones pay scales had to be increased and adjusted to fairly compensate for loss of incentive bonuses.

M. Scott Myers, who has spent a fair amount of his career studying reward systems, has concluded that systems consistent with "ultimate" performance balance three dimensions: (1) individual monetary rewards; (2) group monetary rewards; and (3) nonmonetary recognition, both for groups and for individuals. American companies noted for high performance have gravitated toward this kind of system.[9]

Examples of individual monetary rewards are merit pay, pay-for-knowledge, benefit plans (including tuition refunds, subscriptions, and so forth) and premium pay for night work, travel, or hazardous conditions. Group monetary rewards include various forms of gainsharing, profit sharing, stock ownership, and occasional bonus payments to project teams. Nonmonetary recognition might include time off, flex time, and opportunities for desired transfers or course attendance, besides public citation on both formal and informal occasions. Nonmonetary recognition requires enough imagination that several people may be kept busy with support for various occasions in a large company, but it does not include significant payouts to groups or individuals. Figure 8-1 summarizes this three-dimensional reward system.

Reward systems best promote esprit de corps if status differences between people are not allowed to become polarizing. Exclusive parking spaces and exclusive dining rooms are two oft-cited creators of

FIGURE 8-1

MYERS'S THREE-
DIMENSIONAL REWARD STRUCTURE

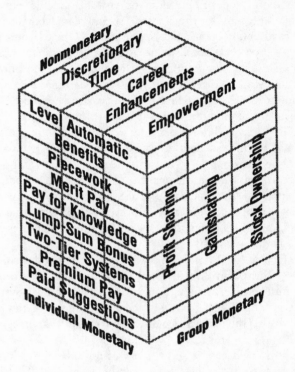

SOURCE: *From M. Scott Myers,* Every Employee a Manager, *3rd ed. (San Diego, CA: University Associates, Inc., 1991), p. 32.*

us-versus-them feelings. So are status-enhancing office layouts and locations and dress codes.

The work function of offices is the major consideration in their design, but it is very easy to justify status symbols as necessary to concentration, proper impressions on visitors, and the like. Private offices are necessary for some activities, and completely open office layouts tend toward being noisy "cattle barns." Office layouts that are more open promote office visibility useful to open-system enterprises. In manufacturing plants, offices are frequently located out on the production floor or adjacent to it (noise is sometimes a distraction), near those with whom frequent communication is desired. One Japanese plant I visited did not provide offices for manufacturing engineers. They used pull-down desks hinged to the wall of the plant so they could not hide in their offices working on projects unknown to those in production.

One American trend is the opposite. All workers have some kind of desk, complete with nameplate and access to a computer. As production becomes more automated, with everyone participating in continuous improvement, almost everyone has times when they need to study or perform analysis.

The effect of these trends on reward systems is also to make them more open. In systems heavily tilted toward individual merit rewards, pay is often considered to be a personal matter. In open-system enterprise, with many costs known to everyone, keeping salaries secret is more difficult. Open knowledge of pay or pay scales has an egalitarian effect.

In publicly held companies, the pay of top officers has long been publicly known—if the revelation could be deciphered. That in itself doubtless contributes to accusations by investors that American top corporate brass are overcompensated. However, another reason why open-system compensation makes sense is that if a chieftain is considered to be overpaid, his or her leadership ability is undermined. Increasingly, the duty of corporate officers is to be leaders of people rather than agents for owners and direct managers of investor assets. The leaders develop associates, and the associates make wise use of assets, which implies widespread knowledge of costs. And associate linkages into customer and supplier companies require leadership of collaborators who figure that overcompensation is at *their* expense.

The usual arguments for secrecy are: (1) privacy—people do not want others talking about their pay; and (2) unnecessary discussion. For instance, executive compensation is sometimes based on complex formulas of profitability, capital ratios, operating ratios, and the like that people will not understand, so they will question it endlessly. But a method of compensation that complicated should be subjected to the five-why routine, beginning with whether it will motivate anyone to do anything in particular or is only a jackass theory raised to a higher power.

Reward systems in open enterprises must build trust. Associates will work toward common goals for mutual survival, but profitability presents a different motivational challenge. Enthusiasm inversions occur if associates do not understand how big the pie is, and dividing it creates suspicion that others profited from *their* sacrifice.

Finally, the bottom line is important to almost any kind of enterprise. One cannot expect empowered associates to share concern for the bottom line if they do not know what it is.

Open-System Organizations

What kind of organization do we want? One that is capable of blowing through a process analysis and reforming itself to run the process effectively. The organization adapts to a changing process, and the process changes in response to customers, environmental needs, and new technical possibilities. The requirement suggests a flat, open-system organization made up of highly skilled people, some with deep specialities, who can participate in cross-functional, cross-industry teams and processes. (Perhaps a "flat-out" organization—from racing vernacular—would be more descriptive.)

In contemplating how they might evolve from their own dependencies on hierarchy, the Japanese refer to "holonic management." This term is derived from Sir Arthur Koestler, the British writer. Koestler used the term "holon" in the context of biological systems. A holon is part of a total system, or of several systems, but having independent internal functions. It is linked both upward and downward to other holons. Each holon is autonomous and self-reliant in responding to external contingencies but is subject to direction by higher-level holons.[10]

Koestler refers to a "holarchy of holons" as a hierarchy of self-regulating holons that simultaneously are:

1. Autonomous wholes in superordination to their parts.
2. Dependent parts subordinated to higher levels.
3. Units adaptive to the local environment.

Another "vision" of open-system organization combines ideas from consulting companies and Japanese manufacturing companies. A large consulting company consists of specialists, yet they must often work as a cross-functional team with clients. Anyone not somewhat of a generalist in addition to being a specialist has difficulty. The consulting company hierarchy is flat and dispersed, consisting of five or six levels: staff, senior, manager, senior manager, partner and managing partner. Primary promotional recognition is awarded independently of current projects or engagements. A high percentage of organizational time is devoted to keeping on the leading edge of practice.

The entrepreneurial spirit of consultants is a plus, but a manufacturing enterprise with a long-term outlook needs a higher level of loyalty than consultants typically show. Partners with money at risk will not walk away on a whim, but unlike the Japanese, consulting companies do not have a history of "lifetime employees." Those with good opportunities can and do opt out.

In manufacturing, lifetime commitments have given companies that need to downsize a big hangover cured only by early retirement and other buyout options. Occasionally, veteran employees that retire early are paid from the retirement fund but continue to work on a more flexible arrangement for an outlay much reduced as recorded on the books.

Security commitments and reward structures to induce highly capable people to commit themselves to an open-system manufacturing enterprise can be devised—if the institution is committed to the open system; that is, if a consortium of companies, with government understanding, commits to making it happen. The concept takes joint planning and effort and the close work of people from across current corporate boundaries. Not all enterprises will succeed in their mission. A consortium of "home-base" resource organizations can provide a safety net for people with placement services and portable benefit plans—but no safety net for failing enterprises themselves. The failures are case studies for benchmarking.

However, the basic motivation for open-system enterprise is not necessarily growth. It is improvement of quality of life—so alien to the assumptions of the twentieth-century system of business and economics that it is difficult to grasp the thought. But grasping it is necessary before one can become enthused about a new soul of enterprise.

Migration to the Open System

Procedure owners can seldom imagine destroying their own role. For instance, a production planner whose job it was to schedule around a production bottleneck compiled a long list of reasons why setup times could not be reduced on a press, though others could see within a few seconds how to begin. An engineering manager whose department spent 30 percent of its time on engineering changes would not hear of designing tooling directly for production trial to reduce time and the number of changes. He recited a dozen incidents to prove his case. (Both true stories.) The objectors had valuable points to be considered, but their vision was obscured by their own fog. Without skillful change leadership, old systems will keep going until they fall of their own obsolescence.

To cut through all this, organizations need champions and change agents. The champions toss out "impossible challenges," like Motorola's six-sigma quality goal or a challenge to reduce tooling cost on an automobile by ten times in five years. An impossible challenge recognizes where processes can be radically changed, then states a goal that cannot be reached without radical change. Champions blow proceduralists out of their comfort zones. A champion is a fomenter of revolution, a status much strengthened if he or she is also the chief executive of today's organization.

A change agent shows people how to make a radical change. Emboldened (or bullied) by a champion, people start an earnest search for the "how to." A champion may also be a change agent, but a champion without change agents is all blow.

Some variation of this process is illustrated by the way many of the Japanese companies "adopted JIT." For example, the top executives of

Kawasaki Motorcycle Division said "we are going to do it." Then, five change agents went to Toyota for a hundred days to bring the know-how back. In other cases outside change agents with experience came to a plant and immediately began turning it upside down. The usual method was to straighten flow paths, reduce setup times, create a few cells, and generally make chaos with little explanation. Only after there was physical evidence to show would they begin to explain the principles of it. (The latter kind of approach is now becoming known in the United States as a five-day-and-four-night program. Learning and accepting quality-improvement processes is somewhat similar, but less dramatic. For instance, after training, if an inspection area is phased out, people must rapidly learn how to perform without it.)

The same approach is necessary in other circumstances. For instance, workers and managers in Russia have been so accustomed to waiting for orders from a planning agency that they cannot bring themselves to sell directly to customers, plan production, and buy from suppliers. Only after seeing Western operations can they truly understand what to do and how to behave.

Successful change quickly jolts people into new ways of performing, somewhat like urging novices to climb mountains or jump from airplanes. ("Whaddaya mean, you can't do this. You're doing it already.") Otherwise, the dangers of muddle, fuddle, and stagnate are great.

This kind of change is paradoxical. The champion and sometimes the change agent behave like dictators at first. But the nature of the change is to empower the people doing the work with responsibility they never before held.

Consultants are sometimes major change agents. Manufacturing companies hire expertise they cannot afford full-time, but they also hire consultants to force themselves to make changes that otherwise could not happen. Radical changes in operating processes require new thought patterns. Nothing can change without process owners taking the perilous leap of relinquishing control. Otherwise, proposals sit trapped in emotional gridlock until something dislodges them.

The most dramatic "acronym" changes have been accomplished by drastic initial sweeps. A more evolutionary approach educates first. In either case, champions and change agents must destroy something old to build something new, so they leave bruised feelings in their wake, but the feelings and politics of every situation are different. Sometimes the conversion of a naysayer is the political key to change—like Nixon going to China. A flaming liberal would have never had enough credibility to legitimize the China opening.

Annual percentage improvements are startling for a few years, but as people become accustomed to new processes, they find barriers they cannot seem to break through. Harley-Davidson, Xerox, Ford, and many others well publicized for operational improvements have all had this experience. After the company weathered a survival crisis, progress stagnated.

The difficulty is the human problem of stretching old limits. As soon as the status system of an organization begins to recast around a new set of procedures, it is already hardening itself against continuing change. Humans being what they are, a certain amount of this is inevitable. The answer is an organization form and a culture that reward successful change rather than status as a guardian of procedure.

Order-of-Magnitude Reorganization

The first stage of the change process needs to occur within functions of a company. The conversion to JIT is at first a shop revolution; then the waves start washing over all the rest of the company. Quality starts in pockets, but after a time it consumes the whole company. Conversion to a team-based organization generally starts in a few areas amenable to it—production and engineering, for instance—and grows to encompass all functions. No company can blow up its entire past at once.

Suppose that the can company (from Chapter 4) conceives a plan to radically depart from past practice developing new container designs. A designer/customer representative from the can company works at the customer's site using software on-line to home base to develop the design. Even regulatory or environmental checking might be done on-line. Supposing such an idea to be technically feasible, it brings the supplier company's processes into the customer, and the customer into the supplier.

If the can is for seasonings sold through ethnic food shops, trial designs might even be transmitted to some shops for their reaction.

Speculating further, interaction on actual container design can be part of market research direct to users of the container—if they don't mind being bothered. If the tooling time for a container is greatly compressed, then a process that in 1992 took weeks is shortened to hours, with no danger to quality. In fact, while the can company is greatly improving quality, the customer is probably rethinking the purpose of the can. That is order-of-magnitude change. It would also result in order-of-magnitude changes in organization.

The technical challenges are considerable, but not unthinkable. However, revolutionizing current organizations and mind-sets to this degree might be impossible. This kind of revolution may take place in organizations not now in the can business, so great are the problems of migrating to an operating mode so drastically different from today. If such a change process took place, it would be a high-tech version of tearing up a shop floor (and its organization) for JIT.

Inability to imagine how to perform in different roles is the human drag on order-of-magnitude improvement. Probing and asking why from many different points of view is highly desired, part of healthy process thinking and necessary to high-quality process innovation. Finding people who can do this is the tough part.

Enterprise Organization

An order-of-magnitude organization is one that can combine and recombine people's roles into an enterprise without great stress—without having half its people in emotional counseling at all times. The structural flexibility required is similar to the matrix organization used in aerospace and other R&D work. It would consist of resource companies—functional centers of technical training and expertise that farm out members to various kinds of cross-functional operating enterprise teams. Resource companies' marketing centers would research new opportunities. Their training centers would prepare people for new assignments. The operating enterprises supported would be taxed to support these source services. Career paths would give people generalist training as well as technical depth. Flat general hierarchies with numerous highly autonomous groups can be organized around products or processes or assigned to operating enterprises as required.

The major asset of resource organizations is skilled people who can fit into numerous teams. The operating enterprises themselves would be designed to communicate using a network cutting across what would traditionally be called a "horizontal slice" through functional departments and a "vertical slice" through a supply chain.

Needed are proposals to form resource companies and open-system operating enterprises of this type. An early version may be the Mayekawa Company of Japan. It makes large refrigerators and freezers for warehouses, stores, and ships. A new, legally chartered company is formed for each order, so each order becomes an "open-system enterprise." The customer buys in, Mayekawa buys in, and major suppliers buy in. A project team, or enterprise team, is formed from all these players. Naturally, the interfacing is much easier if all participating resource companies have "open systems."

The purpose of the enterprise team is to research the customer's need for refrigeration; design, build, and install equipment to meet the need; then engage in training and early-life service. If the result is successful, the customer in effect gets a rebate, Mayekawa keeps a cut, and the major suppliers get their cuts. If the result is unsuccessful, everyone shares in the loss. The financial commingling is intended to stimulate the resource partners to work together rather than argue, and to eliminate many of the routine transactions across the boundaries of the partners.

No mechanism of this organization is new. What is missing is the "soul" to inspire it. Participants in enterprises cannot expect the business to expand forever. Projects terminate, and while a core group from one venture may form another, many participants move on. Each venture must meet high expectations for quality, productivity, and environmental protection. Two of Mayekawa's objectives for creating their enterprise teams were to improve participants' morale and to increase the learning of integrative know-how from one order to the next.

Operating enterprises need socially acceptable means of recognizing venture participants; otherwise, they just grub for money. To jell as a team, each group needs a symbol of its existence, a "tribal totem" to dance around. Since project ventures are temporary, some system must also be used to recognize the veterans of each enterprise, like hash marks or campaign ribbons for military veterans. Major ventures can start with get-acquainted parties and "pump-up." At its end, singing "Auld Lang Syne" may be a bit maudlin for a group of hardened management-by-fact process thinkers, but some rite of passage is needed to cement the values of teamwork.

Migrating Toward a New Enterprise

Various kinds of project teams and joint ventures today may be similar to enterprise teams of the future. Some enterprises may be short-term projects; others long-term services. What is potentially different is the formation of teams with members scattered around the globe—if that proves to be any advantage. (This scenario is a small extension of the current work-at-home-by-computer phenomenon.) What we need in the near future are more actual "experiments" to determine how such visions might actually work. The human side of them is the most difficult to work out, and it is a more significant departure from the past than the physical construction of computer networks.

We cannot migrate toward this new world faster than people can change themselves. Old institutions, mired in inhibitions from the past, have great difficulty making order-of-magnitude changes. If they do, one set of emotional scars has not begun to heal before a new one appears. Figuring out how to build these visions from the ground up, instead of the sky down, requires translating visions to pragmatism and back again. The result will undoubtedly not be quite like the original visions.

No one seems to know who originated the saying that "the business of business is business." The implication is that businesses should not be distracted from concentrating on activities that promote cash flow, profit, and growth. If the assets of a company are truly people, that old adage is severely limiting. In an open-enterprise world, the resource companies that contribute to enterprise have mostly soft assets to contribute: technical expertise, money, software, communications networks, market research, and perhaps databases. Nearly all those assets have value only if people understand them and maintain them.

The business of business is development of people. If a Hewlett-Packard, Allen-Bradley, Motorola, or General Motors actually conducts many of its key product and process developments through operating enterprises, the old corporate carcass becomes a resource company left with the overhead: support operations, venture banking, R&D, strategic planning (visioning), and human development.

Human development is the key. The best companies have always supported development of people. General Motors once had General Motors Institute; McDonald's has Hamburger University. Motorola has Motorola University plus a huge training effort. Much of each company's activity has been designed to keep fresh a critical mass of skills and knowledge.

Japanese companies concentrate on human development in their own way and offer a good lesson for open-system enterprise development. Much of the training of new "freshmen" in Japanese companies has the intent of bonding them to the company's culture. New hires receive insider information on the company and go through similar "boot camp" experiences. (Anyone who has gone through airborne training feels an immediate kinship with others who have done the same, even if the training took place years apart. A few American companies, including AT&T, use "survival training" to achieve a similar result.)

The bonding is important, and it is not just a Japanese cultural phenomenon, such as extended endurance training.[11] For example, Japanese insurance agents (often women), whose training was merely reading a manual, have had turnover rates as high as once a year. With more intense, personal training, the insurance agent retention rate is higher.

Enterprise teams need to jell. Their missions are more challenging than those of almost any prior business if they include such charges as control of a full cycle of material use. They need to agree to a mission statement, not just sign off: discuss it, thrash it out, and have a meeting of the minds. Any time an enterprise is dedicated to doing something that takes extraordinary coordinative effort, an important step in keeping everyone together is to agree on what they are trying to accomplish. Part of their allegiance may be bought by signing contracts "for the duration," but that is not enough. A different kind of spirit is needed in a high-performance innovative enterprise, a tolerance for wackiness combined with team spirit, and discipline where needed. Amid the technical training needs to be some team-building exercises.

Much of the soul of the enterprise, new style, is apt to be something akin to the old school tie. First, investment in a person's education is an expense that can be repaid by an indenturing period, just as the armed forces expect an enlistee who has gone through training to commit to a minimum time of productive service. Beyond that, a common educational experience itself is an opportunity for bonding of teams—particularly if it is a rigorous group effort.

However, such enterprise cannot be motivated by the same urges that have attracted men to piracy for ages. In a resource-constrained world, the prospect for claiming a great pot of booty at the end of a rainbow will not be the emotional driver for very many. It's more like the pride that stimulates people to provide water or electricity of very high quality without fail.

The soul of the enterprise is a strong public-service ethic. It will not work perfectly. Nothing will inspire 100 percent enthusiasm in all participants. However, the multidisciplinary preparation of future enterprise teams should instill an ethic of service entrepreneurship at the same time, and do so without drippy pledges and rituals.

An entrepreneurial service ethic combined with adherence to the scientific method—process thinking—is not mushy sentiment. Most people will probably not think about it much, just as most medical doctors spend little time thinking about the Hippocratic Oath (now taken in the form of the Declaration of Geneva), but most of them live by it. In an open system, this soul must be strong enough to transcend differences in racial, sexual, ethnic, and religious backgrounds. A pluralistic work team has to have a superordinate ethic that bridges the members' differences for work purposes—the soul of the enterprise.

NOTES

1. Harry Levinson, *The Great Jackass Fallacy* (Boston: Harvard University Press, 1973).
2. Paul Rimington, "How We Are Learning to Let Go," *Target* 8, no. 4 (July–August 1992): 4–5.

3. A brief account of the Weirton situation is in "How Can We Be Laid Off If We Own the Company?" *Business Week*, 9 September 1991, 66.

4. David J. Mattingly, "A View from the Other Side," *Target*, 7, no. 5, Winter 1991, 23–27.

5. Two books typical of an emerging genre are Max De Pree, *Leadership Is an Art* (New York: Doubleday, 1989); and John P. Kotter, *A Force for Change* (New York: Free Press, 1990).

6. Anthony Bale, "America's First Compensation Crisis," in *Dying for Work*, ed. by David Rosner and Gerald Markowitz, (Bloomington: Indiana University Press, 1989), 37. Data originally from Prudential Life Insurance Company.

7. Performance Management is a system developed and promoted by Aubrey Daniels & Associates, Atlanta, Georgia.

8. According to surveys by the Center for Effective Organization, University of Southern California.

9. M. Scott Myers, "Rethinking Your Reward Systems," *Target* 7, no. 3 (1991): 25–33.

10. Arthur Koestler, *The Ghost in the Machine* (Chicago: Henry Regnery Company, 1971), pp. 101–102.

11. An example of Japanese endurance training is the "thousand fungo drill" sometimes given to baseball players. Keep a young player scooping up ground balls until he collapses. Then praise his Samurai spirit, tell him that mind prevails over matter, and that collective discipline prevails over raw talent. Overdrilled ball players may be too tired to play well, but that is not what the traditional Japanese fans come to see.

9

CUSTOMERS, SUPPLIERS, AND OPEN-SYSTEM ENTERPRISE

NO COMPANY CAN BE EXCELLENT ALL BY ITSELF. THE CONCEPT OF A "VERTI-cally integrated" fortress company doing it all is outmoded, as are specialty companies that operate as secret compartments encased in transactions. Instead, enterprise must operate as a more open system, horizontally conceived, with every member of it recognizing that it is not the whole.

This kind of enterprise is not really new, so it is not impossible, but it turns a number of twentieth-century business concepts upside down. Ordinary mortals can make it work. The changes are an extrapolation of many ideas now in current practice.

For an open-system, horizontal enterprise to function, its people must lock onto the same mission and goals. Otherwise, it is gridlocked by confusion or quickly undermined by contradictory agendas. An open system must give careful attention to:

1. Common mission and goals.
2. Fair sharing of risks and rewards.
3. Trust among the participants.
4. Acceptance and use of a common improvement process.
5. Common systems of communication.

6. Common systems of performance measurement.
7. Fair rules for entering or departing from the system.

It is difficult to agree on systems of communication and performance measurement with enough common threads to work together. Fairness and trust seem to be mushy sentiments. But without all these, an open system has no meaning. Our old way, alternately cajoling, then threatening suppliers is filled with waste and distrust.

A CEO writing in *The Wall Street Journal* captured the essence of the problem. In the 1970s his company had been the major supplier of plastic coloring materials to a big account constituting a third of its total business. This customer's requirements were much more demanding than the rest of the trade's. Meeting them to a standard acceptable at the time took the supplier five years of effort, extending its process capabilities and developing the know-how.

Without warning the customer began decreasing orders. The supplier did not know why. When confronted, the customer confessed to building its own internal capability to make coloring agents, noting that it could hire all the experts it needed. Not said, but implied, was that the supplier's skill commanded a high margin—a tempting target to a customer feeling utterly dependent on a sole-source supplier and therefore vulnerable to "blackmail." To successfully break this dependence, do not tell the target company of your intentions until you are able to get along without it. So goes the conventional economic wisdom of arm's-length relationships.

The supplier offered price concessions. Not accepted. A buyout of the supplier, or even partial buyout, might have been arranged, but communication never got that far. The customer was already committed to going it alone.

Later, the CEO heard "through the usual sources" that the former customer had greatly underestimated the technical difficulty of duplicating the coloring agents. Downtime was high, and the overhead expensive. Later, the supplier CEO wondered why it was all necessary. He reflected that he would have liked to have joined a "Japanese *keiretsu*," had one existed. However, in such a system, how would his own company have started up in a "market" closed to outsiders?[1]

The customer's management did not appreciate that it was not really purchasing coloring agents but was a partner in the development of the supplier—a partnership thrown away in an effort to replicate the supplier's know-how. The supplier company was not open to the customer either until it was too late. The supplier CEO suffered the usual bitterness when a customer wants to pay only for his product but not his development, engineering, service, and loyalty. The received tradition in manufacturing companies values only "things," not the people and processes that create things.

A better system is possible and practical, and it is in gestation if old instincts do not abort it. The steps shown in Figure 9-1 are neither new nor unknown, but the volume of such activity has certainly increased. The steps describe levels of structured relationships, but they signify something more important—attitude shifts, starting with the notion of becoming a better customer and maturing toward interactive, open-system enterprise.

Internal Customers

Referring to the next operation—the receiver of one's work—as an internal customer has become almost commonplace. The phrase is attractive but meaningless unless internal customers and suppliers—other divisions, plants, and departments, as well as individuals—learn how to directly engage in improvement processes with each other.

Relations between plants or divisions of large companies, and sometimes even between individuals in small companies, are frequently worse than those with external customers and suppliers. Informal hand-raising polls taken at a hundred or more meetings over the past ten years by the author have consistently shown around 80 percent of an industrial audience agreeing with that statement, although with the rise of the quality movement, the percentage has declined to half or less.

A catalogue of the historical ills of internal supplier relations would be interminable. Almost any experienced manufacturing manager in a multiplant or multidivisional company can recite at least one instance of major performance problems being referred to the top of a company for action. A sister division will not pay attention to defects. It ships to everyone else first. It assigns only inexperienced personnel to designing or making something for another division. In short, the internal customer behaves as the internally competitive reward sys-

FIGURE 9-1

STAGES OF CUSTOMER–
SUPPLIER DEVELOPMENT

OPEN
|
| OPEN-SYSTEM ENTERPRISE
| (Resource companies buying into action companies struc-
| tured for collaboration on specific operation missions.)
| JOINT VENTURES
| (With collaboration and improvement processes.)
| PARTNERSHIPS AND COLLABORATION
| (Mutual improvement processes, risk sharing.)
| CONSORTIA
| (Mutual participation in projects or programs of common
| interest with commingling of funds—the National Center for
| Manufacturing Sciences or Sematech are well-known
| examples.)
| LONG-TERM CONTRACTS WITH CUSTOMERS AND
| SUPPLIERS
| (Stop unneccessary uncertainty in relationships.)
| OPEN-EXCHANGE IMPROVEMENT PROCESSES
| (Improvement workshops, network organizations, bench-
| marking exchanges, etc.)
| INFORMAL NETWORKING BETWEEN COMPANIES
| (Sharing of ideas between individuals.)
| ALLIANCES AND INDUSTRY ASSOCIATIONS
| (Standards setting, industry market research, lobbying,
| etc.)
| EVERY BUSINESS FOR ITSELF: STRICTLY TRANSACTIONS
| (Unmitigated "competition" in every relationship.)
CLOSED

While this list does not constitute a linear scale, it does represent moving from a condition of cold, calculated self-interest by independent, arm's-length companies (and by many departments and individuals within each one) to a system of institutions and practices that enable openness and collaboration to be much more the norm.

tem usually suggests it will. It helps other divisions just enough to keep problems from "going upstairs" without making another division look good in the corporate ratings at its own expense.

This problem has existed since the advent of multidivisional companies early in the century. Companies have tried various kinds of fixes with partial success. For example, years ago Black & Decker often made parts in one plant and shipped them to another for assembly. Corporate manufacturing policy was that plant managers' first priority was to keep sister plants' assembly running. If faced with a tough decision, they were to feed parts to the other plants first. Naturally, the policy was sometimes overridden because of customer-service priorities from marketing—an indication that the policy worked much as intended.

If a manufacturing company protective of intellectual capital has good strategic sense, its internal suppliers are vital because its critical expertise is kept in house. However, a company managed only for cash flow may play off internal suppliers against outside bidders just to "stimulate efficiency" without much consideration for strategy. Without internal expertise, it struggles to maintain innovation, much less good performance from internal suppliers.

Decisions based on financial projections often inhibit strategic considerations or mutual improvement processes. When decisions are based strictly on immediate cash flow, firms will outsource a part for a few pennies per part, no matter how vital it is to strategy. Internal suppliers of critical equipment, tooling, and services are even more important, but the same kind of mentality undermines them with more disastrous results. A machine tool story illustrates the issue. Names are disguised to protect the innocent—and the frustrated.

A few years back one of the American car companies developed a grinding machine for a common engine part that was superior in accuracy, surface quality, and machining speed. It was more costly than the existing machines, but also very flexible to set up and could be used on many variations of part design.

The idea was unproven in production, so the project could not be "justified" internally, and it dragged on and on. Since the machine could not be built in house, one was built by a small shop near Detroit. Still, no one at the car company wanted to test it in use after seeing it. Only proven equipment could survive the risk calculus in financial projections (though a whole plant full of automation could be justified on the basis of rosy sales projections of a million or so units in sales to amortize it). The "system" stymied would-be internal production champions.

Meantime a German company observed the machine. It is relatively easy to invent around any design patents, so the company began to build it. It also sold the concept to a Japanese car company, which promptly assigned its trusted supplier of similar equipment the task of developing the machine and proving it in production with it, which the supplier did in just a few years. Now the "trusted supplier" is knocking on the door of the same American car company's manufacturing engineers to sell them back their own idea, production-proven, but probably not with the most advanced tweaks that they have been able to put on it.

Many of the stronger Japanese manufacturers have acquired such expertise in equipment and tooling critical to their processes that they have opened equipment subsidiaries on the side. (This strategy is much more vital to manufacturing than financial *keiretsu*.) The subsidiaries build any critical tooling and equipment for the parent that are not already built in house. Naturally, they also seek the best technology and incorporate that into the parent's machines *first*. In addition, they have a few trusted machine suppliers that work very closely with them. It was to one of these that the Japanese auto company assigned the American design concept for the new machine.

The most important relationship that must exist with either an internal or external supplier is a mutual improvement process designed to make the overall operation "world class"—among the best in a world business that increasingly demands ultimate all-around performance. That, and not a piece of hardware, is what is really important and what is really "sold." In this sense, no one can buy the core know-how of a business without not only learning it themselves, but how to improve it.

Why do American companies have such comparatively big trouble with their internal suppliers? Often because no manufacturing strategy supersedes the dictates of ROI or cash flow. If internal transfer prices are high, they prompt sourcing production out from high overhead, which is then spread across remaining volume, thus increasing internal "prices" again, thus descending into a costing death spiral that hollows out the company.

On the other hand, allowing a nonstrategic supply operation to stay in business just to keep jobs or equipment confers little advantage. As long as the operation is noncompetitive, it is a drag on the rest of the business. Forcing an internal division to bid "below cost" against outside suppliers is no assurance that it will learn how to operate more effectively. All this bidding is perfectly logical if internal divisions are not guided by a mission or strategy and engaged in improvement processes. If they are, the policy starts to appear insane.

(Slashing cash outflows and really learning how to perform are not the same thing. In many lines of work, a skilled crew with good experience in improvement processes will be five or ten times more productive than so-so workers. Construction material fabrication is one such area.)

The more "excellent" large companies have begun to correct these problems in recent years. One action has been to have full operating reviews emphasizing internal quality and delivery, not just financial indicators. Internal improvement processes help all customers. Companies such as Kodak, for instance, appointed directors of "internal marketing" to assure that divisions became better internal customers and worked with supplier divisions to improve internal performance in comparison with that obtainable elsewhere. It is a good start, but only a start.

First Step: Becoming a World-Class Customer[2]

One does not have to form a working relationship to buy and sell onions. Impersonal transactions will do, assuming that buyers and sellers know their onions. That is the usual assumption of classical free-market theory, which is the bottom rung of the customer-supplied development scale in Figure 9-1.

That assumption is impossible when creating, making, and delivering a complex product with all the service that goes with it. It's usually not sufficient even when products or services seem simple. For instance, making starch from corn would seem simple. While it is not as tricky as an integrated circuit, there are hundreds of types of finished starch. Really understanding the corn, the physiochemistry of starch, and its applications in the detail necessary for top-quality performance is far from a quick study.

No one has strictly transactional relations with critical suppliers, just as relations with important customers are not impersonal. One of the great challenges of business is understanding the reasons for this. For instance, department stores rarely operate a successful bridal department (wedding gowns and accessories). Gowns are only the vehicle for the real service, which is tending to the exact details of "the improvement process" wanted by every bride to make the most important occasion of her life come out perfect. Small shops operated by dedicated suppliers are better suited to this challenge, usually because a large organization's bureaucracy frustrates the process.

If a supplier is trying to please, whether the product is wedding gowns or septic tanks, having a good customer helps. Good customers explain what they want and why. If a supplier can learn how to satisfy the demands of a tough but collaborative customer who gives good feedback, it is better able to please other customers as well. A bad customer is chronically confusing, contradictory, uncommunicative, fickle, and greedy—the kind of company that wants to purchase long-term *service* as if haggling over roller skates in a flea market.

A great many large companies no longer browbeat suppliers at every opportunity. Nor are many small companies any longer afraid to give detailed feedback to much larger suppliers, fearing they are simply at their mercy. However, the idea of being a better customer is still novel. The company that wants to be an excellent customer to its own suppliers begins as one trying hard to please its own customers. It must be pursuing its own improvement processes; otherwise, it is limited in the amount and value of feedback it gives suppliers. Figure 9-2 shows a short list of the attributes of a good customer as U.S. companies now conceive them.

In January 1990 Rank Xerox Venray (a part of Xerox in the Netherlands) received the Co-Purchaser Award from Nevat-Missat (Dutch Association of Suppliers), marking the first known time that a group of industrial supply companies had ever selected a best customer. The citation remarked on Xerox's continuous endeavors to improve supplier involvement world-wide. The reasons given for the award were a subset of those listed in Figure 9-2.

Being a good customer is really being a good improvement partner

FIGURE 9-2

CHARACTERISTICS OF A GOOD
CUSTOMER COMPANY (CIRCA 1992)

- They demonstrate, by improvement practices and information sharing, the ability to sustain good customer-supplier relationships.
- They have top leadership committed to open customer-supplier relationships.
- They commit to long-lasting relationships.
- They can be trusted—with proprietary confidentiality, for example.
- They share a common vision and collaborate working toward it.
- They seek mutual prosperity through joint objectives and mutual improvement using common measurements and benchmark goals.
- They expect you to make a reasonable profit.
- They are responsive to supplier needs such as accurate billing, on-time payment, timely transmittal of quality feedback, etc.
  —They ask you what their deficiencies are, and do not punish honesty.
  —They fix the problems—or try to.
- They help you become a better partner—a better supplier to other customers and a better customer to your own suppliers.
- They "show you the same face" in all parts of the company—consistent behavior in all functions and activities.
- They maintain open communication. (It's easy to contact engineers, marketers—and *their* customers when useful.)
- Their measurement of your performance is consistent and designed for your improvement as well as theirs.
- They involve you early in new-product and process development.

Companies are here referred to as "they"—people—rather than the more grammatically correct "it." This list is adapted from one compiled at a meeting of leading purchasing managers and supplier representatives by the Association for Manufacturing Excellence, April 11, 1992.

or collaborator. Serving a supplier in this way is simply an extension of serving a customer. Customers and suppliers are collaborators in mutual improvement. They are part of the same network to serve primary customers and "secondary customers," even if the scope of that enterprise remains vaguely defined.

Many larger customer companies today teach improvement processes to their suppliers. Xerox, Ford, and Motorola have become well known for instructing suppliers. Certainly Toyota, Honda, and other Japanese companies also coach suppliers. However, not all the learning is one way. Good customers learn from their suppliers as a regular process, not just to be bailed out of a jam.

The first step in being a good customer is selecting a limited set of receptive suppliers as partners. One cannot have interaction and improvement processes with a large network of suppliers for the same reason that everyone cannot speak in a meeting with too many people. This concept works in reverse, too. The limited time for collaboration does not permit a supplier company to maintain a close relationship with too many customers.

If relationships with suppliers are mostly transactional, having multiple suppliers is a prudent way to maintain control in an environment of distrust. The customer can play one supplier against another, and losing one does not seem serious. Having a large number of suppliers automatically means that we cannot be a confidant with many of them, and perhaps not with any of them because of the distrust engendered by the methods of keeping suppliers at bay.

Likewise, conventional business wisdom cautions against betting the whole store on a few customers, for then losing one of them is a heavy blow. However, when communication and improvement processes are necessary with customers, a single operating company cannot have many of them either. Having a few good customers and pleasing them is preferable to having a multitude of customers, none loyal, and none a good improvement partner or giving helpful feedback.

Any general formula is impossible. Take the case of Woods Wire, for instance. It produces electrical extension cords and sells them through the normal retail channels, so there are fifty or more major chain accounts, plus many others. The company cannot be a close improvement partner with all customers. Two, three, four or so are more like it. However, all of Woods's customers would benefit from the improvement collaboration of a few.

Suppose an auto supplier reasons that it would rather produce for an aftermarket than put up with demanding OEMs who want to "tell them how to run their business." They lost the inside track to new products. Unless unusually diligent, they also risk lagging in quality and process improvement. A smart industrial supplier wants ties with customers that are "ahead of the curve" in their industry.

Customer companies are also utterly dependent on the sustained high performance of suppliers. Good customers want to be the preferred customer of their suppliers, and that is also a selection process. A company lax in developing relationships with "world-class" suppliers cannot make up the deficiencies all by itself. A few defects from one supplier can force a company to recall its products just as surely as bobbles on its own premises.

All industrial suppliers are part of an integrative process by their customers. A foundry that makes its own patterns is a minimal integrator itself but critical to the integrative efforts of customers. A company like Xerox fabricates very little itself, so that its primary operating forte must be the integration of suppliers into the total plan for a machine—and the service that accompanies it.

The integration process begins inside the customer company itself. One of the attributes in Figure 9-2 is consistent treatment of a supplier across all the customer's processes. A typical problem in even a small company arises when the production function finally tries JIT delivery from a supplier, only to have a controller on a different wavelength decide that cash flow makes it necessary to delay payments to suppliers. Then, not only is the supplier's production cut back to dry up the excess stock in the pipeline but payment for material that is shipped is delayed.

One of the major problems in improving partnerships with suppliers is functional divisions and contradictory reward systems within the customer's own organization. The customer's operating personnel want improvement partnerships, but their reward systems are based on immediately demonstrable results in cost reduction and cash flow, department by department—a highly divisive incentive system.

A good customer is a good partner. In the current environment, the customers and suppliers most aggressive in quality, technology, and process improvement are apt to pair up. Those left out are in danger of watching their business erode, noses pressed against the glass, complaining that the system is unfair.

Types of Partners

A company with close ties to suppliers thinks of suppliers' factories and other operations somewhat as extensions of its own capabilities. Suppliers of materials, tooling, and equipment really work for the customer's factory, but under a different roof. Sometimes they work directly under the customer's roof, as with contract maintenance or PPG Industries operating paint departments inside General Motors plants.

Auditors, architects, and consultants are also suppliers. So are bankers, although they are usually considered to be creditors. Relationships tend to be defined financially and contractually rather than by critical contribution to customer satisfaction or other objectives. The differences between employees, consultants, and suppliers are sometimes blurred. If a consultant is a supplier, is a temporary employee also a supplier? An agency supplying temporaries is a supplier. Unions like to be considered suppliers at contract time.

Distinctions between customers and suppliers are also becoming blurred when companies are defined using the total corporate umbrella. For example, Motorola and Alcatel are simultaneously customers and suppliers of each other as well as competitors in a few lines. Many projects and operations commonly mix personnel from many companies, as in aerospace or construction ventures.

Suppliers exist for the reasons given in economics texts, like economy of scale. "Information contributions" by suppliers, such as knowledge of a foreign customer's regulatory requirements, are increasingly important, or perhaps that only seems so. Most suppliers are specialists who bring something to an integrated effort.

The major human challenge in these arrangements is stability and allegiance to the needs of the joint enterprise and its customers rather than "fulfilling the contract." Regardless of its source of capital, a customer or a supplier is a partner in the same enterprise, working in the same process to serve the same end customer. A differently composed enterprise, perhaps with a cast of characters from some of the same suppliers, may compete for the same customers. To hold each cast of characters together, each of these combined operational enterprises must have a sense of mission—something in common must inspire a collage of people to satisfy the same set of customers.

In this kind of environment, most suppliers perform a service by working with others to integrate a complete result. Many companies have extensive experience assembling teams of consultants, supplier representatives, and core employees (some recently hired) to carry off projects. Such teams may even be fielded to do "excellence turn-arounds." If a mission is well done, diverse participants will unite behind it—something more than acquiring another line on their resumes.

Some suppliers are more critical to the mission and the quality of its results than others. They are the critical suppliers with whom close relationships and improvement processes are essential. Figure 9-3

FIGURE 9-3
CRITICAL AND LESS CRITICAL SUPPLIERS

Traditional Offering of Supplier	Critical to Customer Satisfaction	Less Critical to Customer Satisfaction
Material	Major components	Miscellaneous hardware
	Design partners	
Equipment and Tooling	Steppers (for ICs)	Exhaust fans
	Molds and dies	Racks
Service	Custom software	Office cleaning
	Advertising	Lawn service

The critical suppliers are those with which long-term relationships and improvement processes are needed. Those are not needed for a paper clip supplier. As the need for integrative collaboration intensifies, the critical suppliers are those most useful as joint-venture partners in an open-system enterprise.

classifies suppliers according to their contribution to mission and to customer satisfaction. Assessing which suppliers are critical is not to be done lightly. Under the right circumstances some unlikely ones are critical. For example, if screws cannot be avoided in a design to be assembled by automation, a screw supplier is important to the process.

This discussion of supplier relationships should be close to common sense—no big stretch in current thinking. However, the definitions of a "good" customer, supplier, and competitor slide away from convention.

Customer: A collaborator with key suppliers in improving its own products, processes, services, or satisfaction.

Supplier: A collaborator with the customer and with other suppliers serving the same customer to improve the customer as well as all other partners serving that customer.

Competitor: A party in a separate network providing a potential alternative to the same customer or customers.

Open Systems and Trust

Open exchange is essential to resolving most problems and conflicts, but participants in almost any enterprise will not bare all. (Even married partners don't tell *everything*.) No one expects enterprises to invite direct competitors to coaching sessions, but when people float from company to company within an industry, as they often have, the notion of airtight secrecy is an illusion. Secrecy and the protection of intellectual capital go hand in hand, so in an open system, the concept of intellectual capital is more limited.

Nondisclosure of intellectual capital fundamentally differs from sitting on a gold mine. Most intellectual capital is a set of skills. Sharing technical knowledge does not necessarily enable the average observer to duplicate it. For example, merely watching a golf pro sink a forty-foot putt does not make the feat any easier. Even embedding skills in software does not enable anyone to integrate them into a useful accomplishment. For that reason, collaborators can work very closely without giving away everything. For example, an advisor can work with a customer using software to design an integrated circuit, but the actual process for building the circuit is not in the software.

Suppliers collaborating in design do not need to disclose everything. For instance, designers need to know only the major cost, quality, and process characteristics of frabricators' parts to design to their strengths and avoid their major shortcomings. On the other hand, if knowing exactly how a surface treatment takes place is vital to design, the supplier has to design the part to the customer's needs anyway. In a different context, a company that designs an inductor to harden a part for a customer needs to know the details of part use, part stress, and part metallurgy. The advantage of openness is that participants know their competitive position. In conditions of secrecy, it is easy to believe illusions.

Much intellectual capital is worth little unless you know how to use it to serve a customer. The inductor designer has a skill (and perhaps software) that others need. His real intellectual capital is skill and experience—the ability to apply that skill to a new situation. Even if inductor design know-how were transferred to software, the use of the software still takes expertise, especially if the user is constantly incorporating new learning into it.

Skilled integration is in itself intellectual capital. Learning to combine the best effort of numerous suppliers and specialists in a design project with all the "design for" considerations is not done casually. Today, the premium is on integration. Standoffish specialists, all protecting their intellectual capital inside little fortress companies (or departments) cannot hope to beat a team effort.

The specialists have to build trust in each other through honest give-and-take and data sharing. They must commit to the mission of the total enterprise. The reverse of this is hanging back. Hanging back is typified by "consulting-speak," referring to a team (or enterprise) as they, not we, and using totally detached analysis.

Jelling an enterprise, or even a small project team, is difficult when everyone is mercenary. Putting together a set of suppliers for a long-term effort is similar to putting together a top-flight project team.

The Japanese approach to supplier relations, while not a model to be totally copied, offers a number of insights.

Lessons from Japanese Supplier Relations

The existence of *keiretsu* fogs the lessons from Japanese supplier history. More financial families than operational ones, the *keiretsu* played an important role in Japan's postwar industrial rebirth. When capital was short and companies were struggling to rebuild, the six largest *keiretsu* accounted for more than 50 percent of exports. They now account for less than 20 percent. Their role in the development of Japanese supplier relations has been less vital than the creation of operating relationships, which often cross *keiretsu* lines. For example, human relationships between Toyota and its suppliers enable smooth transfer of machines, material, and personnel between them, not its position within the Mitsui *keiretsu* nor a "leverage position."[3]

In their early days, Toyota and Nissan had few capable domestic suppliers, so they spun off their own. For instance, Nippondenso, now a huge company in its own right, started as a small supplier to Toyota in 1947. Most of the important relationships with suppliers continue to be personal, operational links, not financial ones.

Locating Japanese suppliers nearby began not because anyone decades ago had the idea of JIT delivery but so that technicians from one company could easily run over to another to train people and to help out in case of trouble. That tradition continues. For example, if a supplier in a network incurs damage to a tool or a machine, it can call on engineering departments or tool rooms in the same network for the right expertise or equipment. A part of just-in-time is immediate response to one of thse fire-alarm requests. If one supplier in the network has a problem, so does everyone else unless it is immediately righted.[4]

Auto companies in Japan obtain most of their parts from sole-source suppliers with whom they have long-standing relationships, seldom broken unless a supplier falls behind technically. Electronics companies have fewer sole-source suppliers and are much more likely to switch suppliers when technology changes. Operating practices, especially the relationships between people who work within—and across—the companies, are far more effective than "financial leverage."

All employees throughout a "family" of suppliers speak the same quality problem-solving language. Visit almost any company location, and the presentation is similar. The history of the operating unit and its improvement processes is briefly recounted. The current situation is described, followed by a tour of a plant or other operations. Then the visitors are inevitably asked for ideas for improvement.

Except for new-product development, most information is open, including that in design departments, provided one is allowed to enter. Even competitors are apt to share improvement methods (but not new-product information). A few personnel on station in almost any company are likely to be from customers or suppliers. Customers regularly visit supplier plants, where visibility systems make it easy to see what is really occurring. In addition, where kanban systems are usable, they provide what-and-when visibility between plants. In general, the need for close teamwork takes precedence over close secrecy.

When companies know each other's processes well, they can also estimate each other's costs fairly accurately, and cost sheets are frequently shared when companies jointly study how to improve a process. Likewise, suppliers may have a fair understanding of a customer's costs, too. Therefore, price negotiation is neither a bluffing contest nor an excuse for extortion. The parties are more likely to consider how to share the pain, if that is their lot, or the gain if they have prospered.

Inside Japan, the domestic auto industry's common planning cycles stimulate common learning cycles. Other industries are not as synchronized, but almost all have some form of improvement process in common between customers and suppliers.[5]

Particularly in autos, but also in other industries, subsets of a Japanese company can operate with suppliers almost as a single enterprise. Those who are looking for secretive collusion or governmental policy miss the obvious. It isn't hidden. The operating development of a Japanese supplier family has been an open system, but the actual practice is difficult, and the concepts do not register immediately in minds molded around transactions and deals.

Selecting the Japanese Supplier

Medium and large Japanese firms usually classify suppliers into at least two groups, close suppliers and others. The close ones generally supply the most critical equipment, parts, or tools. Firms search for new long-term, critical suppliers infrequently. When they do, the purchasing department reviews technical and operating performance and the prospect of working closely with personnel in the prospective company. Efficient existing processes or immediate costs are not as important as cooperation and determination to become the best.

If the relationship will be close, the final decision is made by the customer's top management based on the "attitude" of the prospect's top management. Will they commit to a long-term working relationship? Often this commitment is couched in a catch phrase, "coexistence and mutual prosperity." Each will do its utmost to assure the survival of the other in tough times and share the wealth if times are good. Savings from mutual improvement processes are often shared, too.

A key aspect of these relationships is that most of the manufacturing companies are de facto governed by operating managers. That is, the board of directors has few outsiders, and the company is *not* run by the stockholders, unless it is owner-operated. To promote relationships, boards can swap stock between companies if they wish, but mere money does not insure the informal relationships at all levels between suppliers necessary for close operating interchange. Those take conscious effort.

The system is kept vigorous because companies assist each other with technical and operating improvements. They goad each other to improve. Without this, the linkages become cozy and inefficient— like much of the traditional Japanese distribution network.

How does a new company enter a system like this? Based on demonstrated performance, not on a proposal or bid alone. A Japanese customer tests a new supplier's capabilities and attitudes. This ordeal is strange to Western companies that simply think that sending parts that meet specification is good enough. In Japan, simply meeting a contract is not good enough.

Trade pressure has forced Japanese domestic operations to buy foreign parts, materials, and machines. Asked what it takes to induce them to sever ties with an established supplier in favor of a foreign one, Japanese companies almost always say quality or technology not possessed by the existing supplier, and which they cannot quickly match. Overwhelming evidence of high operating performance makes a strong case for a customer to proceed with a change that is the business equivalent of divorce.[6]

Given the normal tendency to favor people who are known and trusted above those who are unknown, the Japanese supplier system is indeed difficult to crack. Government pressure to buy foreign has limited effect. As Western supplier relationships become more long-term and interactive, one can expect the same kind of difficulty cracking in.

Japanese Supplier Associations

Most larger Japanese companies have associations for suppliers. Formally, suppliers do not need to belong, although participation is very helpful to them. In general, associations consist of those suppliers most interested in cooperating closely with a major customer. Members join voluntarily, but it is obviously in their self-interest to do so.

Supplier associations seem to have begun as social groups to promote better working relations. The average association meeting is still a semiannual or quarterly meeting differing little from many business events anywhere. The customer and its suppliers discuss business conditions, new products, and how to mutually work through peak load periods or business lulls. These meetings are usually followed by parties or sports.

The more active associations do much more. Toyota's supplier association has been aggressive in promoting quality, JIT, fast product introduction, and the like. It has inspired a number of other companies to also use their associations to boost supplier network performance.

In these associations, key operating managers more likely meet monthly. Others may attend meetings covering both hard technology and operating techniques. Some have active coaching programs to prepare members for a suppliers' quality award modeled after the

Deming Prize. Others sponsor cross-company improvement teams that travel from operation to operation attacking quality and process problems. A few even publish an association journal. They become mutual improvement societies.

Weaknesses of the Japanese Supplier System

One weakness of the Japanese supplier system is that it is often explained using Japanese cultural tradition. Many practices have universal value, but their ethnocentric development causes them to appear as cultural curiosities, despite the efforts of many Westerners to study the "Japanese miracle" from any angle they can find.

A second weakness—which is also a strength—is the difficulty of someone from outside displacing a close supplier. As long as the existing partners aggressively pursue mutual technical and process improvements, it would be a major challenge for an outsider to demonstrate clearly superior performance. Cracking in is not impossible, but it is a very high hurdle to jump. That seems unfair in an American society in which people have been accustomed to making opportunities by aggressive self-promotion.

Third, because improvement-intensive interchanges primarily enable people to work smarter, but they are easily confused as pressuring them to merely work harder. Companies under cost pressure everywhere find it more expedient to outsource and pressure subcontractors than to engage in aggressive improvement processes. A supplier that misreads an improvement process as merely working harder will soon face demands it does not know how to meet. (Japanese laws prevent large companies from putting small suppliers out of business. If one cannot perform, the customer must ease them out without driving them bankrupt. At least one Japanese transplant has had a similar experience in the United States.)

Fourth, Japanese supplier relations have been motivated by survival and growth (coexistence and mutual prosperity). In flat markets, the soul of enterprise must be motivated more by an ethic of service excellence, a different drive to keep the adrenaline flowing. In other words, Japan is just entering the postgrowth phase of industrial development, and the system will be tested by it.

Finally, the slowing of industrial growth in Japan is stimulating investor interest in profits when they can no longer count on growth premiums. Many Japanese themselves do not understand the nature of the system that their industry has built. Scandals attest that Japanese investors are as avaricious as any. If stockholders decided to take control of the companies and turn them into financial fortresses operating independent-profit tollgates, the system would quickly degenerate.

As the Japanese system matures from a catch-up position to leading-edge, the Japanese will have to dump the cultural explanations of their supplier relations. People from other ethnic systems can adopt visibility techniques and similar methods without Japanese cultural predilections such as endurance training.

The Beginnings of Open-System Operations

The direction of customer-supplier relationships in the West is to open the operating systems between companies. Companies like Steelcase have a long tradition of trust with certain suppliers, using open-ended blanket contracts that have spanned more than a decade. However, the country is filled with contrary examples.

One common small step in opening the operating connections is quality certification of suppliers. Many companies do not want to inspect material sent by suppliers. Instead, they want to assure that the quality practices used by suppliers makes inspection unnecessary. Actually, the volume of material sent to electronics or vehicle-assembly plants has for years been so great that inspecting it all is impossible anyway. Supplier defects show up as end-of-line repair, line stops, or field problems, including recalls. An assembler of complex products must have high confidence in the proficiency of suppliers.

Certification requires the customer to review the operations of each supplier. Reviews have become increasingly tough. Customers do not want to receive defects, nor to pay a supplier to sort out defects before shipping. Therefore, quality reviews have more and more become reviews of a substantial part of a supplier's operations: design, sourcing of material used, production, and quality systems.

If a single supplier serves ten major customers, all ten may troop through periodically for operations reviews. If each of the ten has independently developed its own detailed expectations down to the formats of records used, the paperwork and reviews are an enormous waste to the supplier. Each customer is paying for excessive overhead just to comply with its own audits. Furthermore, the documents each one reviews may be eyewash, not what the supplier actually uses.

Better to simply have a general review of the system the supplier actually uses. In fact, if several customers agree on the basic performance criteria they expect of suppliers, they do not all have to completely review each supplier independently. Each customer can review performance scores and determine whether it wants to take any action.

Industry standards on physical measurements, communication, and many other operating attributes are established and extensive. Common systems of performance measurement (other than financial reports) are not. A start is the ISO 9000 quality standard adopted by the European Economic Community. If a company selling into the EEC passes an ISO 9000 audit by an independent party about once every five years, it will be considered certified for EEC trade. (This is simplistic; actual requirements for certification are a tangled web.) However, ISO 9000 requirements are not high-performance criteria. They do represent the expectations of sound quality practice circa 1990, and they emphasize documentation.

The auto, steel, and electronics industries all have projects that might lead to common systems to measure fundamental supplier operating performance. These would go beyond minimal standards. They would make known to the industry a relatively detailed appraisal of each company's operating capabilities at the time of review, and each firm could compare itself with benchmarks. That's a far more rigorous system than checking whether someone meets a minimum performance standard. Even better is competing to be the *best* in class. That is an expectation of an excellent supplier.

Achieving that goal implies a more important first step: that companies share some common processes of improvement between them. Teams of people from different companies can work on common projects in the expectation that each will use a variation of the same improvement methodology. Most important, firms with high performance expectations make increasingly stringent demands. Too often industry standards or regulations are now tightened only *after* an error or tragedy, and then laggards want to fight it.

However, performance assessment is not a one-way street, customer-to-supplier. Suppliers should also rate customers. Improvement processes are two-way, and performance rating should be also. When a supplier does not perform well, it may be that the customer is not performing well—not communicating engineering changes accurately and on time, for instance.

The objective of common measurements and all the rest of an open system is to build a learning system that spans companies. Sometimes it is believed that common systems stifle creativity. They do stop a great deal of reinventing of wheels. Fast improvement is more implementation of concepts already known to someone than attempting to devise excellent practice in everything from scratch. Few ideas themselves are truly new, and common knowledge of deficiencies does not make them go away, just as the world knowing that a baseball player is in a slump does not by itself help him regain his batting form.

The crucial elements of an open system are commitment to improve performance and *action* to do so. That commitment is a very different motivation from each company forming its own little private fortress, determined to defend its own position and capture its own cash flow. To do something very different takes strong leadership to breech the walls between functions inside companies and open the boundaries between them.

Open-System Enterprise

An open-system enterprise is more than decentralized. Decentralized companies exist in large numbers. McDonald's, Mrs. Fields Cookies, the Pritsker companies, and many others all exhibit some form of decentralization. Some companies exert central control through financial reports, leaving all operating methodology to operating units. McDonald's, however, is quite different. Each unit is on its own, but training and controls assure that a hamburger from one is virtually identical to that from another. That is decentralization with extensive operational training, coaching, and field monitoring.

Charles Handy has referred to decentralized organizations as federations, or "shamrock" organizations. Operating responsibility and the coordination of units working with each other is pushed away from centralized bureaucracies. The result is flat organizations that offer people more opportunity to work in small organizations where they want to live and still contribute through a network, particularly if they do professional work. Handy's explanation is much like the organization envisioned by the twenty-first–century manufacturing scenarios—small, networked operating organizations serving the population in its region, somewhat like decentralizing car remanufacturing to a network of car dealerships.[7]

Other "open systems" currently exist more by computer linkage than anything else. For example American Hospital Supply (AHS), now part of Baxter Health Care, has for several years sold to hospitals by having computer visibility into the hospitals' inventory systems. AHS keeps the hospitals resupplied almost automatically, in effect running part of their inventory systems for them. What's missing is an aggressive improvement process across a total supply chain, or around a full cycle of material use, from manufacturing to disposal.

A larger version of this is Quick Response, the program used by major U.S. retailers to have their suppliers manager their inventory all the way to the store shelf, if possible. For example, Woods Wire, a manufacturer of extension cords, is expected to ship its product in packages bar-coded for the exact Wal-Mart store shelf destinations where it is needed. Just now, that is managed largely by "cross-docking." That is, daily shipments go to Wal-Mart warehouses, where they are immediately resorted into truckloads with other items destined for the same store.

Those Quick Response manufacturers who have not achieved JIT production capability are also left holding finished goods inventory that once would have been shipped to customer warehouses, so Quick Response is a powerful stimulus to also improve manufacturing. However, that arrangement is also a great deal short of instituting cross-company improvement processes or capturing a full cycle of material use where that is useful.

Besides these examples, the country is now filled with various forms of partnerships and consortia. The total number of arrangements by which companies can work together seems almost infinite. Not all of these will be a success.

The influences stimulating decentralization are so powerful that one can hardly see how they can be held back. However, the pressure that will drive organizations to the next stage of collaboration will be the need for "excellence" in all phases of operations throughout a network—virtually error-free cycles of material use. That requires human operational interaction in addition to computer networking, not an organization structured to easily respond to a financial control system. Larger purposes must be served than just pumping cash flow.

Structure of Open-System Enterprise

Most of the prior examples of decentralized organization and database linkage still retain the separate corporate identities of the different companies. If people in a complete material-use cycle are to work closely together and share most information openly, they need to be in the same legal entity and be focused on the same customers. Otherwise, the need to maintain transactional boundaries foils the relationships, and the need to maintain separate marketing identities creates friction.

In the United States, this baggage from prior business practices will reimpose the boundary limitations that everyone is trying to break down. The variety of legal structures possible all have tax and liability implications, which is a subject in itself, but some form of corporation or joint venture should be formed. All the critical partners can combine under this tent. Each can put some money into it, as in the Mayekawa Company example near the end of Chapter 8. Then, people from different resource companies can more nearly function as one team under a relatively familiar type of corporate framework.

The open-system structure would then consist of two basically different kinds of companies: resource companies and operating enterprises. Resource companies would provide seed money, personnel, and expertise to the operating companies. Operating companies would be formed as the integrators to accomplish specific missions. Some missions might be short-term, such as construction projects or the development and marketing of a computer with a limited life cycle. Some might be long-term, such as fielding the manufacturing, remanufacturing, and service for a "three-day car." The long-term variety would represent a fundamental reordering of an industry.

Payments from operating companies to resource companies might be in two forms: service payments and profits. The operating companies would probably be dependent on resource companies for technical interchange, some kinds of training, communications networks, specialized consulting, and other services. A strong operating company could likely do much of this on its own, but the idea is to keep operating companies lean. The overhead would be shared with other companies via the resource companies. That is the direction many corporations are taking anyway.

The resource companies would be "home base" to many people working in operating enterprises. Therefore, they would also serve as personnel development and deployment agencies—not so different from what some company headquarters are evolving toward today. A vital concern of resource companies is preserving and enhancing the intellectual capital residing in the skills of their personnel. When personnel transfer, or when an operating enterprise breaks up, one of the most important factors is preventing a skill base from being totally lost. A resource company recognizing this as its mission is more likely to reformulate effective new operating enterprises than pure spin-off entrepreneurs are. Independent entrepreneurs tend to enter a venture underfunded and with incomplete skills.

The open-enterprise idea is a reformation of business, not just a restructuring. The objective of the reformation is to concentrate on a mission and maximize operating effectiveness, not maximize cash flow to the financiers—although a high degree of correlation should exist between the two.

Without trying an idea as different as this, it is impossible to detail what could or should happen. No one can anticipate every detail, but a form of business something like this is an idea whose time is fast approaching. A few projected comparisons are shown in Figures 9-4 and 9-5.

Example of a Long-Term Open-System Enterprise

Suppose GM converted Cadillac to an open-system enterprise with the mission of designing a new model with tooling costs reduced by 90 percent or more, with customer lead times reduced to ten days or less, and with a design for remanufacturing and recycling—a big leap

FIGURE 9-4
OPEN-SYSTEMS COMPARISONS

Business-as-Usual Open-Market Systems	*Open-System Enterprise*
Companies have different missions and objectives. Often cash-flow-driven.	Each enterprise has a COMMON MISSION. Driven by excellence meeting the mission.
Common financial reporting disclosure format (with auditing standards).	Common financial reporting format. Each enterprise has internally compatible cost accounting systems. Plus operational audit standards that are comparable between similar operations. (Standard benchmark data.) Plus open disclosure of environmental performance.
Common transactional conventions	With many boundaries eliminated, many transactions necessary are entered into the same system. Compatible computer-to-computer communication standards.
Industrial standards For product performance For common parts	Same industrial standards, plus Common quality framework. COMMON IMPROVEMENT PROCESSES.
Similar departmental structures (allows functional specialists to personally change jobs between companies).	SIMILAR CROSS-FUNCTIONAL TEAM CONCEPTS (individuals can quickly form teams inside the enterprise and work boundaries with those outside when necessary).

FIGURE 9-4 (*cont.*)

Independent planning systems	INTEGRATED PLANNING SYSTEMS (closely synchronized).
Sharing of risks and rewards is negotiated. May or may not be considered fair—subject to "leverage."	Most risks and rewards are shared within the same enterprise framework.
Trust between individuals and between comparnies possible, subject to how the parties handle the instinct to maximize their own gain.	Trust between individuals and resource companies can never be guaranteed. It seems more likely with common rewards and common systems.
Rules, such as bidding (with performance provisions) prescribe entry and exit from contractual relationships.	Entry is largely determined when enterprise is formed. ENTRY INTO A PROCESS is subject to more evidence of preparation. Exit for nonperformance or technical obsolescence is always possible. Preparation routes must be genuine and available.

toward the "three-day car." That enterprise would develop the product, lease it, service it in the field—including retrofitting and remanufacturing—and be responsible for disposition of unusable materials. It would manage the full life cycle of vehicles, a totally different concept of the automotive business.

A number of resource companies might buy into the enterprise corporation. GM with its personnel and research resources would probably be the lead partner. Critical supplier companies would also buy in, including some for recycling or benign environmental dis-

FIGURE 9-5

COMPARISON OF INFORMATION
NORMALLY KEPT SECRET

Business-as-Usual Open-Market Systems	*Open-System Enterprise*
Trade secrets, costs	Trade-secret processes are the know-how of the enterprise itself.
Most salaries secret	Salaries generally known.
"Personal" personnel data	"Personal" personnel data
Research and new-product information is confidential.	New-product information is confidential.
Most internal operating data (such as defect rates, etc.) is confidential.	Most operating performance data is open.

posal. One supplier might be GMAC to provide expertise in financing the leases. Very likely the dealers would be exclusive to the enterprise—all their resources committed to it, and therefore having a big voice in it.

Large dealer locations might very well become remanufacturing locations, and if so, they might emerge as the dominant member of the enterprise. They should not be. The "home base" resource companies are the coordinators of the real capital—people. Otherwise, the open-enterprise system is little more than another financial restructuring.

Such an enterprise would not be small either geographically or financially. Only one of many problems is likely to be financing the leases. Some customers will want to shop for a better deal on lease financing, and that can be arranged, provided that control of the physical machine remains with the Cadillac enterprise, just as control of airliners remains with airlines. (A top-quality vehicle of this type would start taking on the attributes of an aircraft.) Good customers work with the company to have reviews and maintenance checks at the right time, and the payment system may reward them for doing so. Another problem would be assigning financial responsibility for damage.

As an open-system enterprise, Cadillac would extend its concurrent engineering practice to encompass dealers (retrofitters, if not remanufacturers), suppliers of parts and materials (some remanufactured or recycled), suppliers of equipment and tooling, and suppliers of services—dealers, transportation firms, and others. To be successful, every participant in the operating enterprise must pledge allegiance to the same mission. They must have a similar improvement process and language by which they can interact. Then they must abide by compatible nonaccounting measurements of primary results. In addition, if the enterprise uses a compatible accounting system throughout, with all the inventory in circulation owned in common, some of the major problems of working together should ameliorate. Each partner stands to gain if the enterprise is successful and lose if it is not. Mustering the best enterprise team possible is in the best interest of each participant.

The stability of the key players on an enterprise team is vital to success. The participating resource companies should not be able to pull their players on a whim, and individuals themselves sign on for a fixed period or through a milestone point, somewhat like signing on with the navy. Individuals who quit fail to receive a termination bonus, or might even pay a penalty for early withdrawal. The concept is a financial arrangement that stimulates a group to work through a long-term program together—unless the enterprise management itself decides that someone is not working out or that a substitute is needed. Both individuals and companies must give earnest thought to the length of their commitments.

The value of this approach is similar to the value of substituting a gainsharing system for the independent contractor foremen in factories of a hundred years ago. It should help override the tendency to compete by partners who should cooperate. If the individuals assigned to an enterprise form a bond, and their performance is judged more from within the enterprise than from without, they should be more cooperative. So should any affiliated, but independent, companies that they must coordinate.

For example, General Motors in fifteen years (if it begins rapid change and retains market share) might look somewhat like twenty or thirty Saturns all under a GM marketing umbrella and interacting with the talent and technology pools in GM R&D centers (which themselves would have research alliances in many directions). The operating divisions would multiply into lean, mean, open-system enterprises highly interwoven with suppliers. In effect, General Motors would cease to be a big operating company and become a marketing, research, and educational campus with umbilical cords to many enterprises, some of which might have more personnel than the core campus.

To exist, a campus must support many enterprises—or a few highly profitable ones. At the campuses, education, research, and investment must be planned for enterprises one to three developmental generations in advance, the same as GM technical centers do today, except in the enterprise system, they must concentrate on advanced concepts—not try to run current vehicle programs. In turn, enterprises cannot refuse to fund long-term improvement by their owners.

Finally, in a society that prides itself on being fair, routes must exist whereby new entries have opportunities to enter the closed-cycle enterprise system, but not through pure self-promotion—not just because they have a good story and a low bid. One can imagine the "core campus" for a number of crack enterprises having a "farm system" to prepare both individuals and new resource companies. New entrants whose forte is technical—say a new sealant for doors—but who lack process-improvement skills would have to be prepared to participate in an operating enterprise network. New technology companies, the kind that have historically broken into the business, would need a process partner or process coaching to prepare themselves for it. They cannot just "sell parts."

Finally, the end customer must in general have a choice of several enterprises to become associated with. The auto industry should make a number of competing service choices available to the public, with key performance data from each one publicly known. In fact, the competition for excellent service should push all the competitors to migrate to a new league of performance.

More than Restructuring

None of the seven open-system requirements listed at the beginning of this chapter (common mission, trust, sharing, improvement methods, communication, performance measurement, and fairness of entry) are met simply by the way enterprises are structured and how the people are rewarded. The lesson is clear. Structuring financial and human relationships for open-system enterprise is very important, but it's only the beginning, and it's probably one of the easier parts of the new industrial revolution once the emotion of discarding the baggage of old structures is past.

That is, it's not unthinkable for GM to reform into "a resource company" feeding "open-enterprise operating companies" after the current operating bureaucracy totally comprehends that the old structure cannot continue.

At the beginning of 1993 GM was trying to combine "lean manufacturing" with old bidding techniques with its suppliers to fuel its recovery. The mix was sputtering. Transition to a different mind set is so tough that an "open system" automobile may be initiated by a player not now in auto manufacturing.

The great challenge is motivating people to concentrate on customer satisfaction and operating excellence, including environmental excellence. The genuine test of this soul of enterprise is translating the soft inspirational mush to concrete methods and systems of work. It is much easier to give business-as-usual a new coat of buzzwords. The demands cannot be underestimated: technically interpreting the detailed needs of customers—sometimes a lone individual—and promptly giving them the newest or best with part-per-billion quality; flexible-flow, tightly coordinated production with a lot size of one; reprocessing hazardous materials; long-term development of people to use multiple skills. The warm, fuzzy concept of open-system enterprise has hard edges as soon as one begins to contemplate how anything like it can actually be implemented.

NOTES

1. Hugh Aaron, "U.S. Business Relationships: Color Them Brutish," *The Wall Street Journal*, 17 June, 1991, Sec. A, 10.
2. The phrase "world-class customer" was first heard from Kenneth J. Stork, formerly Corporate Director of Materials and Purchasing, Motorola Inc.

3. One of the better authorities in the United States on the *keiretsu* families is Mark Eaton of the Microelectronics and Computer Technology Corporation. He had a short but informative overview published as a letter in the *Harvard Business Review*, 68, no. 5 (November–December 1990): 212.

4. Robert W. Hall, and Jinichiro Nakane, *Flexibility: Manufacturing Battlefield of the 90s*, Research Report, Association for Manufacturing Excellence, Wheeling, Illinois, 1990.

5. Ibid.

6. Robert W. Hall, and Jinichiro Nakane, "Family Ties," *Target* 6, no. 3 (Fall 1990): 4–11.

7. Charles Handy, *The Age of Unreason* (Boston: Harvard Business School Press, 1989).

10

SUBSTANCE OVER STYLE

A TOP-RANKED UNIVERSITY WITH IVIED HALLS HAS A STATELY FACULTY DINING room, wood-paneled, hung with paintings of major benefactors and distinguished scholars, tables set with elegance—surely a fitting place to discuss grave matters of deep academic significance. Describing the place to a maintenance man produced an unexpected reaction: "I wouldn't wanta eat there. Rather go to Steak 'n Shake or Taco Bell."

"Too formal?"

"That's not it. We got called twice in the last month to locate a smell in their kitchen. Found dead mice in some holes both times. Several of them, too. It's no wonder. They never really clean the place up. The food's fancy, but I wouldn't want to eat it."

"I presume the brass have taken some action by now," I ventured.

"Nahh. What do they know? *Nobody* is going to tell them anything. Not until they barf."

A few minutes later I got around to asking the whistle-blower what he liked about Steak 'n Shake and Taco Bell. "You can see and smell everything that's going on."

But did the "brass" know about the kitchen problem? An administrator said the condition was minor. The kitchen was closed over a weekend for fumigation. "Happens every fall," he shrugged, noting that it certainly was not necessary to bring it to the attention of the university president, though he was a frequent diner there.

Both observers agreed on the mouse story, that the kitchen had few preventive measures for pests, and that the problem was recurrent. Without seeing the kitchen, inferring causes comes down to whose biases to believe.

The story illustrates several problems in determining whether performance improvement is real or only an illusion: (1) many conditions such as the mouse population or kitchen cleanliness are not regularly checked or measured in any way; (2) no one wants to report bad news upward, and usually not to customers either; (3) making performance visible to everyone adds credibility to any measurements kept; and, (4) measuring, tracking, and actually *improving* performance is a highly disciplined process, and failing to do so is easy to excuse away.

The way performance measures are used is as important as what measures are used—and probably more so. Detailed top-down performance measures are flawed. Managers can watch only a few measures, usually aggregate ones, because a single person cannot possibly pay attention to every detail that can be tended by ten others, much less tens of thousands of subordinates. Even Harold Geneen, the numbers-hawking one-time head of the ITT empire, had a limited capacity for data digestion. Excellence is created when the people doing the work directly pay attention to the details and improve processes until they do not have to pay constant attention for everything to go right.

A manager who understands a small operation in detail can obtain very good results by direct control even if others do not enjoy it very much. One of the most common examples is a restaurant owner who can run one location well by constantly nipping and yapping at the help. If he opens a second location, he does not know how to behave.

Objective measures of performance are important, even if a relatively subjective aspect of customer satisfaction is being measured; otherwise, form wins out over substance. Those who put a "positive spin" on their efforts make themselves look superior, just as in the ancient Olympics, the athlete who ran fastest was not always declared the winner over a slower one who ran with better form.

Properly used, most measurements should assist someone to better meet the mission of an enterprise. Some detailed measurements may only be seen by the one person who uses them. Others are open to the view of anyone interested. Well-employed measurements lead to corrective action or to permanent improvement. Substance wins out over form.

Most measurements should help someone *do* something better. Otherwise, the measurement itself is waste. Excellence is empty prattle unless firms work to improve something that is demonstrable; shorter and more accurate order processing, elimination of out-of-service field calls, product designs, reduced materials movement—something that usually can be represented by a measurement in some way.

Measurements for improvement are often detailed and represent a small contribution to an overall mission. For example, measuring the consistency of impact in a package scorer contributes to eliminating just one customer annoyance: a package that can't be opened with the bare hand. These measurements are coupled with action.

Top-down measurements are for control. If well done, such measures only indicate whether major processes are meeting objectives. Just as a machining process that shows normal variation is made worse by overcontrol, a manager who responds to every little performance blip makes conditions worse. Well done, a leader (not manager, as that term is often construed) develops people, and people control work processes. It's not as easy as it sounds.

Directionless Financial Management

Almost anyone who has ever successfully operated a business will say that cash flow (or sometimes profit) is the most important measure of business health. A multitude of technically astute entrepreneurs have gone broke because they did not make a business plan, or could not hold to it if they had one. Oblivious to cash-flow implications, entrepreneurs can spend themselves into oblivion in a few months' time. That's the business side of operations.

Millions of financially educated managers have now learned this lesson well—sometimes too well. Financial discipline is basic and essential. Even churches and schools must exercise it, but their primary mission, presumably, is not to make money. However, if the only mission a measurement system conveys is financial discipline, an organization is directionless. If the nature of its business is obvious, it may prosper despite this, but it is virtually impossible for it to be excellent compared with organizations dedicated to serving target customers and achieving continuous operating improvements using different measurements in a different way.

Control of a company almost exclusively by financial and accounting systems assumes that control of assets carries the potential of wealth. It is an illusion that financial control of plant and equipment equates to permanent wealth, just as the graceful appearance of Tara, Scarlett's plantation home in *Gone With the Wind*, symbolized the illusion that control of land assured permanent wealth.

Financial measures emphasize profitability of inert assets over any other mission of the company. They do not recognize the emerging leverage of soft stuff—skilled people and employment of information—as the new keys to high-performance, near-perfect customer satisfaction. Therefore, good stewardship of human capital is key to quality of life in the emerging era.

Financial controls do not assure a clean kitchen. A shortage of cash may stimulate all kinds of improvement, but it does not give much direction. Customer satisfaction or environmental security is not obtained by financial management. Many accomplishments needed to satisfy customer-satisfaction or quality-of-life objectives are inadequately represented by a dollar sign. Removing the Tara illusion brings everyone closer to reality.

Some of the new measures of performance excellence are dollarized—sort of a hybrid measurement to wean the financially oriented away from excessive dependence on cost measures. One is cost of quality. To determine it, firms attempt to approximate the losses from internal failures, external failures, inspection, and prevention. Figures derived for this purpose usually depend on numerous approximations and allocations. Once convinced that excellent quality is vital, quality measures expressed in dollars no longer carry as much importance.

Much the same can be said of the holding cost of inventory. Once convinced that inventory itself is a sign of waste somewhere, one no longer needs to put a dollar sign on it to be convinced that action should be taken if possible.

Dollar measures tend to dominate in financially controlled companies. They exist in common forms such as ROI formulas, both the discounted cash-flow variety and the simple ratio estimates, and the stack-up of measurements represented by the Du Pont Investment Formulas.[1]

Perhaps the most significant consequence of the Tara illusion is that performance measures for ownership interests dominate all others. In the information age the performance challenge is much broader. Measurements must track progress toward goals important to customers, whether primary or secondary, internal or external.

The know-how to achieve order-of-magnitude improvements toward customer satisfaction or quality-of-life goals is not directly related to profit maximization, just as the profitability of major league baseball teams does not necessarily depend on their won-loss record, and vice-versa. Neither does a ballplayer's salary have a big effect on the quality of the game. For example, in 1991 major league baseball players earned salaries 1,900 percent higher than in 1976 because of free agency and television.[2] However, the performance of both individual players and teams is recorded by the deluge of statistics that commentators recite in the slow parts of the games. Few baseball fans would argue that baseball performance has improved as dramatically as salaries.

Control by Misbegotten Measurements

Back in the not-so-good old days, before quality reviews and hefty product liabilities, I was once asked to search a shop floor for all orders of custom-built industrial chain more than six months overdue. Half the orders in the shop seemed to be that late or later. After a few hours, a long list of orders was checked with the customer-service department, which chose to expedite very few of them. They assumed that any customer who truly needed an order would "scream" and suggested that I concentrate my effort on orders more than a year overdue.

When asked why so many orders were overdue, the customer-service manager's response was enlightening: "Most customers add six months or more to our quoted lead times because they know we are always late! We do not want to build too soon because once their projects have moved to where they really need it, they might change the order."

I asked why customers did not send the order later accompanied by a scream. The response: "Probably figure we would charge a premium if they were in a hurry. Probably right too." While not exemplary, only a few years ago this company was not unusual. The finer points of systematic deceit had become so ingrained in the culture that upstanding people had built careers on them.

In this setting nonfinancial performance measures had limited meaning. If the company was taking orders, building orders, and making money, all must be well. Other than cash balances and engineering specifications, embarrassing performance indicators could be redefined to become socially acceptable. For instance, an inventory count within 10 percent could be considered accurate, and if an order had finished the last shop operation, production could record it as complete, even if unacceptable to ship.

The only performance measures with a semblance of rigor were financial, because debits and credits must at least balance. No wonder the company became financially driven. Nonfinancial performance measures had to relate to dollars to be taken seriously.

For years this organization chewed up reformers intent on improving delivery-to-schedule, lead-time reduction, and so on. All met the same reception as a rookie cop shooing away streetwalkers. Career climbers learned to create enough stir to brighten a resume, then move on, leaving little permanent change in their wake. Operating performance improved enough for the company to survive, but the financial-control culture remained in place. It made money. Even as high-labor-cost products were outsourced, the company continued to make money. In that sense, the financial controls worked, but they also suppressed major operating reforms. Those were too risky.

This company is a relatively extreme case, but the same disease affects thousands more to some degree. The system of control is designed to extract profit from the existing modes of operation, slashing expenses when that status is threatened.

In this company, as in thousands of others, the only universal performance measurement is budget variances. Nonfinancial performance measurements tend to be relatively narrow and assigned by function. For instance, sales is responsible for sales volume, engineering for product performance, and production for plant efficiency. In production, efficiency is emphasized because it is presumed to relate to immediate fulfillment of budget goals.

This form of accounting-derived control not only narrows the perspective of all the functional specialists but reinforces their behavior by giving them bonuses for meeting such goals as efficiency. At its worst, the people who exercise this kind of control are so mesmerized by it that they cannot see a different vision. Shop reforms obvious to people who work there are passed over because if direct labor is not reduced, no one can "prove" a payoff from a change.

These kinds of issues have been belabored by a number of awakening accountants in recent years. One form of accounting that avoids the worst blind spots of direct labor costing is called activity-based costing (ABC). However, a recognition is that while ABC allocates overhead in less distorted ways, any cost number is constructed by a model, and all models have weaknesses. The beginning of wisdom is the insight to penetrate the assumptions of cost formulas to factor in each model's biases.[3]

The quest for "unbiased" cost systems, or for cost systems that translate quality practices to dollars, is a quest for a Holy Grail. If readers have limited understanding of customer needs, products, equipment, distribution, or processes, a set of cost numbers does not sharpen their judgment very much—no more than rheological test data conveys to someone inexperienced with polymers and their applications. At its worst, this results in remote-control management by the numbers. Operating personnel distort their pursuit of organizational objectives to achieve artificial numerical goals.

Numbers are only indicators of reality. They are not reality itself. But to those fixated on cash flow, hardly any reality exists except the numbers presumably describing it.

Types of Performance Comparisons

Performance comparisons fall into roughly four classes:

1. *Comparisons with Our Own Past Performance.*   Most manufacturing companies engaged in improvement rely greatly on these comparisons because information is relatively easy to obtain. Even then, most companies have not tracked data that later they wish they had.

Production improvements are indicated by the trends of defect rates, materials lead times, productivity ratios, space used, distances moved, actual costs, and the like. But a company starting to improve process capability may not compile "baseline" data on it.

Today, many companies are justly proud of the improvements shown by these indicators. Sometimes they show progress by quantum leaps. However, the companies may still not be keeping up with competitors or satisfying customers.

2. *Comparisons with Others' Performance, or Benchmarking.* Comparing operating practice with the best found elsewhere has become one of the hottest topics in American business. Well done, it produces ideas and incentives to do better. Poorly done, it is just another exercise in comparative business analysis that ends with nothing but excuses that "we are different." Measurement data needs to be in a similar form, and firms have to examine contrasts to learn how to improve an environment that is inevitably somewhat different. Learning how to do something better is the objective. Benchmarking at its best is simply built into improvement processes. It's the first two stages of the Deming Circle.

Benchmarking is the antithesis of not-invented-here thinking. It seeks to learn from the best practices of others. In large, multidivisional companies, it begins internally. Processes are compared between divisions or between plants. Everyone learns from the best. (Large companies have seldom compared processes in detail.)

The next step is to benchmark from best-in-class operations from other companies. They do not have to do the same thing. The most storied of all comparisons is Xerox learning how to improve its distribution processes from L.L. Bean. Today, the companies well known for best-in-class processes are reluctant to admit people who are simply on "fishing expeditions." They bring no data on their own operations. They share nothing about their own learning process. They just want to pick their hosts' brains and go away, not having an internal improvement process from which they can ever give something back to the "benchmarking partner" that they have troubled.

Benchmarking is sometimes considered to be only a comparison with competitors. Some companies interpret it as only a teardown and reverse engineering of competing products. Those are important, but they do not always reveal how the competitor is obtaining superior results—if those are observed.

Comparative learning, or benchmarking, is described in many ways. One of the better frameworks is by Michael Spendolini, who explains it in five steps:

I. Determine what to benchmark. That is, determine who is going to use the information and how they might employ it. Define the specific processes to benchmark. (Just knowing that a similar company has one tenth the order-entry errors of yours says very little. The learning comes from defining how their process of order entry is different. It is best done by those who are experienced in your own order-entry process—and who *want* to make changes.)

II. Form a benchmarking team. Even something like order entry is not a one-function process. Benchmarking itself is a process that should be organized with specific roles to play, and with time lines set up—a planned and controlled project or series of projects.

III. Identify benchmark partners. Seek the organizations to learn from. A great deal of preliminary information can be found from published information; some can come from industry networking. The partners may not be unquestionably the best in the world. That is often too tough to establish to be worth the effort. They just have to demonstrate points you can learn from. Conversely, they may learn something from you.

IV. Collect and analyze information. Use a protocol, which provides an easily understood approach and methods of comparison, defines what you want, and offers feedback. One of the initial frustrations is learning that other companies keep data using different definitions in different formats. Some of the most useful information is very detailed—how an order-entry format works in different situations or contexts, for instance—and is best reviewed by persons who are deeply into the subject.

V. Take action. While it is best if those who must take action actually do the learning firsthand, that cannot always be done. The initial learning is by a small subset of them, so reports or evidence must be organized to convince the other "customers" of benchmarking that the results are valid. Acceptance of the need to take action is the first objective. After that, it's a matter of dedication to an improvement process.[4]

3. *Comparison with Customer Needs or with the Mission of the Enterprise.* One can benchmark such things as how to manage warehouse input-out using bar codes only to realize that what the customer wants is direct shipment, bypassing all the warehouses. Another problem is comparing mostly costs and cost ratios before realizing that benchmarking must dig deeper than that.

The first axiom of the Adam Smith school of economics is that no objective of the firm supersedes the mandate to make money, so to the true believers, the dominant measures of performance are all financial. However, an enterprise competing with others on excellence in customer satisfaction must have performance measures that center on customers. Moreover, it must measure whether it is attaining all missions required of it, including the environmental ones.

Mission-oriented performance measurement is an attribute that distinguishes open-system enterprise. Only part of its constituency is interested in whether it makes money. The rest want to know whether it is fulfilling its mission and obligations. Measuring the extent of customer satisfaction has proved to be an unfulfilled challenge of companies that have won the Baldrige Award and that have thus demonstrated unusual dedication to that mission. Measuring environmental impact is at least as challenging.

4. *Comparisons with Ultimate Performance.* Setting a goal of perfect performance (like absolutely zero defects) seems impossible unless people understand how it is possible for them to reach it. Ultimate performance usually means fail-safe product or process reliability so that reliability is virtually perfect in ordinary use. For example, a Motorola Bravo pager has a mean time between failures of about 156 years. If run over by a lift truck, a pager probably will not work, but only one or so in a million will glitch in ordinary service.

If all the pagers offered by the industry had such ultimate reliability, operating quality would cease to be a customer concern. Competitive advantage would hinge on other features. But if enterprises began to take ultimate reliability for granted, it would return as a customer issue. It cannot be neglected, just as ultimate safety cannot be taken for granted by airlines.

Achieving near-ultimate performance assures that for all practical purposes, competitors cannot better it. However, it does not prevent being blindsided by a competitor's new technology or by different concepts for customer service. For example, Motorola could make pagers to last five thousand years only to have them made obsolete by wristwatch telephones.

Measurement for Improvement

Even a manufacturing enterprise with a few hundred persons may have thousands of measurements, many of them technical. The performance record of one particular part or machine may require considerable data. The mass of detail cannot be comprehended by any single individual. Some measurements kept by computer are never reviewed by any human unless something goes amiss.

However, a number of operating-performance measures are kept for review and control. Efficiencies, sales quotas, budget variances, and the like are usually part of control methods. Most tightly run companies have such measurements. Nothing is usually wrong with any single measurement itself. The shortcoming is in how they are used. "Control" accompanied by fear of denigration does not encourage mass improvement. It often encourages only manipulation and cover-up.

Measurements related to budgets and cash have to have a sense of control attached to them. After all, no enterprise can long spend more than it takes in, so control is not an evil in itself. However, if control is so obsessive that it stifles achievement of mission or improvement of performance, it is counterproductive.

As a subject of management study, nonfinancial performance measurement is in its infancy. It is broader in scope and more difficult than cost and financial measurements—difficult as those may be. Furthermore, the average individual cannot pay careful heed to a welter of performance measurements. Attention can be given only to a few improvement processes at a time. However, performance measures should be kept on many processes from many perspectives. True performance improvement is shown by a favorable change in one or more indicators with no corresponding unfavorable changes in another.

For instance, the time to ship orders may be decreased simply by adding people and having a decline in productivity and perhaps in quality. The decision may be good business, but it is a trade-off decision. Process improvement should not be a trade-off.

This concept of improvement attacks the Achilles' heel of most optimization strategies. "Optimization" is a concept borrowed from economics and mathematics (and a term often used sloppily in business parlance). It redirects resources so that the best result occurs— but usually within constraints and by making trade-offs. Making the best use of existing processes has value, but it is not the same as fundamentally removing waste from processes or radically changing them—eliminating the constraints.

Measures used for improvement should relate to the overall mission of the enterprise or to a fundamental improvement goal. For instance, if the overall goal of improvement is to make all processes have a C_{pk} of 2 or higher (a measure of process capability), then any measurement of machine variance, or even error rates in order entry, should relate to this goal.

A superb performance measure is an indicator having several improvement purposes. An example that is becoming classic is factory work-in-process inventory expressed as days on hand (or hours on hand). It is an indicator feeding into working capital investment, quality feedback time, customer-response time, and other desirable outcomes. However, to serve these purposes, those using the indicator must understand how it relates to the processes being studied and improved.

That is, in a mission-oriented enterprise, the heavy-duty performance measures must indicate the degree to which the firm's activities are furthering its mission and how its processes are progressing toward goals that enable it to better perform that mission. One of the primary missions—always—is customer satisfaction. Performance includes development of capability, not just achievement of results. "Results-oriented" traditional managers, unaccustomed to grass-roots improvement processes, have a difficult time understanding the importance of such indicators as time to increase production volume.

Balanced Performance Measures

We measure what we think is important. Cash almost always falls in that category. Other measurements depend on what questions seem to need answers. Since financial analysts demand a forecast of whether a company will show a profit in the next year or next quarter, publicly held companies keep a forecast and measurement system that attempts to be a crystal ball for investors.

Otherwise, measurements kept are usually the results of what someone has wanted to know for some reason. If OSHA wants to know the light level in lumens falling on each person's work area, someone may actually measure and track it. However, a company buried in data may still not be able to answer a seemingly simple question like, how many associates are certified welders?

The kind of measures that seem important depend first upon which stakeholder is being served. Ownership questions differ from those asked by customers and from those asked by suppliers. Each stakeholder and each function within a company is likely to pay much more attention to some measurements than others. A detailed set of measurements on effluents and emissions gives a different picture of a company than a survey of customers does.

Figure 10–1 gives some examples of a balanced set of measures under eight headings crossing a broad scope of performance. Issues of where to classify some measurements within the headings never end. For instance, where would a vital measurement like customer credit ratings be classified?

An individual cannot pay equal attention to a broad set of measures at all times. A baseball player thinking about a welter of statistics while at the plate is not concentrating on the ball. However, a few of his personal statistics may themselves suggest points on which he can improve. The same is true of associates as they program interface software, listen to customer requests, or perform preventive maintenance.

In a complex enterprise different teams and associates pay attention to different areas in detail. They must also pay attention to integrating the whole. To do it, they must be integrative learners as well as specialists. They must pay attention to a broader array of performance indicators, but they cannot pay attention to very many.

Traditionally, control has been exercised by splitting specialized performance measures by function so that integration has to be done by centrally made trade-off decisions. Functional specialists easily become myopic. Subdivided measurements reinforce that. Sometimes CEOs also concentrate on a narrow set of indicators, poring over

FIGURE 10-1

EXAMPLES OF A BALANCED
ARRAY OF PERFORMANCE MEASURES

	External	*Internal*
1. Quality	Returns, complaints	Yield, scrap rates
	Customer loyalty	Process capabilities
	Ratings versus competitors	Percentage of processes fail-safed
2. Dependability	Arrival on time	Ship on time
	Service reliability	Working to schedule
	On time from suppliers	Adherence to promises
3. Resource Use	Power efficiency of products	Labor productivity
	Ease of product use	Percentage of equipment ready
		Value-added ratio (time)
4. Environmental	Effluents/emissions in use	Effluents and emissions
	Recycling potential	Safety
	Product safety	Associates' health
5. Flexibility	Customer lead times	Throughput times
	Lead-times-to-change	Setup times
	Service lead times	Support function lead times
		Supplier lead times

FIGURE 10-1 (cont.)

	External	*Internal*
6. Human-Resource Improvement	Training given to customers Team interaction with customer personnel (percent, quality)	Percentage of associates cross-trained Learning-curve rates Suggestion rates Attendance, etc. ("morale" indicators)
7. Innovation	Percentage of product-line turnover Feature comparisons with competitors First-to-introduce rank in industry	Time-to-market indicators Percentage of product custom-designed for unique applications
8. Financial	Price to customers Debt service Rate of return to owners	P&L and balance sheet Cash flow

hundreds of field sales reports or thousands of accounting variances, always looking at the elephant from the same angle.

No single metric is a "magic answer," nor is any single category of metrics. Restructuring a cost accounting system may be helpful, but cost numbers themselves cannot convey the context for their own interpretation. If a company concentrates on quality measures to attain C_{pk} of 2 in all processes, it cannot be sure that everything else will work out.

Genuine improvement advances some aspect of operating performance without a corresponding decrement elsewhere. That is why attention to a balanced set of performance measurements is important. In a data-driven enterprise, where the total number of measurements kept is mind-boggling, excess measurement and reporting is in itself a significant waste, and it is very easy to keep measurements that add little or nothing to progress. Part of an improvement process is to review measurement collection and information flow from time to time and eliminate useless measures. Before computers, a useful rule of thumb for shop floors and often for offices was to keep the primary performance measurements at the point where the data was collected. Then, first-line operatives were more likely to understand them and to rely on them. Furthermore, the waste of poorly done or excessive measurements was more likely to be questioned—if anyone would listen.

With the rise of electronics and computers, more and more measurements have become captured automatically—and often acted on automatically. The only data brought to human attention is that which software presents for human attention. The primary work of many persons is evolving into process observation, but the objective is still the same. Those responsible should keep appropriate measurements and use them for process improvement, meanwhile being aware of important performance indicators kept by others—like the amount of effluents entering a plant waste-recovery system or the number of misreads by a bar code system. Excellence in achieving difficult, complex missions is not attained by emphasizing a narrow scope of performance measures used for control.

From Vision to Reality

A management adage is that you do not get what you want, you get what you measure. That old saw may presume that more measures are used for control of people than are used by people to control processes, but even in the latter sense, it has a ring of truth to it. Our measures reflect our objectives and our comprehension of processes. A hundred years ago no one comprehended statistical control of processes or tested effluent streams for part-per-billion contamination.

If we have a different vision, we emphasize different processes. We emphasize different measurements to help us achieve the vision. Measurements help clarify processes and control them. A broad vision presumes use of a broad scope of performance indicators. The study of comprehensive performance measurements used in this way has now progressed about as far as the study of industrial cost accounting had around 1880. At the time, a number of effective manual systems were in use, but accountants had just begun to compare them. Only after breaking the internal contractor systems and becoming integrated did the manufacturing companies of that time begin to develop standard systems, including costing.[5]

Tracking a rigorous, comprehensive set of performance measurements—demonstrating improvement using a balanced set of "facts," as nearly as one can get them—does much to foil claims from hype artists cloaking themselves in "excellence jargon," just as manufacturing companies a century ago were escaping from the worst excesses of process concealment from their own foremen. A familiar example is a claim that 100 percent of shipments are made on time. However, if labeling mistakes or shipping delays occur, the customers do not receive shipments where they need them when they need them. And if every part must be present at the right place at the right time, as in a complex assembly process, the same supplier may still be stopping its customers' lines. The *total* process is still not in control.

Furthermore, the use of comprehensive operating measurements clarifies a fluttery vision. The popularity of the Baldrige Award criteria in the United States is stimulating a new consciousness of operating performance. Self-assessment using Baldrige criteria gives a company a "wart report" that can then be used to guide a broad range of improvements. For now, most companies cannot absorb anything much more demanding than that.

How measurements are presented also makes a big difference. If the measurement itself suggests how to improve, a major step has been taken. Some of the newer performance-assessment systems themselves provide substantial clues to what must be *done*. This attribute is the unique feature of the Motorola Corporate Quality System Review (QSR), for instance.

The direction of improvement is suggested by a "maturity index." The concept behind a maturity index is shown in Figure 10–2. Both IBM and Motorola use maturity indexes in performance assessment but the Motorola one is more specific, and it evokes a review pattern to evaluate each item assessed based on approach, deployment, and results. An example from the Motorola QSR is in Figure 10–3.

A maturity index describes performance on a scale from poor-for-the-present to excellent for some ultimate point envisioned at the time. The "excellence" point will move as visions extend. The "poor" category of the index may move too. Over time, performance represented by the mid-range may no longer be acceptable and become "poor." The Motorola index in Figure 10–3 is contemporary. It does not envision an open system enterprise or a full-material-cycle enterprise.

Establishing performance measures helps to clarify what people need to do. The "excellent" end of a maturity index (or vision index) forces people to clarify a vision in more detail. Defining the scale of various indexes forces them "to draw a road map" that clarifies how to reach the vision. Selection and design of measurements is a form of detailed long range planning that has benefit in itself. Many measurements may be adopted or adapted from others so that comparisons are possible, but some may also originate from those whose performance is to be measured. Then the measurements can be used to check whether progress is being made. Use of a rigorous measurement system helps translate a vision into action.

Figure 10–4 represents a basic concept of human achievements in manufacturing and in other kinds of endeavor. Just as children begin life with the most basic of abilities and keep adding to them, people in their work life can individually and collectively raise the level of their achievements, some of them technical, some of them social.

FIGURE 10-2

MATURITY MATRICES
FOR QUALITY ASSESSMENTS

MOTOROLA

Evaluation Dimensions

Score (points) ↓	Approach	Deployment	Results
Poor (0)			
Weak (2)			
Fair (4)			
Marginally Qualified (6)			
Qualified (8)			
Outstanding (10)			

A supplier performance review examines ninety-nine items in ten categories. Each item is evaluated using the maturity index above. For each item a list describes the evidence that would designate each of the six scoring levels. The approach-deployment-results side of the matrix is directly from the American Baldrige Award assessment framework. The system is easy to use and improvement actions are automatically hinted by the scoring levels higher than the one given for each item.

SOURCE: The Motorola Corporate Quality System Review Guidelines, *Motorola Inc., Tempe, Arizona, March 1991.*

FIGURE 10-3

AN EXAMPLE
PERFORMANCE RATING
USING A MATURITY INDEX

Is there an effective supplier certification program or
equivalent supplier continuous quality improvement program?

Considerations:

a. There is a system for certifying suppliers.

b. There is a process which ensures continuous quality improvement
of procured material and services and the rewarding of suppliers for
their involvement in programs.

Scoring for Element 3.9 (Note: The scaled rating below is a maturity index.)

Poor:	There is no supplier improvement program.
Weak:	The organization is beginning to define their needs for supplier quality improvement. A few areas of the business are working with specific suppliers to improve the quality of procured materials.
Fair:	A program has been defined for the continuous quality improvement of procured materials and services. Some major areas of the business actively utilize this program with their key suppliers. Some managers are supportive of supplier quality improvement efforts.
Marginally Qualified:	The organization's procured materials and services quality improvement program includes supplier certification procedures and criteria. Most areas of the business participate in the program and a few suppliers have been certified.

FIGURE 10-3 (cont.)

Scoring for Element 3.9 (Note: The scaled rating below is a maturity index.)

Qualified: Most of the organization's suppliers are active
in the supplier quality improvement program.
Many key suppliers are certified. There is
evidence that the supplier improvement
activities are having positive results on total
cost of quality and improved product quality.

Outstanding: The supplier quality improvement program is
exceptionally well defined. Certification of
suppliers has resulted in quantified cost
savings. There is evidence that certified
suppliers are rewarded as preferred suppliers
when making sourcing decisions. All suppliers
are involved to some extent in the certification
and/or continuous quality improvement
program.

SOURCE: The Motorola Corporate Quality System Review, Motorola Inc., Tempe,
Arizona, March 1991.

Today the companies most successful making a transition to Total Quality, JIT, or whatever recognize that they are engaged in a
process of human development. They must also achieve real
progress, rather than merely attaching progressive-sounding names
to old practices. Use of open, verifiable, balanced measurements is
one of the primary ways to avoid substituting smoke and noise for
genuine achievement.

Few leaders will want to explore open system enterprise unless
convinced that the enterprise can maintain its direction. Companies
start by accepting today's challenges, such as order-of-magnitude improvement goals, like six-sigma quality and extreme reduction of lead
times. Open system enterprise begins when it becomes obvious that
further improvement cannot be reached without a basically different
kind of organization.

FIGURE 10-4

ACHIEVING QUALITY OF LIFE AND ENTERPRISE VISIONS IS A CUMULATIVE DEVELOPMENT OF OURSELVES

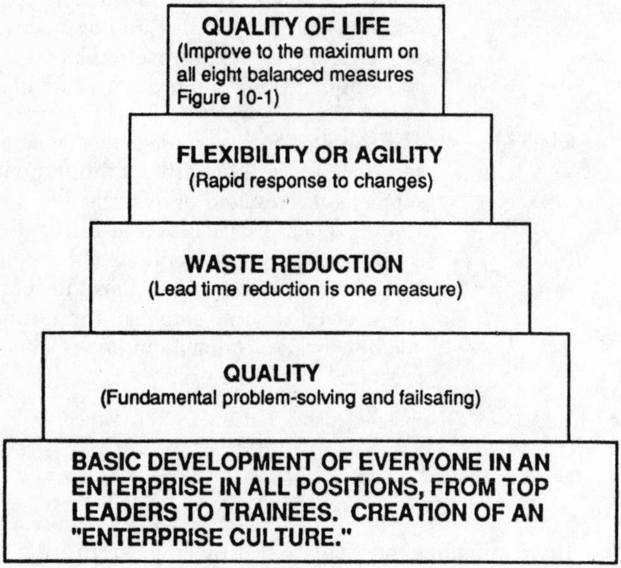

QUALITY OF LIFE
(Improve to the maximum on all eight balanced measures Figure 10-1)

FLEXIBILITY OR AGILITY
(Rapid response to changes)

WASTE REDUCTION
(Lead time reduction is one measure)

QUALITY
(Fundamental problem-solving and failsafing)

BASIC DEVELOPMENT OF EVERYONE IN AN ENTERPRISE IN ALL POSITIONS, FROM TOP LEADERS TO TRAINEES. CREATION OF AN "ENTERPRISE CULTURE."

This stack-up can be labeled in many ways. Each level summarizes more detailed development than anyone can comprehend at once. A collective human development, like a stick built house, must start with a foundation and build-up.

The diagram represents the layered accumulation of human skills, not necessarily a sequence of programs striving for "excellence." Those who start trying to reduce waste soon find that they must improve quality processes and vice versa. This type of diagram was first seen as drawn to illustrate the improvement strategies of Japanese manufacturers from 1960–1985 by Professor J. Nakane, Waseda University, Tokyo.

Vision Deployment and Performance Drivers

A single leader cannot put a complex enterprise together. Vision-driven leadership is more likely to be several leaders combining resources. The leadership group may initiate a vision, but it must communicate it so that others participate in it, or else the vision is not driving anything. A vision becomes more specific through performance measurements.

A performance driver is an aggregate performance measurement that embodies a vision, or a part of it at a point in time. Since people cannot coordinate effort system design and improvement while working toward many goals at once, the purpose of a performance driver is to focus effort. Well done, a good performance driver makes a complex undertaking become simple in principle.

One of the best-known performance drivers today is six-sigma at Motorola. Thousands of performance measurements in many areas contribute to six-sigma. Other companies use Cpk=2 (which is the same as six-sigma) as a driver, and many more use cycle time (lead time) reduction. Interestingly, in order to improve quality, the companies driving on Cpk=2 must drastically reduce lead times, and those with a lead time driver must drastically improve quality. Both reduce costs. The operating relationships allows a well-chosen driver to drag performance improvement in many areas in its wake. No performance measurement system should encourage trading performance on one dimension for that in another unless it is urgently needed for strategic reasons.

Open-system enterprise will be partly achieved by project-style, big-step progress, and partly by human evolution, which is normally done by small-step continuous improvement progress. Both are important, and performance measurement is vital to each. A driver should measure processes, not human performance per se. As Dr. W. Edwards Deming notes, measuring human performance has limited effect if people are not in a position to influence the processes with which they work.

To start a system of measurement, the leadership must convert a vision to a specific mission, or a series of them over time, then devise a soundly conceived performance driver for each mission. One driver at a time is better because it helps the various teams to focus their effort and fill out the measurement system. Well done, a performance measurement system yields strong, consistent feedback whether a mission is being achieved. The development of such a measurement system is roughly presented in Figure 10–5.

Reducing a comprehensive vision to practice is a tough challenge— perhaps *the* human challenge. It is more multifaceted than pure budget discipline for profitability, or driving for increased market share. The process of vision deployment and measurement deployment are akin to "policy deployment," or *hoshin kanri* as the Japanese call it, and those processes run afoul of the command and control structure of twentieth-century companies.[6]

The performance-measurement system will undoubtedly vary in use, depending on whether it is applied to an operating company as currently organized or to some other form of enterprise. Some enterprises would simply be ongoing operating organizations, like the Cadillac example in Chapter 9. Others would be formed and disbanded, as with the Mayekawa example in Chapter 8, in which a company is formed for each order of a major refrigeration system. Others might be fast-migration enterprise organizations, as might form up around an evolution of a computer family going through a complete birth-to-death cycle of service in a couple of decades or so.

However, another of the major attributes of performance measurement would be to allow enterprises in formation to quickly appraise the capabilities and prior performance of individuals and entities recruited. To participate in advanced-capability enterprise one needs an operating track record—an operations version of a Dun & Bradstreet report today. Access to the data might cost money, but it would be open and subject to audit. Common performance measures are a form of common language.

Toward a Universal Operating-Performance Assessment

The structure of open-system performance measurements is now evolving from the quality prize criteria beginning with the Deming Prize checklist, then the Baldrige Award, and broadening with the European Quality Award. From these are evolving all manner of self-assessment checklists, the most comprehensive to date probably be-

FIGURE 10-5
VISION DEPLOYMENT
AND PERFORMANCE DRIVERS

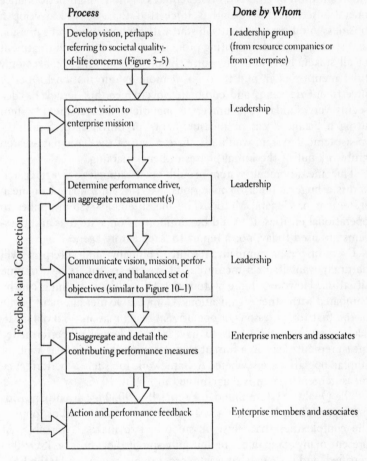

Process	*Done by Whom*
Develop vision, perhaps referring to societal quality-of-life concerns (Figure 3–5)	Leadership group (from resource companies or from enterprise)
Convert vision to enterprise mission	Leadership
Determine performance driver, an aggregate measurement(s)	Leadership
Communicate vision, mission, performance driver, and balanced set of objectives (similar to Figure 10–1)	Leadership
Disaggregate and detail the contributing performance measures	Enterprise members and associates
Action and performance feedback	Enterprise members and associates

Feedback and Correction

A deployment process is a leadership art. Thousands or millions of detailed activities contribute to the overall mission. The total number of performance measurements kept somewhere in some process by someone (or a computer) is probably unknowable. The art is keeping the core mission and performance driver so simple that a scattered, diverse collection of associates can unify their effort around it.

ing the one compiled by the National Center for Manufacturing Sciences, as noted in Chapter 3.

The future evolution of these measurement systems is important to the realization of any vision that requires rigorous, high-performance operations. Peter Drucker has forecasted that we will develop a business-audit practice that will start with an operating unit's mission and strategy, include operating proficiency, and finish with treatment of all stakeholders and, of course, financial results.[7] He makes only brief mention of it, and thinks of it more as information for better investment decisions and corporate governance, but Drucker's idea seems very similar to a universal operations measurement system using a balanced set of measurements. A universal performance-measurement system would also take much of the basic data-search grubwork out of the initial phases of benchmarking.

This measurement system would be meaningless if aggregated across a huge number of operations, like the consolidated financial statement of General Motors. The measurement system applies to operational entities. It would be an information system as audit systems are used today, not a report to a regulatory agency.

Every operating company, resource company, and enterprise will naturally want its own measurement system to suit its own unique situation. However, if the system is totally unique, nothing can be compared with other organizations. Comparable measurement is one of the first tough lessons of operational benchmarking. To obtain it, each operating unit needs to have a basic kernel of performance measurements kept in a format that is compatible with that kept for similar operations elsewhere. A framework for such a performance measurement system is diagrammed in Figure 10–6.

The Quality System Standards series ISO 9000 is currently providing a preview of how such a system might be used—and of some of the complexities that must be smoothed to make it workable. At present many companies are not quite sure if they must be ISO 9000 certified, and if so, in what way in order to be recognized by the EEC and any other countries that require certification to participate in certain kinds of business within them. If the criteria of performance measurement were greatly broadened, these problems would expand.

The objections to a universal performance-assessment system are many. They begin with doubt that operations can be generally com-

FIGURE 10-6

FRAMEWORK OF A UNIVERSAL
PERFORMANCE-MEASUREMENT SYSTEM

Total Measurements

On Unique Operations	Compare with our own history
On common, but industry-unique, operations	Compare with competitors or near-competitors
On core operations common to many organizations	Compare with anyone's similar *processes*

pared. That is a rational apprehension, because if interpretations of data are poor, a great deal of time is spent explaining why order-entry processing lead times have increased recently, for example. The same kind of objection was once used to justify keeping financial data secret.

Trying to make fine distinctions using operating data is useless. If two plants are roughly comparable, but one has a total productivity 30 percent better than another, the difference may or may not be meaningful. The difference in local work content or in the intentional features of products and service may easily account for the difference. On the other hand, if one of two roughly comparable plants is beating another by two or three times in total productivity, it is worth asking deep questions about differences in operating approach. If an open system of operating-performance data is to be used, people must learn how to interpret the data and not pester other operating units with useless questions. In other words, they must learn to be civilized, competent benchmarkers following accepted protocols.

Developing a universal performance-measurement system is more than just an evolution of the metrics themselves, and that is difficult enough. It must be accompanied by universal education in how to use the data and the system. The rise of public financial reporting was accompanied by growth in understanding of how to use it, too. Interpretation of financial data is greatly aided when the analyst understands the kind of business being studied or compared. A more comprehensive set of performance data demands even more of a background from which sound interpretation can be made.

A second objection is that no set of universal measurements can possibly convey everything that someone wants to know about an operating unit that is being considered for partnership. That is not possible. The universal system is only a starting point. It should convey whether the unit should be included in a set for serious consideration.

Finally, the performance assessments should be audited by a trusted party. In financial reporting, that is the function of certified public accountants. The prospect is enough to make auditing companies drool. However, the development of organizations qualified to do this for operating performance is barely in its infancy. Management audits are nothing new, but they vary greatly in rigor and methodology. Even today, most of the quality reviews that larger companies give their suppliers concentrate more on documentation than on direct verification of key performance indicators. A much tougher methodology is required.

At present, many companies cannot even agree on a common system to audit the core quality practices of suppliers within their industry. For instance, the automotive industry objects that trusting a third party to monitor quality assumes some legal risk. If the supplier screws up so royally that its oversights lead to product liability suits, the customer could be held accountable for improper monitoring if it did not check that supplier's quality methods itself. Legal paranoia is a bane of most cooperative ideas, and it can only be allayed if third-party verification of performance is rigorous and trustworthy. (ISO 9000 examiners are already being sued in liability cases.)

While universal performance measurement now seems almost as farfetched as the concept of the three-day car enterprise, many trends are hopeful. Enough people are knowledgeable to be very skeptical of claims not supported by data and demonstration. For instance, critics of the U.S. Army's plans to dispose of chemical weapons by burning them know enough to question the validity of the testing and scale-up of incineration in the absence of operating-performance data from actual pilot-plant operations. An error in this process would not only be costly, it might be fatal to large numbers of people.

When people realize that they are utterly dependent on the technical proficiency and service performance of operating units, they do start to become seriously interested in how well those units perform. At that point, sales pitches and confident assurances are not sufficient to convince skeptics that operations are extremely flexible and virtually failure-free. The only way a more open system of enterprise can work effectively is through an open system of measurements. Those are currently underdeveloped and they will never be perfect, just as the system of financial reporting has never been free of scandal. Despite the problems, capabilities and accomplishments have to be verified so that interested parties can be sure that claims are not just self-advertising.

NOTES

1. For a more detailed treatment, see Robert W. Hall, H. Thomas Johnson, and Peter B. B. Turney, *Measuring Up* (Homewood, IL: Business One Irwin, 1991). Chapter 2, "Our Measurements Model Our Mindsets."

2. Stephen Jay Gould, "The H and Q of Baseball," *The New York Review of Books,* 24 October 1991, 47–52.

3. For one of the more insightful analyses of cost and measurement issues, see H. Thomas Johnson, *Relevance Regained* (New York: Free Press, 1992).

4. Benchmarking has become an extensive subject. Most of this discussion is a very brief and inadequate synopsis from Michael J. Spendolini, *The Benchmarking Book* (New York: AMACOM, 1992).

5. Robert S. Kaplan and H. Thomas Johnson, *Relevance Lost* (Boston: Harvard Business School Press, 1987), Chapters 2–4.

6. Ernest C. Huge and Brendan Collins, *Management by Policy* (Milwaukee, WI: ASQC Quality Press, 1993). This book describes policy deployment in a contemporary context.

7. Peter Drucker, "Reckoning with the Pension Fund Revolution," *Harvard Business Review* 69, no. 2 (March–April 1991): 107–14.

11

TRUST BETWEEN
THE STAKEHOLDERS

"THE CORPORATION HAS NO SOUL," IS A FAVORITE EXPLANATION OF THE DIF-
ference between a legal corporation and a living individual. Having no
soul is sometimes an advantage in explaining unpleasant actions taken
to preserve cash flow: reductions in force, reductions in customer
service, discontinuance of suppliers, suspension of dividends, renego-
tiating of debt, and so on. These are more easily and impersonally
accepted if mentally justified by "that's business" or "the market
rules."

No system of business can avoid the need to sometimes take action
unpleasant to its participants. Nothing lasts forever, and "continuous
improvement" does not guarantee continuous cash flow. Beyond that,
the emotional side of "improvement processes" is creating urgency to
perform at a high level for many reasons other than cash: customer
satisfaction, environmental protection, quality of life. The circumstances of technically based business are more demanding than ever.
If a new form of business organization is to be an improvement over
the old, it must have discipline built into it from more directions.
Alarm bells should stimulate action for reasons other than profitability and the nagging of regulators.

Building and sustaining this organizational discipline is one of the most difficult aspects of open-system enterprise. The investor is not the only stakeholder whose interests should stimulate an adrenaline rush for high performances. The open-system enterprise is dedicated to a mission. High performance in attaining a mission, particularly in low-growth conditions, takes great trust between the stakeholders.

In almost any company today, the various stakeholders may disagree on how to cut a pie, but resolving differences is much easier when the pie is expanding so that everyone gets a bigger cut. Fairly dividing a constant or shrinking pie is more difficult. Keeping the trust of various stakeholders then requires evoking within them a vision of something worth sacrifice. Usually the vision is of a resumption of growth: "Some day we'll be back in fat city." A vision of just making a better quality of life for the participants (including customers) is possible, but this makes little sense to go-go investors.

A long legal history affirms that the primary purpose of a business is profit, and that obligations to other stakeholders are vested in ownership, the party presumed to have the greatest self-interest in treating others fairly. Laws inhibit owners from making money by deceiving other stakeholders, but they do not guarantee compliance. Adversarial behavior does not create genuine trust, for trust is an implicit confidence that *people* try to be "fair" and perform to the best of their ability—whether legally bound to or not.

Governance of a business refers to ownership's oversight through a board of directors. Most boards of publicly held companies are concerned with fairness and financial performance, so they tend to be populated by people experienced in those areas. However, most actions affecting stakeholder trust are actually taken by management. Given the current sociology of boards, if a management's actions do not accord with their words, an outside director can learn of it only through nonboard contacts. If the financial condition of a public company is perilous or if a buyout bid is offered, the liabilities of directors are high. Well-qualified people may deem that the risks of serving on a board of directors outweigh the rewards.[1]

The current rules of corporate governance presume that the primary goal of a company is maximum value to ownership. Unfortunately, investors usually view the primary assets of manufacturing companies as inert things—buildings and equipment. But in open-system enterprise the major asset is people and their development.

However, the fundamental importance of investing in people is not unfamiliar. Anyone investing in professional athletics, entertainment production, or other talent-dependent businesses automatically recognizes that most of the key assets are human, although such recognition does not guarantee successful investment. Far from it.

Investors and financial institutions are slow to recognize that people—the team—are the primary success factor in any high-performance enterprise, whether it is a service business or a manufacturer. This imperceptiveness is the source of many current troubles. High performance is needed, but traditional business reasoning presumes that nearly all of it comes from management and investment. From that mind-set, "justification" of investing more than the bare minimum of trust, time, or money in people is impossible.

A Small Manufacturer's Plight

Labeco is a microcosm of 1990s small American industry. Its core expertise is designing and building dynamometers to check drivetrain and emissions performance of vehicles and aircraft—a small, cyclical niche business. Labeco also builds test stands for army tanks, heavy transmissions, helicopter drivetrains, and even the mechanisms to control heavy fire doors for buildings. Virtually all automotive companies in the world obtain their large dynamometers from Labeco, Shink-Pegasus in Britain, or Onasoki in Japan. Over half of Labeco's sales are exports.

The people of Labeco have a unique skill set. Silicon Valley might not view it as high-tech, but several years' experience are a big help in integrating the latest motors, gearing, sensors, and computers into a test stand, and getting it right the first time. Enough pitfalls lurk to prevent high-tech customers from doing it themselves. Labeco's experience and capabilities are its real stock-in-trade. They cause customers to override concerns for their financial jeopardy to work with them.

When the automotive market went flat in the 1980s, test stand sales stagnated, and profits went flat. To boost growth a subsidiary ventured into ultrasonic medical diagnostic equipment. Intellectual-capital royalties and venture-capital premiums convoluted the financing, as often happens. Transforming licensed designs into marketable machines was more difficult than expected, and it was tough to market to a different kind of clientele. By 1990 the subsidiary had folded. (It has since been trying to restart.)

By 1991, about a million in bank debt plus direct losses from the subsidiary reverted directly to Labeco's balance sheet, transforming working capital and retained earnings to negative numbers. Although cash flow from remaining operations remained positive, Labeco became the kind of example bank examiners use in lectures on risky loans.

If Labeco liquidated, the bank could get only about fifty cents on the dollar. Other investors would get nothing. Its American customers could only get this kind of test equipment from one of the two remaining competitors. What is the value of preserving Labeco's expertise, and what is the reward for doing it?

Because people can walk away, bankers seldom count them as assets, but the skills of Labeco's little band of technicians is the only assurance of continuing cash flow. Quality in execution is an absolute must. Time cycles of projects must compress further, which means improving both the effectiveness of the technicians themselves and their work with partners.

In 1991–92, the core investors were genuinely concerned for the people of Labeco. Others just wanted their money back or hoped that eventually they would receive handsome dividends. To keep the confidence of all stakeholders, the president, Jack Sweeney, had to motivate the technicians to a higher level of performance. A backlog indicated that customers had confidence. The technicians stayed. Sweeney promoted continuous improvement, reassured customers, and otherwise led a traditional kind of recovery.

At Labeco, governance was strongly influenced by the bank, which minimally recognized the value of human development or team development. Forget giving associates any reward that smacked of a bonus. Training time was acceptable only if a check did not have to be written for it.

Despite the obstacles, in 1992 Labeco increased sales and made enough cash to substantially pay down the bank notes. In 1993 sales are expected to decrease, but the company will remain profitable. Labeco is in an increasingly common high-skill, but flat-growth environment.

Labeco is not ready to participate in open-system enterprise networks. Neither are its customers. However, patient investment is needed, meaning financial supporters must recognize the need to increase the overall skills of the people. The current Labeco team can serve the market for heavy test stands with less risk than bankrolling a new start-up to do the same thing. A new set of people would have to work through a substantial learning curve. Any one of several ideas for a spin-off business might increase revenues, but growth in worldwide demand for dynamometers is problematic. Newly industrializing countries need them, but established industrial countries mostly have replacement demand, not virgin growth. Need for increased environmental testing *might* increase sales. No one forecasts runaway growth for all three competitors in this small industry.

Were the people of the company themselves ready, one cannot imagine Labeco's bankers approving the money for them to participate in open-system enterprise. The fixation is still on cash payments. De facto, the business system needs to be able to put its investment into people, organization, and expertise, and find ways to take new venture risks that do not sap the strength of healthy operations. Once upon a year, that was the intent of a capitalist financial investment system.

The Big-Company Example: General Motors

General Motors is a company in a fishbowl, and yet the empire is so big that it is difficult to comprehend what is happening because of its size and complexity. The story of GM is the embodiment of much that has happened—and will happen—to American industry. Downsizing at GM is a soap opera at times. Because of its size, age, and history, GM has difficulty figuring out what it is trying to migrate into.

A decade ago the company did not slim down when Ford and Chrysler did. Then in the mid-1980s the company blew billions of dollars by automating without first simplifying operations. Then it agreed to a complex jobs bank agreement with the UAW that gave members partial pay even when their work was not needed. Then it held an unannounced competition between assembly plants to see which ones would be kept. Tacitly, a huge number of excess midlevel staff and management were also kept on.

All these policies are from a heritage in which GM's market share and scale of operations allowed it to buy its way out of almost any problem. The policies do not work anymore, prospects of quickly increasing market share are dim, and GM is struggling to move itself into lean manufacturing while saddled with a mass-production mindset largely driven by accounting-based decisions.

The company has no shortage of talent. Throughout GM a number of "excellence" practices have taken hold. Top management has been exposed to almost any "vision" of the future that has been concocted. Different approaches have been tried in different locations, depending on the convictions of the local champions of change. Saturn, Cadillac, Buick City, and several lesser-known parts locations have been publicly recognized for substantial improvement. But as a whole, GM is waffling as it tries to move from mass production to lean production.

Many people have now tilted at this windmill. One of the most publicized was H. Ross Perot, who vociferously recognized the need to increase discipline and cut the bloat, but beyond that seemed to have few specific ideas. The infusion of EDS computer experts accomplished little. Streamlining by computer does not help when problems start with the basic processes to be computerized. Many of the EDS newcomers in the mid-1980s had little detailed understanding of either mass production or lean manufacturing.

By early 1992 the shortage of cash began to exercise its inevitable pressure for fast results, but GM had few quick options. By reports, the GM board first forced CEO Robert Stempel to make Jack Smith president, then six months later ousted him with Smith in charge. Smith had headed GM operations in Europe and soon brought over a Spaniard, J. Ignacio Lopez de Arriortua to head up worldwide purchasing. Lopez entered like a bullfighter to the ring and immediately abrogated all existing supply contracts and threw them open to new bidders, inviting European suppliers, among others, to have a run at them.

Lopez demanded double-digit cost reductions from suppliers, and the first number should not be a one. The savings were supposedly to come from shop floor JIT, which GM called "synchronous manufacturing." Teams from GM swooped in for one-week coaching sessions on suppliers that, in many cases, were well ahead of GM's progress.

Reactions from suppliers were swift and mostly ugly. One was reportedly asked to supply a part at below its cost to purchase the material for it. Reportedly, GM also wanted the suppliers to pay for the tooling, something GM had done in the past. Suppliers feared that the cost-cutting would gut their R&D, and that at worst, GM or rivals would steal their proprietary technology. At the same time, GM belatedly embarked on a program to standardize part designs and reduce their total number by up to 40 percent. That would make global sourcing easier, but common worldwide configurations are not easy because of different design and regulatory requirements.

Many observers speculated that Lopez was goading the suppliers in preparation for taking the knife to GM's Automotive Components Group (ACG), which paid workers about $35 an hour (fully loaded) compared with a rate closer to $15 an hour at many suppliers. Many of the surplus UAW workers had been sent to ACG. In addition, if a low cost for volume production on most parts was the goal, suppliers in neither Europe nor North America could compete with plants in third-world countries, and long supply trails into other countries would hardly speed the delivery process or add to flexibility. The first reaction of almost anyone familiar with the way quality is achieved in manufacturing today is that GM was taking the first steps back to quality mediocrity.

In Europe, Lopez had broken a supplier cartel. In the United States, his actions threatened to start one of sorts. Some thought that suppliers would appeal to the GM board. Others thought that the stockholders of one or more suppliers would sue GM on the grounds that GM should not extort profits from other companies. (The Japanese went through this phase years ago and legally bar large customers from starving small suppliers. They must practice "coexistence and mutual prosperity.")[2]

Observers were treated to the spectacle of a company trying to quickly obtain the financial benefits of lean production without going through the pain and learning. The need to downsize meant that *all* GM's stakeholders should cut back, while at the same time, they would be asked to spur their change into lean manufacturing—a shift that depends on high trust between stakeholders at the grass-roots level. A further transition into open-system enterprise is not yet contemplated. But the adversarial positions taken with suppliers, and sometimes with the UAW, seemed almost calculated to undermine that critical ingredient—TRUST.

The difference between this and the Japanese approach is that the Japanese first demand process, not results, and they show the supplier how to do it. As a rule, the customer company is first lean and tough internally—not the case at GM. GM now seems to be going for price first, which is a negotiating posture, not an improvement process. Japanese instruction has often been a boot-camp experience. They give the existing supplier tough target prices and expect collaboration in aggressive process improvement. Their suppliers may disengage from the customer because they are unable to keep up with them technically or in improvement discipline; they are not thrown out in favor of a rival with an unsubstantiated bid. And that practice is still part of lean manufacturing, not open-system enterprise.

GM appears to be attempting to force a transition from fat mass production to the trappings of lean manufacturing, but without its financial masters loosening any particle of their grip on the company—a grip that investors want to continue in order to assure that cash will be dutifully thrown to them. It is a self-contradictory strategy. The kind of performance desired from lean production, or from open-system enterprise, depends on the willing collaboration of the operating stakeholders, not their subjugation.

Furthermore, if GM could arrive at some semblance of lean manufacturing, the result might not be very profitable. In anything close to free trade, GM's U.S.-built econoboxes cannot compete against Mexico or Malaysia on cost unless the American economy becomes like theirs, or vice-versa. The social factors that contribute to an advanced quality of life—insurance, research, health care, education, criminal justice, infrastructure, environmental protection—are not social overhead that is easily shrugged off. A different concept of the company is necessary, and perhaps a different concept of an economy to go with it. And in that, as its former CEO "Engine Charley" Wilson once noted, "What's good for General Motors is good for the country." To do that takes more than the passing of the mass-production mind-set in engineering and factories.

The Investment Mind-Set

The investment mind-set has minimum regard for any objectives other than return on investment. Behaviorally, such mental concentration is what is meant by maximizing ROI.

Economists have long twitted sophomores with the question of whether return should be maximized in the long run or short run. The way that ancient question is put misses the point. Unless a company (or enterprise) has a mission other than financial return, it is strictly a numerical investment, like a savings account. All the human purpose and adventure have been abstracted out of it. While many financial types are both brilliant and broad-minded, those afflicted with the investment mind-set see results only as financial box scores.

This is not a new affliction. Remote-control management was fortunate to have wrung a profit from the Boott Mills for a century without having a better vision for it than "going south." Management by the numbers creates insights not seen by those who deal directly with customers and products, but it too has its own myopia. One is confusing elimination of apparent cost with elimination of waste. Fiats to slash accounting-measured costs do not differentiate between eliminating waste and eliminating value. Low initial cost does not equate to low lifetime cost. With little thought given to identifying the non–value-added steps in processes, they are frequently stripped of safety, quality, and environmental features, not waste. A dictatorial cost-control system stifles imagination and quality of life. Classic symptoms of nonquality appear. Concern for the customer seems to cost too much, problem solving responds only to obvious crises, maintenance is deferred, research projects are starved, and people in the action positions become spread too thin. The human foundation for high performance is eroded—or never built.

The beginnings of this mentality start with the investment system. Investment today is dominated by professional investment managers. Pension funds, insurance funds, and similar sources own 40–50 percent of all stock in publicly held companies. Institutions hold a big chunk of corporate debt, including so-called junk bonds. In addition, banks are the sources of many loans. One way or another, the lion's share of corporate financing is done by people who concentrate on maximizing the gain to their institutions.

Money managers have fiduciary responsibilities. Despite a few Ivan Boeskys, most of them have good intentions. They want an assured return for their institutions' customers (pensioners in the case of many funds), so their loans and investments must perform. Until very recently, most fund managers had little interest in the intrinsic missions of the companies in which they invested. If a company seemed to have little promise, they sold shares and tried to invest where the balance of risk and return seemed appropriate.

Most funds do not want a major position in any one company, just as banks do not want their loan portfolios too concentrated either. That is prudent risk taking. Those who took flyers in the 1980s got burned. However, as a result, investment managers and loan officers are portfolio managers. The system intentionally keeps them several layers removed from the real action in the companies they finance.

As returns from many former blue-chip companies deteriorated in the 1980s, a number of fund managers became much more interested in taking an active role in the governance of these companies. Most of them want stable returns, not adventuring, but this mind-set shows when they state their goals of governance.

The most publicized governance issue among fund managers is excessive executive compensation to managers whose companies are not giving much value to the owners. While this is a complex issue, soaring executive salaries are thought to partly result from cozy board compensation committees simply pegging the pay formulas to survey results from other companies. Consequently, executive pay went into a competitive upward spiral even as company financial performance was lackluster.

However, investors also want executive compensation tied to results—for them—and therein lies a contradiction. To do this, compensation must be related to stock price or dividends at some point in time. Consequently, an executive can sell stock previously acquired and profit nicely while the current condition of the company is dismal. Some of the convoluted pay formulas do not result in the rewards desired anyway, and they have been less than fully disclosed to investors. Much of the excitement about this issue is less about the percentage of corporate revenue that goes to top executives than the principle of the thing. Highly paid executives leading companies that give little value to the investors do not retain the trust of financial stakeholders.

However, high pay does not create trust between executives and the other stakeholders either. One of the major reasons why executive pay should not be "exorbitant" is that it also undermines the leadership status of the executive *inside* the company. In an age when teamwork is becoming more and more important to attain the performance needed for any profit whatever, well-meaning investors that confer a big reward on "their agent" are forgetting that results come from many people, outside the company as well as inside, not from a single leader.

In the past few years, I have been invited more than once to join in a turnaround effort at a poor-performing small manufacturer. The idea is simple. Participate in a leveraged buyout, go in, and pump up people. Train them to do lean manufacturing: quality, cell layouts, kanban systems, uniform load schedules, faster time-to-market by concurrent engineering—the whole bit—and turn everyone into a customer-conscious salesperson, too. After three years or so, when the company is stomping its competition, sell out and pocket a bundle.

If successful, this scenario is an investor's dream. Unfortunately, it has a fatal flaw. (All the invitations were declined.) From its inception, the plan's intent is to deceive the personnel of the company— profit from what they create. Sell out to whom, and with what consequences to them? After the buyout craze of the 1980s, many employees in all positions are wary of such schemes. In company after company, would-be associates are suspicious of transient ownership that will leave them in the lurch. If there is to be a new quality-of-life prosperity, investors *must recognize* that their most important role is establishing a form of governance that inspires trust.

In *Power and Accountability*, Robert Monks and Nell Minow present an investor's view of corporate guidance. They assert that the CEOs of public companies are accountable to no one but themselves. The basic issue is an old one. The seminal Berle and Means study on professional management in 1932 concluded that 44 percent of the then top two hundred nonfinancial corporations were controlled by managers, not ownership.[3] For much of this century, many arguments have been made that the system of professional management is not a problem; to the contrary, the system made it more likely that capable, broadly qualified persons would head large companies instead of founders whose own success had led them out of their depth. That was before trading pressure for short-term results and management-by-the-numbers became big issues.

Rather than creating short-term pressure on companies by trading away from earnings laggards, Monks and Minnow recommend that institutional board members take a longer view and aggressively seek seats on corporate boards. Once there, they should limit their attention to ownership issues: officer compensation, dividends, and business expansion or continuance—and to seeing that companies obey the law. However, without modification, the influence of the investor mind-set may not be the medicine needed, for it focuses on profitability and results, not on process building and trust.[4]

Take the case of Cummins Engine Company, which makes Monks and Minow livid. The company has long been noted as a rather patrician benefactor of its headquarters town, Columbus, Indiana ("being a good corporate citizen" is how management would prefer to describe it). But like most Rust Belt manufacturers, Cummins has had a belly full of problems for fifteen years: fuel economy, exhaust emissions, soft markets for its truck engines after trucking was deregulated, and high-quality-low-cost competition from the Far East. In addition, their U.S. competitors have become much more formidable in the domestic truck market in recent years.

In the early 1980s Cummins had to reduce costs substantially (Komatsu could build the same engine for 30 percent less). Downsizing and outplacement quickly became familiar terms. The main engine plant was a big, slow job shop, one of the toughest conversions to fast-flow production imaginable. Cummins has had consultants on everything from TQM to TPM, and there have been some successes. Consolidated Diesel, the Cummins-Case joint venture, is one of the best engine plants in North America, if not the world. But everyone else has improved, too. Core manufacturing operations are barely competitive in a much tougher market, and new engines have been slow coming out. The chief problem is the same as at most old companies. Throughout Cummins, many people now know what to do. Many new midlevel managers with new ideas have come—and gone. Basic control from the top is still through the "financial system" with the intention of wringing out a profit. That creates reward systems that inhibit the trust people need in each other for vigorous change.

Meanwhile Cummins's dismal financial performance invited take-over. Two foreign groups purchased stakes and began playing games. ("No, we have no interest in acquiring the full company," and so forth). Coming on the heels of takeover raids on Goodyear and other companies, the immune systems of Cummins and the state of Indiana began counterattack. No one trusted the raiders to change to a management that would lead the company to "world-class" performance, or even give it a chance.

Ford, Kubota, and Tenneco came to the rescue: $250 million for a 27 percent stake. That stabilized ownership with the old guard in control, which in the opinion of Monks and Minow allows Cummins to continue thumbing its nose at investors. They would have a no-nonsense board change top management. A change in leadership might be helpful, but if the board expects management to financially control the company for them and exerts pressure for dividends now, not later, a critical problem is reinforced. The people of the company may trust investors on the board no more than its management to lead them in the kind of endeavor that seems necessary.

Another interesting case is the performance of Kohlberg Kravis Roberts & Company representatives on the boards of companies in which they have substantial stakes. They install CEOs that will pump growth and profits. They press for divestiture of unprofitable, neglected divisions. They assist in the restructuring of capitalization. And by their own criteria, they have been successful more often than not. For instance, a new marketing team at Motel 6, coupled with a new formula to build units at lower after-tax cost, quickly led to a doubling of the chain's operating profits.[5]

However, these policies have basically built a fire under traditional management approaches. Returns-driven control does not build trust. The KKR-controlled companies have had to repair employee relations and customer relations in their wake. The investor mind-set has to change if teamwork-based approaches of the future are to succeed.

A company does not have to be "investor controlled" to exhibit the investor mind-set. Any remote-control management that applies pressure for results mostly through financial goals and incentives is operating the same way. GM is one case. The scandal at Sears Automotive Centers is another. The use of commissions, job "piece rate" pay, and tough quotas pressured service representatives to run up the charges, which led to accusations of consumer fraud. Sears eliminated the commissions, but denies that abuses were systemwide. (In a bygone era, similar compensation plans at Sears worked, but they do not work now when Sears is competing against retailers that concentrate on customer satisfaction.)[6]

Despite the pervasiveness of financial control systems, financial officers are beginning to learn that while their job may be to minimize their companies' cost of capital, improvement processes and attention to customers fuels their companies' success. Chief financial officers who gathered for a *Business Week* workshop noted that they had to remain aware of increasing their companies' assets of every kind, including people and information. There's hope.[7]

A little tinkering with outside investors in corporate governance is insufficient. What is needed is a different concept of the role of investors—in practice, not just in theory. Investors need to understand that they are investing in human development and organizational missions, and not just regard investments as shares in cash-flow machines.

Profits and Interest Used as a Tax System

Because in the advanced industrial countries so much investment today is by institutions, the need of these institutions for money is a prime contributor to their behavior. Why do they need money? One reason is that their own customers will leave them if they do not perform well. A second is that the prime benefactors in many cases are people whom "the system" must support in some way. An insurance company has policyholders and beneficiaries to pay. A pension fund has payouts to make. When bank interest rates dropped in 1991–92, savers living off the interest saw their income drop by more than half in a year. Many were retirees.

Just looking at retirement rather than other uses of investment income, the prospects in the advanced industrial countries indicate continued increases in funds to invest. First, the various government social security systems (about 11.8 percent of GDP in Europe, 7.2 percent in the United States, and 5.3 percent in Japan) were often "sold" as investment plans. Actually they are transfer payments from current workers to the pensioners, usually at about the poverty level.

Had Social Security actually been set up as an investment plan, payments, which were regarded as a tax, might have been too high to be politically acceptable. Certainly the investment policies of such a stupendous-sized fund would have been controversial. But perhaps the founders of Social Security merely deferred the thorny issues to the private retirement funds decades later.

Because of the inadequacies of Social Security, retirees fortunate enough to have personal savings income or private pensions are relieved—and dependent on them. The number of people retired is now between 15 and 20 percent of the working-age population and will increase in the next century. By one forecast, pension funds in the industrial countries will grow from $4.2 trillion in 1990 to $11 trillion by 2000, although the percentage of Americans in pension funds fell from 49 percent to 43 percent between 1979 and 1991 and appears to still be dropping. Where will these funds be invested? One prediction is that a high percentage will go to developing nations where growth (and profits) will take off, not to the advanced countries that will be struggling to retain a high quality of life in slow-growth conditions.[8]

The increased size of institutional funds also portends a reckoning on the issues of how investment decisions are made and how institutional investment affects companies. Driven by a fiduciary duty to seek steady, stable flows of funds, fund representatives influencing companies may function more as tax assessors ready to exact their due from the operations. Indeed, before the decade is out, the United States may see sharp political conflict between those who are fortunate enough to be the beneficiaries of this "private tax system" for pensions, medical treatment, education, and so on, and those who are left out.

If boards of directors insist on a steady flow of dividends while suppressing the costs of human development and operational transition, they set a downward spiral in motion. So far, that is too often the direction of the investment mind-set. By pushing for more profit and lower costs using traditional business logic, both investment and jobs head for low-cost regions. If this drives more and more domestic American working-class people out of the private investment and benefits system, one can see the pressure building toward explosion. Unless the mind-set of many of them changes, being a fund manager in another ten years might be less popular than being a tax investigator.

The usual defense of investment policies is that if they are practical, in due course the markets will balance things out. Growth will resume and happy days will be here again. That's counting on future development being the same as in the past—and that we only have to wait for it, rather than make changes. Better to recognize right away what we must invest in—primarily process improvement and reorganization across all kinds of businesses as currently conceived, applications of technology, and most of all, ourselves.

It is easier to think of investment in terms of how we spend our time. In an advanced society, skilled people spend the first twenty years of life, and often more, in basic preparation for adult responsibility. Some are in formal education until past thirty. For many, peak skills are not reached until well after thirty. After that, in organizations where the need for upgrading is recognized, 10 percent or so of work time is spent on skill improvement. After thirty or forty years of this, another ten or twenty are spent in retirement. In more and more cases, some of that time is spent back in the same condition of dependency from which we begin, only the cost is higher.

In an advanced society, nearly half of the life of highly skilled and professional workers is spent in preparation, or in setup. (How much time does a pilot, MD, master machinist, or circuit designer spend in setup compared with his or her actual activities? However, the investment mind-set wants to recognize—and pay for—only the time spent in direct action unless "the market" demands it.) In addition to professional teachers, many housewives and others spend most of their life helping someone else prepare. Because there is no direct payment, the value of a "nagging mother" is unrecognized by those for whom money is the prime symbol of status, but the majority of us do not become productive people without having had a series of prodders, mentors, and helpers at the right times.

The point of all this is not that housewives should receive a stipend to signify that they have status, too. It is that an advanced technical society has a huge social overhead. If such a society is to sustain itself, the overhead has to be carried. Our thinking is still carried over from New England mill-girl days, when if hands were not needed at the mill, they could easily return to forest and farm and essentially live off the land.

That is an ancient instinct. The Chinese mandarins survived for centuries because most of them retained connections to the country-side whence they could return if life turned harsh in the cities. As late as the 1930s that was still feasible in much of the United States, but we are passing that point. Today, the equivalent is returning to basic service work or living by our wits off the "flea market" economy.

These kinds of problems were unknown or ignored in the high-growth industrial age. In an industrializing society, life in a factory may be hard, but it beats most alternatives—like scraping by on the land. That is so hard that millions of people all over the world drift into cities and live however they can rather than endure it.

The problem now is that if we want a better society than this, we must create the conditions for it. That kind of society has to maintain a high social overhead, meaning that the financial system must find mechanisms that pay for it.

One mechanism is high taxes as in social-welfare societies. Another is a high margin demanded of businesses to support the preparation and life-style of those who are its beneficiaries. The high tax system confers benefits on everyone regardless of merit or attitude, which turns off "conservatives," but since World War II countries like Sweden have generally been internationally competitive despite conservative railings. If ownership and its benefits are narrowly held, the high-margin system creates a privileged class and offers little opportunity to those outside it. Neither approach sits well with Americans. About the only alternative is sharing the risks and rewards of ownership where it counts—with the associates of the company.

Using any system of financial support, the advanced society has to support a high social overhead. That overhead must be taken into account in any business. High-margin businesses, no matter whether the margin is profit or tax, cannot compete on cost against those that do not carry the same burden. A value-added type tax, regardless of its regressive nature, does have the benefit of somewhat equalizing the burden between companies. Likewise, if the institutional ownership of companies needs money for "social" purposes, that, too, had as well be recognized, and the role of the investor representatives should take it into account. That is done by recognizing that the basis for competition is human development that creates high value-added products and services.

Lessons from Japan on Governance

Most of the public commentaries on Japanese *keiretsu* look at Japanese practice as it was, not as it needs to be. After World War II, *keiretsu* banks financed penniless companies, and companies helped finance each other when capital was short. In addition, company pension funds needed to be invested in something *keiretsu* members understood. Where better than in companies with which they did business and had connections?

Today, the needs of Japan are changing. Despite the bust of land values and stock prices, capital is more available, and the collaboration between high-tech, high-performance operations in global environments needs to be more flexible. Japan's social overhead is also rising. Previously, Japanese education could be "financed" by the promise of future growth, but a graying population presents a different problem, and Japan will soon have a higher percentage of senior citizens than anyone. More people with savings want to draw on the earnings. Consequently, Japanese companies must pay more attention to profit margins rather than betting so much on market-share growth. Besides, a maturing Japanese economy will not grow so fast.

The postwar Japanese manufacturing corporation has not really been governed by its ownership. The board of a Japanese manufacturing company is mostly top managers representing all the stakeholders of the company, not exclusively the owners. Since the goal has usually been growth, not profit, there was little incentive to reward managers for making a premium profit for owners. That's one reason the pay of Japanese CEOs has been anemic compared to that of Americans. The other reason is that huge compensation would make CEOs "stick out," thus creating a social gulf between them and the people they should be leading, so they are paid at the top end of the employee compensation scale.

Many large manufacturing corporations (like Toyota) are still controlled by the founding family. Most of the other large ones are institutionally owned. If performance is mediocre, an investor institution may replace the CEO to turn it around. However, change is usually regarded as improving the performance of the people (sometimes with drastic action) rather than financial restructuring. Mergers and acquisitions have usually been seen as people-change processes.

As long as the objective was growth, not profitability, it was non-divisive because growth is a win-win objective for everyone. During postwar development, all stakeholders sacrificed to achieve it. Unless it is shared, profitability is a divisive objective, so the typical Japanese manufacturer pays about a third of annual compensation in semiannual bonus payments tied to overall unit performance (although when the practice is routine, it can also be regarded as withholding a big chunk of pay for later payment).

The general approach to governance was designed to reinforce commitment and reduce risk by all key parties. "Lifetime employment" never applied to the total work force and is an informal understanding, not a contractual agreement such as the GM jobs bank agreement with the UAW. The real assurance of job security is not the present company but general insistence that employees become so skilled and versatile that they can easily be placed elsewhere if need be. However, when distressed companies take pains to look after displaced employees, they demonstrate that companies are for the employees, even if base pay is poor and working conditions harsh.

In this system employees realize that in many ways *they* are the company. Mutual support arrangements that would be considered "patriarchal" or cozy in a profit-first system do not evoke that reaction when the goal is growth. People work unreported overtime for *their* company, but if they need money, they may also report overtime that is not worked.

Why has the Japanese manufacturing company not been run as a cozy employees' club? First, employees easily saw that superior performance was essential to sustain a lifeline of exports to demanding customers against tough competitors by a country with few natural resources. The main asset had to be skill and organization. Second, the manufacturing governance system easily unified its participants around the goal of growth. That is a triumph of the system. An abundance of financial scandals demonstrates that the Japanese as individuals have no cultural aversion to personal gain.

Companies that have not seen themselves as in the vanguard of skill or growth have not been so vigorous. Lacking a driving goal to improve or to serve customers, the Japanese National Railway became flabby. Traditional arrangements in the Japanese distribution system have been notoriously cozy and inefficient. The moral: To motivate people to high performance, the business system has to unite its participants around an easily accepted common goal. The enterprise has to have a soul.

The new Japanese challenge is how to create a unifying motivation in a slower-growing economy that is both high-tech and that must carry a heavier burden of social overhead. Therefore, institutional investors are becoming less willing to obtain their returns through growth and want a higher payout. The Japanese industrial experience offers useful lessons, but the old Japanese system of building mutual trust and allegiance within companies and among networks of companies must be modified. Their new status and the nature of their problems are closer to the American ones. In fact, the basic situation may not be radically different in all the older, more technically advanced regions of the world.

The New Financial Order

The essential problems of the new financial order are:

1. How to combine research, technology, and very fast-flow operations know-how with marketing in an open-system enterprise.
2. How to organize and finance open-system enterprise.
3. How to draw more people into such an environment so that we do not wind up with a two-tier society.

In the United States, a company's core incentive has been the motivation of owners for profit and growth—in 1980s idiom, "maximizing shareholder value." In old-style industry, it isn't working very well. In theory, outside board members assure that top management does not serve themselves or other stakeholders at the expense of owners. That isn't working either. Stockholder activists become wrought up when they discover that board members are seldom effective doing that.

That basic concept of corporate governance and purpose is becoming archaic because it is based on the concept that companies must keep each other at arm's length rather than participate in open-system enterprise. Unless this concept is mitigated, it leads to a financially driven company with conflicts between the stakeholders. As often as not today, a good CEO must shield employees, suppliers, and other stakeholders from impatient investors who do not understand the evolution taking place. Otherwise, no one has time to develop his or her capabilities.

If margins are high enough, all stakeholders can get a nice cut. If the pie is shrinking, cutting it is more contentious. Investor reaction is to disinvest in human development—payout takes too long. Bring in talent if it is needed. The usual prescriptions are to divest losers, spiff the product line, rev up marketing, and cut the costs. Short run, it primes the cash-flow pumps if they are not sunk in a dry hole. Long run, strong corporate governance does not lead *people* toward a different concept of the business. Well-run companies today need commitment between owners and the other stakeholders well beyond an industrial plantation system. Governance by ownership representatives who regard the other stakeholders as resources for their benefit rather than as partners cannot cope with today's needs, much less forge an open-system enterprise.

Entrepreneurship and the Open-System Enterprise

Most cost systems and financial mind-sets today are still attuned to a bureaucracy managing and controlling a large direct work expense. So different is open-system enterprise from their usual rut that many investors mired in this mind-set have little chance of jumping far enough out of it to think seriously about what is being proposed. The more entrepreneurial ones are the hope of the future, but even then a different kind of entrepreneurship is needed—one that invests in process and technology, but most of all in people. The "system" must be devised so that the investment in people is obvious, and this aspect of open-system enterprise is probably the most difficult challenge.

Numerous routes to financing can be thought of. For instance, return to the example of Cadillac as an automotive open-system enterprise. Investors would put money into a resource company, Transportation Technology Inc. This company would have advanced R&D, market research, access to capital, and a cadre of people. The cadre would be capable of creating concept cars that could be turned into service vehicles for the market. They might also provide consult-

ing services offered by personnel between stints in operating enterprise. Such a company would be in a prime position to guide capital
into promising new enterprises, but without question, its key assets
would be talent, experience, and intellectual capital.

Transportation Technology would be a source of talent as well as
capital for lead partners and integrators in transportation enterprises,
like Cadillac—sort of a human bank as well as a financial one. This
company would also serve as an absorber of talent released from
enterprises. If an enterprise failed—nothing lasts forever—it would be
responsible for arranging a workout. A new enterprise might be formed
to take over the failed operations or simply to decommission them
and parcel out customers, personnel, and physical assets to healthy
enterprises.

This is really just a reformation and downscaling of auto companies
to concentrate on the core responsibilities they need to assume to
operate differently. A few companies have done something approaching this. For example, Honda years ago split itself into Honda Manufacturing and Honda Engineering. They work very closely together,
but the reason for the split was to assure that technology and human
development never was shorted out inside Honda. However, the incentive for an even more radical change might not come from an old
car company struggling to shed its past but rather from a coalition of
larger dealers having the vision to change market approach and take
on the requisite technical expertise. The big change is less in the
structure than in the attitudes—the soul of the enterprise.

However, under this scenario, the responsibility for obtaining a
return to pay the social overhead would lie with Transportation Technology. The difference between this institution and a conventional
investment pool or bank is that responsibility for human development
and financial flows to keep everything going is clearly with the same
party. If the job is done well, Transportation Technology would doubtless be a stern disciplinarian when necessary.

Besides a resource company for lead partners or integrators, one can
also visualize other resource companies in materials, equipment, software, fuels, and other areas. These would support the major supplier
partners in automotive enterprises and in other kinds of enterprises.
Where economy of scale in production can be greatly reduced, these
companies might spin off personnel to operate plants that serve a

single enterprise or a limited number of them. Where that is not feasible—or capital requirements prohibit it for a long time—the company may simply "dedicate" personnel and parts of facilities to certain enterprise customers. This is a not very big deviation from the direction of current practice. Again, the big shift is human attitudes and responsibilities. Those allow the technologies to be used to full advantage.

Cadillac would hopefully be an open-system enterprise with longevity. One cannot imagine environmentally sustainable transportation from come-and-go organizations. A long-term enterprise would also have a pool of capital if it were successful, but probably not much. Most of the excess cash would go to the Transportation Technology parent charged with sustaining the flows of human, technical, and financial capital. This scheme of things is not going to work unless some institution—half investment bank, half a personnel development and placement agency—is charged with paying the social overhead and maintaining the system. That again is simply organizing to carry out a responsibility that the current system is drifting into without being overtly conscious of it.

The differences between resource companies, open-system enterprises, and conventional business are the sharpest in the area of governance. A very serious social duty of a resource company is to earn a return to pay the social overhead, but a second one is to sustain the human development necessary to preserve the system. Thesefore, the aims of governance are broader than maximizing value to the investors. Turning on the afterburners for a three to five year payout is no longer adequate, just as counting on growth to solve the problems is ineffective when the chief resource is human.

The governance of an operating open-system enterprise is straightforward. It belongs to representatives of the stakeholders in it—primarily the major partners that have been bought in. Stating the qualifications of someone to serve as a director of a resource company is more difficult—like listing the qualifications needed to be president of the United States. Nobody living completely measures up, but just holding title to capital is insufficient. Directors need to have the experience to make judgments about human, technical, marketing, ecological, and organizational issues, as well as financial ones.

The position is analogous to being the director of a hospital, university, or research institute rather than a company as it is thought of today. The director has to consider the positions of all stakeholders. The expertise in combining and recombining companies has to be based on technology and human factors, not just some assumed financial synergism. Such a person is more likely to emerge from a resource company after a diverse career than from fund management after a career picking stocks, as in the 1980s. The board of a resource company should consist of people with rounded experience in the industry plus outside representatives of communities or customers. If people spend much of their career working in cross-functional teams, the pool of such people will become much larger than it is at present.

The fear that such a board will not "maximize profit" is probably misplaced. Achieving the margins needed to keep such enterprises going and pay the social overhead would be an unceasing concern.

The proposal for resource companies and operating enterprises is a major shift from the current practice of separation between fund managers, investment banks, and other financial institutions and operating companies. However, the big, old industrial companies today have acquired their own financial arms of various kinds. They could restructure into something like a resource company rather easily, but restructuring is easy compared with reforming mind-sets and attitudes. That is the major change.

These proposals are not very different in intent from Michael Porter's recommendations in his report for the Council on Competitiveness (the executive-run group that grew out of the Young Commission, not the vice president's group by the same name). Porter also recommends that institutions be allowed to hold bigger, longer-term stakes in companies and that they should learn more about their investments.[9]

Even Porter's recommendations are considered utopian by many in the financial community, so accustomed are they to remote investment and growth pumping. The instinct of investor-oriented people to push for quick-hitters has to be resisted by institutions that can take a broader view as well as a longer one. Something more is needed than building an American version of German and Japanese methods of generating long-term commitments in institutional investments. Those institutions are also in need of change to reach what open-system enterprise is capable of. Again, it seems more likely that an upstart institution will rise than that the current governance guiders can quickly learn a new mind-set.

Buy-In

Reports of 30–40 percent productivity improvement and order-of-magnitude quality improvement in *production*, while not the norm, are now so common that they are not big news in manufacturing. These achievements are only a precursor to much more astounding productivity improvements in white-collar work. If a process of new-product definition that once took thirty people in three functions six months now takes a five-person team and their software support a couple of days—well, everybody has to go somewhere.

When the waste goes out of processes, much of it is in wages and salaries to persons whose jobs, in whole or in part, consisted of "wasted" activity. In most cases no waste was intended. People worked by methods that were efficient for the time. But when the total structure and relationships of an industry change, the entire system of financial allocation goes with it. The financial allocation includes the cut for investment—whatever that is coming to mean in an era of computerized, amorphous capitalization by instruments with stipulations that were impossible to calculate in a precomputer age. Financially and economically, the challenge is to reinflate the system—stop the downward spiral to low-price mass-produced goods and enable an upward spiral into high-quality, environmentally sustainable customer service. It isn't going to be done by givebacks, layoffs, and everyone working out of his or her house as a consultant.

Nothing lasts forever. A well-run enterprise like a Cadillac should be a long-term operation. The same people could stay there thirty years, but it might not be the best choice for them or for the enterprise. Most people should not expect that their career in an operating open-system enterprise will last a lifetime. The problem is binding their allegiance to an operating enterprise long enough to generate momentum. Having something like a resource company to fall back on and inspire them through a tradition is important.

Rewards to the individual should reinforce the system. Since a good system should be balanced, performance has to be measured in a variety of ways besides profit. Furthermore, a well-designed human reward system should be a mix of monetary rewards and nonmonetary recognition, which should promote both group achievement and individual achievement. There are no ideas in this that are really new. The crucial point is the willingness of investors to cut the individuals into the company. Give them a short-term and a long-term reward for an enterprise that generates and sustains high margins: profit sharing, and some of that with a delayed payment, so people do not feel rich with the first flush of success. Unless enterprise gains are rewarded in some way, some version of a union arises to obtain them in the form of big compensation.

From gainsharing to profit sharing to stock distribution, the variations in plans to give associates an interest in the financial success of an enterprise are infinite. None is perfect. The trick is to build a system that gives associates an interest in their own long-run security—an assurance that the system as a whole will not run down or deflate. That is a human incentive problem as well as a financial one. More than enough financial ingenuity exists in the United States to devise such systems if financial architects gain the vision and inspiration to work on it.

The hitch in profit sharing or employee partial ownership is that many employees are not entrepreneurial, nor do they necessarily exercise long-term judgment. If they like sharing in profits, but not losses, organizations dominated by employees are more conservative than those dominated by owners. Conditions are even worse if they want to pay themselves the money and not use it to promote their own future improvement. From any stakeholder's viewpoint, paying for the human development to cope with an uncertain future is a tough mind-set to acquire and maintain, but that's the objective of the system.

NOTES

1. William A. Sahlman, "Why Sane People Shouldn't Serve on Public Boards," *Harvard Business Review* 68, no. 3 (May–June 1990): 28–35.
2. Among a number of accounts of this is David C. Smith and Marjorie

Sorge, "Why 'Inakiphobia' Grips GM's Suppliers," *Ward's Auto World*, July 1992, p. 27.

3. A. A. Berle, and G. C. Means, *The Modern Corporation and Private Property* (New York: Commerce Clearing House Loose Leaf Service, Division of the Corporation Trust Co., 1932).

4. Robert A. G. Monks and Nell Minow, *Power and Accountability* (New York: HarperCollins, 1992).

5. George Anders, "The 'Barbarians' in the Boardroom," *Harvard Business Review* 70, no. 4 (July–August 1992): 79–87.

6. Julia Flynn, "Did Sears Take Other Customers for a Ride?" *Business Week*, 3 August 1992, 24–25.

7. "Building the Future of Corporate Value," *Business Week*, 20 July 1992, 82–83.

8. "Tomorrow's Pensions," *The Economist*, 20 June 1992, 19–21.

9. Michael Porter, *Capital Choices* (Washington, DC: The Council on Competitiveness, 1992). This study and several others are encapsulated by Porter in "Capital Disadvantage: America's Failing Capital Investment System," *Harvard Business Review* 70, no. 5 (September–October 1992): 65–82.

12

ESCAPING
THE BLACK HOLE

As THE TWENTY-FIRST CENTURY NEARS, TECHNOLOGY ALLOWS MARVELOUS feats to become routine business. Productivity and quality improvement allows the essentials of food, clothing, and shelter to be provided by a fraction of the available work force. But something seems to be amiss. Manufacturing folk in advanced economies who have endured all the performance revolutions realize that performance excellence alone is not enough. They sense another yet-unnamed dread. Call it the black hole of negative economic growth.

Economic stagnation in the early 1990s has not treated Americans as severely as it did in the 1930s. Despite gaps, social safety nets now catch people much more effectively, but they may also retard recognition that fundamental change is occurring. Efforts to revive economic growth will have some effect, but growth will not kick-start as it once did.

In already developed economies, growth as an end in itself appears to have reached a limit. We need to define our problems differently:

- In business strategies and public policy, we need to build an economy based on the ideas of this book, summarized in Figure 12-1. Simply "making money" or priming growth are not sufficient indicators of achievement.

- We must learn how to work together much more effectively—a different form of voluntary capitalism, not an old form of socialism.
- All the advanced industrial countries have similar problems. The issues are worldwide.
- Worldwide, capital increasingly is in short supply. To build financial capital, we need to build human capital.

We do not know how to run this new kind of world. Too many of our economic policies and business motivations depend on growth from increased use of resources—easy payment of today's debts by tomorrow's growth—whether the debt is public or private. In this, the old American political divide between "conservative" and "liberal" is meaningless except to invoke traditional passions.

We are crossing a new divide. Americans have little choice but to promote growth in underdeveloped countries. Trade with Mexico only happens to be the case in closest proximity. A free-trade agreement requires wrestling with provisions for sustainable ecology, American job loss, and other issues, but some form of relatively open economic interchange is necessary. Otherwise, population growth in a poverty-wracked Mexico will drive millions of additional Mexicans north. Americans cannot hang on to an old standard of living and wish that the rest of the world's problems would go away.

All the advanced countries adjoin some form of this problem. The United States next to Mexico. Western Europe and neighboring Eastern Europe. Japan near China. And the rates of development (and quality of life) are disparate within the advanced countries. Parts of the United States resemble the third world.

How bad could it get? While futurists like John Nesbitt picture rosy changes, many others, like Alvin Toffler, see high-tech fortresses surrounded by chaos: fragmented nations, ethnic strife, sectarian disputes, environmental disaster, high-tech the handmaiden of the haves, and guerrilla warfare by the have-nots.[1] Fortunately, the future is partly what we make of it; we do not need to let it wash over us.

Manufacturing (and many service businesses) is presently sinking into the black hole of getting lean just for survival: productivity improvements by all the "excellence" methods, delayering, wage reductions, outplacements, early retirements, use of temporary help having limited benefits (even in professional positions), and reluctance to

FIGURE 12-1

ELEMENTS OF THE OPEN-SYSTEM ENTERPRISE

The first elements illustrate why this is no mere structural transition. We the people
must see ourselves differently. Those new perspectives are the essence of a new
"soul of enterprise."

1. A different view of ourselves and of companies: from highly
egocentric individuals in stand-alone, fortress companies to being one
part of a mosaic. From doing what we wish in a small part of an
infinite world to participating in the improvement of a finite world.

2. From an economic system dependent on growth to one
driven by quality of life.

3. Ubiquitous use of information-age technology. Most computer systems and software can interact.

4. Maintaining a sustainable environment as a vital part of a
high quality of life. Environmental protection no longer seen as a
"drag on growth."

5. Open-system organizations with few secrets. Information
limited only by human perceptual capacity.

6. Distributed, interactive operating organizations, each unit
much smaller than mass-production organizations of the twentieth
century, with the distinctions between functional specialties blurred.
Many common, interactive human processes and systems.

7. Recognition of the importance of human capital—that
most of our limitations are us. Investment in developing human capital so that many individuals understand at least one technical specialty in depth but are also generalists so that they can participate in
the integration of the whole.

8. Highly flexible (or agile) equipment, tooling, and software
systems not only in engineering and production, but in order entry,
service (or remanufacturing), and elsewhere. Ability to deliver products in lot sizes of one, tailored to individuals, with efficiency at least
equal to lean manufacturing, and with much higher overall effectiveness.

9. Products designed and built for remanufacturing and upgrade. (A prime strategy to both conserve capital and prevent environmental damage.)

FIGURE 12-1 (*cont.*)

10. Ability to incorporate foreseeable technical advances into existing products. Ability to integrate complex technology.

11. Education and development of knowledgeable consumers capable of contributing to the process (prosumers).

12. Development and deployment of universal systems for measuring overall operating performance. These might not be one system, but a set of similar ones adapted to different kinds of operations and administered not by a governmental "big brother" but by people involved in operations in the broad sense and stimulated to improving them.

13. Development of a different kind of economy loaded with high-margin enterprises so that we have a system that can maintain itself. Dedication of enterprises to earning high margins, not just for investors, but to cover the social overhead.

14. Constant creation and refinement of "visions" that can be used as guides to where this new world is going.

---

spend capital. Since the basic excellence practices work equally well anywhere, a commodity-products manufacturer finds it difficult to clearly best a smart third-world competitor.

However, the black hole does not exist just because of foreign competition. Companies vying for strictly high-tech, advanced business find themselves competing much more vigorously in high-tech rat races. Easing the competition is no answer; one only falls further off the world pace. The American Big Three auto companies had high costs and relatively cozy competition for years. They were not pressed hard enough to serve their customers—or to meet any other challenge.

A basic-products manufacturer can "do all the right things" and still find that revenue per person is only $50,000 or $60,000 per year. That is insufficient for a high quality of life. Deduct the materials cost (about half), capital costs (running on used equipment), and other operating expenses, and at 1992 costs the leftovers do not support take-home pay plus retirement benefits, health benefits, day care, taxation, and so on.

A more advanced manufacturer might have revenue per person in the $150,000- to $200,000-per-year range and still be troubled. Factor in the pay or direct expense required to obtain the services of highly trained people and keep them at the edge of the state of their art. That business is also marginal.

Simply stated, for a high quality of life, economic enterprise has to have a high revenue per person and a high margin while maintaining vigorous attention to customer service, technical advance, environmental concerns, and the like.

The problems in former Communist countries are a clear illustration of a vital point about the United States, where the situation is still somewhat murky. Technology is present, or can be introduced relatively quickly. Capital is short, but it can be attracted when conditions are promising. The critical factor is learning how to work in a radically different system as quickly as possible. But that goes slow even when people are eager to do it.

Black Hole Economics

Our patterns of economic thought greatly influence our management thinking. The old economics is not working. Fundamental change is making obsolete the models usually assumed by macroeconomics.

By convention, growth of gross national product (GNP), the sum of national income accounts, indicates an addition to wealth. (Many other countries use a similar measurement, Gross Domestic Product [GDP].) After World War II, GNP growth gradually became part of the daily news as economists demonstrated that it was related to jobs and income. Politicians encouraged policymakers to hypo GNP growth with a suitable Rx of interest rates, money supply, tax levels, and government spending.

GNP is criticized on many grounds, some old, some new: Lags in data collection and statistical inaccuracy make initially reported change numbers suspect. Vital activity, like house-spouse labor, is not captured by a transaction-driven model. GNP measures only income, not the value of resources themselves, or losses of them. For instance, it does not factor in the value of topsoil lost each year. It is fixated on growth in activity measured by transactions.

However, GNP or GDP is still a major guide to policy because its growth seems to correspond to overall economic well-being. Overreliance on GNP is akin to one-dimensional financial guidance of companies, for GNP reveals waste no better than corporate financial statements do.

No one knows how much GNP is waste, but any estimate would surely be astonishing. Material purchased, never used, and packed off to landfill still counts as an addition to GNP. Repair services and spare parts have been high-margin operations padding GNP and bottom lines. Engineers paid to make drawings that toolmakers rarely need (a real case) still add to GNP. However, an economist will simply say that one person's waste is another's livelihood and continue counting any dollar-recorded activity as GNP.

Clerical and managerial work are a big repository of GNP waste. Most clerical work is simply for *control*—for planning, preventing fraud, or insuring fairness. Some waste, like idle time and double-handling of paperwork, is easily identified. Some is well intentioned, like keeping detailed health care records for third-party payers.

Overbuilding of office space in the 1980s was primed by favorable depreciation tax rules, not just anticipation of growth in clerical and managerial work (but it added to GNP). Now these jobs are prime candidates for wastebusting. A drastic attack on waste in clerical control functions accompanied by rapid decentralization of management might prolong the commercial real estate depression in addition to adding to the glut of white-collar job seekers.

Many of us—perhaps most of us—make our living from waste. An inefficient distribution system is highly wasteful, but every participant in the chain receives a markup (if they are astute enough not to be beaten out of it). Such a system is a series of tollgates providing income to many people. It is possible to see how to improve the efficiency of distribution in ways similar to that of manufacturing, but eliminating jobs might create considerable opposition. The Japanese economy is noted for inefficient distribution, but the inefficiency also creates something to do ("underemployment incomes") so that "reforming it" is unpleasant. Likewise, "reforming" family farms runs into emotional opposition.

Distribution is only one area plentiful in waste. Unfortunately, the aggregate elimination of waste in a relatively flat-growth economy also eliminates income. Those with little or no income create social overhead without contributing to it—another way of saying that unemployment is bad. The counterarguments are always that those displaced will be absorbed by more efficient enterprises—that productivity improvement always leads to more growth, which will take care of the problem.

However, if growth is no longer an automatic solution, we have a black hole. A short-run public policy that might ease the import pressure is a value-added tax (applied to domestic goods and imports, but not exports, and always opposed by consumers who want rock-bottom prices), an old favorite used by several other advanced economies. A value-added tax does not change the basic situation, but it might be more imaginatively used. The detailed rethinking of the economics of this new world is beyond the scope of this book.

Inflation and the Value-City Economy

The evils of inflation have long been a favorite editorial topic. Commentators can easily wrap the vilification of whatever irks them in a package of inflation theory. Most of these theories center on markets and money: demand exceeding supply, interest rates too high or too low, government deficits, high taxes, excess money supply, excess wage demands, cost of regulatory requirements.

Many of the editorials simply voice reluctance to pay some form of social overhead, using an inflation theory to explain why monetary flows directed one way or another would be disastrous. However, despite the worry that it would get out of control, inflation has not been so bad as long as it was accompanied by "real" growth—more jobs and more things to buy. And as long as that was the case, theories of inflation presented by economists also concentrated on financial flows.

Structural theories of inflation have never been popular either in classrooms or in editorials, but in a time of fundamental change they should receive more attention. One structural theory is that with industrialization, productivity grows unevenly. Businesses with high productivity (such as manufacturing the "high-tech" products of the time) find themselves commanding high margins. Soon the workers in these industries demand their share of prosperity, and their wages increase.

Eventually, people working in areas with less productivity improvement want parity. Waiters, hospital aides, and other personal-service workers find fewer ways to improve productivity compared to those who harness more energy and better methods of controlling it. To buy the output of factories, they need tickets entitling them to consume. If their wage increases exceed their rate of productivity improvement, they contribute to inflation.

That kind of inflation is necessary to propel consumption, or else mass-production factories churn out goods that few people can buy. The result is a low-level inflation that seems necessary to lubricate a growing economy. (Arguments about how much inflation beyond this is excessive are interminable.)

For four decades after World War II, wage increases prevailed. Almost everyone acquired an expectation of higher incomes, cost of living increases, and steady appreciation in the value of real estate and investments. The economy inflated.

As manufacturing (and other high-productivity growth industries) stopped expanding, low-productivity services soaked up jobs. U.S. manufacturers also began to compete against nations with high-productivity growth industry but lower wages and lower social overhead. Not only is direct labor in the third world cheaper; salaries are lower in construction, trades, and the professions.

When American companies compete using wage givebacks and outplacement, people with less money still want to buy goods, so they increase retail sales price pressure, which reverts back to the manufacturers supplying them—a downward spiral. No wonder that discount retailing has grown rapidly. One might even term the U.S. economy of the 1990s the "Value City economy."

An article of faith is that if productivity improvement resumes, so will growth. Productivity is improving in American manufacturing and in other industries, but when the United States competes against high-productivity growth in a world economy, growth is far from assured. Some plants are the most productive they have ever been the day the doors close.

Even productivity growth figures themselves can be deceiving. For example, during the 1960s, one of the highest-productivity growth industries in the United States was railroads, but among the major reasons for the phenomenon was that they were tearing up track and eliminating their least-productive operations as rapidly as the regulatory process would allow. At the time the rails were certainly not noted for either growth or improvement of service.

In distribution, the major retailers' Quick Response initiative may allow the shrinkage of inventory and the streamlining of transportation until a high percentage of goods is shipped much like UPS operates today. The streamlining will probably improve productivity but not increase jobs in the aggregate. The Wal-Marts of retailing will grow at the expense of the laggards.

Both manufacturers and retailers can gain margin if Quick Response allows promotion of more style goods than commodity goods. However, the pressure for lower prices transmitted to manufacturers of Value City–type products squeezes costs. To some extent, the producer can compete through lean manufacturing. A faster route is cutting the marketing expense—stopping heavy promotion of manufacturing brand names or simply making goods under a generic label.

Continuance of this forces manufacturers to compete with newly industrializing countries where the old formulas still work—for the present. Taken together, all such factors run the system down because nothing is built in to assure paying the social overhead. Long run, something different is necessary.

What Has Changed?

Many prescriptions for economic "recovery" in the United States place too much trust in the forces that fueled the growth of an earlier era: that more investment will create more jobs. For instance, low interest rates stimulate housing, but $7-an-hour construction workers cannot afford the rock-bottom $75,000 starter homes they build even if the interest rate were zero. Growth pumping helps, but conditions have changed in the past thirty years. It will not usher in a new era.

In 1990 GDP per capita in developed countries was roughly three times what it was in the former Communist bloc countries and well over ten times higher than in Africa and China. From 1980 to 1990, per capita GDP in African economies actually dropped over 20 percent. Eastern Europe and the USSR collapsed and groped to rebuild economies in a different mold. Much of the world is struggling toward institutional reform of some kind. The most successful formulas created a newly industrializing (NIC) economy, like Thailand and South Korea. These countries doubled their GDP per capita (as did mainland China). Creating a cadre of technically competent professionals and a basically educated population has been part of the strategy of each of them, much like the United States during its industrial rise.[2]

However, the GDP figures organized by political boundaries do not reveal large differences in income within countries. In the parts of the United States resembling the third world, a strategy similar to developing an NIC might be appropriate if creating and distributing more goods were the only goal. However, these regions are tied to advanced monetary scales and high social-service expectations. They have a big social overhead. If these areas are neglected and left "outside the advancing system," the result is a two-tier economy and, probably, severe political problems.

The factors that prevent undeveloped regions from industrializing rapidly is lack of education and absence of appropriate concepts of work and service. Developing the human conditions takes time. When they are present, both infrastructure and industry develop significantly in about a generation. The "Asian tigers" are evidence of it.

Suppose standard growth pumping, combined with keeping the value of the dollar low to boost exports, is applied to mature industrial areas. It works to some extent, but it assumes that manufacturing workers are competing on cost with exporters from elsewhere, and sometimes with people eager to prove themselves in places like Indonesia and Chile.

Growth pumping does not by itself solve the problem of creating a high added value from the work. While some high-value services are also exported, some of them (technology licenses, for instance) also assist the ability of foreign operations to compete. Just boosting the dollar attractiveness of that which already exists does nothing to relieve the cost pressure creating the black hole—deflation in wages and social overhead.

An example of this deflation is maneuvering to shift health care payments from employers. A more subtle form of it is improving the efficiency of the health care system, which might improve health at less cost but also displace jobs now performing waste functions.

In the United States, the standard growth stimulants are inhibited by the size of the federal deficit, much of which is underfinanced social overhead. Foreigners who buy Treasury issues help keep American tax rates down and support our social overhead. Pumping up consumption also boosts imports. The trade deficit boosts other nations' exports. Investment tax breaks tip investment decisions, but by themselves they do not assure that investment creates high-margin enterprises. In short, the tools that have been used for growth pumping now have substantial leakage, a situation common to other international economies.

State and local governments use aid packages to bid for both foreign and domestic companies on the rationale of buying jobs and paying off the investment through future taxation. Usually they bid for jobs with a high value added in comparison with existing work, but sometimes it is just to maintain work that is marginal.

Growth of 5–6 percent GNP per annum, led in the "traditional" sense by manufacturing, is unlikely to recur in the United States. Fundamental worldwide structural changes are against it. At the beginning of the century, our land, resources, and labor were relatively cheap. Now they are not. In addition, an advanced economy almost by definition has to figure out how to carry a high social overhead.

All countries reaching industrial maturity have similar problems. The export-dependent Japanese increasingly run into trade friction and cannot compete on mass-production costs with the NICs. Their strategy is to become a high-tech center, presuming that advanced products will command the high value-added margins that ensure continuing prosperity. That strategy also has leakage. Nothing prevents the spread of high-tech elsewhere, and companies must cooperate internationally to stay on the edge, as is now being done with semiconductor consortia.

Would something like high-density television (HDTV) fuel a new industrial boom in the traditional sense? Not a big one. If HDTV were part of an information network, building the hardware would be a short spurt of virgin growth, much like the spurts with TV or personal computers, followed by steady-state replacement and upgrade.

Can software or other mass-produced service markets take over from hardware? New-concept software is a high-margin business, but as software markets become competitive, those growth spurts also subside. Advanced services also depend on advanced skills in consumers.

A high–quality-of-life society must be able to carry its social overhead. The social overhead includes research, education, health care, and a variety of activities that will please most tastes. Recently, the United States has been trying to inflate the economy by rekindling traditional growth. Instead, we need to reinflate the economy through high–value-added enterprises. We need to inculcate what quality performance is, both in commercial enterprise and in social services, so that people insist on it, understand how it is created, become capable of providing it, and are able to pay for it.

Reinflation with High-Margin Business

As Cassius said in the play *Julius Caesar*, "The fault, dear Brutus, lies not in our stars, but in ourselves." If we want a high quality of life we must learn how to pay for it. In macroeconomic terms, if a minority of the work force can supply the basic needs of the whole, what kind of economy is left for everyone else?

On the surface, high productivity would seem to be the best of all possible worlds. Either a high percentage of the population has the luxury of living in leisure, or everyone has a great deal of leisure time, or a combination of both. However, we do not know how to grasp a high quality of life when the possibility for it is within reach. When an old form of thinking has reached its limit, it's time to look at the problem differently, more as a service economy, not one powered by virgin manufacturing capturing new sources of energy, materials, and jobs. If the real capital is human, even in manufacturing, we should study it directly.

The answer is basically within us. A high quality of life is not something one gets. It's something one does.

Economically, we should stop looking at monetary flows so much. They are important, but just as important is how people spend their time. Look at the economics of people, not money. How do people spend their time to assure a high quality of life?

Return to the personal time example of Chapter 11. For most of us, the first eighteen to twenty-two years of life are primarily spent in preparation to serve others in some way. During those years, many people have to invest some of their time in us, and if we are diligent students (both formally, and informally in various activities and odd jobs) we invest time in ourselves. Sometimes, the time is paid for by direct tuition. Often it is paid indirectly through taxation—or not recorded by any transactions whatever.

During the next forty to fifty years of a normal adult life, we spend a great deal of time on others. That's apparent if we happen to be in a service occupation dealing directly with people. Parents do the same with their children, only it's not considered an occupation—no transactions mark the economic value. As adults, others still spend some of their time on us too, depending on our needs.

In old age, we're more of a receiver again. Others must increase the time they spend on us. That's obvious if we are infirm and need constant care. It's less obvious if we are simply retired and enjoying "leisure" activities, doing much as we please. With increasing life spans this period can last another twenty years or more.

Our system has to pay for the time we must invest to have a quality life. It's that simple—and that difficult.

To keep it simple, perhaps too simple, suppose everyone's time is valued equally. Then on average we must invest enough in others in a forty-year work span to compensate them for investing in us for another forty, youth plus old age. More important, the quality of the time is important. We do not want someone who can only hold our hand if we need to learn servo-feedback systems or to have a pacemaker put in.

But everyone's time is not valued equally. A basic principle of business is to sell one's personal time only if it is seen as worth much. An established doctor or lawyer can command a high price per minute. Easily appreciated is the value of their years of preparation to make a difference in another person's life in just a few minutes.

In other occupations, the perception is the same. Someone in maintenance may draw a fat premium for fixing a crucial breakdown in a crisis. A comparative pittance would have been earned if the same time were spent earlier avoiding the breakdown. The same is true if one merely spends time making sure that drawings are accurate or that a label clearly conveys vital information. Personal time is valued when it is heroic or when its value is multiplied many times over—like a star sports figure on television.

We need to improve public perception that preventive skills have great value for quality in a high-tech world. Traditional business advice is to multiply the value of one's time by using it to make or purvey something of great value: jewelry, custom-built cars, or prosthetic devices—or by taking the risks and rewards of owning a business. The point of such commonsense observations is that for most of us to have a high quality of life, our time must be worth something. The keys to quality of life (or to a high-tech, open-enterprise system) are first to learn how to perform so as to actually obtain it, and second, to value that performance. If we want this kind of world, we must invest in our own improvement.

This investment is not confined to the producer side of either service or manufacturing. One needs skill to be a good prosumer. One can imagine some auto prosumers spending hours in different kinds of auto simulators—advanced, virtual-reality "arcade games" that simulate racing (against human drivers in other simulators), driving in extremely rugged terrain, or simply predriving parts of a trip (like driving in Tokyo). To afford this, a prosumer's time must also be worth something. That is, the prosumer has to be a valued participant in the economic system.

If a large percentage of people are unable to make their time worth something, almost any dazzling future imaginable is confined to the rich in high-tech enclaves. In such a condition, even the quality of life in an enclave is tenuous. What of the wreckage outside?

Without high skill, both technically and behaviorally, a high-tech quality of life eludes us. So does ability to sustain a world environment, socially as well as ecologically. Public policy has to focus on creating the skills. Macroeconomic policy has to stimulate high-margin enterprises.

Much of that margin may be siphoned off to the social overhead. That's inevitable in a quality-of-life world. Our illusion is that undefined economic "growth"—meaning some poor sap at a later time—will pay for it.

This illusion stems from older eras. Under feudalism, the serfs needed no special development to do what was needed to keep the gentry in relative comfort and in control. Under old-style mass production, semiliterates could do the grunt work. Their time was not worth much, but so long as material waste was tolerable, almost everyone could participate in the enjoyment of it. This new world will not work that way.

Investing in Human Capital

- What does all this mean to the individual business—or the individual open-system enterprise? That people must pay a fat premium for quality of life. That business will have to stop competing on price and compete on quality and service—much easier said than done. If the margin is slim, there's no surplus to pay for human development. If it goes only to a few owners, the system runs down.

Especially if they are hard-pressed for money, many manufacturing companies delude themselves that talent simply appears. Perhaps they think that the schools should produce it fully mature or that experience and hard knocks simply create it. The better companies spend freely on development of their own people, recognizing that a percentage of them will be lost to other opportunities elsewhere, and they sponsor external schools and other sources of education.

On few issues is business so united today as on the need for great improvement in K-through-12 education. By all accounts, the performance of average high school graduates in math and science is inadequate to participate in on-the-job problem solving. While the present status of public funding promises no great increase in school budgets, the uproar will probably lead to some degree of improvement. (Here too, a "Total Quality" approach seems likely to suggest improvement without major funding, and multimedia instructional programs, as with "UltraComm," will begin to offer more exciting education if funding is made available.)

However, much of the work force that must climb the mountain toward open-system enterprise is already at work. Schools for the young are but a start on lifetime learning. Almost everyone now agrees that adult education is a high priority. Some of this instruction is formal, acquired through courses in colleges, vocational schools, professional societies, and elsewhere. Some of it comes from previously unconventional sources, such as labor-management councils, consortia, centers of excellence, and roundtables. A huge network of educational institutions is in the making.

However, the most important place to learn about work is at work.

Among people actually engaged in quality-centered, team-based work, one of the most commonly heard phrases is, "I learn something new every day."

While capital for new equipment and for physical improvements of all kinds is vital to any form of manufacturing, old-style or new, investment in equipment is undermined without attention to human development. One cannot deal with technology or techniques that are not understood and on which one cannot personally make some form of improvement. In such a condition, both workers and managers are mired in a hopeless system.

In a complex world, ordinary mortals cannot understand the technology in every product. However, it is not only possible, but critical, that every enterprise intimately understand not only its own product technology but also the process technology used to make it or modify it. The hands-on version of that knowledge must be possessed by the people doing the work. A technology organization will be incapable of reaching the levels of performance required in the future if most of its people can only follow steps A to Z, as directed.

To learn, part of everyone's *work* time must be devoted to learning, one-to-six weeks of paid time per year, or more, in improving either the people themselves or the processes they work with. (The effectiveness of any specific off-line educational time is another question, and on-line learning from the work itself should be highly effective.) Future knowledge workers and knowledge enterprises may have to invest more time—20, 30 percent or more of total payroll on educational or improvement time. Accountants are not likely to classify payroll as a capital expense, but everyone should recognize skill development as the engine that pulls everything else.

The High-Margin Enterprise

There many ways to achieve a high margin. One is by being a technology leader. Pharmaceutical companies are the classic example of dependence on R&D for temporary monopoly position. Essentially, they are research dependent. The research has to create high enough margins to sustain itself. (The margins may also allow considerable laxness in noncritical operations, but that can be dealt with through performance comparisons and other means.)

Another high-margin business strategy is to turn a product into a fashion that commands a premium—a little technology and a lot of marketing: turning discount sneakers into high-status athletic shoes; converting jeans from a cowboy's work garment into a fashion statement. One can easily see such products becoming prosumer businesses.

However, the classic condition for a high margin is through monopoly, either permanent or temporary. Monopolies are always suspect because, if not monitored, nothing stimulates either efficiency or high-quality service, but actual examples under regulation vary. For instance, AT&T as a monopoly was fat, but in its time service was "good," and the margin was always high enough to sustain such resources as the Bell Labs.

Monopoly status needs to be reconsidered if high-margin, high-performance businesses are to become a rule and not an exception. Already, for example, the reliability of service from electric utilities has to be nearly perfect to satisfy computerized customers. Outages that cause computers to crash are disastrous. The operating performance of utilities can be measured and compared with the effectiveness of companies maintaining their own generating systems to bridge outages or brownouts. Benchmarking of practices and quality-improvement processes between utilities has barely begun.

Pressure for performance can be applied without the necessity for direct competition. Demanding customers comparing the performance of different utilities can exercise considerable influence. If the utilities are customer-driven enterprises, they pay attention. Threats to buy from elsewhere are not the only ones that are credible. Penalties for poor performance are possible—especially if applied to responsible individuals. Simply "bringing in another team" to show how it's done is a blow to esteem, and in a tough case of recalcitrance, teams can be replaced.

If utilities or other monopolies were run as open-system enterprises rather than on the model of financially governed fortress companies, both the measurement of performance and the exercise of governance would be very different. To reach twenty-first–century levels of performance, changes in this direction may be necessary.

This rethinking is important because if intense performance competition is to exist in industries (with several competitors) that collectively have high margins, sanctions for poor performance should not degrade the system to be effective. Most high-margin businesses depend on enjoying some form of monopoly or oligopoly position.

Prosumer businesses would not be pure monopolies, but well run, they would approach monopoly position because their technology, models, features, or services would be tailored to specific customers. Consider the automotive prosumer. Once embraced by an auto-service enterprise, that organization's database defines *that prosumer's* favorite seat, *his* favorite ride-response package, the coating for *his* custom-colored body panels—and *his* lifelong history of preferences. Even if such materials and data easily transfer between competing enterprises—a lot to hope for—the servicing enterprise always has a substantial edge over a would-be competitor.

That condition is another reason why twenty-first–century enterprises have to be fundamentally different from those of the twentieth. While high-margin, they cannot be the sole possession of investors claiming the total margin. That creates the conditions for the ugly monopolies of the past. One can even foresee the prosumer himself having some "right of ownership" over the databases that define him.

The ideal is to evolve into high-margin, high-tech businesses. ASICs, UltraComm computers, and three-day cars would be high-margin service enterprises, but many other parts of the economy could also go that way. (Imagine a scenario for a high-margin, "three-day house.") No matter what scenarios emerge for prosumer-focused enterprises, the business codes of the time will have to grapple with maintaining high operating performance without relying on the competitive exercises (bidding, for example) used today. A challenge at least as tough as the technology is migrating to a new mental territory with our business customs and mores.

We can expect to enjoy the benefits of both high margins and demanding operating performance only if we learn how to handle near-monopoly business conditions by methods different from today. Nonperforming monopolies deserve to be broken up. However, enterprises that effectively satisfy the needs of both customers and environmental sustenance to near perfection need the margin of monopoly to endure.

The emotion of this issue can hardly be understated. The mind-set of the twentieth century by both economic "conservatives" and "liberals" is that, in the abstract, monopolies are inherently fat, lazy, arrogant, unresponsive to customers, resistant to change, inefficient, wasteful, and inept. Conservatives want to break them up with competition and liberals want to control them with regulation. Instead, we must learn how to put monopolies under the operating governance of the people they serve, starting with customers as well as investors. This cannot be done if "quasi-monopoly" enterprises are allowed to keep their operations in virtual secrecy, as monopolies did a hundred years ago. The transition will be painful to civil libertarians, but perhaps we can find ways to preserve individual privacy in areas of life where it is meaningful—times and places where people can go "off-line" (the new phrase for taking a break or a vacation).

Private Taxation

One way to increase margins is through social pressure. Mandating that enterprises pay for the health care system is one way to require an increased margin while siphoning the money to a social purpose. However, the current insurance system displaces its "customers" too far from the system that is supposed to serve them. The customers must evolve more into health care prosumers, and they might be stimulated to do so if the system made it clear that preventive medicine had a direct impact on their own pocketbooks and the competitiveness of their own enterprise. The complex system of third-party carriers must be greatly simplified and accompanied by a private review system to improve performance.

One improvement would be to pay medical professionals to conduct operating reviews and suggest benchmarking comparisons. Everyone involved might learn and improve a great deal, and this approach might start turning medical operations into a more open system. Jawboning and nitpicking the billings only aggravate such complex activity. However, even after considerable simplification, high-quality health care is costly.

The same is true of retirement benefits. Or various kinds of education costs. Or costs to dispose of waste material. However the transfer payment system is organized, it has to stimulate a higher level of responsibility by those "paying." The system cannot create the illusion that someone else is paying the bills or has total responsibility for improving the quality and productivity of social services.

A system of private taxation needs to be much more thoroughly thought out, although a number of current practices tend in that direction. One of the more interesting angles of it is that importers of goods into an advanced economy might be required to contribute to the "social funds" of the industry in which they compete. This idea is similar to a reverse form of value-added tax, and it helps to offset the exemption of value-added taxes on goods shipped from elsewhere to cheapen imports. That will take international negotiation, but the ideal is to not permit aggressive trading to undermine quality of life in either the country of import or export.

Migrating to Open Systems

Achieving anything like this different kind of world is a challenge of wrestling with the unknown. So far removed is agile, open-system enterprise from the perspective of 1980s business that the ideas are difficult to grasp, much less practice. One must have traveled the road to "excellence" and ascended the first foothill to glimpse the mountain that soars beyond.

This point is important because while the number of people ready to start this migration is considerable, it is only a small fraction of the population. Hopefully, that fraction will grow considerably.

The summary of this new world in Figure 12-1 can be supplemented by Figures 2-1 and 2-2. Such complex projections have value only if they are convincing and if we collectively pour enormous energy into reaching them.

The technology necessary for this new world is within our grasp. Missing are the human capabilities needed. Achieving them will take far more than a restructuring of financial assets or a repositioning of companies in markets. That is a strictly financial view of change to restart cash flow. In a larger sense, no quick fix exists when no one really knows what to do. Investors cannot remain dispassionate onlookers of the need for drastic operating improvement or the human upheaval needed for it. They have to invest in a human future, not just a future stream of cash flow.

Such drastic change is generally accompanied by severe emotional jolts. Even changes of lesser magnitude, such as full deployment of Total Quality Management, require an overhaul of organizations and attitudes. Companies find that they are not "implementing techniques" but making basic changes in themselves. Many of these companies refer to the shift as "a journey with no final destination." If that form of change is a journey by basically one company, a shift to agile, open-system enterprise is a migration—a movement by many people, companies, and institutions.

Large bureaucracies have the toughest time. Ample resources and advanced technology do not necessarily convert to practice. IBM, Sears, and GM today represent much-publicized behemoths surrounded by faster rivals, and competition using flexibility has barely begun. In their present form, the bureaucracies cannot carry their own weight, and so are ill-conditioned to make a migration without making initial changes in form—breaking into lightweight operating units.

We cannot suddenly transform. Rather, we must build up the basic practices and infrastructure, accompanied by trials by new-style organizations ready to venture into them. Some of the basic human challenges of this migration are:

"Visionary" Guidance. The value of a common vision is direction, not precision. It enables diverse people to stumble in roughly the same direction by different paths. When people are trying to arrive at the same location from different starting points, a common vision is necessary. A single leader can guide a single organization, and sometimes several of them. A single leader cannot guide a migration because a number of journeys must meet in the same place.

The importance of vision is such that we must doubtless invent new words for it as we tire of the old. By whatever name, vision is important to keep everyone reminded that, for instance, they should be designing both products and processes for "agility," which assumes an understanding of both the human and technical ideals for it. Learning the specifics will take trial and error.

"Open-System" Information. Of course, computer systems must universally talk to each other, but today we still have islands of automation, CAD/CAM systems that cannot communicate, and EDI linkages that are really used as fax machines. The problem is far deeper than

hardware and software compatibility. Intellectual capital derives its name from the assumption that if we know something unique, the world must come to us to buy it, and we protect that opportunity through nondisclosure.

That assumption turns on us when we find that what we do adds value only if it will fit into a universal system. In the nineteenth century railroads discovered that none of them added value unless each used the same width track. In this century, we simply expect any telephone to connect to all other telephones. In the twenty-first century virtually any system must interact with other systems, and that is first a problem of humans perceiving that it is necessary.

Open systems are necessary for many reasons. They enable dispersed operations to function almost as one. They are the major way that society can monitor "monopolistic high-margin operations." And without them, the world will probably snarl in a ball of competing complex systems, none of which accomplishes very much by itself.

Decentralized Interactive Organization. This shift has begun today with emphasis on flat organizations and teams of every kind: functional, cross-functional, and cross-company. If team members are remote and computer connected, they begin to build "virtual companies." Even an auto business—a big-scale enterprise by any standard—will likely consist of much smaller operating units with tight linkages between entities operationally focused on separate processes from raw material to customer service—and back again.

A transportation-service enterprise might be one of the more permanent ones, but a characteristic of all enterprises is transience, even if the nature of their transition is not foreseeable. Many will arise for a specific purpose as project or program teams and disband when that purpose is accomplished. Even the longer-term enterprises, like the transportation service and UltraComm ones, will go through constant shifting.

The churn of change itself is not a new experience. It's common in the twentieth century. What will be different is the evolution toward people working as a team at a distance. Even there, the twentieth century has precursors who work through fax, phone, and computer. It's a matter of figuring out how to do this effectively and efficiently—

beginning with the formation of better human links between people physically remote but electronically close.

We have to find security in operating units that float in a shifting world and attach allegiance to "the enterprise network," or whatever it may be. Perhaps by instinct, we prefer the protection of fortress companies (with impressive headquarters buildings). Perhaps the human change will be to simply maintain a consciousness that we are never the center of the economic universe but only a part of the total fabric of it.

Common Interactive Human Processes.   Whether the new human organizations are called networks, holons, virtual companies, or buckyballs, they cannot function unless work habits and customs have a common framework, but one that allows individuals to exercise freedom and creativity. Otherwise, enterprises can never link up through all the "culture clash."

Human systems include everything from expectations of normal work times to common drawing conventions. They are "the way we learn to get things done." No one unlearns a lifetime of experience quickly. Such basic changes force us to put at risk whatever small career status we may have acquired, learning by doing and discovering anew "what really works."

We have barely begun to use information technology in all its possible forms as an interactive tool. Today, we still often work with programmers as an armless carpenter telling someone else exactly how and where to drive each nail. We must learn different concepts by which things get done. Forget the four-part purchase requests, mandates for three stages of a new product prototype, and clear distinctions between the turfs of large functional departments. Learn how to function more as interactive entrepreneurial organizations, but networked by compatible practices.

Those interacting in the same network must have common visions and strategies, and at least three practices in common: (1) a method to diagnose and solve problems—bedrock TQM; (2) a shared sense of common systems (for example, common conventions to describe products and more precise concepts for how operations should mesh. We now think of meeting shipping dates instead of how our total sequence of work meshes with everyone else in the same network; and finally (3) a common concept of good operating performance or operating excellence.

Common Standards of Excellence. ISO 9000 is an early form of common standard. Much tighter, more comprehensive codes of performance will become necessary and include total enterprise practices. Self-assessments, external reviews, and recertifications will be done regularly. Reviews should be somewhat easier when many activities leave a trail of data and software. The standards will be high. For example, the expectation will be that all critical processes have fail-safe methods built in, so a defect from them will be so rare "it should be reported in the news."

The importance of these reviews goes beyond fairness in financial and investment decisions. That's a twentieth-century concern that financial audits were intended to allay. The concern of the twenty-first century will be whether operating units are operationally competent at a high level and whether they are net contributors to the quality of life. Eventually, that will be the purpose of regular, rigorous operating reviews.

The official reviews are best done by third parties paid by the customers through a premium on the price of "certified" products and services. The system may have to be enforced by the government on occasion, but the money transfers from customers to the review organizations. (Politicians can thereby stimulate social improvement while disclaiming that they have raised taxes.)

Forging Ahead

Today, we cannot effectively use the technology we have, much less any that is coming. We need to revise how we think about work and the institutions that are built on old concepts rather than counting on economic growth to wash away our problems. To do this, more than forecasts and analyses are necessary. We need a different inspiration—a different soul of the enterprise.

Nothing presented in this book presumes that a final answer has been found. That is the presumption of a utopian treatise, and no system can be devoid of faults and controversies. A great deal of thought needs to be given to these issues. If there is any lesson in open-system enterprise, it is that the time when a single charismatic leader could impose a social order or economic system has passed. The information wave is too complex for that.

There are infinite ways to fail even if one has a comprehensive grasp of how to proceed. The companies doing best with their current journeys to excellence recognize that they must accomplish something specific and measurable. They cannot merely talk. They must try something. But the trials themselves are a continuing process of developing people.

Human development dictates the speed of migration. We can go no faster than we can change ourselves, and changing ourselves is more than merely achieving intellectual grasp of new concepts.

What to do? Discuss the issues. Flesh out the half-formed ideas. And try an experiment in open-system enterprise—or whatever it may be called. Without trials we will never go anywhere.

Five centuries ago European explorers began to set sail in significant numbers to unknown lands pictured only in their imaginations. Some, like Columbus, never actually reached where they set out for. Those that arrived at their intended destination never found a reality that precisely matched their vision. Likewise, the new explorers of human capabilities and forms of enterprise will never find exactly what they expect. Though the new exploration is within us, it is no less uncertain.

NOTES

1. Alvin Toffler, *Powershift* (New York: Bantam Books, 1990).
2. *World Economic Survey 1990* (New York: United Nations Dept. of International and Social Affairs, 1990), p. 3.

INDEX

Absentee owner, 37–38
Acronyms, 30–32, 64–65. *See also specific acronyms*
Activity-based costing (ABC), 293
Agile manufacturing. *See* Holistic remanufacturing
Agile Manufacturing Enterprise Forum, xiv, 44, 47, 112
  three-day car concept and, 61–62
Agility, 44, 364
Agricultural wave, 96
AIDS research, 203
Airlines, 83. *See also* Boeing 777
Air pollution, 143–45, 147
Alar, 145
Alcatel, 265
American Greetings, 101
American Hospital Supply (AHS), 277
American Society of Mechanical Engineers (ASME), 14
American system of manufacturing, development of, 9–19
Application-Specific Integrated Circuits (ASICs), 48–50, 172, 178–79, 361

Arkwright, Richard, 11
Army, U.S., 315
Asbestos, 149
ASICs. *See* Application-Specific Integrated Circuits (ASICs)
Assembly line, 15–16
Associates, statement of company policy toward, 71. *See also* Empowerment
Association for Manufacturing Excellence, 200–201
AT&T, 26, 182, 251, 360
ATMs, 218, 224
Attendance, 238
Auditioning, of performance measures, 314–15
Auto industry, 52–64
  CAD/CAM and, 219
  design for disassembly (DFD) and, 158
  electronic data interchange (EDI) and, 218–19
  enterprise and, 34
  environmental issues and, 52
  evolution of, 4–6

Auto industry (*cont.*)
    example of long-term open-system
        enterprise in, 279, 281–85
    flexible processes in, 196–97
    innovation in, 177–78, 258–59
    intelligent body systems and, 55–56
    Japanese, 52–54
    in newly industrializing countries
        (NICs), 52–54
    niche and custom markets and, 54
    option packages and, 181–82
    product development in, 54
    quality growth in, 97
    in South Korea, 53
    three-day car and. *See* Three-day car
    times-to-change in, 119–21
    tooling time in, 195–96
    workers in, 55–56
Automotive prosumers, 58
Autonomous dispersed system, 129–30

Baldrige Award, 67
Banking, consumer, 217–18
Battelle Institute, 172
Baxter Health Care, 277
Bell, Daniel, 7
Bell Laboratories, 76, 182
Benchmarking, 20, 160, 212–14, 294–95
    sharing and, 213–14
    steps in, 295
Berle and Means study, 327
Bhopal, India, 148
Biological diversity, xiii
Black art, 15
Black & Decker, 192, 258
Blount, Inc., 22, 81
Blue Cross/Blue Shield, 93
BMW's Z1 sportster, 158
Boards of directors. *See* Investors
Boeing 777, 68, 193, 196, 220
Boott Mill, 11–12
Brewer, Chuck, 232
Buffet, Warren, 110
Buy-in, 341–42

CAD/CAM, 196
    software for, 219
Cadillac, long-term open-system enter-
    prise scenario for, 279, 281–83,
    337–43

Campus, 284
Capital, intellectual. *See* Intellectual
    capital
Carcinogens, 145
Carnegie, Andrew, 12–13, 16
Carnegie Steel, 12–13
Cars. *See also* Auto industry; *specific
    cars*
    solar, 97
    used, 87–89
Carson, Rachel, 143
Carter, Art, Sr., 235
Centers of excellence, manufacturing
    and, 4
CFCs, 156–57, 161
Champions, 245–46
Change
    agents for, 245–46
    order-of-magnitude reorganization
        and, 247–48
Charts, organization, 106–7
Chemical industry, green manufacturing
    and, 50–51
Chemicals, unknown hazards of expo-
    sure to, 148
Chevrolet, 120
Chinese ethnocentric view, 41–42
Chrysler, 57
Citizen's Clearinghouse on Hazardous
    Waste (CCHW), 155–56
Civic virtue, 26
Clinical pathways, 93–95
Closed-loop cycles of material use, 152–
    54, 165–66
    problems of, 157
Closed systems, consequences of, 202–6
Clozaril, 204–5
Collaborators, improvement, 81, 83
Communications
    JIT and, 118
    in time-based organizations, 111–12
    UltraComm and, 47–48
Communism, 227
Company mission statement, 71
Comparative learning. *See* Benchmark-
    ing
Competition
    benchmarking and, 294–95
    open system enterprise and, 210,
        220–24

Competitor, definition of, 25, 267
Computer industry
  Application-Specific Intergrated Circuits (ASICs) and, 48–50, 172, 178–79, 361
  disk drives, 178
  integrated circuits and, 178–79
  need for standardization in, 25–26
  software. *See* Software
Computer integrated manufacturing (CIM), 129–30, 217, 219–20
Computers. *See also* Information wave; UltraComm
  chemical industry and, 50
  greetings business and, 102–3
  lean manufacturing and, 23
  open-system information and, 364–65
  personal computers, 6
  smart chips and, 46
  software as dominant feature of, 45–46
  visibility systems and, 129–30
Computer shopping, 45
Concurrent engineering teams, 189–91
Condie, J. Thomas, 186
Consortia, research, 184–86
Consultants, 31–32
  as change agents, 246
  open system enterprise and, 244
Consumers. *See* Customers
Consumption, information wave and, 96–97
Continuous improvement, 37, 115–16
Contractor-foremen, 14
Control of service cycles, 204–6
Cooperation, 25
Corporate governance, 318–20. *See also* Investment; Investors
  in Japan, 334–36
  motivation and, 335–36
  open system enterprise and, 339–40
Cost
  of inventory, 290
  of quality, 290
Cost systems, performance measures and, 293
Cost-time profiles, 105
Council on Competitiveness, 340
Cpk=2, 309
Credit arrangements, 108

Cummins Engine Company, 328–29
Cumulative learning, 115–16
Customer requirements, product/process design and, 193–94
Customers, 254–58
  classification of, 81–82
  definition of, 267
  good, 88, 260–65
  as improvement collaborators, 81, 89
  internal, 256, 258–60
  lead times and, 123–24, 127
  limitations of, innovation and, 179–82
  as partners, 24–25, 45. *See also* Customer-supplier relationship
  primary, 81
  as prosumers, 45
  responsibility of, 78
Customer satisfaction, 8, 35–36
  quality as, 78
  service and, 223–24
Customer-supplier relationship, 82, 254–76
  consistent treatment of suppliers across customer's processes and, 264
  critical suppliers and, 266–67
  intellectual capital and, 267–68
  internal customers and, 256, 258–60
  internal suppliers and, 258–60
  in Japan, 269–74, 324
  as partnership, 265–67
  performance measures and, 274–76
  trust and, 321–24
Customization. *See also* Niche markets
  Application-Specific Intergrated Circuits (ASICs) and, 49
  auto industry and, 54
Cycle time, 121, 133. *See also* Lead times

Dale, H. K., 171
Davidson Rubber, 166
Decentralization, 276–77, 365–66
Defense Department, U.S., 61–62
  R&D and, 187
Deflation, 353–54
Deming, W. Edwards, 20, 74, 76–77, 208, 309
Deming Circle, 20
Deming Cycle, 74–75

Deming Prize, 84, 86
Design, robust, 194. *See also* Product design
Design engineering, 195
Design for assembly, 194
Design for disassembly (DFD), 158–59
Design for manufacturing (DFM), 117
Desktop publishing, 102
Development. *See also* Research and development (R&D)
    individual quality of life and, 91
    sustainable, 138–42, 145, 147
    virgin, 145
Diagram
    relationship, 123–24
    time flow, 123, 125–26
Diemasters Manufacturing, 232
Dirt-to-dirt cycle, 152–54
Discipline, 238, 317–18
    social, 37
Disk drives, 178
Dow Chemical Company, 161
Dow-Corning, 149
Drucker, Peter, 20, 26–27, 312
Drug industry, 204–5
Dual-role researchers, 187–88
Du Pont, Pierre, 16

Economic challenge, quality of life as, 95–99
Economy, Value City, 351–52
Economy of scale, 54
EDS, 31
Education, 65, 358
    manufacturing in, 4
Electronic data interchange (EDI), 218–19
Electronic greetings industry, 102–3
Electronic light bulbs (E-lamps), 154
Emissions, 161
Employee involvement, 20. *See also* Empowerment
    availability of information and, 24–25
    in improvement processes, 83–84
    intellectual capital and, 183
    lean manufacturing and, 22
    management and, 228
    visibility systems and, 128–30
Employee-owned companies, 233–34
Employees. *See* Workers

Empowerment
    fake, 232
    hierarchical organization and, 230–31
    trust and, 232–35
Endangered species, 145
Energy consumption, rating products by, 162–63
Enterprise, 33–34
    Honda as, 34
    mission-oriented, 296, 298
    open-system, 37
    organization of, 40
    performance and, 38–39
    soul of, 8–9, 27, 35–37
Enterprise integration, 222
Enterprises. *See also* Open system enterprise
    building, 251–52
    high-margin, 359–62
    human development as business of, 250–52
    recognition of venture participants in, 249–50
Enterprise teams
    bonding and, 251
    public-service ethic of, 252
    recognition of, 249–50
Entrepreneurial service ethic, 252
Entrepreneurship, open system enterprise and, 337–41
Environmental accidents, 168
Environmental impact statements, 163–65
Environmental issues, xiii, 6, 8, 24, 35–36, 136–68. *See also* Green manufacturing
    auto industry and, 52
    environmental impact statements and, 163–65
    excellence practices and, 165–68
    growth and, 138–42
    limits of regulations and, 161–63
    material-use cycle and, 152–54
    media and, 145
    movement of raw materials and, 165
    NICs and, 143
    open system enterprise and, 159–61
    rating products by energy consumption, 162–63
    recycling and, 46, 153–56
    remanufacturing and, 46, 153–56, 159

risks and unknowns and, 147–51
selling of service process vs. products
    and, 159
sustainable development and, 138–42,
    145, 147
three-day car and, 64
zero-discharge manufacturing and,
    46–47, 50, 152
Environmental Protection Agency
    (EPA), 162
    Toxic Release Inventory database, 161
Equipment subsidiaries, 259
Ethnocentrism, 41–42
European Economic Community
    (EEC), 275
European Quality Award, 85
Excellence, common standards of, 367
Executive compensation, 326
Expansion as soul of American system,
    9, 11, 13, 16
Expected quality, 79
Exxon, 149, 162

Factory America Network (FAN, or
    FANit), 47
Factory-control systems, 15
Fail-safe methods, 86, 98
Fake empowerment, 232
Feigenbaum, Armand, 76–77
Female life expectancy, 142
Financial measures, 289–93
Financial order, new, 336
Fisher, Sir Ronald A., 78
Flexibility, 44, 54–55
    design process and, 196–97
    lead time and, 120–21
Florida Power & Light, 84
Ford, Henry, 15–16, 21, 72, 107, 115,
    221–22
Ford, Henry, II, 17
Ford Motor Company, 15–16, 83, 263
    concept of quality at, 79
    Model Ts, 120
    Willow Run aircraft plant, 17
4950th Test Wing, 92–93
Future, projections for, 44–47
Fuzzy logic, 181

Gainsharing, 14, 342
Galbraith, John Kenneth, 20

Galvin, Paul, 67
Galvin, Robert, 36
Geneen, Harold, 17, 288
General Electric (GE), 32, 111
General Motors (GM), 16–17, 31, 63,
    81, 93, 237, 251, 265
    Automotive Components Group
        (ACG), 323
    customer-supplier relationship at,
        321–24
    EDI and, 218–19
    lean manufacturing at, 323–24
    long-term open-system enterprise sce-
        nario for, 279, 281–85
    Saturn, 57, 158, 177–78
    Williams Technologies and, 209
Germany, material-use cycle laws in,
    157
Gettysburg Address, 36
Gibbs, Lois, 156
Global warming, 148
Good customers, 88
Goods and services, command over,
    quality of life and, 91
Governance, corporate, 318–20. See
    also Investment; Investors
    in Japan, 334–36
    open system enterprise and, 339–
        40
Governmental agencies, quality im-
    provement processes in, 92
Green manufacturing, 50–51
Greeting card companies, 101–3
Gross Domestic Product (GDP), 348,
    352–53
Gross national product (GNP)
    life expectancy and, 139–40
    waste and, 348, 354
Growth. See also Quality growth
    benefits of, 139–41
    decline in, 1–2
    environmental issues and, 138–42
    limits of, 344–45
    mass production and, 4–6
    in newly industrializing countries
        (NICs), 353
    quality of life and, 97–98
    as soul of American system, 9, 11, 13,
        16
    virgin, 17–18

Hallmark, 101
Handy, Charles, 276
Hardware, 45–46
  incompatibility of, 216
Harrington, Sir John, 139
Hasbro, 233
Health, quality of life and, 91
Health-active consumers, 93, 95
Health care
  growth and, 140–41
  quality improvement processes in,
    93–95
Hewlett-Packard's HP Way, 71
Hierarchies, organizational, 229–31
High-density television (HDTV), 354
High-margin enterprises, 359–62
Highways, smart, 63
Holistic remanufacturing, 9, 23, 44
Holonic management, 243
Home appliances
  with fuzzy logic programming, 46,
    181
  self-adjusting, 46
Honda, 53, 115, 119, 263
  as enterprise, 34
  split-up of, 338
Hoshin kanri, 310
House, three-day, 361
Human development, 307
  as business of business, 250–52
  disinvestment in, 337
  investment in, 318–21, 358–59
  quality of life and, 308
Humanity. See Soul of the enterprise
Human processes, interactive, 366–67

Iacocca Institute, 61
IBM, 34, 183, 304
  control of service cycles and, 205–6
Improvement, performance measures
    for, 289, 297–98, 302–4
Improvement collaborators, 81, 83
Improvement cycles, 114–15, 130–32,
    134
Improvement processes, employee in-
    volvement in, 83–84. See also
    Quality improvement processes
Ina Tile Company, 194
Incentive systems, 14–15
Income, decline in, 4

Indifferent quality, 79
Individual development, quality of life
    and, 91
Industrial wave, 8, 96. See also Mass
    production
  growth and, 139, 141
  paradigms of, 40
Inflation, 350–51
Information. See also Openness; Open
    system enterprise; Visibility sys-
    tems
  availability of, 24–25, 39
  open-system, 364–65
Information waste, 116–19
Information wave, 7–8
  consumption and, 96–97
  improvement processes and, 74–75
  quality of life as soul of, 35
Innovation
  academic research and, 186–89
  in auto industry, 258–59
  consortia and, 184–86
  customers' limitations and, 179–82
  dual-role researchers and, 187–88
  funding of, 175–76, 182–84, 186–89
  ideal system of product/process de-
    sign, 189–97
  incentives and, 171–73
  liaison programs and, 188
  originality and, 174
  patent systems and, 174
  as process, 172
  Saturn and, 177–78
  sharing risk and expense of, 183–84
Integrated circuits, production of,
    178–79
Integration, enterprise, 222
Intellectual capital, 173–77
  definition of, 173–74
  internal suppliers and, 258
  learning attitude and, 211–12
  monetary rewards for, 188
  in open system enterprise, 267–68
  originality and, 174
  protection of, 176–77
  transitory value of, 178
  work force and, 183
Intelligent body systems, 55–56
Interactive human processes, 366–67
Interest used as tax system, 330–34

Internal contracting, 14
Internal customers, 256, 258–60
Internal suppliers, 258–60
International Standards Organization
    (ISO), 214
Inventory, cost of, 290
Investment
    in human development, 318–21,
        358–59
    profits and interest used as tax system
        and, 330–34
    resource companies and, 248–49,
        337–40
    short vs. long-term return and,
        325–29
Investment mind-set, 325–30
Investments, short vs. long-term return
    and, 340–41
Investors, trust and, 318–19
Inward growth, 98–99
Ishikawa, Kaoru, 76–77
ISO 9000 quality standard, 275, 312,
    367

Japan
    adoption of JIT in, 245–46
    auto industry in, 52–54. See also
        specific companies
    customer-supplier relationship in,
        269–70
    improvement cycles in, 132
    three-day car. See Three-day car
    tooling time in, 195–96
    benchmarking by, 213
    corporate governance in, 334–36
    customer-supplier relationship in,
        269–74, 324
    human development in, 251
    improvement processes in, 76–77
    innovation in, 174–75
    interdependencies in manufacturing
        system of, 202–3
    job security in, 232
    keiretsu, 334
    lean manufacturing and, 20
    liaison programs and, 188
    Manufacturing 21 Project, 47
    organization in, 230
    quality improvement processes in,
        76–77
    slowing of industrial growth, 273–74
    solid-waste disposal in, 154
    spirit in, 20
    supplier associations in, 272–73
    trade with, 272
    visibility systems in, 193
Japanese National Railway, 335
JC Penney, 36, 77–78
Job loss, lean manufacturing and, 22
Job security, 232–35
    open system enterprise and, 244–45
Johns-Manville, 149
Johnsonville Foods, 69
Juran, Joseph, 20, 74, 77–78
Justice, personal, quality of life and, 92
Just in Time (JIT), 20, 103–4, 127–32
    adoption of, 245–46
    closed-loop cycles of material use and,
        165–66
    communication and, 118
    customer-supplier relationship and,
        269
    improvement cycles and, 130–32, 134
    kanban system, 160
    learning and, 114
    visibility systems and, 128–30

Kanban system, 160
Kano, Noritake, 78–80
Kawasaki Motorcycle Division, 246
Keating, Charles, Jr., 37
Keiretsu, 334
Know-how, loss of, 2, 4
Kodak, 179, 260
Koestler, Sir Arthur, 243
Kohlberg Kravis Roberts & Company,
    329
Komatsu, 77, 120

Labeco, 319–21
Landfills, 154–56
Lasch, Christopher, 26
Lead time
    definition of, 121, 133
    flexibility and, 120–21
    in time-based organizations, 121–27
Lean manufacturing, 20–22
    at GM, 323–24
    paradigms of, 33
    quality growth and, 21–22

Lean manufacturing (*cont.*)
   Taylorism vs., 21–22
Learning. *See also* Benchmarking
   cumulative, 115–16
   during product/process design, 197
   time-based organizations and, 112–16
   unlearning and, 211
Learning attitude, 211–12
Learning cycles, 134. *See also* Improvement cycles
Learning organizations, 208–12
   characteristics of, 208–9
   time-based organizations as, 112
Learning processes, 75. *See also* Improvement processes
Lehigh University, xiv
   Iacocca Institute, 61
Leisure, quality of life and, 91
Levinson, Harry, 228
Liaison programs, 188
Life expectancy
   GNP and, 139–40
   in industrial regions throughout history, 142
Light bulbs, electronic (E-lamps), 154
Lincoln, Abraham, 36
L.L. Bean, 294
Long-term development, 111
Lopez de Arriortua, J. Ignacio, 322–23

McDonald's, 251, 276
Machining standards, 15
Madison, Wisconsin, 92
Malcolm Baldrige National Quality
   Award, 85–86, 160, 194
Male life expectancy, 142
Management. *See also* Corporate governance
   Deming's definition of, 75, 92
   employee involvement and, 228
   executive compensation and, 326
   holonic, 243
   pay of, 242–43, 327
   postwar approach to, 17
   recognition by, 234–38
   sharing of risks by, 232–35
   Taylorism and, 14–22
   vision-driven, 309
Management consulting, 31–32
Managers, professional, 11, 38–39

Manufacturing. *See also* Remanufacturing
   decline in, 2, 4
   development of American system, 9–19
   sustainable, 24
   training programs in, 4
   zero-discharge, 46
Manufacturing excellence, 20. *See also* Lean manufacturing
   environmental issues and, 165–68
Manufacturing 21 Project, 47
   three-day car, 56–61
   working group, xiv
Market expansion, end of, 45
Marketing, selling vs., 203
Markets
   maturation of, 4–6, 24
   media and, 45
Marshall Field, 75
Marx, Karl, 8, 227
Massachusetts Institute of Technology (MIT), Media Lab, 188
Mass media, fragmentation of, 45
Mass production
   assembly line and, 15–16
   evolution of, 12
   growth of, 4–6
   in newly industrializing countries (NICs), 46
   paradigms of, 33
   World War II and, 16–17
Material losses, 164–65
Material requirements planning (MRP), 216–17, 219
Material-use cycle, 278. *See also* Control of service cycles
   closed-loop, 152–54, 165–66
   definitions of, 153
   design for, 157–59
   environmental impact statements and, 163–65
Maturity index, 304, 306–7
Mayckawa Company, 249
Mazda, 119
Measurement deployment, 310
Media
   environmental issues and, 145
   markets and, 45
   waste and, 116–17

Media Lab, 188
Medicare Diagnostic Review Group, 93
Mexico, 345
Microelectronics and Computer Technology Corporation (MCC), 184–85
Microsoft, 192
Milliken, 85
Miners, 236
Minow, Nell, 327–29
Mission-oriented enterprises, 296, 298
Model Ts, 120
Monks, Robert, 327–29
Monopolies, 360
Morgan, J. P., 13
Morgensen, Allen, 19, 21
Motivation, 228
  corporate governance and, 335–36
  soul of the enterprise and, 35–36
Motorola, 34, 36, 67, 85–86, 183, 251, 263, 265, 296, 309
  Bandit Project, 174
  Corporate Quality System Review (QSR), 304
  Model 55, 67–68
  six-sigma quality and, 67, 71
Myers, M. Scott, 240–41

Nakane, Jinichiro, xiv
National Center for Manufacturing Sciences (NCMS), 86, 184–85, 312
National Power, 182
National Toxics Campaign (NTC), 155–56
NCR Corporation, 158
Nesbitt, John, 345
New financial order, 336
Newly industrializing countries (NICs)
  auto industry in, 52–54
  growth in, 353
  mass production in, 46
  pollution in, 143
Nigeria, 143
NIMBYs (Not-In-My-Backyard), 155
Ninnemann, John L., 186
Nippondenso, 269
Nissan, Intelligent Body System of, 55
NOPEs (Not On Planet Earth), 155
Not-invented-here (NIH) syndrome, 174–75, 184

Object-oriented programming (OOP), 215–16
Oceana (Harrington), 139
Omakr Industries, 22
One-dimensional quality, 79
Open computing systems, 214–16
Openness, 24–25, 39. See also Open system enterprise
  consortia and, 185
Open system enterprise, 37–41, 159–61, 254–58. See also Enterprises
  advantages of, 206
  arguments against, 222–23
  benchmarking and, 160, 212–14
  closed systems vs., 201–6
  competition and, 210, 220–24
  control of service cycles and, 204–6
  customer-supplier relationship and, 254–76
  discipline necessary to, 317–18
  elements of, 254–55, 346–47
  entrepreneurship and, 337–41
  executive pay and, 242–43
  features of, 39–41
  governance of, 339–40
  improvement collaborators in, 81
  intellectual capital in, 267–68
  as learning organizations, 208–12
  limits of, 207
  long-term, 279, 281–84
  migration to, 245–46, 363–67
  need for, 108, 110
  need for information in, 159–61
  new form of business and manufacturing required for, 216–21, 223–25
  open computing systems and, 214–16
  operating enterprises as component of, 248–49, 278–79, 340
  organization of, 243–45
  public-service ethic of, 252
  quest for, 201
  regulations and, 206
  resource companies as component of, 248–49, 278–79, 337–40
  responsibility for material-use cycle and, 157
  selling and, 201
  standardization and, 206

Open system enterprise (*cont.*)
  structure of, 278
  trust and, 108, 203–4, 232
Open system for interconnection (OSI), 214
Open system information, 364–65
Operating enterprises, 248–49, 340
Operating performance, 39
Operations, comparing, 160
Optimization strategies, 298
Order-of-magnitude reorganization, 247–48
Organization charts, 106–7
Organizations. *See also* Hierarchies, organizational
  decentralized, 276–77
  Japanese, 230
  order-of-magnitude, 248
  processes and, 231
  process flow, 124
Outsourcing, 2
Owner, absentee, 37–38
Ozone holes, 148

Partners, customers as, 24–25, 45. *See also* Customer-supplier relationship
Patent systems, 174–75
Pay and reward systems, 236, 238–43
PCBs, 149–51
Performance. *See also* Operating performance; Quality performance
  enterprise and, 38–39
  ultimate, 296–97
Performance comparisons, 293–97
Performance drivers, 309
Performance Management, 237
Performance measures, 274–76, 287–315, 367
  auditioning of, 314–15
  balanced, 298–302
  benchmarking and, 294–95
  comparison with communications own past performance, 293–94
  cost of inventory and, 290
  cost of quality and, 290
  evolution of, 310, 312
  financial, 289–93
  implementing, 303–7
  for improvement, 289, 297–98, 302–4

maturity index and, 304
  mission-oriented, 296, 298
  nonfinancial, 292
  performance drivers and, 309–10, 312
  processes and, 237
  top-down, 289
  types of performance comparisons and, 293–97
  universal system of, 310, 312–15
  use of, 288–89
Perot, H. Ross, 322
Person, revenue per, 347–48
Personal computers, 6
Personal safety and justice, quality of life and, 92
Personnel issues, 238
Perspective, broadening, 41, 43
Peters, Tom, 26
Pharmaceutical companies, 359
Photo CD System, 179
Physical environment, quality of life and, 91
Picking up process, 239
Planning cycle, definition of, 134
Poke-yoke, 86
Policy deployment, 310
Pollution. *See also* Environmental issues
  in newly industrializing countries (NICs), 143
  visible, 147
Polymerization, 51
Pontiac Fiero, 57, 158
Pontiac Saturn, 57, 158, 177–78
Population explosion, 142–43
Porter, Michael, 110–11, 340
Positive reinforcement. *See* Recognition
Power, time and, 106–8
Power and Accountability (Monks and Minow), 327–29
Power density, 195
Power retailing, 183
Private taxation, 362–63
Process design. *See* Product/process design
Processes, performance measures and, 237
Process flow organization, 124
Process variance, 93–94
Product design
  design for disassembly (DFD), 158–59

fasteners and, 158
material-use cycle and, 157–59
Product development, in auto industry, 54
Productivity, measuring, 2
Product/process design
  concurrent engineering teams and,
    189–91
  consistent objectives and, 192–93
  customer requirements and, 193–94
  flexibility and, 196–97
  freezing designs and specifications
    and, 192
  ideal system of, 189–97
  as learning experience, 197
  power density and, 195
  robust design and, 194–95
  time as driving measurement and,
    195–96
  use of established parts and processes
    and, 192
  visibility and, 192–93
Products, selling of services vs., 159
Product tracking, 46
Profits used as tax system, 330–34
Profit sharing, 14, 342
Prosumers, 72, 361
  automotive, 58
  quality of life and, 92
Public-service ethic, 252
Pull-flow systems, 118
Push-flow systems, 118

Quality
  categories of, 78–80
  cost of, 290
  customer satisfaction as, 78
  definition of, 68–69
  expected, 79
  global vision of, 69–74
  indifferent, 79
  one-dimensional, 79
  redefining, 78–81
  unexpected, 79
Quality control, 76
Quality Function Deployment (QFD),
    193
Quality growth, 21–22
  definition of, 68
  inward growth and, 98–99
  responsibility and, 98–99

Quality improvement processes
  benchmarking and, 20, 160, 212–14,
    294–95
  customer-supplier relationship and,
    261–62
  in governments and services, 92–95
  information wave, 74–75
  in Japan, 76–77
  practicing, 75–77
  stepwise, 71
Quality of life, 26–27, 35–36, 68
  definition of, 73, 89–92
  as economic challenge, 95–99
  human development and, 308
  revenue per person necessary for,
    347–48
Quality performance measures, 84–86
  fail-safe methods and, 86, 98
Quality reviews, 274–75
Quality System Standards series ISO
    9000, 275, 312, 367
Quick Response, 118, 154, 277, 352

Radio, 117
Railroads, 11–12, 25–26
  Pennsylvania Railroad, 16
Rank Xerox Venray, 261
Rate-of-return, 11
Raw materials, movement of, 165
Rebuilding, 153
Recognition, 234–38
  of enterprise teams, 249–50
  pay and reward systems and, 236,
    238–43
Recovery, 352–54
Recycling, 46, 153–56
Refrigerators, 6
Regulations
  environmental, 161–63
  open system enterprise and, 206
Reinflation, 355
Relationship diagram, 123–24
Remanufacturing, 46, 153–56, 159
  holistic, 9, 23, 44
  of three-day car, 64
Reorganization, order-of-magnitude,
    247–48
Research, academic, 186–89
Research and development (R&D),
    175–76. See also Innovation

Research consortia, 184–86
Researchers, dual-role, 187–88
Resource companies, 248–49, 337–40
Responsibility, 24, 37–38. *See also* Empowerment
  for environmental protection, 156
  quality growth and, 98–99
  of workers, 26, 227–28. *See also* Employee involvement
Retailing, power, 183
Retrofitting, 46
Return on investment (ROI), 325
Reuse cycle, 153
Revenue per person, 347–48
Reverse utopia, 143, 151
Reward systems, 236, 238–43
Rimington, Paul, 232
Risks
  environmental, 147
  sharing, 232, 235
Robots, 202
  chemical industry and, 51
Robust design, 194
Rust belt, 18, 63

Safety
  manufacturing excellence and, 166, 168
  personal, quality of life and, 92
Sandoz Pharmaceutical, 204–5
Savage, Charles, 112
Schwartzkopf, Gen. Norman, 238
Self-interest
  civic virtue vs., 26
  holistic considerations vs., 23
Selling
  marketing vs., 203
  open system enterprise and, 201
  sharing vs., 203
Sematech, 184–85
Senge, Peter, 112, 208
Service cycles. *See* Control of service cycles
Services
  customer satisfaction and, 223–24
  quality improvement processes and, 92–95
  selling of products vs., 159
Shainan, Dorian, 77
Sharing
  benchmarking and, 213–14

of risks, 232–35
  selling vs., 203
Shewhart, Walter, 74, 76
Shingo, Shigeo, 103
Short-term thinking, 11, 110–11
Silent Spring (Carson), 143
Silicone implants, 149
Silicon Valley, 18
Six-sigma, 67, 309
Slater, Samuel, 11
Sloan, Alfred, 16
Smart chips, 46. *See also* Application-Specific Intergrated Circuits (ASICs)
Smart highways, 63
Smith, Adam, 8, 227
Smith, Jack, 322
Social concerns, quality of life defined as, 91–92
Social discipline, 37
Social opportunity, quality of life and, 92
Social overhead, 355, 357, 362–63
Social Security, 331
Software, 45–46
  funding R&D for, 176, 183
  pirated, 176, 183
  word-processing, 87
Solar, cars, 97
Soldiering, 14
Solid waste disposal, 154–56
Soul, use of term, 35
Soul of the enterprise, 8–9
  definition of, 35–37
  spirit of inquiry and, 27
South Korea, 353
  auto industry in, 53
Space race, 18, 25
Spendolini, Michael, 295
Spirit, Japanese, 20
Spirit of inquiry, soul of the enterprise and, 27
Stakeholders, performance measures and, 299
Standardization, 25
  open system enterprise and, 206
Stayer, Ralph, 69
Steel industry, 233
Steelmaking, 13
Stempel, Robert, 322
Stock distribution, 342

Stork, Kenneth J., xv
Stress, technical progress and, 25
Subsidiaries, equipment, 259
Superfund Amendments and Reauthorization Act (SARA), 161
Supplier associations, Japanese, 272–73
Suppliers, 254–58. *See also* Customer-supplier relationship
   classification of, 81–82
   critical, 266–67
   decreasing, 117
   definition of, 267
   as improvement collaborators, 81, 89
   internal, 258–60
   as partners, 25
   quality certification of, 274–75
Supply chain, 34. *See also* Enterprise
Sustainable development, 138–42, 145, 147
Sustainable manufacturing, 24
Sweeney, Jack, 320
Synchronous manufacturing, 322. *See also* Just in Time (JIT)
Systems-thinking, 43

Taguchi, Genichi, 77, 194
Taiwan, 143
Takt time, 21, 131
   definition of, 133
Taurus, 79
Taxation, private, 362–63
Tax system, profits and interest used as, 330–34
Taylor, Fredrick Winslow (Taylorism), 13–22, 76, 78, 84, 98, 131–32, 161
   concepts of, 18
   lean manufacturing vs., 21–22
   as obsolete and dysfunctional, 18
Teamwork, pay and reward systems and, 236, 238–43. *See also* Enterprise teams
Technical Data Interchange (TDI), 219
Technical progress, stress and, 25. *See also* Innovation; Intellectual capital
Technology-transfer organizations, 185. *See also* Consortia
Telephone companies, 26. *See also* UltraComm

Televisions, 6, 117. *See also* UltraComm
   high-density (HDTV), 354
Tennessee Eastman Company, 237
Textile mills, 11–12
Thailand, 353
Third Wave, The (Toffler), 7
Three-day car, 47, 52, 56–64, 172, 222, 361
   American version, 61–62
   challenges of, 56
   customer involvement in, 57–59
   engineering, production and delivery of, 59–61
   implications of, 62–64
   modular design of, 56–57
   ordering a, 57–59
   remanufacturing of, 64
Three-day house, 361
Thurow, Lester, 26
Time. *See also* Cycle time; Lead time; Takt time
   different senses of, 110–11
   as measurement driving project teams, 195–96
   power and, 106–8
   quality of life and, 91
   value of, 355–58
Time-based organizations, 104–34
   communication in, 111–12
   as floating crap game, 111–12
   improvement cycles and, 130–32
   improvement cycles in, 114–15
   information waste and, 116–19
   JIT and, 127–32
   lead times and cycle times in, 121–27
   learning and, 112–16
   times-to-change and, 119–21
   trust between people in, 108
   as virtual companies, 112
Time flow diagram, 123, 125–26
Times-to-change, reducing, 119–21
Tobacco companies, 110
Toffler, Alvin, 7–8, 72, 345
Top-down, performance measures, 289
Total preventive maintenance, 20
Total Quality Control (TQC), 76–77
Total Quality Management (TQM), 8, 20–21
   environmental issues and, 166
Towne, Henry, 14

Toxic Release Inventory database (EPA), 161
Toxic waste, 136–37, 155–56
Toyo Engineering Corporation, 51
Toyota, 63, 272
    governance of, 334
    improvement cycles at, 114–15, 130–32, 134
    JIT and, 165–66
    lean manufacturing at, 21, 23
Trade with Japan, 272
Trust, 25, 318
    consortia and, 185
    customer-supplier relationship and, 321–24
    empowerment and, 232–35
    executive pay and, 327
    investors and, 318–19
    job security and, 232–35
    open system enterprise and, 108, 203–4, 232

Ultimate performance, 296–97
UltraComm, 47–48, 175, 178, 215, 361
Unexpected quality, 79
Union Carbide, 148
United Mine Workers, 236
United States
    Department of Defense, 61
    manufacturing in, 9–22
        expansion as soul of, 9, 11, 13, 16
        Taylorism and, 13–22
        recovery in, 352–54
Universities, research in, 186–89
Unlearning, 211
U.S. Steel, 13
Used cars, 87–89
Utilities, 360
Utopias, 44, 139, 141, 152

Value City economy, 351–52
VCRs, 24
Venture participants, recognition of, 249
Virgin development, 145
Virgin growth, 17–18
Virtual companies, 47, 365–66
    time-based organizations as, 112
Visibility systems, 25, 128–30, 193

Vision deployment, 41, 43–44, 310–11, 364
Vision-driven leadership, 309
Vlahos, Michael, 26

Wallace Company, 85
Wal-Mart, 277
War production, 16–17, 25
Waseda University, Tokyo, xiv
Waste. See also Solid waste disposal; Toxic waste
    gross national product (GNP) and, 348, 354
    information as, 116–19
    JIT and, 103
Weber, Joseph, 210–11
Weirton Steel, 233–34
Westinghouse, 105
    PCBs and, 149–51
Williams Technologies, 201, 209
Wilson, Charley, 324
Woods Wire, 263–64, 277
Word-processing software, 87
Work cycle, definition of, 133–34
Workers, 227–52. See also Associates; Employee involvement; Employees; Empowerment; Enterprise teams
    in auto industry, 55–56
    buy-in and, 341–42
    education of, 251–52
    hierarchies and, 229–31
    pay and reward systems and, 236, 238–43
    picking up process and, 239
    recognition and, 234–38
    responsibility of, 26, 227–28
    selection of, 238–39
Working life, quality of life and, 91
World War II, production during, 16–17
Wright-Patterson Air Force Base, 93

Xerox, 85, 212, 261, 263–64, 294
    Business Products and Systems Group, 35

Zelco, 174
Zero-discharge manufacturing, 46–47, 50, 152